S0-EXH-764

THE NORWEGIAN-AMERICAN HISTORICAL ASSOCIATION

THE NORWEGIAN-AMERICAN HISTORICAL ASSOCIATION

John A. Johnson

John A. Johnson

An Uncommon American

by AGNES M. LARSON

1969

The Norwegian-American Historical Association

NORTHFIELD • MINNESOTA

PRINTED IN THE UNITED STATES OF AMERICA AT THE
LUND PRESS, MINNEAPOLIS, MINNESOTA

Foreword

Shortly before her death in January, 1967, Professor Agnes M. Larson had completed a well-structured biography of John A. Johnson, pioneer Wisconsin manufacturer, whose many-sided career in business, politics, and cultural life is the theme of this study. The Norwegian-American Historical Association feels privileged in issuing her book as the seventeenth volume in its Special Publications series and as the forty-ninth to bear its imprint.

I am happy on two counts to have had the opportunity to supervise and to participate actively in revising, checking, and seeing this work of an esteemed colleague through the press. Such tasks have seemed a fitting tribute to a teacher and scholar whose precepts and examples, both in and out of the classroom, have influenced countless persons in ways too many and too profound to find expression in the printed word. It is of interest, too, that Dr. Larson's biography is the Association's first publication to deal specifically with an immigrant businessman, and thus to contribute significantly to a neglected phase of American history.

Many individuals have given invaluable assistance in the preparation of this book for publication. Professor Ralph L. Henry of Northfield, Minnesota, served from the start as associate editor and assumed the initial task of revision, in addition to reading proof, preparing the index, and conferring almost daily with the editor for a period of about a year and a half. Professor Henrietta M. Larson, the author's sister, formerly of Harvard University and now a resident of Northfield, assumed the role normally assigned to the author in the editing process, and drew on her rich background of experience in offering wise counsel. Helen Thane Katz, Association editorial assistant, St. Paul, read page proofs and advised in the late stages of publication. Mrs. Dorothy Boettcher typed the final manuscript copy.

It is difficult to express adequately the Association's gratitude to Mr. George H. Johnson, grandson of John A. Johnson and former president of the Gisholt Machine Company, Madison, Wisconsin, for acting as the prime mover in the undertaking that resulted in the present volume. His assistance to Professor Larson, offered in many forms from the early 1950's, was such as to buoy her spirits through a fatal illness, when she completed the manuscript against heavy odds.

The Gisholt John A. Johnson Foundation, of which Mr. Johnson is president, provided grants in aid of research to the author and also assumed a major portion of the cost of publishing this book. Dr. John R. Wrage, its secretary, and his indefatigable assistant, Mrs. Norma Beckman, in addition to advising Dr. Larson and supplying her with Johnson materials, have also made levies on their time and energy to assist me by securing new information, providing photographs, and reading proof.

Dr. Wrage, when asked to comment on his relations with Professor Larson, replied: "It is my firm belief that those who have lived a full life with the greatest satisfactions have rubbed shoulders with great people. Dr. Agnes M. Larson was such a person. The longer we worked together, learning all we could about John Anders Johnson, the more we came to admire him. It was a thrill to talk to those who had known him and to secure records that identified him as a man of integrity, of conviction, and of moral strength. Dr. Larson's physical and mental suffering was intense, yet she worked on diligently. I was often reminded of the saying, 'I admire you so much, not only for what you are but for what I am when I am with you.' May this biography of a great man by a great woman inspire those who read it as it has inspired those who participated in its preparation."

Finally, I wish to acknowledge the generosity of the Gisholt John A. Johnson Foundation in delivering its large collection of Johnson papers to the archives of the Norwegian-American Historical Association. To the Foundation and its officers, our warmest thanks.

KENNETH O. BJORK

St. Olaf College

Acknowledgments

Throughout her manuscript, the late Professor Agnes M. Larson repeatedly expressed gratitude to many people for assistance given her in the preparation of this biography. A few of her acknowledgments, deemed essential to specific items of information, remain in the footnotes. The editor has thought it desirable, however, to delete others from the manuscript and to bring them together in the kind of statement that she doubtless would have prepared had she lived to assist in the final stages of bookmaking. She especially wished to thank the following persons and institutions:

Mr. George H. Johnson, grandson of John A. Johnson and president of the Gisholt John A. Johnson Foundation, Madison, Wisconsin, for promoting and supporting the preparation and publication of this volume and for assisting her in countless ways during many years of work on the project.

The directors of the Gisholt John A. Johnson Foundation; its secretary, Dr. John R. Wrage; and Dr. Wrage's assistant, Mrs. Norma Beckman. The Foundation put the Johnson letters and other documents at Professor Larson's disposal and provided financial aid for research. Dr. Wrage and Mrs. Beckman were untiring in assembling Johnson materials, hunting out additional information, and, like George H. Johnson, drawing on their rich knowledge of John A. Johnson, his family, and the businesses he directed.

The author's sisters, Dr. Henrietta M. Larson and Dr. Nora L. Larson, and her niece, Emilie G. Larson, for their interest, encouragement, and assistance in the preparation of the manuscript.

The librarians and staffs of the University of Wisconsin Library and the State Historical Society of Wisconsin; Mr. Gerhard B. Naeseth of the University of Wisconsin Library, for the passenger list of the "Salvator" and for data concerning members of the John A. Johnson family; the Reverend Olav Kr. Strømme, pastor of the Cathedral Church in Kristiansand, and Mr. K. J. Helland Hansen, for information about the Kildahl and Holgersen families in Norway.

Engineer Erling Gjærum of Oslo, Norway, for data concerning John A. Johnson's birth and birthplace and the emigration of the Skibsnæs family; Mr. Clarence B. Hagen, Whitewater, Wisconsin, for information about the Heart Prairie Church; Mr. Harold K. Hill, register of deeds, Dane County, Wisconsin, for documents dealing with the purchase of the John A. Johnson farm.

Mr. J. F. Driscoll, corporate secretary of the St. Paul Insurance Companies, and Mr. Martin F. Raynoha of the department of insurance, state of Wisconsin, for information about the acquisition of the Hekla Fire Insurance Company by the St. Paul German Fire Insurance Company.

Mr. Robert R. Bolin and Miss Jean Dorman of the University of Wisconsin staff, for data concerning the John A. Johnson scholarships; the Reverend Dr. Morris Wee, former pastor of Bethel Lutheran Church, for use of the records of his congregation and for background information; Mr. Henry Wolf, former treasurer of the Fuller and Johnson Company, for a review of marketing plans for a farm pump gasoline engine; Messrs. Fred W. Coombs, George E. Gernon, David Wright, Clem Affholder, and others, for information—written or spoken—about the Gisholt Machine Company.

Mrs. Amelia Sønneland of Los Angeles, for a description of the old log schoolhouse at Pleasant Springs, written by her aunt, Mrs. Caroline Johnson Stuverud; Mr. Maurice A. Edwards of Madison, grandson of Oliver Johnson, for information about his grandfather and great-grandparents; and Mr. James Eckman of the Mayo Clinic, Rochester, Minnesota, for data concerning that institution.

Mrs. Mathilde Houkom and Mrs. Marian L. Anderson, for typing the manuscript.

K.O.B.

Contents

JOHN A. JOHNSON

CHAPTER I

Old-World Moorings

The last shot of the War of 1812 had hardly been fired when there began the greatest folk movement in the Western world since the barbarians invaded the Roman Empire. For a generation the focus of the migration was on that heartland of America known as the Old Northwest. From nearly every village and town of the northern coastal region of the United States, someone or some family joined the trek westward. The promise of new land also stirred the imagination of restless folk across the Atlantic. Soon a flood of immigrants began to come from the Old World, at first mainly from northern Europe: from Great Britain, Germany, Norway, Sweden, Denmark, and even from Switzerland. In a few years they occupied the land north of the Ohio River to the Mississippi, except the plains between Lake Michigan and the Father of Waters.

Rich in nature's bounty, these western lake plains were still in the hands of sullen Indian tribes. In the late war they had been allies of the British and now were a threat to anyone who might despoil them of their lands. The issue was joined in the Black Hawk War of 1832, the last stand of the Sac and Fox nations in northern Illinois and in what later became southwestern Wisconsin. The outcome of the struggle for territory was tragic for the Indians. At last they realized how futile was any effort to resist the white man. The defeated tribes no longer had any choice: they must move from the valleys, forests, and streams they loved to lands beyond the Mississippi.

The way for farther advance was now clear. The region that became

Wisconsin Territory in 1836 and a state in 1848 was the mecca for many settlers. The earliest history of Wisconsin chronicles the coming of explorers, fur traders, and lead miners, but most of the immigrants who arrived in the 1830's and 1840's sought land. In southern Wisconsin, with its broad valleys and fertile prairies, they formed old-world colonies, creating a unique society whose social and economic ways were to be modified in time by the impact of the frontier and a culture different from that of their homeland. The census of 1850 counted 107,000 persons in Wisconsin who had been born in Europe.

Among the immigrants who came to Wisconsin was a twelve-year-old Norwegian boy, an alert, sensitive, gentle lad. He arrived with his family in 1844. Aboard ship on the Atlantic, he had been listed as Jens Anderson Jensen Skibsnæs, but his name was soon to become Americanized as John Anders Johnson. Wisconsin was to be his home for the rest of his long life. To the building of that state, throughout the last half of the nineteenth century, he was to give generously of his ability, his energy, and his material means.

Two patterns in the life of John A. Johnson were to join to form a third. His old-world experience and culture and the influence of America, which had become his home, merged over the years into a new design. Like so many immigrants, before his time and later, he helped to create a new pattern of culture, of living, of working—in a word, a new civilization that came to be known as American.[1]

The old-world moorings of Johnson's family and his own childhood were in southern Norway. They came from Telemark, a district in Bratsberg—a romantic land, a land of poet and painter, a region of lofty mountains. The highest peak, Gausta Mountain, is beautifully majestic, its snow-clad crown reaching above the clouds. It washes its feet in the Rjukan River, the largest of many streams that course through this rugged area, forming numerous waterfalls and shimmering lakes. Telemark has not one but a multitude of fertile valleys. Lying between thickly forested walls

[1] Some of the information included in this chapter was obtained from John A. Johnson's "Memoirs," written in hand on loose pages tied between stiff covers. The manuscript is among the Johnson Papers formerly in the possession of the Gisholt John A. Johnson Foundation, Madison, Wisconsin, and now in the archives of the Norwegian-American Historical Association at St. Olaf College, Northfield, Minnesota. As only a few of the pages are numbered, reference to this valuable source is difficult. It will be assumed hereafter that Johnson's reminiscences, unless otherwise indicated, are taken from this document.

of rock, they still give shelter to snug, quaint hamlets and carefully tilled farms, the latter passing on generation after generation from father to son. Now, in the second half of the twentieth century, the driving energy and humming life of modern industries have harnessed the ancient waterfalls. Today, life in the valleys of Telemark has two facets: its idyllic rural quiet and the press of a surging industrial economy.

Historically, this part of Norway, sequestered by its stony ramparts, was long set off from the rest of the country. Isolation fostered distinctive characteristics: self-reliance, a spirit of independence, a love of liberty. The men of Telemark were quick to use their weapons when their freedom was endangered. Separateness also nurtured local folk tales, music, and poetry and gave the inhabitants a distinct dialect and a culture which has survived and still contributes richly to Norwegian life.

The universe of John A. Johnson for the first twelve years of his life consisted of the valley cradling one lake in southern Telemark. Norsjø was a beautiful body of water — some twelve miles long and up to a mile wide — bounded in some places by steep rock walls and in others by green fields, meadows, and pleasant farmsteads. Its waters emptied into a river on its way to Skien, Porsgrund, and the sea. Like that of most of the Telemark valleys, the land surrounding the lake was widely renowned for its fertility.[2]

John was born April 15, 1832, on a small farm called Eik [3] located on the eastern shore of Lake Norsjø. He was baptized Jens Anderson, Jens the son of Anders. Eik had long been a part of a larger farm called Gjeitebua, on which John's forefathers had lived as leaseholders or cotters since the seventeenth century. At the time of his birth, Gjeitebua included an extensive cultivated area carved out of a forest of spruce and pine. It took its name from a large shelter (*bua*), where goats (*gjeite*) and goatherds on their way to or from mountain pastures in the spring and fall found protection from the rain and cold.

Gjeitebua had historic significance reaching back to the age of the Vikings — that stirring period which stands as a kind of watershed between legendary and historic times. On the highest mountain in the area, com-

[2] Werner Werenskiold, ed., *Norge vårt land*, part 2, p. 124 (Oslo, 1941); Amund Helland, *Topografisk-statistisk beskrivelse over Bratsberg Amt*, part 2, p. 300 (Kristiania, 1900), vol. 8 in Amund Helland's *Norges land og folk topografisk-statistisk beskrevet*.

[3] Sometimes spelled *ek*, the word means oak. A large stand of oak trees gave the farm its name.

manding a panoramic view of Norsjø, the men of Telemark built a huge cairn and assembled in it a pyramid of logs from the tallest spruce trees in the forest. When watchmen saw enemies approaching below, they set ablaze a mighty signal fire calling the farmer soldiery to battle in defense of their home valleys.[4]

John's paternal grandfather was the son of Mari Jensdatter Gjeitebua; his grandmother Aavet Hansdatter came from the neighboring valley of Vassdalen. It was his grandfather who in 1799 leased the land at Eik. On this farm in later years lived John's parents, Anders Jensen and Aaste Bjørnsdatter Killingkoven.[5]

The small farm where the family of John's mother lived was a cottage allotment on the Solberg estate located on the east side of Lake Norsjø, not far from Eik. The Killingkoven family had come from Rauland, a forested district in northwestern Telemark. Its members spoke a slightly different dialect from that common in southern Telemark. John's maternal grandfather was a forester and lumberman recognized as an able craftsman and as a hard-working, considerate man. He had served in the Napoleonic wars; during his soldiering his resourceful wife had managed the home and cared for the young children. One of these was Aaste, later to become the mother of John A. Johnson.

When John was barely two years old, his parents moved to the west side of Norsjø to become innkeepers at Skibsnæs in Holden Parish. Favorably situated at the upper end of the lake, the spot was a crossroad of sorts for people traveling between East and West Telemark. Standing on a bluff-like promontory, the inn was often buffeted by strong winds and storms, but fortunately its heavy timbers and strong foundation held the elements at bay.

For hundreds of years wayfarers on the lake, with their goods, had been transported in boats, often rowed by women. Year in and year out, there was constant traffic. The whole day through one could hear the rhythmic splash of oars. Hostels along the shore offered shelter and food, and the Skibsnæs Inn was an especially busy one. There travelers transferred to boats for other points on the lake and off-duty oarsmen rested. In stormy weather travelers had to seek shelter, sometimes for days at a

[4] S. Ytterbøe, *Holla: Historisk skildring av bygda og dens utvikling*, 620 (Oslo, 1925).

[5] Ytterbøe, *Holla*, 410. Killingkoven is now spelled Killingkåvan, a variant also current in the earlier time. John's mother's father was Bjørn Halvorson Killingkoven; his maternal grandmother was Svanaug Olsdatter.

time. The elements ruled. The frozen lake in winter became a highway and the inns were crowded with visitors stopping to warm themselves and to eat and rest.[6]

Anders Jensen Skibsnæs and his wife never owned the inn, but they continued to lease and operate it from 1834 to 1843 — the years in which their son John grew from a toddler to a boy of eleven. Early in this period word spread that Aaste Jensen served the best coffee on all Norsjø. Customers responded and the reputation of Skibsnæs Inn as an orderly, well-kept hostelry grew. Travelers often brought their own food; so it turned out that lodging, coffee, and other beverages provided the innkeeper's family with its livelihood. A night's "keep" with only the simplest comforts cost two Norwegian skillings — a couple of pennies — as did a drink of whisky or a "bowl" of coffee.[7]

In spite of the modest success of the inn, John's mother had an uneasy feeling that it was not a good place to rear children. Her reservations on this point undoubtedly explain the fact that young John, the family's eldest, spent a great deal of time with an aunt and uncle who lived on a farm known as Gisholt, on the east side of Norsjø.[8] Ingeborg Jensdatter, sister of Anders Jensen, had married Ole Arnesen Gisholt, a wealthy member of the local council of Mælum.[9] These prominent relatives on his father's side provided the boy from Skibsnæs with a stimulating change of environment and an important early association with people of high standing in the community. The Gisholts had no children, and, becoming attached to their nephew, they at one time considered making John their

[6] Ytterbø, *Holla*, 152, 155. Holden Parish is now called Holla. Skibsnæs has itself been written in many variant forms. The early occupying Danes spelled it Skibsnæs or Skibsnes; in the Telemark dialect it was pronounced Skiffsness and today the spelling is Skefsnes. In the United States, after many a change, the family name is now Shipnes. Until the family moved to America, they were usually known by the patronymic Jensen.

[7] A Norwegian skilling at that time was worth less than half a penny in British money, about a cent in American.

[8] Ytterbøe, *Holla*, 155. There were two Gisholt farms on opposite sides of the lake: Eastern Gisholt and Western Gisholt. A *holt* is a grove or small wood.

[9] J. Birkenes, *Solum Herred gjennem 100 aar 1837–1937*, 39 (Skolfoss, Norway, 1940). O. Rygh, in *Norske gaardnavne i Bratsberg Amt: Oplysninger samlede til brug ved matrikelens revision*, p. 158 (Kristiania, 1914), explains that the name Gisholt may have been derived from the name of a man. His name, Geitir, may have been changed to Geitirsholt at a remote time in history. This is volume 7 in Rygh's classic study *Norske gaardnavne*. A. Michelsen, in a letter to Dr. John R. Wrage of Madison, Wisconsin, November 30, 1962, also refers to Rygh's interpretation. Michelsen is technical manager of Brødrene Sundt, who for a long period have sold Gisholt Machine Company products in Norway.

heir. There is no doubt that the boy loved this spot in his native Norway. Often, later on in America as a teen-age immigrant working for others, he cried himself to sleep, homesick for Gisholt farm and the warm love of its owners.

Gisholt had had a long history. It is referred to in Bishop Oystein's record at the close of the fourteenth century, when it was a landed estate (*gaard*) of the Catholic Church. From it had come the income of St. Michael's Church, located on the Gisholt estate. This place of worship for early Christians was a dry and comfortable cave in the nearly perpendicular granite wall of the mountain, about two hundred feet above Norsjø. Its entrance was eighteen feet high and twenty-four feet wide. The interior, both higher and wider than the "doorway," extended inward for one hundred and twenty feet. In the Middle Ages, St. Michael's – named for the patron saint of mountain-cave churches – had had its own priest and an altar complete with lights and golden ornaments.[10]

During the Protestant Reformation, control of the national religious organization passed to the king of Denmark-Norway, and the government took over all church land. The ancient estate of Gisholt, under Lutheran masters, was subdivided into small farms. On one of these, the property in modern times of Ole Arnesen Gisholt and his wife Ingeborg, the young John A. Johnson found almost a second home.

Gjeitebua, Eik, Skibsnæs, Killingkoven, Eastern Gisholt – these were familiar to the boy. All around, he saw natural beauty worthy of the artist's brush: in the foreground Lake Norsjø and, rising behind, snow-capped mountains. In the larger setting, his eyes took in sheltered valleys, covered with spruce and pine and dotted with green fields, meadows, and neat farmsteads. In this close-knit social milieu, not greatly different from that of his forebears, he spent his most formative years.

There were psychological and spiritual influences, too, flooding down out of the remote past. The intriguing history of St. Michael's Church on the Norsjø and the legends of dwarfs and giants who once lived among mountain crags and in forest depths kindled John's youthful imagination. He knew the story of Father Sylvester, the last priest to serve the church in the cave. When Denmark-Norway separated from the Catholic Church, Sylvester became a wanderer in foreign lands. Sick with longing for Nor-

[10] Helland, *Bratsberg Amt*, part 2, p. 321; Jens E. Kraft, *Historisk-topographisk haandbog over kongeriget Norge*, 316 (Christiania, 1848); Rygh, *Bratsberg Amt*, 158, 162; *Madison Democrat*, May 29, 1901.

way and for his parish home, aged and infirm, he returned by stealth to his former haunts. While other men slept, he climbed the steep rocks to light the candles in the cave and to pray at the altar. People saw the lights and spoke of supernatural happenings.

One night the Lutheran Bishop Povel, investigating the mystery of the lights, encountered Father Sylvester in the rock-bound church. There the bishop, listening to the old man's story, exclaimed compassionately: "Your speech goes to my heart. If you are in want, kindly make these wants known, for they shall be supplied." Sylvester answered: "God reward you for your kindness. The little I need is supplied by the Gisholt people and, when I die, they have promised to bury me in the sacristy of this little church." Soon there were no more lights, and the last priest of St. Michael's Church was laid to rest by parish folk in the place he had loved so well.

Even as late as John's childhood, superstitious people around him clung to belief in tales of supernatural folk who dwelt in remote places where normal men dared not set foot. In his later life, John A. Johnson wrote: "These myths formed the most charming children's entertainment in my boyhood days." Even in America, Norwegian folklore followed him. In his father's house in Wisconsin, he encountered an old man from Norway, known as "Coal Aslak" because he made charcoal for blacksmiths. This old-country character was adept at relating fantastic tales of people and places in his homeland. "We boys laughed heartily," Johnson wrote in his "Memoirs," "but we were most eager listeners. It is clear that our ancestors lived and moved in a semi-mystical world wholly different from ours." He added that neither his father nor his uncles — nor his grandfather, for that matter — believed in such stories.

By 1843 the family of Anders and Aaste Jensen included four sons and a baby daughter. The parents, looking to the future, saw ahead pressing problems attending their inferior economic position and its direct bearing on the educational opportunities of their children. In Norway there would be possible only such training as the parish school afforded — at best rudimentary and giving little hope for a better life. Hard manual labor and a meager living were all the father and mother could foresee for their promising children. Looking about them, they could see people physically and mentally enervated for want of sufficient nutritious food and adequate shelter. In those days, the thought of emigrating to America was often in the minds of Anders and Aaste. What should they do? The two were of different minds. At first the husband, more conservative, resisted the idea of crossing the sea and setting themselves up in a strange land. Persistently his wife took the lead in urging the change. After careful consideration, they decided to go to America.[11]

Other more remote but complex and interrelated factors had been influencing the keepers of Skibsnæs Inn at the very time of their anxious debate over emigrating to America. In the early 1840's, Frederik Stang, minister of the newly established department of the interior in Norway, had initiated a series of economic reforms. Following its policies, he moved quickly to modernize communications by building roads and introducing steamboats on the lakes. Such modern vessels were to make a strong impact on the life on Norsjø: slower rowboats would no longer be wanted and the shoreline inns would suffer. Skibsnæs Inn was especially vulnerable. It would cease to be a transfer point or an important hostel, and patronage would fall off. Housewife Aaste saw all these things clearly and realized that the future of their family in Norway was not promising. It was one of her strongest arguments.

Now that the die had been cast, letters from America whetted their interest in the New World. A year earlier, the families of Ole Søgaard and Hans Milebaand, close friends, had left Holden Parish in a party bound for the United States.[12] Their letters, eloquent with favorable reports of fresh opportunities across the Atlantic, were eagerly studied. Copied and recopied, they were passed from hand to hand. Norwegians who had gone to Wisconsin were especially pleased with their new location. Messages like these accelerated the flow of Norsemen to the new western states — first to Illinois and Wisconsin, then to Iowa, Minnesota, and the Dakotas. Certainly they helped shape the plans of the Jensen family.

John himself read these letters with interest when he was not yet twelve years old. His reading ability was excellent despite his meager schooling. He had attended school, in private homes, a few days in each. But his parents had been persistent in teaching him, and Grandmother Killingkoven at the spinning wheel had had him sit by her side reading to her as she

[11] Fate may have hastened their final decision. On a bleak March day in 1844, in a fierce gale, the Skibsnæs Inn burned. The Jensens lost all their household goods and all their clothing except what they were wearing. This catastrophe loosened the ties binding them to their ancestral homeland and undoubtedly clinched their resolution to start over in the New World.

[12] George T. Flom, *A History of Norwegian Immigration to the United States: From the Earliest Beginnings Down to the Year 1848*, 289 (Iowa City, Iowa, 1909).

worked. Later in life he recalled that as a boy he had never seen anyone in Norway who could not read.

Some Norwegian newspapers did not hesitate to tell the plain truth about migration to the United States. A letter dated January 1, 1844, and printed in a paper in Skien, Telemark, called emigration and conditions in America the popular themes of the day. Even earlier — on June 3, 1839 — *Christianssandsposten* had declared in an editorial that the average man in Norway had usually accumulated only debts and that financial success was a rare and individual accomplishment.[13] New political and religious forces were also at work, causing discontent among the farmers (*bønder*). Norway was overpopulated and its economic development lagged. Opportunities to earn a livelihood were severely restricted, and thus the prospect of material betterment in America drew Norwegians like a magnet.[14]

America, however, was far away. The Jensen (Skibsnæs) family thought only vaguely of the distance in miles, but the overwhelming cost of the trip for seven persons was of real and immediate concern. Children could travel across the ocean for half fare; passage for adults ranged from $25 to $38.[15] Johnson writes in his "Memoirs" that his parents actually paid $25 each for their fare on the ship, and $12.50 each for the boys — a total of $100.00. Inger, a babe in arms, required no ticket. To this amount they had to add something like $14 per person for transportation from New York to Wisconsin — the land so enthusiastically praised in the letters of their friends in the New World. The total cost was frightening. An auction of the family's worldly goods yielded only enough money to pay the Atlantic passage. Where — how — could funds be raised to take them to Wisconsin? Mother Aaste was determined. She would find a way.

In the extremity she thought of Ole Vale, wealthy owner of a farm in the neighborhood. There was a special reason for her to turn to this friend for help. Ole Vale was head of the local governing body, spokesman for the community, a public-spirited citizen highly respected for his intelligence and integrity. Moreover, the Vale family already had a particular interest

[13] Theodore C. Blegen, *Norwegian Migration to America, 1825–1860*, 138, 157 (Northfield, Minnesota, 1931).

[14] Blegen, *Norwegian Migration, 1825–1860*, 138. Telemark was one of the regions from which large numbers migrated to America in the decade ending in 1845. Of the 6,200 emigrants in this period, nearly half came from Bratsberg, of which Telemark was a part. More people left from this province than from any other in Norway in the early period of migration.

[15] Flom, *History of Norwegian Immigration*, 224.

in America: two years earlier, a son and a daughter had crossed the ocean to settle in Wisconsin. Their letters had been so intriguing that Ole and his wife, seized with "America fever" themselves, had decided to follow their children. Neighbors were aghast that such well-established people should give up the good life they had known for the rigors of a pioneer existence. But Ole Vale had sold his farm in 1843, and now everyone knew that one of the most substantial families in the community was yielding to the call of the New World.[16]

Thus it was to Ole Vale that Aaste went to inquire about the possibility of a loan to finance her family's journey inland from New York to Wisconsin. She found Ole kind and generous: the loan was granted. Thus the last obstacle was surmounted — and on April 4, 1844, the Norwegian government issued the official emigration certificate to the Jensen family. Now there could be no turning back.

An emigrant family crossing the Atlantic in 1844 had to provide its own food and water. Obviously the preparation of rations for eight people — four of whom were growing boys — for a sea voyage that might stretch out to twelve weeks was a staggering task for any household.[17] Both quantity and quality were of prime importance; nothing that might spoil could be included. Aaste Jensen, following standard practice, relied heavily on Norwegian *flatbrød* as a basic food — a brittle flatbread made of dough rolled thin and baked on top of the stove. This staple was very dry, but it had lasting qualities. Added to it in the food pack were butter, cheese, and salted dried beef. Such fare might be monotonous, but it had twin virtues: it was simple and it was good.

All his life John remembered in sharp detail the day the family said goodby to Norway. The scene was not wholly unfamiliar to him. As a boy, he had watched boatloads of emigrants — the younger Vales, perhaps — with their traditional red-painted chests, on their way to Skien to board ship for America. He had not realized then that *he* would later on join the band of pilgrims journeying to America. Now, in May, 1844, his family was leaving Skibsnæs and Gisholt and Gjeitebua, St. Michael's Church in the cave, and the Norsjø. The parting came hard — the breaking of family

[16] Ytterbøe, *Holla*, 134, 372.

[17] The eighth member of the family group was Aaste's younger sister, Mari Bjørnsdatter Killingkoven.

ties, the tearing up of old, deep communal roots. For John, eldest son and most attached to the familiar haunts of his youth, the experience etched a poignant and lasting picture in his memory.[18]

The voyage of the Jensen family was to be a relatively uneventful one. Their ship, the "Salvator" out of Porsgrund, was a sailing vessel of 380 tons carrying on this trip 151 passengers, all from Telemark. These folk were exceedingly fortunate in their commanding officer, Captain Johan Gasmann of Gjerpen, himself from Telemark, a master with a warm personal concern for his passengers. In a letter to an official at Porsgrund a few months before the voyage, he had described the facilities of the "Salvator" and had set forth helpful suggestions for emigrants. He had urged them to pay strict attention to personal hygiene – to air their sleeping quarters, to scrub them frequently, and unfailingly to take the prescribed exercise on deck. He had warned them to beware of unscrupulous travel and land agents in New York. And – significantly for the Jensen family – he had strongly recommended Wisconsin as a place of settlement.[19]

Captain Gasmann's admiration for inland America and the institutions of the country was based on firsthand data from a brother who had settled at Pine Lake in Waukesha County, Wisconsin, in 1843. Hans Gasmann was no ordinary immigrant. He had been a well-known property owner in Norway and had twice been elected to the Norwegian parliament. Many wondered why he had gone to America, but the fact that he had thirteen children may suggest the reason. He had sold his farm in Norway and, with the proceeds, immediately on his arrival in Wisconsin, had bought 160 acres of land and soon after an additional thousand acres, which he quickly subdivided into extensive farms for his four grown sons. Glowing with the success of his venture in America, he wrote letters extolling the virtues of his new life – to his brother, Captain Johan, and also to others. He had achieved his goal, he wrote – "a higher welfare for all my children." His reputation in the homeland guaranteed that his letters would be published in newspapers there. They carried great weight, thus increasing the personal influence of his brother, the master of the "Salvator."

[18] Many years later, John A. Johnson wrote: "Though but twelve years of age, I had a good cry when the final parting came."

[19] A transcript of Captain Gasmann's letter, dated December 18, 1843, is in the archives of the Norwegian-American Historical Association; Carlton C. Qualey, tr. and ed., "From New York to Wisconsin in 1844," by Johan Gasmann in, *Norwegian-American Studies and Records*, 5:30–49 (Northfield, Minnesota, 1930).

Wisconsin is no doubt indebted in no small degree to the Gasmanns for the early growth of its flourishing Norwegian settlements.[20]

Incidents during the voyage across the North Atlantic soon relieved the inevitable monotony of a long journey. As the "Salvator" passed Lindesnæs, the westernmost point of Norway, everyone strained to keep the shore in sight as long as possible. Then the coast receded, and a mood of sadness overtook many who until then had held up well. There was a brisk wind as the ship crossed the North Sea; then near the Shetlands they encountered rain and fog. The ship rolled and some, including John, were "uncomfortable." The sight of icebergs created considerable concern, but all went well. A bit travel-worn, the passengers looked forward to making the Newfoundland banks. There might be fishing for cod – and a welcome change from a salt-meat diet. The fishing tackle was brought out, but Captain Gasmann held to the course. The wind was favorable; they must keep sailing. On July 4, 1844, the "Salvator" arrived in New York harbor after a crossing lasting six weeks.[21]

Shipboard experiences of the twelve-year-old-boy – soon to be known by the Skibsnæs name – had been memorable. Stocks of food and water had grown smaller and the supply of wood for fuel scanty. It had been stowed in the hold of the ship under a cargo of iron bars, and the approach was so narrow that only small boys could crawl in to pull the sticks of firewood out. There could be no light because of the fire hazard; so the youngsters had to feel their way. As the ship rolled, the iron bars clanged together, making a noise like a tolling bell. The experience was frightening, but John did the work well and was tapped for duty several times. He was permitted to climb the mast, and he enjoyed the exalted view from on high. He liked this sensation much better than creeping along the bottom of the boat under the iron cargo. The ship and the sea intrigued him, and he dreamed of becoming a sailor.

As they set foot on American soil, members of the Skibsnæs (Jensen) family – each in his own way – doubtless experienced strongly rising emotions in which exaltation and fear mingled. They were typical immi-

[20] Blegen, *Norwegian Migration, 1825–1860*, 151, 178, 206–208. Quotations from Hans Gasmann's letters were published in *Christianssandsposten*, December 22, 1843, and in *Morgenbladet* (Christiania), December 19, 1844.

[21] Gerhard Brandt Naeseth, *The Naeseth-Fehn Family History*, 4 (Madison, Wisconsin, 1956). The ship actually docked on July 5, according to the passenger list of Captain Gasmann, but John A. Johnson later recalled flags flying and evening fireworks on the day the ship sailed into the harbor.

grants of the 1840's. Anders Jensen was forty; his wife Aaste Killingkoven was thirty-six. The four boys ranged in two-year steps: John was twelve, Oliver ten, Hans eight, and Ole six. Their sister, Inger Andersdatter, was a baby a year old. Aunt Mari was twenty-two. Now hand in hand they all stood in the legendary land of America ready to explore its newness and its promise.

At best, New York was only a halfway house. Immigrants bound for the Upper Midwest had little understanding of the immense distance they still must travel. It would be interesting to know what Aaste Skibsnæs was thinking as she said her farewell to kindly Captain Gasmann and left the temporary shelter of the "Salvator." Now the Atlantic was behind them – and still farther behind lay Norway. Ahead were tedious weeks of journeying and many hardships before they would reach their new home.

Immigrants headed for the West were being routed by boat up the Hudson River to Albany, there to connect with the Erie Canal traversing the state of New York to the eastern shore of Lake Erie. The Skibsnæs family were not alone on the river boat; with them – also bound for the West – were most of the folk who had sailed on the "Salvator." The short trip on the Hudson was a new experience, but not a particularly pleasant one. The boat was heavily loaded and the night chilly. Aaste tucked her children in as best she could on deck amidst the baggage. Perhaps the young ones slept under their scanty covering, but the parents kept vigil most of the night. In the early morning they arrived in Albany, ready to be transferred to the canal, the famous artery that carried thousands of immigrant travelers on their way to the Midland Empire.

Traveling in a boat pulled by horses on shore proved to be a novelty, but the pace was deadly slow – a mere four miles an hour. Accommodations on the canalboat were poor; fares varied and the family, hoarding their resources with care, had to choose the very cheapest. Milwaukee was still far away. Adventures enlivened the dull days: they passed 83 water gates, they bumped another canal boat, and finally they ignominiously stuck fast on a mud bank. The week-long haul of 363 miles was an enormous test of patience. Writing of it many years later, Johnson called it a "lazy life." Arrival in Buffalo marked another milestone, but three great inland lakes – Erie, Huron, and Michigan – seemed still to push their goal farther into the unknown.[22]

[22] John B. McMaster, *A History of the People of the United States: From the*

John called the lake steamer they boarded at Buffalo a "rickety old propeller for Milwaukee." This was the largest ship they had ever seen. It crowded in a thousand passengers, all types of people; the immigrants realized that now indeed they were in the land of the melting pot. Unlike Captain Gasmann, the ship's officers showed no concern for the passengers. The captain was intent on maintaining a schedule. Speed was the watchword. The Skibsnæs family settled down on deck rather than in the hold, their only other choice. Their spirits rose as the vessel finally steered southward into Lake Michigan. On the right they saw the shoreline of Wisconsin. Now the land of promise seemed a reality – no longer a mirage in the doubtful distance. Here was the port of Milwaukee after three monotonous and uncomfortable weeks of travel from New York. Nine weeks had passed since the May day when they bade farewell to Norway.

The last lap of the journey had to be traversed on foot. Their funds now exhausted, the family had no alternative but to walk the forty-five miles to Heart Prairie near the present site of Whitewater, Wisconsin. Their meager possessions, brought so many miles by water, were stored in Milwaukee until money could be found to pay for transporting them inland. So they set out with Mother Aaste carrying little Inger and Ole riding pickaback when his short legs grew weary. The three older boys trudged along behind their parents. On the way, they slept in barns and ate the last powdery crumbs of *flatbrød*. The July weather was fair and warm. There were no delays, no serious difficulties. With grateful hearts, the travelers from a faraway land at last saw ahead a beautiful little prairie. This was the place.[23]

They were welcomed by the two families who had come from their neighborhood in Norway the previous year. Johnson later recalled the scene: "In due time we arrived at Søgaards, who met us with a hearty greeting." Hans Milebaand turned his modest house over to the newcomers. It was only ten by twelve feet; what mattered was not the size of the dwelling but the bigness of heart that put it in their hands.[24]

The parents looked about them in the new land for whose promise they

Revolution to the Civil War, 5: 135 (New York, 1902); Hjalmar Rued Holand, *De norske settlementers historie*, 68 (Ephraim, Wisconsin, 1908).

[23] Heart Prairie lay in the southern part of Whitewater Township and the northern part of Richmond Township in Walworth County. Six miles away was Sugar Creek, another settlement of immigrants from Telemark.

[24] Milebaand and his wife moved to a pioneer cabin on another piece of land owned by them.

had left their homes, their kindred, and the graves of their forefathers. To reach it, they had sold everything that could be turned into money; they had even gone into debt. What did the future hold? What would this chosen place do for their children? Would their own old age be happy and contented? The discomforts of the weeks just past had represented to them a sort of purgatory, an interval of endurance through which they must pass on their way to paradise.[25] They realized that from their old-world inheritance they must summon inner strength to meet the challenge that a richly endowed frontier offered. As the test began, the family were all in excellent health. To cross the ocean and half a continent had been a giant undertaking. Success in that great adventure now stood as a measure of their capacity to make a place for themselves in their new environment.

[25] The fact that immigrants often referred to America as "Paradise" reveals the depth of their emotional commitment and the profound sense of fulfillment they felt when they reached their destination in the New World.

CHAPTER II

An Immigrant Family

Wisconsin was in the early stages of settlement when the Skibsnæs family arrived in the summer of 1844. Only a dozen years before, the United States had secured from the Indians title to the land south of the Fox and Wisconsin rivers, thus making possible the opening of the region to settlers. Wisconsin Territory had been organized in 1836, a vast expanse of prairie and forest reaching westward to what are today the Dakotas. In the heart of the forest lay the capital city of Madison.[1] Into this virgin area, the immigrant boy John A. Johnson and his family came with the wave of pioneers who were to lay the basis for the growth of a great commonwealth.

Like a sleeping giant, the future state awaited the arrival of men with the strength, imagination, and capital to awaken it. It was a land of rich and varied resources. Great waterways led to distant markets – to the vast interior of the continent and to the growing port cities of the Atlantic coast. The network of Wisconsin rivers emptying into the Mississippi opened a highway of commerce reaching to St. Louis. Already an important center of trade, this burgeoning city served the huge basin drained by three continental rivers – the Missouri, the Mississippi, and the Ohio. Lead was shipped to St. Louis from the mines of southwestern Wisconsin. Lake Michigan was the first link in a chain of waterways stretching eastward to American centers of manufacture and trade, and to ships carrying products to the Old World. When the Skibsnæs family

[1] John B. McMaster, *A History of the People of the United States: From the Revolution to the Civil War*, 7: 201 (New York, 1910).

arrived, Wisconsin wheat was already reaching the rapidly increasing market created by the industrial revolution in England and on the European continent.[2]

Land was the resource that contributed material necessities to the immigrants from Norway—land in what is now southern Wisconsin, a rich black soil that produced an abundance of wheat. When the Skibsnæs family arrived, they found a considerable number of other newly settled immigrants: by 1850, two years after Wisconsin became a state, nearly half of the Scandinavians in America were living in its eastern and southern counties.[3] They had been drawn there by the seemingly endless stretches of fertile land that could be bought for very little: in 1844 the price of government land was $1.25 an acre. Walworth County, where John and his family made their new home, was near Lake Michigan, the great highway to the East. The new settlers could haul their wheat to Milwaukee in *kubberuller*, crude wagons with wheels sawed from large oak logs.

Anders Skibsnæs had no money to buy land—even at $1.25 an acre. Complicating his financial situation was the fact that he owed a modest sum to Ole Vale, who had advanced part of the money that had brought the family to Wisconsin. Resolutely they chose to forgo all other expenditures in order to pay this debt. When they decided to remain in Walworth County, their good friend Milebaand urged them to extend their stay in his log house until they could provide permanent shelter for themselves—and the generous offer was accepted. Thus the tiny dwelling on Heart Prairie became John A. Johnson's first home in America.

For a time John's father worked for "Americans"; he also helped Ole Vale build a house, thus by late fall discharging half his debt. But just as things seemed to be going well, the father was taken ill with malaria, with the near-tragic result that he was disabled for six months. Unfortunately, the children too were sick and Aaste, the mother, had to assume the care of the family and at the same time to earn their bread. Often she walked a half dozen miles and back to do a day's washing for others, carrying on her return the provisions she had received for her work. Her sister Marie (Mari) also contributed her earnings. In this manner, they found a way to live through the first difficult months in the new land.[4]

[2] Shipments to England became especially significant after the repeal of the Corn Laws in 1846.

[3] *Wisconsin: A Guide to the Badger State*, 160 (New York, 1941).

[4] John A. Johnson, *Fingerpeg for farmere og andre* (Hints for Farmers and Others), 148 (Chicago, 1884). This is a book of 166 pages intended to give advice

In the emergency twelve-year-old John, up from his sickbed, also began to contribute to the support of the household. He went to live with an American family, working for board and room — a fortunate enough move, for his new friends treated him kindly and sent him to "English school," as the immigrants called the public school. There was a dark side, too: he was dreadfully homesick, so unhappy at times that he could not eat. "I would have given anything to be back in Norway," he wrote later. Clearly the acquiring of a feeling of being at home in an alien wilderness meant for him a painful adjustment.

By the spring of 1845, Anders Skibsnæs had recovered his good health. Seeking gainful employment, he went to Mineral Point, Wisconsin, where he earned fifty cents a day — which he considered "good wages" — helping to build houses for men working in the lead mines. John, now turning a sturdy thirteen, accompanied him; the boy's knowledge of English, the new language which the father so far had not learned, proved of immediate practical value. As Mineral Point was a Cornish settlement, anyone who could not speak English was at a great disadvantage; so young John served as an interpreter. He had the further experience of working for his board in a combined grocery store and saloon, where he had to learn to mix and serve drinks. Here he saw drinking, gambling, and the rawness of a frontier community. What he observed disturbed him, and he tried to persuade other boys of his age not to drink — the beginning of a lifelong stand against the use of alcohol.

The opportunity for profitable work at Mineral Point ended after only six weeks. Johnson later wrote, "Father and I returned home, he then being a capitalist to the extent of 16 dollars."[5] With that small fortune safely pocketed, father and son set out on the hundred-mile trek to Walworth County. They walked the whole way, not lingering in spite of early summer heat or the lack of good drinking water. Small wonder that John remembered the trip as "difficult." The travelers spent the second night in Madison, where they slept in the barn of the Lake House Inn for twenty-five cents. Little did he dream, Johnson wrote years afterward, that Madison would one day be his home, and that he would occupy an office in the court house and sit in the state capitol as one of the lawmakers. In the afternoon of the fourth day, Anders and John found them-

to immigrants from Norway who wanted to become farmers in America. It was widely circulated without charge by the Fuller and Johnson Manufacturing Company. Hereafter it will be referred to as *Fingerpeg*. See also Johnson's "Memoirs."

[5] Johnson's "Memoirs." See also his *Fingerpeg*, 148.

selves in the family home at Heart Prairie with Mother Aaste, who in their absence had managed courageously and well.

How to spend the sixteen dollars was the question now facing the Skibsnæs family. They still owed Ole Vale a final payment. But there was another even more compelling consideration: they did not have a cow. "Working out" for others, they were often paid in meat, flour, corn, and vegetables. A cow to provide milk would fill a pressing need, especially when the young children were considered. Because milk was so important, Anders Skibsnæs went to Ole Vale and set the problem squarely before him, requesting additional time to pay the remainder of his debt. And Vale, goodhearted man that he was, readily assented.

Years later, Johnson wrote that it was he who had noticed a "mouse-colored" cow with a black and white heifer calf; now, their Mineral Point fortune intact, he and his father went to the owner. For ten dollars they acquired the two animals—their first property in America. Later the cow was transferred to Ole Vale as the final payment on the obligation incurred in coming to the New World. The calf in time became the nucleus of a future herd for the family.[6]

John and his father did not return to work at Mineral Point. For the next five years the boy was employed summers by farmers in the Heart Prairie region, his usual wages being three dollars a month with board and room. During the winter months he worked for his board and room and attended "English school." The reading he had done at his grandmother's knee and in the home of Ole Arnesen Gisholt now gave depth and richness to his later learning.

In Norway John had read the Bible, even including the Apocrypha. He had cherished it chiefly for its stories; and these he had read many times until they had become very real—Joshua, Samuel, the Kings and Chronicles, Daniel, the Maccabees. He also knew the Psalms, the Gospels, the Acts, the Epistles, and Revelations. He wrote in his "Memoirs," "Those who miss reading the Bible, especially in early life, miss what must be very difficult to replace in any other way." It is clear that childhood familiarity with Scripture was a strong formative influence throughout John A. Johnson's whole life. The persistence of his parents—and of others in the family—in encouraging him in his youth to seek out the values of books had introduced him to wide horizons.

[6] Johnson's "Memoirs." See also his *Fingerpeg*, 148.

Once settled in their American environment, the parents of John A. Johnson were eager that their children should attend the frontier "English school" during its few months of winter sessions. In such a school a well-trained teacher was a rarity, but this mattered little to John. His eagerness and industry compensated for all deficiencies. And for such a student, certain instructors opened vistas of what learning could mean. In his "Memoirs" he referred to "an excellent lady teacher" who was skilled in arithmetic and under whose direction he became a fair reader and a good speller. One winter a man who taught the district school stressed "orthography" and "orthoëpy." Under such teachers the young immigrant learned to speak English correctly, with a sensitive ear to inflections and with no trace of an accent. To increase his vocabulary, John took to Webster's *Dictionary* every unfamiliar word encountered in his reading. This practice helped him acquire verbal proficiency and at the same time trained his memory. The English language became for him a medium in which – in the words of a great Norwegian-American novelist – "one's emotional life can move . . . freely and naturally." [7]

John finished his schooling in 1850 at a "little high school" in Fort Atkinson, where for part of a year he studied algebra and grammar. Though this marked the end of his formal schooling, his education was to go on – for some years on the other side of the desk. At the age of eighteen he was certified as well qualified to teach district school – the first vocation that lay open to him.[8]

Anders and Aaste Skibsnæs brought with them to America the strong influence of an old-world religious heritage – an important link with their own youth and one which they fervently desired to preserve in the life of their family. The year they arrived at Heart Prairie, Norwegian Lutheran pioneers there had formed a congregation with the Reverend Claus L. Clausen as pastor. On the shore of lovely Whitewater Lake, the immigrants built a small brick church and provided it with a bell to call people to service. In this congregation, at the age of sixteen, John A. Johnson was confirmed by the Reverend J. W. C. Dietrichson, a clergyman educated in Norway.[9]

[7] Theodore Jorgenson and Nora O. Solum, *Ole Edvart Rölvaag: A Biography*, 115 (New York, 1939). For an excerpt from Johnson's "Memoirs" describing his school days, see the Appendix, p. 277.

[8] Teaching seemed the natural occupation of members of John's family: two of his brothers and his two sisters were at one time or another to teach in public schools in Wisconsin and Minnesota.

[9] Johnson, "Memoirs." A larger church has been built in the city of Whitewater,

The Skibsnæs parents also sent their children to a Lutheran parochial school, but in pioneer days such schools could be held only when a teacher was available. John's father was a charter subscriber to the first Norwegian Lutheran church paper published in the United States – *Maanedstidende* (Monthly Times), whose first issue came off the press in Racine, Wisconsin, in March, 1851. Its first editors were the pastors Claus L. Clausen, Hans A. Stub, and Adolph C. Preus. It was the organ of the Norwegian Evangelical Lutheran Church of America, later to be known as the Norwegian Synod. It is clear that from the first the Skibsnæs family believed strongly in the values of a close-knit religious organization and faithfully supported their pioneer church paper.[10]

The Reverend C. L. Clausen soon felt the need for a paper not wholly limited to church matters. His goal was the education of the immigrant in American affairs, and to that end he took the initiative in organizing a press association in which both pastors and laymen of the Norwegian Synod participated actively. In order to establish a paper on a firm financial basis, the association sold shares, the majority of which were bought by laymen.

Clausen became the first editor of the Norwegian-language secular paper called *Emigranten*; the first issue was published on January 23, 1852, at Inmansville, Wisconsin. It was the crusading editor's avowed intention to hasten the process of Americanization among his immigrant countrymen – and he attacked the problem with fiery zeal. "We want to be one with the Americans," he wrote in an early editorial. "In this way alone can they [*the immigrants*] fulfill their destiny and contribute their part to the final development and character of this Great Nation." In the turbulent decade preceding the Civil War, *Emigranten* was inevitably drawn into the arena of national politics. The paper first announced itself

but in the summer services are still held in the old building. See "History of the Heart Prairie Church," in *Forward: The Centennial Book, First Lutheran Church* (Whitewater, Wisconsin, 1958). The old church has been carefully preserved and the cemetery well kept.

[10] Olaf M. Norlie, *History of the Norwegian People in America*, 225 (Minneapolis, 1925). *Maanedstidende* continued in regular publication except for the years 1854–1855. In 1874 it changed its official title to *Evangelisk Luthersk Kirketidende.* The press on which it was originally printed was later moved to Inmansville, Wisconsin. Names of the original subscribers are to be found in the "Record Book of the Subscription List of *Maanedstidende*," in the archives of the Norwegian-American Historical Association, Northfield, Minnesota. See also Theodore C. Blegen, "The Early Norwegian Press in America," in *Minnesota History Bulletin*, 3:513, 515 (November, 1920).

as Independent-Democratic. But, as the question of slavery stirred the Norwegian people and the Kansas-Nebraska Bill became a heated issue, Clausen took a determined stand against slavery and for the preservation of the Union – and moved his paper into the Republican ranks.[11]

The influence of Clausen and *Emigranten* confirmed and strengthened the concern of Anders and Aaste Skibsnæs and their sons about slavery. John, who was twenty years old the year the paper began publishing, read English-language newspapers as well as the one in Norwegian. His parents, however, like many other recent immigrants, welcomed *Emigranten* in their native tongue and relied on it for information on national events and issues. When a proposed constitution for Wisconsin was rejected in 1847, John and his family were still living in Walworth County. In this part of the Territory, the Negro suffrage provision, submitted to the voters at the same time, was approved. Significantly, the only three counties to vote in the affirmative on that particular provision were areas in which Norwegian immigrants predominated.[12]

John A. Johnson and his parents continued to hold firm convictions about slavery, and they found in *Emigranten* an exemplar and guide in their developing philosophy as American citizens. John early bought shares in the paper; in time he became an able contributor on matters of concern to immigrants. In his writings he stressed the importance of preserving the Union. He was equally firm in his belief that the institution of slavery was not in harmony with the principles of the Declaration of Independence.

Four years after their arrival in Wisconsin, the Skibsnæs family felt secure enough in their new environment to think seriously of acquiring land on which to establish a permanent home. The boys were growing up and contributing more each year to the family coffers. But the best land in Heart Prairie had been sold earlier to moneyed settlers from New York and New England; these people were now well-established farmers. The

[11] Theodore C. Blegen, *Norwegian Migration to America: The American Transition*, 307, 308 (Northfield, Minnesota, 1940); Arlow W. Andersen, *The Immigrant Takes His Stand: The Norwegian-American Press and Public Affairs, 1847–1872*, 12, 16, 17, 23 (Northfield, Minnesota, 1953).

[12] Kendric C. Babcock, *The Scandinavian Element in the United States*, 158 (Urbana, Illinois, 1914). The constitution and the provision concerning Negro suffrage were both printed in English and Norwegian newspapers. Copies of these documents in Norwegian can be found in the archives of the Norwegian-American Historical Association.

only land for sale when John's family felt ready to buy was of marginal quality. In spite of their discouragement, Anders decided to buy what could be had: 40 acres of poor government land, swampy and rough, for which he paid $50 – borrowed at 40 per cent interest! Soon he added another 40 acres of still poorer land adjoining his first purchase. There was plenty of open cattle range on the tract and wild meadow land providing hay for their herd. The father and boys found work as "hired men" on nearby farms and were able in this way to earn a meager living. But there seemed no promise at all for the future. John, nearing his majority, had to make plans. Finally the family decided to sell the farm for whatever it would bring – "even to abandon it rather than to stay on it." [13]

Now that they were determined to leave Heart Prairie, John's parents were strongly influenced to move to the Koshkonong area in Dane County – for them a cross-country trek of about fifty miles. This region, settled by immigrants of Norwegian descent as early as 1840, enjoyed a fabulous reputation. Its pioneers were so boastful of its rich and bountiful soil that something of a legend had grown up about it. Corn there attained a growth unknown elsewhere, the prairie grass grew as tall as a man, the marshes provided excellent grazing ground for cattle, and from the woods came fuel and lumber in abundance. Paraphrasing Horace Greeley, an enthusiastic settler advised a young immigrant who had reached eastern Wisconsin: "Go farther west; not until you reach Koshkonong will you find America." [14]

The language was perhaps a bit extravagant, but there was much to endear the Koshkonong area to immigrant families like that of Anders and Aaste. There was the largest Norwegian settlement in Wisconsin, including many friends from Telemark. John and his parents felt sure that in its friendly environment – among people whose dialect, legends, ballads, and dress would be happily familiar – they would find an opportunity to make a successful new start.

Of prime importance to the Skibsnæs family was the personal tie drawing them to Dane County. In Koshkonong lived Aunt Marie, Aaste's sis-

[13] Johnson, "Memoirs." The Skibsnæs eighty acres were located near Bass Lake, five miles due south of Whitewater. Land records in the National Archives show that "Andras Johnson" secured title to the first acreage on July 13, 1848, and that "Andrew Johnson" bought the second tract on October 11 of the same year.

[14] Theodore C. Blegen, *Norwegian Migration to America, 1825–1860,* 144 (Northfield, Minnesota, 1931); Carlton C. Qualey, *Norwegian Settlement in the United States,* 52 (Northfield, Minnesota, 1938).

ter, now married to Peter Halvorson. All the family, grateful for her help in earlier emergencies, longed to be near again to their only close relative in America. And so when an invitation came to John from the Halvorsons, they immediately decided on a preliminary step: John, representing his parents, brothers, and sisters,[15] would go to Koshkonong on a visit. At the same time he would scout for available land at a price they could pay.

Armed with a sum of money and the full confidence of the family group, twenty-year-old John in early April, 1852, set out on horseback on his quest. Before the month had passed, he was in the process of buying an 80-acre farm near his uncle and aunt. He had hoped that he had enough cash for the initial payment on the land. But in this he was disappointed — it was not nearly enough. Making a real sacrifice, he offered to surrender his horse as well. Still not enough — and John was heartsick, for here was an eminently desirable piece of land in the middle of the soil-rich Koshkonong prairie. In this desperate impasse, Aunt Marie and Uncle Peter Halvorson found a way.

John A. Johnson later wrote: "Uncle Peter very generously gave me a mortgage on his farm on which to raise $200 [more] for the first payment on our land. I went to many places to get the money, Milwaukee and other places. I finally got it by paying 30 per cent interest." With the money received from one John Bell, who held the mortgage, John completed the sale. The land of which Anders and Aaste Jensen Skibsnæs now became owners was situated in Pleasant Springs Township, Dane County.[16]

In the summer of 1852, the family moved from Walworth County to their new farm. In every way it was a fortunate step and a milestone in the lives of all concerned. Here the four sons and two daughters would live until they set out on their own. Dane County would be Johnson's home for the rest of his life — and he would give of his strength and ability to its development. Looking back many years later on the important move from Heart Prairie to Pleasant Springs, he wrote: "All the boys turned in to help pay for father's farm. Our first concern was to make our parents reasonably comfortable. The new farm was a very good one. In due time

[15] A second sister, Caroline, had been born in Walworth County on April 1, 1846.

[16] Peter Halvorson and wife to John A. Johnson, in *Mortgage Record*, office of register of deeds, Dane County, Wisconsin, vol. 5, 674 (Madison, Wisconsin, April 28, 1852); John Johnson in *Deed Book*, office of register of deeds, Dane County, Wisconsin, vol. 15, 282 (Madison, Wisconsin, April 14, 1852). Although the deed was in John's name, he had purchased the land for his parents. John A. Johnson paid in full the mortgage held by Bell on March 29, 1855.

comfortable buildings appeared and my parents spent their last days in modest comfort." [17]

It was time for John to make his own start in life, and in this process his ingrained habits of industry and thrift stood him in good stead. Late in 1854, at the age of twenty-two, he purchased about 140 acres of land in Pleasant Springs Township from John Spear Nicholas of Baltimore, Maryland. For this property he engaged to pay $1,482.76 in three installments, the last in November, 1857, with interest at 10 per cent. To finance improving the land and building a house, he secured another loan on which he paid 12 per cent interest. The panic of 1857 caught him, and there were those who predicted that he would lose his farm. But he did not lose it. Accustomed to working hard, he was also trained in economy. In summer he worked on his farm; in winter he taught the Pleasant Springs school, in a building located near the Skibsnæs farm. As a side line, he sold farm machinery for a firm in Beloit, Wisconsin. Having weathered the panic, he emerged at the end of 1860 – aged twenty-eight – as the owner of a debt-free, productive Dane County property.[18]

In 1856, two years after he had first established himself as a farmer, John brought to his new home a bride, Karen Kristine Thompson. His family and hers had been friends in the Old World, where they had all lived in the vicinity of Lake Norsjø. Karen had been born in Norway in the same year as her future husband. As children they had crossed the ocean together on the "Salvator" and with their families had come to Heart Prairie. Karen's father was Hans Thomason Vale, known in America as Hans Thompson – a prominent farmer of some means and a leader in developing the Heart Prairie community. Now the early friendship between the two Norwegian immigrant families was strengthened by a closer tie through the marriage of Karen and John.[19]

John did not neglect the duties of citizenship in his community. Wisconsin in 1848 had adopted a liberal constitution which enabled foreign-born white men to become voters upon taking a simple oath of allegiance. With

[17] Johnson, "Memoirs." Still called "the old Skibsnæs farm," the property is now owned by Oscar Berge.

[18] The deed for John's farm, dated December 15, 1854, was recorded on April 4, 1855.

[19] Information from *The "Salvator" Passenger List of 1844*. A copy is in the Johnson Papers. The Thompson family made Heart Prairie their permanent home. Their log dwelling there was the meetinghouse of the original congregation until the Heart Prairie church was built.

a lively interest in the world about him, he eagerly availed himself of this opportunity to identify himself politically with local administration in his new state. He immediately qualified as a voter and soon as a township and county officer. Two years after he had moved to Pleasant Springs, he was elected town clerk, at the age of twenty-two. Successively he held positions as assessor, justice of the peace, and supervisor in the township. Later he became chairman of the town board, a position which made him *ex officio* a member of the Dane County Board and chairman of a number of the important committees of that body.[20]

Not long after assuming his first township office, John took the next logical step leading to political activity in a wider field. On November 19, 1856, he became a citizen of the United States, renouncing and abjuring his allegiance and fidelity to Oscar I, king of Sweden and Norway. Two immigrant neighbors at Koshkonong testified concerning his character: Gunnar Torgersen Mandt, who had come from Telemark in 1842, and Lars Knudson, who in the same year had emigrated from Numedal. Instead of the original name of Jens Anderson Jensen Skibsnæs, the new citizen's naturalization papers bore the name of John A. Johnson.[21]

Politics continued to interest John's active mind. In Walworth County he had lived among New Englanders and families from New York state. These "Yankees" were generally Whigs and John grew to respect their political philosophy.[22] Like almost all of his Norwegian immigrant associates, however, he had strong leanings toward the Democrats. Until the slavery question thrust its ugly head upward, the Democratic party in Wisconsin could definitely count on a solid bloc of Norwegian votes. But abhorrence of the evil of slavery drove John and his friends to favor first the Free Soilers and eventually the Republicans. There was a complete revolution in Norwegian allegiance over the red-hot issue posed by the Kansas-Nebraska Bill. To the dismay of the local Democratic organization, Pleasant Springs almost to a man joined the antislavery cause.

Johnson entered Republican politics at the grass roots. The township of Pleasant Springs was one of five comprising the southeast district as-

[20] *Emigranten* (Madison, Wisconsin), October 1, 1860.

[21] Hjalmar Rued Holand, *De norske settlementers historie*, 155 (Ephraim, Wisconsin, 1908). There is a copy of John A. Johnson's naturalization documents in the Johnson Papers. Before his certification as a citizen, John had used the name Johnson, but in his home community he was still referred to as John Skibsnæs and sometimes as Jens Skibsnæs.

[22] In his "Memoirs," looking back on this period of his life, he characterized the Whigs as "a glorious old party."

sembly of the newly formed party organization in Dane County. Representatives of this group met at Utica, Wisconsin, on May 29, 1856, to elect delegates to the Republican state convention. John, still youthful and a neophyte in politics, took a prominent part as one of three members of the resolutions committee. From this committee came a document vigorously opposing all attempts to "nationalize" slavery, deploring the infringement of state's rights by the "general government" in Washington, "reprobating" the principles of the Know-Nothing party, and urging support of Republican candidates soon to be chosen at the 1856 national convention in Philadelphia.[23]

Johnson's ability to state his position in clear and forceful language undoubtedly impressed the Republican assembly at Utica. He was first chosen one of two delegates to represent the county's southeastern townships, and then one of eight delegates to go to the state Republican convention to speak for Dane County. So there was twenty-four-year-old John on the floor of a major political meeting in Madison on June 4, 1856. Here again slavery was the focus of discussion. Head-on attack was directed at the Missouri Compromise – "that act of legislative perfidy." The convention's banners flashed a fighting slogan: "Eternal Hostility to Slavery Extension." The Wisconsin convention took a strong civil rights position: "All men, irrespective of nativity or religion, are entitled to equal rights." It adopted resolutions against the whole institution of slavery and elected delegates to represent the state's Republicans at the party's national convention.

A prominent role in two Republican conventions within a week's time gave the name of John A. Johnson political currency during the summer of 1856. John himself was busy on his farm, but, as he recalled in his "Memoirs," "politics were getting warm," and he went in his working clothes to nearby Stoughton to see what was going on at the Republican nominating convention for southeastern Dane County. Intending to be merely an onlooker, he found himself quickly drafted as one of the delegates from his township. That day he probably served in his overalls.

Pleasant Springs had no candidate for the Wisconsin state assembly to match ambitious office seekers from Albion, Rutland, and other townships. Johnson's friends encircled him, begging him to be their man. At

[23] *Madison Daily State Journal* (Madison, Wisconsin) June 6, 1856. The direct political attack of the Southeast Dane County resolution was centered on the policies of the administration of Franklin Pierce, which its framers felt to be weak and vacillating on the slavery issue. A copy of the resolution is in the Appendix, p. 278.

first he refused to run; he was not yet twenty-five years old and he felt too young and inexperienced. But the persistence of his eager backers broke down all objections, and finally he gave his consent. Perhaps rivals from other townships looked askance at the "boy intruder." In the end, however, John won the nomination to become the Republican candidate to represent five townships of Dane County. One Madison paper described him as Norwegian by birth, "intelligent, capable, and faithful . . . in every way a worthy and honest man." In the November election, Johnson defeated his Democratic opponent, James Allen, by a vote of 744 to 335.[24]

Johnson's initial experience as a member of the Wisconsin legislature of 1857 was to participate in the election of a United States senator. Two worthy candidates had announced themselves: Judge Timothy D. Howe and Judge James R. Doolittle. The young assemblyman admired both men and found it difficult to decide upon his personal choice. Howe was honest and frank, but his leaning toward state's rights was disturbing. Years later, recalling the contest for senator, Johnson wrote: "A slight concession on the states rights by Judge Howe would have won him the election." Howe would make no concession. And, since Doolittle's position on slavery and state's rights coincided with his own, Johnson voted for him and was pleased when his man, after a long and close political battle, was chosen by the assembly to represent Wisconsin as a United States senator in Washington.[25]

Of all legislation debated in the assembly of 1857, none was as important to Johnson as a proposal to extend the suffrage. As a test of national feeling, the bill embodying this change attracted wide attention in both the North and the South. It proposed that the right to vote be granted to all persons at the age of twenty-one without reference to sex, color, or birth. The real issue was Negro suffrage. True, there were not many Negroes in Wisconsin, but to Johnson the principle of equality was the heart of the matter. Representing what he knew to be the wishes of his Dane County constituency, he spoke and voted for the bill. In the assembly it received a favorable (40-33) vote, but it failed in the state senate. Again and again in later debates, he would be found on the antislavery side. He never deviated from his belief in the basic equality of all men.[26]

At the time Johnson entered the Wisconsin state assembly, the "Booth

[24] Johnson, "Memoirs"; *Madison Daily State Journal,* October 25, November 12, 1856.

[25] Johnson, "Memoirs"; *Madison Daily State Journal,* January 23, 1857.

[26] *Madison Daily State Journal,* March 2, 3, 1857.

case," a cause célèbre of two years earlier, was still exercising strong influence toward antislavery thinking in the state. In 1855 the supreme court of Wisconsin had declared the Fugitive Slave Law unconstitutional and had twice released, by writs of habeas corpus, an editor named Sherman M. Booth who had been convicted in federal courts for violation of the law. Scorn and bitterness arising from this jurisdictional clash still lingered, but many Wisconsin leaders — John A. Johnson among them — were proud to live in a northern state which had dared to defy the federal government in a matter involving so clear a moral issue.

Although Johnson himself wrote later that his influence in the legislature was very modest, it is clear that he left evidence in that body of his intelligence and good judgment — and of his enormous capacity for preparation and hard work on all assignments. He was one of a five-man committee on charitable and religious institutions, which had responsibilities for the state's prisons, mental hospitals, schools for the deaf, dumb, and blind, and the so-called "house of refuge for juvenile delinquents." He took his duties seriously, developing concern for the human problems he met. Evidences of his experience and solicitude in the whole area of social legislation were to appear often in his later life.[27]

Among Johnson's colleagues and associates in the Wisconsin assembly were a number of able men, destined to be his lifelong friends, who were to play a prominent role in Wisconsin affairs as the years passed. John C. Spooner, a lawyer who became a United States senator, was one of these. Forty years after their first acquaintance, Spooner wrote a helpful letter to his friend: "If in your trip abroad you run across any Diplomatic or Consular officer of the United States who knows me or of me, and would be willing to do me a kindness, you will please present this letter as a request from me that he show you such courtesies as he may be able, and that I shall regard any kindness shown you as a kindness to me, and will remember it as such."[28]

The young assemblyman also formed a lasting friendship with S. D. Hastings, a member of the 1857 legislature and later state treasurer. Twenty-eight years after their earlier association, Hastings wrote to his former colleague: "Ever since I first formed your acquaintance . . . I have had for you high esteem and regard. I have watched your course all the years since that time and I have always found you the outspoken

[27] *Madison Daily State Journal*, January 17, 1857.
[28] John C. Spooner to Johnson, May 28, 1897.

friend of all that was good and the unflinching oppressor of all that was wrong in the community. . . . I have always admired the candid spirit in which you have discussed public matters and the frank and fearless manner in which you have given expression to your views." [29]

Philetus Sawyer was another close longtime friend from the early days in the assembly. Of Sawyer, who also became a United States senator at the height of his career, Johnson wrote many years later. "[He was] a man of middle age as quiet and reserved as I was." In his "Memoirs" Johnson always expressed respect for courageous and principled men who would rather go down to defeat than betray their convictions.

After his term in the state legislature, Johnson returned to his acres in the attractive Koshkonong community. From his youth he had liked farming. It was the business he understood. Now he planned that he and his wife would live out their days there. It was a good plan, but other events were shaping themselves. John did not long remain a farmer.

On September 24, 1860 — in his twenty-ninth year — John A. Johnson was nominated by the Republican party of Dane County as clerk of the county board of supervisors. He was the only nominee of Norwegian descent on the ticket of either major party. Hans Borchsenius, his Democratic opponent, was a printer who had come from Denmark and who had become editor and publisher of *Nordstjernen*, a Democratic paper supported by Scandinavians in Madison. His residence in America had been brief, and he had had no experience in county politics.[30]

In spite of his love for the life of a farmer, Johnson threw himself actively into the campaign for the desirable new office. He wrote to his brother Ole on October 4 that he had "hopes of election" and added, "Can you lend me your watch during the fall as I am in want of a timepiece when I am out electioneering? If you can spare it send it by express." There can be little doubt that John was relying for first-line support on the loyalty of his own family. It is a virtual certainty that Ole's watch timed him through the remainder of the campaign.

He had other valuable backing. *Emigranten*, widely circulated among Norwegians, supported his candidacy. Hans C. Heg, Wisconsin prison commissioner, lent his energy to Johnson's campaign. Of Norwegian descent and a state leader among the immigrants, Heg possessed political

[29] S. D. Hastings to Johnson, February 17, 1885.

[30] *Emigranten*, October 1, 1860; O. N. Nelson, comp. and ed., *History of the Scandinavians and Successful Scandinavians in the United States*, 2: 326 (Minneapolis, 1897).

acumen and a knowledge of state and county affairs that made him a valuable ally. His personal confidence in the candidate enabled him to make telling stump speeches wherever he appeared. Another Norwegian, Dr. Christian E. Dundas, a highly respected Koshkonong physician, also gave generous help in speaking and canvassing the countryside.

On election day, November 4, 1860, Johnson received 4,760 votes for clerk of the county board, and Borchsenius, 4,208. Writing to his brother that he had been elected by a majority of about 500, John revealed his elation in a single word: "Glory!" In Pleasant Springs he had almost exactly doubled his rival's vote.[31]

Though success seemed to wait upon John at every turn, sorrow had come to him in the loss of his wife. On March 16, 1860, Karen died, leaving her husband with a newborn daughter, their only child. Four happy years were at an end. To one of his brothers he wrote in June, three months after his wife's death: "I have nothing to strive for except my own and my child's physical subsistence and the education of the latter. This will be my aim, my only care." But the daughter, given her mother's name in baptism, was to live only six months. After the baby's death – on September 19, 1860 – John sold all personal property on the farm. He did retain the land for several years, but the next January he left the home in Koshkonong, never to return to it to live. He was moving to Madison to bury himself in new duties as clerk of the county board.

The change of base represented a fresh start in Johnson's career. The challenge of the new life, with its opportunities to extend his horizons, was a kind of anchor at a time when the future seemed uncharted and empty. Certainly the concern of his parents, brothers, and sisters sustained him. He wrote often to his younger brothers. In office less than a week, he reported that he did not find the duties "onerous." Later he mentioned that he had attended the Dane County Cavalry Ball – the first amusement that he had known in two years. He joined the Good Templars, a society requiring its members to abstain from all use of intoxicants. He admitted that he was lonely and that he felt the need for sociability lest he become a recluse.

Early in his new experience, John confided that he worked in the office "from 7½ a.m. to 11 p.m." The long hours – no doubt self-imposed –

[31] *Emigranten*, November 19, 1860; Johs. B. Wist, ed., *Norsk-amerikanernes festskrift 1914*, 36 (Decorah, Iowa, 1914).

left little time for a program of reading which to him meant continuing his education. On a typical Sunday, he wrote one of his brothers, he got up at seven-thirty and read Plutarch's *Pericles* before breakfast, went to church, played chess in the afternoon, and after supper attended a temperance lecture. A few days later at a book sale, he bought Plutarch's *Lives*, Smollett's works, and Sears' *History of the United States*. He was intrigued by *Don Quixote*; Cervantes' hero inspired him to "become a good and valorous knight." Characterizing the book as "most laughable but at the same time most excellent," he declared that he would find a Dulcinea at whose feet he could lay all the trophies of his great valor. He felt that the great seventeenth-century Spanish novelist had successfully burlesqued the follies of all ages: nineteenth-century dandies were about as rational as Don Quixote.

During his first months in Madison, John also made an avocation of language study, particularly of German. He regretted that no good teacher of that language was available: by himself he could learn the grammar and improve reading comprehension. But it distressed him that he could not master proper pronunciation without drill in the use of the spoken word. Here in the rough was the making of a true scholar. In his capacity for intellectual development and in his delight in learning, John A. Johnson reminds one of Benjamin Franklin—another young American for whom a college education was not possible.

Although he often advised his brothers in his letters, John's tone was one of genuine concern, never scolding. After visiting his parents at Pleasant Springs, he would report to Ole and Hans, who lived at a distance. He told of the father and mother, of Oliver and Inger and Caroline, all still at the family home. Following his trips to Koshkonong, he spoke of how the wheat was growing, the need to cultivate the corn, the road work to be done. "The grain looks remarkably well," he wrote to Ole in May, 1861. "Corn is backward, but a week of such weather as we had yesterday will bring it right along."

John cherished a special fondness for Ole, six years younger, and wrote more frequently to him than to the others. The two had a common interest in their love for learning. At one time the younger boy had been a pupil in the "English school" when John was the teacher. Later Ole attended Milton Academy and Albion Academy; then, following in his older brother's footsteps, he had taught in the district school.[32] Now aged twenty-three,

[32] A statement by B. H. Adams, town superintendent of schools, recommended

he was at Beloit College. The older man — from his office in Madison — found particular delight in Ole's study of Greek and often began his letters "Dear Adelphos." The fact that *adelphos* meant a brother in the ancient language intrigued him. "How simple these words seem," he wrote, "when the meaning of the component parts is made clear." He cited the words *emigrate* and *immigrate*: how the addition of the prefix *e* or *im* changed the meaning of the root verb *migrate*.

At times John assumed his older-brother and former-teacher roles. "Take pains, for a decent handwriting is a good recommendation," he admonished Ole. "Procure the best of ink and paper. . . . Your writing is improving, but very irregularly. Your *p's* are horrible looking characters. Take pains. Perhaps if you had a pen like mine you could do better."[33]

Writing to his brother as mentor, Ole often posed questions he wanted help in answering. One such question: Was England justified in promising Norway to Sweden during the Napoleonic wars if Napoleon were defeated? John's answer, based on sources with which he was familiar, indicated his belief that England had been right — the end justifying the means in this historic case. The brothers discussed their religious beliefs. John's letters reveal that at this developing period of his life he held religion to be a deep, personal — almost secret — matter. He indicated clearly that he definitely believed in a divine creator and in eternal life.

The two brothers grew very close as John shared Ole's college experience. The insecurity of the immigrants' purgatory was past. This was paradise — the era of self-realization and joy in the growth of each member of the family. The youngest and the oldest sons of Anders and Aaste Skibsnæs were to continue a warm relationship, soon to be revealed more vividly through their common devotion to the Union cause in the Civil War.

The careers of others in the close-knit Johnson family were rapidly developing — always in the spirit of all for one and one for all. Hans, the third son, like John and Ole, first became a rural schoolteacher. Soon, however, he turned to farming, his abiding interest. In the spring of 1860, he traveled to Goodhue County in Minnesota, utilizing the various modes of transportation typical of the period. Hans left home in Stoughton, Wisconsin, on a Wednesday and spent the night with John in Madison. Early

Ole C. Johnson for a position as a teacher in Pleasant Springs Township, October 15, 1859.

[33] John to Ole C. Johnson, June 1, 1861. The family letters were circulated among the various members. Many of them are in the Johnson Papers. For Ole's correspondence, see the Johnson Papers.

the next morning he took the train to Prairie du Chien on the Mississippi River. There, at 8:00 p.m. the same day, he boarded a paddle-wheel steamer, the "Golden Era." Against the stiff spring-season current, the traveler made slow progress; it was more than twenty-four hours later when he reached Red Wing, Minnesota, where he spent the remainder of the night at a hotel. Saturday morning he set out on foot for a farm in the western part of Goodhue County, where at midday he was welcomed by his friends, the Gundersons. In a letter home, written from Minnesota on May 1, Hans gave as his expert opinion that the deep rich soil there was superior even to that of Dane County. He would like to buy a farm in the area, and he intimated that perhaps others in the family would help finance the purchase.[34]

Hans did not underestimate the strong family feeling that would help him get his Minnesota farm. The financial problem was solved, and soon he bought 120 acres of Goodhue County land at $1.50 an acre. "This is as good as any land around here," he wrote a few weeks later to Ole at Beloit College. To the family at home he relayed news of friends from Norway who had come to America with them on the "Salvator" sixteen years before: the Huseths, Langemos, Westermoes, and Knut Aaker. All were doing well and living "happy and contented." He added that Pastor B. J. Muus was a good preacher — lest there be worry that his spiritual welfare was suffering in the western wilderness. Nor did Hans hesitate to criticize his younger brother's letters. "You have misspelled a word in your letter to me," he complained — the implication being that a college man should not make such a plebeian mistake.[35]

As the older brothers forged ahead in the world, they thought often of the lively little sister at home — Caroline, the only one in the family born in the United States. Letters of the period attest that she held a favored place in their hearts. To her sister Inger she wrote in Norwegian. To Ole at Beloit she gave a glimpse of her spirit: "Dear Brother: I now take the opportunity to address a few lines to you. I am here at Stoughton going to school but we have only one week left. Mr. Burlow is our teacher. He is very kind he very seldom scolds us but a lot of us have to stay after school

[34] Goodhue County, Minnesota, has the Mississippi River as its eastern boundary. It was settled in part by Norwegians, many of whom came from Telemark.

[35] Hans to Ole C. Johnson, June 13, 1860. The Reverend Bernt Julius Muus was a pioneer Lutheran pastor in Minnesota and later one of the founders of St. Olaf College.

a few times for not knowing our lessons. . . . I have written a composition, they were very poor too. John came home yesterday." [36]

Although John A. Johnson had gained a wide professional and social acquaintanceship during his years as a county official in Madison, he had led what was for him a lonely life. This was to change. On October 31, 1861, he was married to Kaia Nicoline Marie Kildahl of Milwaukee, the youngest of eleven children. Her roots – like those of her husband – were in Norway. In 1848, when Kaia was ten years old, her family had made the long move from their ancestral seaport city of Christiansand to the United States. This was the year that John and his family were moving from the hardships of Walworth County to the comparative affluence of Pleasant Springs. Now at the time of her marriage to John she was twenty-three years old.

Behind Kaia Kildahl Johnson lay an interesting family history dating back to the sixteenth century in Norway. The original Kildahl farm [37] was situated in a valley called Otradalen in the county of Hægeland, about twenty miles north of Christiansand. It lay on the shore of a bay in the Otra River. Here the founder of the family lived, and from this base four of his grandsons, venturing beyond the encircling mountains, migrated to Christiansand and later to Denmark. Today his scattered descendants live in Australia, New Zealand, Ireland – in all parts of the United States and in Norway.[38]

In the Kildahl family story, the remarkable achievements of the four brothers who first left their prosperous ancestral home has special significance. They apparently came from an environment highly unusual for the time and place, a home where books – mainly of a religious nature – were a part of their cultural inheritance. With strong intellectual vigor, all four studied at Christiansand, Helsingør, and Copenhagen. At these centers of learning, they prepared themselves for service to the state church,

[36] Caroline to Ole C. Johnson, June 17, 1861. At the time of this letter Caroline was fifteen years old.

[37] The name is derived from the word *kill* which means a small, deeply enclosed bay. Various spellings have been used – Kiledalen, Kildale, Kiildal – and most recently Kildal and Kildahl. See Arne Kildal, *Slekten Kildal fra Otradalen*, 5-10 (Oslo, 1942). For the earliest records concerning the farm, see also Jon Asen, *Hægelands boka*, 376 (Kristiansand, 1951).

[38] A genealogical chart of the Kildahl family is in the possession of George Hopkins Johnson, former president of the Gisholt Machine Company, Madison. The chart, entitled *The Family Kildahl of Kristiansand, Norway*, was prepared by Gunhild Johanne (Hannah) Kildahl Johansen, a grandniece of Kaia's father.

and from them went on to noteworthy careers as pastors in northern Norway. One of the brothers became a missionary to the Lapps, and he translated the Bible from the Hebrew and Greek into their native tongue.[39]

Kaia's own direct ancestor, a younger brother of the famous clergymen, remained at home to inherit the farm. His name was Kristen. This early forebear figures in the ancestral line as the father of Tarjerd Kristendatter Kildahl, the great-grandmother of Kaia. Tarjerd married Nils Kristenson Engeland, and her family moved from the original home site to a farm called Engeland in the neighboring district of Øverbø. There they prospered and "had the means to educate and prepare their children for the professions."[40]

The children of Nils and Tarjerd, like others in the clan, felt the strong pull of distant places. Two of their sons migrated to Ireland. But Kaia's grandfather, Jon Engeland, taking his mother's name of Kildahl, moved from Øverbø to Christiansand to make his permanent home. There is a legend that the change of name was favored by Jon Kildahl because of the grandfather and granduncles who had given it such prestige all over Norway. However that may be, Jon was a worthy inheritor of the family tradition. In Christiansand he was known as a master shoemaker and merchant at the time his son, Nils Severin Jonsen Kildahl, was born on September 18, 1787.[41]

Nils Severin, the eldest son of Jon and Anne Sørensdatter Kildahl, enters the story of John A. Johnson in America personally, though briefly. A month after he had settled his large family in Milwaukee, Wisconsin, he died at the age of sixty-one. In the last years of the eighteenth century, he had been enrolled in the Cathedral School in Christiansand, and in 1801 he had attended the Latin School in that city. Later he had studied architecture in Dublin and London.

Kaia's mother, Friderike Marie Holgersen, was married to Nils Severin Kildahl on December 30, 1817. She was the daughter of Friderick Holgersen, a merchant of Christiansand and a manufacturer of copper goods, who, it was said, had been the owner of vessels confiscated during the Napoleonic Wars. During Severin's years in his father's mercantile business

[39] *Hægelands boka,* 376, 377; Kildal, *Slekten Kildal fra Otradalen,* 10–12; *The Family Kildahl of Kristiansand, Norway,* 1, 2.

[40] Tarjerd's name was sometimes spelled Tarjer or Terjer (*Hægelands boka,* 378); Jon Asen, *Øverbø boka,* 506, 507 (Kristiansand, 1951).

[41] *Øverbø boka,* 506, 507. The records in Kristiansand (Christiansand) variously refer to Jon Kildahl, Jon Nilsen Kildahl, and John Kildahl.

in Norway, eleven children were born to him and Friderike. In this busy family, transplanted to America and presided over by the widowed mother, Kaia Kildahl grew up.[42]

In family biographical sketches, both Nils Severin and Frederika are appreciatively remembered, the latter particularly for her beauty and graciousness in old age. After she was forty-five, she always wore a handmade lace cap of her own workmanship. A widow for thirty-two years, she lived until 1880 – to see her children well established in their homes in America. Of Nils Severin, one of his grandchildren wrote: "Grandfather was said by his daughters to have been a tall stunning man." [43]

John A. Johnson's second marriage in 1861 marked a turning point in his life. Kaia was a woman of quality who was to become a constant helpmate throughout his career over the next forty years. With Kaia he was to travel in Europe and visit Kildahl relatives in Ireland and Norway. A new link with his native country was to develop through the exchange of warmly affectionate letters, particularly with Hannah Kildahl Johansen of Christiansand. In the year of his marriage, however, the compelling immediate issue was the Civil War, already in progress. In this terrible struggle, Johnson's well-known conviction on the slavery issue was to lead him to wholehearted commitment to the cause of the North as a leader among his Norwegian countrymen.[44]

[42] *Kirkeboken for Kristiansand 1778–1818* (Statsarkivet i Kristiansand). The bride's name in this church record is spelled Friderike. Elsewhere it is spelled Frederikke and Frederika.

[43] See particularly Ida Johnson Fisk, "The Kildahl and Holgersen Families." This short article is in the "Family Scrapbook" in the Johnson Papers.

[44] The influence of Kaia Kildahl Johnson in her husband's career recalls to mind the sentence in Ibsen's *Peer Gynt*: "Der stod kvinder bag dem" (Women stood behind them) – notably true in the story of John A. Johnson's life.

CHAPTER III

Caught Up in the Civil War

On the fateful twelfth of April, 1861, three days before he was to be twenty-nine years old, John A. Johnson wrote to his brothers: "A telegram was read announcing that war had actually commenced. The rebels have fired on Fort Sumter and the fire has been returned. The cause is a righteous one. I know that we are apt to feel very courageous when we are far from danger and perhaps that may be the case with me now, but it certainly appears to me as if I should not be afraid of death. I fear that our mother will be greatly disturbed, but she is a courageous woman and has inherent love for that which is just and right and noble. We [grown sons] have strong and vigorous frames, and I think, an average quality of pluck." As a lighter touch, he added: "Who knows but that one of us might be a Napoleon, the other an Alexander, or more noble, one a Washington, the other a Fabius. Or if not as high as that, a captaincy or colonelship might have to answer."

President Lincoln's call for volunteers to preserve the Union stirred a strong feeling of personal responsibility among the liberty-loving Norwegians in Wisconsin. They realized that the causes of the Civil War were complex, but most immigrants who answered the president's message did so for one compelling reason: They felt that the United States could not endure as a great democracy if Negro slavery were to continue within its borders. In full sympathy with the consensus of their fellow Norwegians, the Johnson brothers debated the question of enlisting, Ole and Hans urging that, because they were younger, they should volunteer instead of John and Oliver.[1]

The deep concern that the brothers felt about the progress of the war permeated their correspondence in the spring and summer of 1861. To the others, John wrote from Madison: "Our lot has fallen on exciting times. The rebels have the first victory, meager as it is; I hope it will be the last. The slaughterers of the French Huguenots in the terrible night of Saint Bartholomew were patriots and philanthropists in comparison with these. If I am to die I could never die at any better time nor in a better place than in the defense of human liberty and my country. God grant that the war may be short and in order to be short it must be vigorous."

Then came the news of the defeat of the Federal army in the Battle of Bull Run on July 21. Its significance was clear – a serious setback for the North and the realization that the war would be much longer, more bitterly contested than anyone on the Union side had dreamed it could be. Such men as Hans C. Heg, state prison commissioner, and John A. Johnson had already considered organizing a Norwegian regiment. The German immigrants had formed the Ninth Wisconsin and the Irish the Eleventh. In view of the fact that Wisconsin had a larger Norwegian population than any other state, it seemed to immigrant leaders that it should have a separate Scandinavian unit. Soon the movement reached a head. Governor Alexander W. Randall on August 20, 1861, issued a call for five additional regiments, and Johnson felt that the time had come for action.

On August 31, acting on the hopes he had shared with Heg and others, Johnson appealed for volunteers for a Scandinavian company of at least eighty-three men. Two weeks later a Madison Norwegian-language newspaper reported that the call had met with an eager response. Following Johnson's lead, a group of prominent Norwegians, meeting at the state capitol in Madison on September 25, adopted a resolution in favor of the immediate formation of a "Scandinavian Brigade." Included in the resolution was a recommendation that the "Honorable Hans C. Heg" be commissioned as colonel of the regiment. The document was at once sent to the governor. No time was lost. Governor Randall quickly endorsed the committee's proposal, and on October 1 he offered Heg the commission as colonel of the new regiment, now officially designated the Fifteenth

[1] As the men of the Johnson family considered enlisting, John was a county officer in Madison, and Oliver, aged twenty-seven, was being relied upon as the manager of the home farm.

Wisconsin. Though called Scandinavian, the unit was preponderantly made up of Norwegian immigrants, with a sprinkling of Swedes and Danes.[2]

Earlier, when Heg had revealed that he intended to enlist, Johnson had tried to dissuade him, arguing that Wisconsin could ill afford to lose its prison commissioner. The two men went together to take counsel with the governor, but at the office door, so the story runs, Heg stopped, stood quietly for a moment of decision, then turned away. Soon thereafter, his resignation as a state official was in the governor's hands. At first Randall would not accept it, but Heg refused the nomination for another term, making clear his determination to serve his country by joining the Union army.[3]

General approval followed the choice of Colonel Heg to lead the Fifteenth Wisconsin. He had won the respect of everyone in the state for his competency as head of prisons. In this position he had instituted changes aimed at rehabilitating convicted criminals so that they might reinstate themselves in society. He had pioneered in introducing the indeterminate sentence, later to become general. Now that he was assuming military command, his associates gave him their unqualified trust. *Emigranten* summed up the confidence felt by all: "The young gifted colonel, you can be assured, will lead you to honor and victory."[4]

The establishment of the Norwegian regiment was largely the result of John A. Johnson's fervent belief in the cause its men were pledged to defend. Now the war came personally much closer: Governor Randall called Ole C. Johnson, fresh from his studies at Beloit, to serve as recruiting officer for the Fifteenth Wisconsin. At the age of twenty-three, this young immigrant, possessed of many qualities of leadership, gave up his cherished hopes for an education to throw in his lot with the other volunteers. Ole, both a scholar and a man of action, was an admirable choice. He had excellent command of both English and Norwegian; he was well built, strong, in excellent health; he was known for his dependable quali-

[2] *Emigranten*, September 2, 16, October 7, 1861; O. A. Buslett, *Det femtende regiment Wisconsin frivillige*, 8, 15 (Decorah, Iowa, 1894); Theodore C. Blegen, ed., *The Civil War Letters of Colonel Hans Christian Heg*, 24, 25 (Northfield, Minnesota, 1936). John A. Johnson's signature as a committee member is the second of the group of seven framers of the resolution. The full text of the document is in the Appendix, p. 278–279.

[3] Blegen, *The Civil War Letters of Colonel Hans Christian Heg*, 20, 21.

[4] *Wisconsin Daily State Journal*, October 1, 1861; State Prison Commissioner, *Annual Report 1866*, 1, 2, 7; *Emigranten*, December 23, 1861.

ties. Because he was of Norwegian descent, it was thought that other immigrants would be influenced to enlist under such an attractive young officer. As it turned out, he found recruiting a disagreeable task. Not all the men he talked to could feel the patriotic pull to leave home and risk their lives. There were phases of human nature that made him realize how young and inexperienced he himself was.[5]

Ole C. Johnson's "Memoirs" reveal the emotional tensions that dominated his thinking during the summer of 1861. He had hoped to study law, and he felt sure that if he went to war the ambition of his life must be abandoned. Yet, like his older brother John, he was idealistic, strongly inclined to support the moral issue for which he believed the Union cause stood. The Battle of Bull Run crystallized Ole's thoughts and emotions—and he enlisted at once. "My time had come," he wrote, "for I had made a pledge to myself that whenever the government needed my services I should go, college or no college. Nothing but the greatest necessity would reconcile me to this sacrifice. To say that the sound of fife and drum, the sight of marching squads through the streets, and the appeals made at the nightly meetings held, wrought powerfully upon my excitable and patriotic nature is putting it mildly." A tear trickled down his mother's cheek when he told her of his decision, but Aaste spoke no word of objection. "She could not ask or urge me to go, nor even suggest it, yet she felt it was my duty and she could only bid me Godspeed." [6]

Ole, abandoning his attempts at recruiting, was shortly made captain of Company B of the Fifteenth Wisconsin Regiment. This unit, made up largely of volunteers from his home area of Koshkonong, was called, a bit romantically, "Wergeland's Guard"—named for the Norwegian poet whose stirring verse was filled with sympathy for the oppressed and for patriots fighting for freedom. In keeping with Wergeland's theme, the Wisconsin immigrants hoped to strike a blow in the best poetic tradition. But after Bull Run all began to sense the grim nature of their mission. "We [now] knew," Ole wrote later, "that it would not be merely a holiday tramp into the Southern States and a triumphal march home again, but that it meant months and years of hard toil, days and nights of weary

[5] See John A. Johnson, *Det skandinaviske regiments historie*, 16 (La Crosse, Wisconsin, 1869).

[6] Ole C. Johnson, "Memoirs," 1, 2, 4, 7. This document is in the possession of the daughter-in-law of Ole C. Johnson, Mrs. Bessie Shipnes, 1417 Green Bay Road, Highland Park, Illinois. Ole often used the original family name, which his descendants spell Shipnes.

marching, suffering from wounds and disease, and to very many thousands, death itself." [7]

Soon it was known that the third son of the family, Hans, leaving his recently purchased farm in Goodhue County, Minnesota, had volunteered and had already joined the Third Minnesota Regiment. Like his brothers, Hans had been moved by the ringing words of President Lincoln's inaugural address. "I think he has taken a noble stand," he wrote early in the year, "for all the [Minneapolis] Tribune does denounce him. . . . Yours for the Union." Now the two youngest sons of Anders and Aaste Skibsnæs — seventeen years after their childhood immigrant march into Wisconsin — had been caught up in the opening phase of a great war. To John, going on with his work in Madison, what happened to them was, for months to come, a daily source of involvement and concern.[8]

By the fall of 1861, the seriousness of the situation was apparent to every informed citizen in Wisconsin. From his vantage point in Madison, John A. Johnson continued to play a leading part in the war effort — particularly in securing enlistments for the new immigrant regiment. He was concerned that Americans should realize that Scandinavians in the United States were willing to bear their share in the struggle. Understanding the power of the printed word, he prepared a long article which *Emigranten* published in its issue of September 30, 1861: "Scandinavians!" he wrote. "Let us understand the situation, our duty and our responsibility. Shall the future ask, where were the Scandinavians when the fatherland was saved?" Other prominent Norwegians — Hans C. Heg, Knud Langeland, and K. J. Fleischer — attached their names to Johnson's eloquent plea for support of the Union cause.

He went on to provide information about military service, answering many inquiries addressed to him personally. Through *Emigranten*, he made known the pay of different army ranks, ranging from $13 per month for a private to $118.50 for a captain. Johnson carefully explained in the Scandinavian newspapers all new announcements of military regulations coming from either national or state headquarters. To every enlisted man the state of Wisconsin would add five dollars to his base army pay. In clear terms he dealt with the subject of pensions for widows of soldiers killed in the war. By crossing the language barrier in this way, he rendered a serv-

[7] Blegen, *The Civil War Letters of Colonel Hans Christian Heg*, 52, 53; Johnson, *Det skandinaviske regiments historie*, 110; Ole C. Johnson, "Memoirs," 7.

[8] Hans to Ole C. Johnson, March 6, 1861.

ice of inestimable value in troubled times, both to the distraught immigrants and to the country of their adoption.

Johnson's skillful use of the Scandinavian-language press to spur recruiting quickly produced tangible results. Immigrants from Illinois, Iowa, and Minnesota — in addition to Wisconsin volunteers — threw in their lot with the Fifteenth Wisconsin. Kiler K. Jones had already aided in recruiting a troop of Scandinavians in Chicago — soon to be known as Company A of the regiment. From across the Mississippi, sixty-five Norwegians from northeastern Iowa joined the Wisconsin unit in 1861 and 1862, and Minnesota recruits, headed in the same direction, gathered in Red Wing under the direction of Johnson's good friend, Lars Knudsen Aaker. The Fifteenth, however, had a solid core of Wisconsin men, many of whom had been influenced to enlist by John A. Johnson and other Norwegian leaders like Colonel Heg. With many volunteers in other regiments, it is estimated that between three and four thousand immigrants of Scandinavian descent fought in the war.[9]

The recruits, gathering at Camp Randall in Madison, found discouraging conditions. The poorly constructed barracks let in the winter cold and rations were scanty. The fumbling department of war in Washington had not yet perfected the machinery for paying its soldiers, and charge accounts allowed volunteers by Madison merchants had to go unpaid. The men chafed under accumulating frustrations and for long weeks in midwinter morale declined. The regiment reached its full complement of men in January, 1862. Still no pay and the call for action did not come. Finally in late February the federal paymaster reached camp with back wages for all. The long-awaited orders soon followed. On Sunday, March 2, at eight o'clock on a dark, rainy morning, the Fifteenth Wisconsin Regiment marched in formation to the Madison railroad station. Among those who bade farewell to family and friends was Captain Ole C. Johnson of Company B.[10]

As young men in the immigrant communities of Wisconsin and other states in the North prepared for war, there developed in their home church

[9] Jones, though not a Norwegian, served for a time as lieutenant colonel of the Fifteenth Wisconsin Regiment. See *Emigranten*, October 7, 1861; O. N. Nelson, *History of the Scandinavians and Successful Scandinavians in the United States*, 2: 68, 119–121 (Minneapolis, 1897); Theodore C. Blegen, *Norwegian Migration to America: The American Transition*, 389 (Northfield, Minnesota, 1940).

[10] Ole C. Johnson, "Memoirs," 14, 15; Johnson, *Det skandinaviske regiments historie*, 16, 17; Buslett, *Det femtende regiment Wisconsin frivillige*, 20.

bodies a sharp controversy concerning the institution of slavery. In 1861 leaders of the Norwegian Synod found themselves in an internecine debate involving doctrine and conscience. Through the columns of *Emigranten*, pastors and laymen could reach four thousand homes and several times that many readers. The result was a journalistic build-up of an issue threatening "the quiet, the peace and the unity of the Church." [11]

The controversy must be viewed as something of an anomaly. Why should the Norwegian Lutheran church in the North be drawn into any debate over the subject of slavery at the very moment when its younger members were volunteering to take up arms to put down the evil institution once and for all? The answer lies in an accident of geography and in the tensions generated by a national upheaval.

In 1857 the Norwegian Synod had made an arrangement with Concordia Seminary of the German Lutheran Missouri Synod in St. Louis. Under the provisions of this seemingly natural and advantageous alliance, young men from the North training to become pastors in the Norwegian Synod were to study at Concordia. To strengthen the tie, the Norwegians had sent as their representative on the seminary faculty one of its ablest men, Laur. Larsen, later to be the first president of Luther College at Decorah, Iowa. When Fort Sumter was fired on, Professor Larsen was teaching theology at the Missouri Synod seminary.[12]

As the war began, the border state of Missouri was embroiled in acrimonious divisions of loyalty. In St. Louis, Concordia Seminary became a center of controversy, and Laur. Larsen, a Northerner in a hotbed of secession, faced most difficult personal decisions. Writing to *Emigranten* in

[11] Blegen, *Norwegian Migration to America: The American Transition*, 421. During the Civil War, *Emigranten* was published in Madison under the editorship of Carl F. Solberg, who had come from Norway in 1853. His fine literary style and wide-ranging news coverage gave the paper of this period a particular distinction and a wide readership.

[12] Gerhard Lee Belgum, "The Old Norwegian Synod in America, 1853–1890" (an unpublished doctoral dissertation presented to the faculty of the graduate school of Yale University in 1957), 256–257, 351–366. The history of the controversy over slavery in the Norwegian Synod has been developed in a number of books: Karen Larsen, *Laur. Larsen, Pioneer College President*, 126–155 (Northfield, Minnesota, 1936); Blegen, *Norwegian Migration to America: The American Transition*, 418–453; E. Clifford Nelson and Eugene L. Fevold, *The Lutheran Church among Norwegian-Americans*, 1:169–180 (Minneapolis, 1960); J. Magnus Rohne, *Norwegian American Lutheranism up to 1872*, 202–222 (New York, 1926); H. Fred Swansen, *The Founder of St. Ansgar: The Life Story of Claus Laurits Clausen*, 154–168 (Blair, Nebraska, 1949).

the spring of 1861, he made it known that Concordia students had been sent home, the Norwegians as well as the others.

Editor Solberg, responsible for *Emigranten's* official stand, reacted vigorously to the news. On May 6, 1861, he published in his newspaper an article entitled "Concordia College," in which he referred to Professor Larsen's announcement. In his editorial, he dared to raise a leading question. He urged Laur. Larsen to tell readers in the North what position the faculty of Concordia Seminary had taken toward slavery and the breakup of the Union. Going further, the editor noted the well-founded rumor: Northern students arriving home had reported that the faculty in St. Louis favored the South. Solberg implied that the Norwegian Synod should sever its connection with the Missouri Synod and Concordia Seminary. He concluded by saying that a statement from Professor Larsen, the Synod's representative, would clarify this important issue.

When no reply came from Laur. Larsen, John A. Johnson was concerned over what he considered a serious and untenable situation. To him any suggestion that the Norwegian Synod should be thought to condone teachings favorable to slavery and secession was unthinkable. On June 3, 1861, *Emigranten* published a strong anonymous letter taking a definite stand against all political and social arguments advanced by adherents of the Southern cause. To his brothers, on June 1, he had written: "I have been urged to write this statement, but it was strictly in accordance with my own inclination."[13]

Johnson's letter to *Emigranten* of June, 1861, crystallized all his earlier thinking into a well-reasoned, eloquent whole. From his early years in America, he had thought, spoken, and written of his abhorrence of human slavery. He had affirmed his admiration for the Declaration of Independence and the federal constitution, with their emphasis on the tenet that all men are created free and equal – a principle to which men like Washington and Jefferson had adhered in both public and private life. He had rejoiced that England, Denmark, and Holland had all abolished slavery in their dominions, and he had fervently hoped that his adopted country would follow their enlightened example. Now the United States was hopelessly divided: across a yawning gulf of prejudice North and South were threatening to tear the Union apart.

Addressing himself directly to the Norwegian Synod, Johnson took a

[13] Many years later he referred to his letter on the slavery issue in *Emigranten* and to his motives for writing it. See his "Memoirs."

definite stand on two points. He strongly opposed the familiar Southern position that the Bible did not specifically condemn slavery. And he attacked the point of view — widely held in the South — that opposition to the constitution and laws of the United States was legitimate. Turning to theological concepts, he flatly charged that slavery was indeed a sin, declaring that the spirit of the Bible as a whole was against this monstrous evil. Did not the Scriptures teach men to do unto others as they wished to be done by? As for secession, he pointed out that every officeholder — in a modest township position or in the top echelons of the federal government — must swear to uphold the constitution. Making a particular point for immigrant citizens, he recalled the oath each foreigner must take to accept and abide by the laws of the land. His conclusion was direct. If the teachers at Concordia Seminary in St. Louis accepted the proslavery philosophy, if in their hearts they harbored secessionist beliefs, then the Norwegian Synod should withdraw from its relationship with the Missouri Synod and build its own seminary.

Professor Larsen and other Synod leaders still debated the slavery issue. They were earnest young men to whom the literal language of the Bible was sacred. When the Bible referred to the institution of slavery as an accepted practice in earlier times in history, the trained theologians could brook no compromise. They took refuge in the firm position that the church should not enter the political arena — it might not work toward the abolition of slavery, which they admitted was a social wrong. Johnson found that this reasoning led to a disheartening impasse. Many years later he wrote of the sadness he had felt over the disruption in his church: "The position these men took was certainly very unfortunate. At the same time they were conscientious in the views they took. But like so many scholars they looked too much at the letter and not enough at the spirit. The controversy lasted for many years even after slavery and secession had long been buried and probably caused an estrangement that was the indirect cause of the later split in the Synod." [14]

There were roots in Johnson's Norwegian heritage that reinforced his strong antislavery stand. The struggle in Norway between a mainly rural or peasant culture and the cosmopolitanism of the cities impelled many immigrants with democratic leanings to migrate to America. Anders and Aaste Skibsnæs had experienced political and religious unrest in the

[14] Belgum, "The Old Norwegian Synod in America, 1853–1890," 358; John A. Johnson, "Memoirs."

1830's. As common folk, they had listened sympathetically to the words of Hans Nielsen Hauge, lay evangelist and reformer, who urged the people to take a greater share in the life of Norway. The parents of John A. Johnson had come to the United States seeking a brighter future for their children in a land where the ideals of liberty and equality were respected and cherished. Such people could not accept slavery. The spirit of individualism and anticlericalism, already creating problems within the Lutheran church, shaped their attitudes toward the abolition of human bondage everywhere in the world. Significantly, when the time came in America, immigrant laymen rather than the clergy led the way in the movement to put an end to slavery.

As a boy in Norway, John had only vaguely sensed these cross currents — social, religious, and political. But after taking the oath making him a United States citizen, he experienced a growing emotion of pride in the democratic society to which he had sworn allegiance. Alert to all developing national trends, he saw with dismay that slavery in the South was establishing itself as a permanent economic and political institution — and he hated it. The buying and selling of human beings brought no credit to a country founded on the basic tenets of liberty and freedom. The concept of a slave as a chattel was abhorrent to him. He had stood with the Free Soil party in 1854, and he continued as a Republican to support the political philosophy opposing slavery and defending the Union.

In championing the cause of antislavery, Johnson found a natural ally in Pastor Claus Laurits Clausen, a pioneer clergyman twelve years his senior. Clausen had been the first president of the Norwegian Synod and later had become chaplain of the Fifteenth Wisconsin Regiment. While the new recruits were in training at Camp Randall in the winter of 1861-1862, Johnson and Clausen found themselves drawn together by their agreement on all phases of the slavery issue. They stood side by side in the liberal wing of the Synod against the formal theologians, who could not bring themselves to engage in any political action against the South. Writing many years later, shortly after Clausen's death, Johnson paid a warm tribute to his friend: "A more honorable and Christian-minded person would be hard to find; his influence on his countrymen was both great and constructive. For those who knew him, his life will always stand as a light that makes the way to the eternal home easier." [15]

[15] John A. Johnson, "Minder om Clausen," in *Skandinaven*, March 30, 1892.

Whatever the theological differences back home, by the spring of 1862 Wisconsin men were quartered in enemy territory, and for them the deadly phase of the war was near at hand. John A. Johnson continued to be very close to what was going on. From Island No. 10, a Union outpost in the Mississippi River near the Tennessee shore, Colonel Hans C. Heg forwarded letters to Johnson. More than one asked for advice. The governor of Wisconsin wished to transfer a Captain McKee from the Second Wisconsin to an important post as lieutenant colonel of the Fifteenth. Heg, who did not know McKee, was disturbed by the prospect. He confided to Johnson: "I shall certainly look upon it as a very strange proceeding for the Governor to appoint one that we have never seen or heard of and without consulting us at all. I trust you will look into this matter. I trust you will use your influence in our common welfare. . . . The Governor is a politician and will make his selection on political grounds—this is all wrong." [16]

With two younger members of the family in the Union army in the South, John and his parents gave daily thought to the war. From Hans with the Third Minnesota Regiment, John heard regularly. The young Minnesota farmer wrote on March 26, 1862, from Nashville, Tennessee, that he had heard Andrew Johnson at the state house give "a masterly speech" which Hans predicted would have a good effect on the people.[17] Now approaching sixty, Anders and Aaste Skibsnæs were heavily burdened with worry over their sons at the front. The father, who previously had not learned to read English, taught himself during the early war years enough of the strange language to follow the daily newspaper dispatches.

When the news reached them in Pleasant Springs that Hans had died in a military hospital, the father and mother gave way to tears. In his "Memoirs," written many years after the war, John recalled that they found comfort in their loss in the realization that the sacrifice had been for their adopted country. Hans, who had enlisted in Minnesota in October, 1861, had served less than a year. He died on July 5, 1862, and was buried in Murfreesboro, Tennessee. He was twenty-six years old. [18]

[16] Hans C. Heg to John A. Johnson, March 26, 1862. This and other letters from Heg in the South made Johnson one of the best informed men in Madison concerning the progress of the Fifteenth Wisconsin in the field.

[17] In 1862 Andrew Johnson, later president of the United States, served the Union by taking over the difficult post of military governor of the border state of Tennessee.

[18] Buslett, *Det femtende regiment Wisconsin frivillige*, 313; C. C. Anderson, ed., *Minnesota in the Civil and Indian Wars, 1861–1865*, 1: 185 (St. Paul, 1890).

Complementing the contribution of the men of her family, Mrs. John A. Johnson threw herself vigorously into the women's war project: gathering funds to send supplies to soldiers at the front. She used the money collected to buy comforts for the men — at one time a purchase of groceries costing $30.55. Following one large shipment sent to the South, Kaia received a letter from Chaplain Clausen of the Fifteenth Wisconsin Regiment: "Barrels containing sanitary stores which you were kind enough to send to Cairo several months ago for the use of the sick in our Regiment have been forwarded to Louisville." This particular consignment, however, could not reach the men of the Fifteenth, who had already moved on to Nashville, Tennessee. Fortunately the gifts of mercy were not wasted. As had been suggested by Mrs. Johnson, Chaplain Clausen turned them over to the Hospital Sanitary Commission of Louisville.[19]

Ole C. Johnson had a long and dramatic career in the war. Serving at first as a company captain in the Fifteenth Wisconsin, he took part in the bloody battles of Perryville and Stones River in Tennessee. Promoted to the rank of lieutenant colonel — under Hans C. Heg, by then a brigadier general — he commanded the Fifteenth in the Battle of Chickamauga. This fiercely fought engagement on September 19-20, 1863, cost the life of Heg, a dedicated officer and a friend whom all the Johnson family respected and loved. Long years after the desperate, crashing hours of conflict along the Tennessee River had passed from men's minds, John A. Johnson wrote in his "Memoirs": "His loss was to me like that of a brother." [20]

The responsibilities of Ole C. Johnson in the critical Battle of Chickamauga were heavy. The nearby city of Chattanooga, of immense strategic importance to the South, was to be defended at all costs against Union forces pressing it from the north. After weeks of deploying for advantage, two great armies flung themselves at each other along the banks of the Chickamauga, a small tributary stream of the Tennessee River. The Fifteenth Wisconsin, Lieutenant Colonel Johnson's regiment, had orders to throw a pontoon bridge across the Tennessee and to plant batteries on the other side to protect troops as they crossed. Wisconsin woodsmen

[19] *Emigranten*, September 8, 1862; C. A. Clausen to Mrs. John A. Johnson, November 24, 1862.

[20] Johnson, *Det skandinaviske regiments historie*, 110; *Emigranten*, October 10, 1863. A grim significance has long been associated with the Chickamauga, for its Indian name means the stream of death, because of battles fought there before the white man came.

knew how to use the ax: the bridge was quickly in place, and the regiment was the first to cross the river to plant the Union flag on soil held by the enemy.[21]

The fighting on the first day of the historic battle was indecisive, despite the early advantage won by the Wisconsin regiment. After the grim struggle of the second day, news from the front slowly trickled north to Madison and the anxious Johnson family. Its burden was tragic. The Fifteenth had entered the battle with a complement of 176 men. Now it was cut to pieces – its casualties 111 killed, wounded, or missing, a terrifying 65 per cent of its effectives lost. Those who remained were completely exhausted and disheartened by their failure to overcome the enemy.[22]

Late on the second day of the battle, when the remnant of his regiment could be regrouped under Major George Wilson, Lieutenant Colonel Ole C. Johnson was reported missing. Later it was learned that he had been captured and forced to deliver his sword, according to military ritual, to a staff officer in the Confederate army.

What happened next was subsequently revealed in a series of letters which Ole wrote from a southern military prison to his brother John in Madison and in detailed accounts of his captivity written after the war. The ordeal began the night after the battle ended. With other captured soldiers, the young Northern officer began a long, painful trek to Libby Prison in Richmond, Virginia. Forced to travel sixteen miles on foot, without food or water, the exhausted men at last reached a detention camp. There they were herded like cattle into corrals where they slept on the ground without overcoats or blankets. After several days the prisoners were packed into boxcars of an almost ruined railroad and sent on their way without sufficient food to sustain them. By a circuitous route – via

[21] Details of the battle included in this chapter are based on Buslett, *Det femtende regiment Wisconsin frivillige*, in which a personal account written by Ole C. Johnson occupies pages 95–102, and on an eloquent address by Colonel Johnson delivered after the war at Albion, Wisconsin. The address, written in longhand and 50 pages in length, is the property of Mrs. Bessie Shipnes of Highland Park, Illinois. For a vivid and poetic excerpt describing the first afternoon's fighting, see the Appendix, p. 279.

[22] *Emigranten*, October 5, 26, 1863. The Battle of Chickamauga was a costly victory for the Southern forces. Casualties on both sides were disastrous – an aggregate of 27,000 suffered by the two armies. Historians regard September 19–20, 1863, as the two bloodiest days of fighting in the Civil War. A monument on the Chickamauga battlefield commemorates the sacrifice of the men of the Fifteenth Wisconsin Regiment.

Atlanta – they reached Richmond, Virginia, where, on September 29, they entered the gates of Libby Prison. "The whole setting struck terror in all our hearts," Ole wrote after the war. "It gave us the impression that we had just reached the port of Hell." [23]

Libby was indeed a horrible place. An old stone warehouse standing on the banks of the historic James River, it still bore the sign "Libby and Son, Merchants." Richmond had no need for wholesale houses now, for the war had ruined all trade. The forbidding structure stood three stories high. Each floor, 100 feet by 200 feet, was divided into three large rooms. Into each of these, the guards crowded upwards of 200 men.

By the time Ole entered the prison, the South was losing the war, and the progressive breakdown of production and transportation worked increasingly to deteriorate already harsh conditions. The men slept on the bare floor in their filthy, ragged clothes and suffered each night from the cold and dampness. Exercise outside was prohibited; there was almost no chance to breathe fresh air. The regular fare was corn bread and pea soup, both often wormy. "But hunger spices the food," Ole wrote, adding that as a special delicacy they would be given "a small piece of beef and rye-coffee."

As malnutrition took its toll, Ole observed the men – some from his Fifteenth Wisconsin Regiment – weakening under the evil conditions until serious sickness and death became commonplace. Prison authorities, aware of what was going on, finally advised the prisoners to write to their families for food and clothing. This tardy act – undoubtedly based on both humane and economic considerations – probably saved lives, for in spite of slow transportation, mail and packages did get through. Once a week a boat steamed up the James River bringing "cases" of comforts from home. "There was an air of suspense," Ole wrote to John, "when we saw through the barred windows the white flag coming up the stream." Not all heard their names called when the packages were distributed, and their disappointment saddened the lucky ones. Ole himself was fortunate. Constant in their care and concern for him, John and others in the family sent him food, clothes, and books. "After the packages began to arrive," he wrote after the war, "I suffered no real need in Libby Prison." [24]

[23] The account of Ole C. Johnson's experiences in Libby Prison given here is based on his letters to his brother John and on Buslett's *Det femtende regiment Wisconsin frivillige*, in which a personal narrative written by the young colonel is included on pages 204–291. A copy of this recital is in the possession of George H. Johnson, Madison, Wisconsin, a grandson of John A. Johnson.

[24] Buslett, *Det femtende regiment Wisconsin frivillige*, 208–214.

There is ample evidence that Ole C. Johnson reacted to the monotony of prison life with resourcefulness, making the best of a bad situation. Two young officer friends joined him in making a niche for themselves in a corner of one of the large rooms. With walls on two sides and a stairway on the third, the trio was comparatively secluded. Here they set up "housekeeping," relying on food from home rather than on the vile rations served by their keepers. In spite of primitive conditions, Ole, who took charge of preparing their food, managed to provide a reasonably satisfactory diet. In one first-floor room stood eight stoves on which hundreds of prisoners were expected to prepare whatever warm food they could manage. Getting up early each morning, Ole was regularly on the job before anyone else. By this industry, he contrived to have enough to eat to maintain his strength — and at the same time to earn a reputation as one of Libby's best cooks.[25]

To pass the time in the Richmond prison, Ole fell back on his earlier penchant for reading and the cultivation of his mind. He began the study of German, using books John sent through to him. On one occasion he wrote home that he anticipated reading Hume's *History of England*, promised in the next package. He learned to play checkers — sometimes one match lasted for days. He did not play cards but enjoyed watching the game. The prisoners enlivened their drab life by staging Negro minstrel shows, particularly enjoying burlesqued impersonations of certain prison authorities.

Writing letters was the most common pastime. Prison rules were stringent: each man was allowed to send out one six-line letter a week, a restriction intended to reduce the work of the censor. So harsh was this requirement that fertile minds were soon at work to circumvent it. By dissolving soda in water or using onion juice, the prisoners could produce invisible writing between the lines or on the back of an innocent-looking six-line letter, which could not be detected unless it was held over heat. Through prisoner friends who were exchanged, Ole C. Johnson was able in a roundabout way to notify his family to "get wise to the invisible writing on the back of my letters." The underground correspondence worked. John and the others at home learned the trick — and when Ole's letters arrived there would be a gathering of relatives and friends to hear the real news from Libby Prison.[26]

[25] His two "roommates" were a Captain Gustavson of the Fifteenth Wisconsin and Lieutenant G. W. Buffum of the First Wisconsin.

[26] Buslett, *Det femtende regiment Wisconsin frivillige*, 219. Four of Ole's asso-

Most fortunately of all, Ole possessed inner resources that helped him to survive even such an ordeal as Libby Prison. From his corner he wrote to his sisters of the lovely view he had of the James River through the barred windows. "How beautiful it is! Even despite all the tumult strife and bloodshed, that continually plagues men's plans. Still nature in its iternall [*sic*] quiet way will make a laughingstock of men's efforts. The day is just like a warm March or April day in Wisconsin. A day that one feels glad to be alive, and gives one the feeling that everything is not too dark. . . . If you have never lived behind prison walls, let us hope that you never have the experience. When one is lying, twisting and turning on the prison floor thinking about freedom, home and the loved [ones] there. What a farce it is to hear the guards call out All is Well." [27]

Lieutenant Colonel Johnson knew that all was *not* well during the sad winter of 1863-1864. Contagious disease had broken out in the prison and men were dying in appalling numbers. The Eleventh Kentucky Regiment in three months had lost 40 out of 89 men. His own Wisconsin boys were dying. He hoped against hope that some of them, suffering from serious illness, could yet be saved. In his letters he complained bitterly that the government in Washington had shown so little interest in working out a more effective system of exchanging prisoners. He urged his brother John to bring the horrible conditions at Libby to the attention of Wisconsin state authorities. His heart went into these appeals, for he believed — with ample evidence before his eyes — that many of his fellows were destined to end their service to the Union cause by dying miserably within the walls of a prison. Again and again, he asked himself the bitter question: Had they all been forgotten?

By design Libby authorities shut their prisoners off as far as possible from what was happening in the world. The censors cut all news of the war from incoming letters; they allowed no visitors or newspapers inside the walls. In spite of this surveillance, the Union men could tell from the worried looks on the faces of their guards that the Confederate armies were gradually being pushed farther south. From what scraps of solid

ciates in the prison, upon their release and return to the North, acted as his messengers to let the family in on the new letter-writing technique: a Dr. Hawley of the Thirty-fifth Illinois Regiment; Oran Rogers of Cascade, Wisconsin; Fred West, a conductor on the Milwaukee and St. Paul Railway; and Dr. William How of Palestine, Illinois.

[27] Buslett, *Det femtende regiment Wisconsin frivillige*, 204–291. Letters which Ole C. Johnson wrote to his family, dated December 7, 1863, and January 26, 1864, are included in the Appendix, p. 280–283.

news the prisoners could gather, they learned that Grant's victory at Chattanooga in November, 1863, had countered their own unhappy defeat at Chickamauga. On their fingers they ticked off Vicksburg, Gettysburg, and Chattanooga—and exulted over the Union's successes during the last half of 1863. When, in March, 1864, Grant pressed Lee and his Army of Northern Virginia back toward Richmond, the men in Libby began to dream of a military rescue.[28]

It was a vain hope. Fearful that Richmond would indeed fall, the Confederate government made a drastic decision: to move all captive officers in Libby to the South's other great Civil War prison at Andersonville, Georgia. On May 7, 1864, the commissioned officers who had served in the Union Army were marched from Libby to the Richmond railroad station and herded into a train headed southward. It was a slow, desperate journey putting an end to all hope of rescue. As the prison train rumbled on, thoughts of a joyful reunion with his family and of the new horrors of the infamous Andersonville Prison crystallized a decision in the mind of Lieutenant Colonel Ole C. Johnson. He would risk his life in an attempt to escape.[29]

In his plan to outwit the Confederate guards on the way to Andersonville, Ole had the help of two trusted friends who had endured with him the eight months in Libby: Captain Hunnicutt and Lieutenant Hodges, both of the Second Tennessee Regiment of the Union army. Weakened by over two years on a succession of battlefields and by the deprivations of prison life, all three men felt that their life-or-death attempt must be made now, while they still had enough strength and energy to endure whatever hardships they must face. This they agreed was the best chance to survive the war.

On May 13, while the train stopped at Charlotte, North Carolina, in the late evening, their opportunity came. In changing from one train to another, the three Union officers managed to make their way to the end car. This would be the best spot from which to jump off. But to their dismay other cars were added to the second train. Fortune was with them, however, for the rickety car they had entered had a hole in its floor big

[28] Buslett, *Det femtende regiment Wisconsin frivillige*, 313.

[29] Buslett, *Det femtende regiment Wisconsin frivillige*, 254. In this account, written after the war, Ole revealed that a happy dream one night on the train trip from Richmond encouraged him to make a break for freedom: "I dreamed that I was at home with Mother and Father and my sisters and brother, and that there was no more war or prison with bars."

enough for a man to crawl through. Quickly they threw a coat over the hole and sat down close by.

When the train stopped at the little South Carolina town of Chester to take on water and fuel, they crawled down through the hole to the narrow space between the rails. Ole was the last to make the breath-taking move. Soon the train lurched slowly on its way. The brake rods ripped the buttons from Ole's coat, but he and the others emerged unharmed. From the last car, guards caught sight of their prisoners running for their lives and fired wildly after them. The train stopped and its armed escort made a perfunctory search in the woods nearby. Soon they gave up. In the friendly darkness, Johnson, Hunnicutt, and Hodges lay low until their moving prison vanished down the tracks. They had escaped from Libby — they would never enter the stockade at Andersonville.

To reach the Union lines near Knoxville, Tennessee, the trio of fugitives had to travel on foot northwestward for hundreds of miles. They scaled high mountains, crossed rivers, and worked their way around swamps and through deep forests — a journey to test the strongest physique and the most determined will. Of prime importance was the fact that Hunnicutt and Hodges were Southerners, natives of Tennessee, who knew the countryside and the habits of the people — whose very language would not betray them. Starting in the Confederate state of South Carolina, they were in constant danger, still surrounded by the enemy. A barking dog paralyzed them with the fear that bloodhounds might be on their track. Traveling only at night, guided by the moon and stars, they made but slow progress. The half pound of corn bread and the pound of dried apples they had been able to withhold from their prison-train rations were soon exhausted. For three more nights they trudged on with nothing to eat. Now they began to realize how prison life had dangerously sapped their strength. They could not go on another day unless they could find some kind of food.

Where could they dare ask? In desperation they approached an isolated hut, crawling so close in the darkness that they could see through the chinks between the logs the light of a fire on dark faces. A Negro family — it would be safe to talk to these folk so lately blessed with the hope of freedom. They knocked on the door and explained that they were fleeing Yankee prisoners. Could they have food? "Yes," was the answer, and the woman gave them milk, corn bread, bacon and eggs. In return Ole gave her his gold ring. Later the man of the family walked with them to a spot where they could cross the Broad River in western North Carolina. Continuing on their way night after night, they dodged details of Confederate troops and bands of desperate rebel deserters who would shoot any strangers on sight. By lying low, sometimes for days at a time to escape detection, living off the land as they went, they edged westward hoping their luck would hold.

The first definite objective of the fugitives was the farm of Captain Hunnicutt's uncle, Peter Hunnicutt, in the area of Burnsville, North Carolina, very close to the Tennessee border. The captain had visited his relative as a boy years before, but now he remembered only that the farm was on Jack Creek half a dozen miles from Burnsville. It was a touchy matter to make inquiry, for Peter Hunnicutt was a Union man and one false move would be fatal for all concerned. But for three days, as they drew near to their goal, the men had eaten only a handful of onions, poached from a handy field. Their situation was again desperate. Finally they encountered a man alone, who gave them directions to Burnsville, mentioning Jack Creek in the process. These two words were the key. The next day they knocked on Peter Hunnicutt's door. The farmer answered with extreme caution: the ragged trio might well be a rebel patrol. When the captain called him "Uncle Peter," the two men embraced with tears streaming down their cheeks. Ole never forgot the touching scene nor what it meant to him.

Although the fleeing Union officers felt comparatively safe in this haven of refuge, they realized that their dangers were far from over. From Uncle Peter they learned that rebel picket lines were near and that he was being watched. It would not be safe for them to stay in the farmhouse. So, after a good meal, furnished with plenty of blankets, they were taken to a hiding place in the woods behind the house. There they stayed for the night and the next day, while the family kept constant vigil that no prowling rebels came near them. In the darkness of the second night — well supplied with bags of food — they set out again, their hearts full of gratitude to the family which had risked dangerous reprisals to aid in their escape. The next morning they crossed the state line and set foot in Tennessee.

Step by step they approached freedom. The thought that they were near the Union lines buoyed them up for a final effort. Shortly they met men in blue uniforms and saw the Stars and Stripes moving in the breeze. On June 10, 1864, they trudged into Strawberry Plains, headquarters of the Union army in eastern Tennessee. "Dirty, tired, and ragged as we were," Ole reported later that summer, "there was at that moment not one creature in the whole world that I envied." In twenty-eight days they had traveled 300 miles, in a zigzag course, often over wild and difficult terrain. The commander-in-chief of the Tenth Ohio Cavalry received them, and hundreds of men shook their hands in admiration of their courage and stamina. What they had done was recognized as one of the boldest exploits of the war.[30]

Back in Madison, *Emigranten* published a report of particular interest: Ole C. Johnson had escaped from Libby Prison, had made his way to the Union lines, and was now home on a 20-day leave. His brother John wrote: "I rushed home in short order. Our meeting can better be imagined than described." After his leave, Lieutenant Colonel Johnson rejoined the Fifteenth Wisconsin near Atlanta. Now reduced to 82 effectives, the regiment had become part of General William Tecumseh Sherman's famous army that was to march through Georgia to the Atlantic seaboard. Reunited with his old comrades, Ole served only a few months more. On February 10, 1865 – brevetted a colonel in recognition of his long and distinguished service – he was mustered out at Chattanooga, Tennessee.[31]

During the years of Ole's service in the Union army, John A. Johnson in Madison continued to follow events with deep concern – not alone for the fate of his two brothers but also for the great issue facing the country. On the Fourth of July, 1864, John gave an address. He stressed at first the founding of the United States on the new principle that governments existed for the benefit of free citizens in contradistinction to the theory of the divine right of kings. Turning to the issue of slavery and the threatened disruption of the Union, he traced the step-by-step victory of the North in a terrible internal struggle. With Sherman at the moment nearing Atlanta and Grant hammering at Richmond, he urged all loyal Americans to supply the men and means to complete the war. "Never shall this glorious country," he said in conclusion, "be disgraced by rebel rule, but shall remain the asylum of the oppressed and the home of the free and the brave for many, many generations, and the names of the men who have secured

[30] *Emigranten*, July 16, 1864.

[31] Buslett, *Det femtende regiment Wisconsin frivillige*, 314; *Emigranten*, August 15, 1864. In the family annals, it was always felt that Ole's war experiences had aged him beyond his years, had impaired his health, and had shortened his life.

this noble heritage will live through all time in the hearts of a grateful people." [32]

After the war, it fell to John A. Johnson to compile the record of the Fifteenth Wisconsin Regiment. For this project he enlisted the aid of many individuals – especially officers of the unit and others who had helped to establish it and to stand behind it throughout the war. The result was a 160-page book entitled *Det skandinaviske regiments historie.*[33]

In an introductory section, Johnson traced the growing sectional division over slavery. In the author's mind, knowledge of the long national debate was essential to an understanding of the Civil War: the cause and central issue was slavery. The major part of the book contains an account of the history of the Fifteenth Wisconsin, written or related by the men who had been a part of it. Most of this section was composed by Colonel Ole C. Johnson, but parts were also contributed by Major George Wilson and Captain Mons Grinager. There are eyewitness descriptions of battle after battle, ranging from hand-to-hand fighting to tactics and overall strategy. Also included are accounts of life in Libby Prison, the siege of Atlanta, and Sherman's march to the sea. Chaplain C. L. Clausen, the independent-minded frontier pastor, added his observations on moral and religious phases of military life as experienced by men of the regiment. This history is both a factual account and a subjective document.

Another chapter is made up of thumbnail biographies of officers, surgeons, and chaplains. Many of these are by Johnson's own hand. The life story of Colonel Hans Christian Heg – which Johnson often praised as having unusual merit – was written by Knud Langeland.[34] Privates in the ranks are given their due along with the officers. From Company A to Company K, the last recruited, the name, rank, home, date of enlistment and age at that time are given to bring each man into the regiment. Each is followed through the war to the time of separation from the unit: the date, cause, and place of death for those who gave their lives, the date and place of being mustered out for those who survived.

In view of John A. Johnson's unswerving devotion to the cause of the

[32] A copy of this address is in the Johnson Papers.

[33] The book, written in Norwegian, was published in 1869 in La Crosse, Wisconsin, on the printing presses of *Fædrelandet og Emigranten.* A copy of the volume is in the St. Olaf College library.

[34] Knud Langeland, editor of *Nordlyset*, the first Norwegian-language newspaper published in America, later became the editor of *Skandinaven.*

Union and recognizing his early promotion of and close association with the Fifteenth Wisconsin, it was eminently fitting that he should compile its history. The volume is not alone a human story of men at war. More than that, it affords a rare insight into the story of men caught up and carried beyond themselves in a defense of human freedom as against the ancient tyranny of slavery.

CHAPTER IV

Business and Politics Beckon

After eight years as clerk of the board of supervisors of Dane County, John A. Johnson in 1869 declined the nomination for a fifth two-year term. At the age of thirty-seven, he no doubt felt that the time had come to break away from the relatively drab office routine to which he had accustomed himself. Widely known as he was in Madison, the capital and hub of a variety of activities, attractive alternatives beckoned him to a more challenging pattern of life. To be free to choose one of these alternatives, he dropped out of politics for a time to try his hand at something that might provide a more interesting future.

He thought of farming and the law. Both appealed to him. Earlier he most certainly would have gone back to his farm, for it is clear that love for the land, which had brought his family to America, was always in his blood and had been a formative influence in all his experience. "Life on the farm," he wrote in his "Memoirs," "did give one a certain amount of leisure for reading, study and self-culture. . . . And the farm would be the best possible place to rear a family. I had always thought if I could be the owner of a well-equipped farm and have a modest surplus at interest, I would be abundantly satisfied. This I could now have if I went back to the country." [1]

Had he still owned the Pleasant Springs acreage — once so attractive and prized as the planned site of his permanent home — Johnson's life story might well have been that of a successful farmer. But he had sold

[1] Johnson, "Memoirs."

this farm in 1863 upon his first re-election as county clerk. In 1869 he would have had to buy somewhere else and start over again — a difficult decision to make even though, from the proceeds of his earlier sale, he had a sum of money to invest in such a venture.

He also gave consideration to becoming a lawyer. Though he was not formally trained, he felt himself equipped by study and experience to hold his own with men already established in the profession. His duties in the Dane County office had brought him into association with many of the best legal minds in the state. He had moved freely with such men and was accepted by them as an equal. He had become so familiar with tax law, titles, and contracts that he was regarded as an authority in such matters. He had spent some of his spare time in the study of law, and it seems clear that he could have been successful as an attorney.

As he debated his course between a return to farming and a plunge into the law, a third opportunity presented itself — an attractive invitation to enter the agricultural machinery business. In 1869 Chauncey C. L. Williams of the well-established firm of Fuller and Williams, distributors of farm implements, urged Johnson to take a position as a salesman with the Madison company. After weighing the matter carefully, he accepted the offer. The decision was to prove a major turning point in his life.[2]

Williams had not chosen blindly. Like others in the Madison circle in which Johnson moved, he had admired the intelligent attention that the county clerk had given every detail of his official duties, as well as his legal acumen and writing and speaking ability. In the employer's mind, these qualities overweighed the fact that Johnson did not have specific training in salesmanship or a large amount of money to invest in the business. Williams shrewdly recognized that his man had capital of another kind.

John, of course, had had some early experience with machinery. At the age of sixteen, he had worked in Esterly's Heart Prairie machine shop and on his 600-acre farm. There he had observed experiments with harvesting machines called headers. By the old hand method of cutting grain with a cradle, two men — a cutter and a binder — could cover only three acres a day. Esterly aimed at perfecting a harvester that could cut twenty acres a

[2] At this time, Johnson associated himself with a successful group of Madison businessmen headed by Morris E. Fuller, Edward M. Fuller, and Chauncey C. L. Williams. In 1867, R. G. Dun and Company, New York, in the *Mercantile Agency Reference Book*, listed M. E. Fuller and Company as worth between $50,000 and $100,000. The company's credit rating was high.

day, but other reapers then coming into use had pre-empted the market. John's association with an inventive farmer-machinist, however, interested him early in the possibilities of constructing machinery to ease the back-breaking labor that farmers were enduring, and to speed up and make more financially rewarding many phases of farm production.

Before he was twenty, he had operated a threshing machine and had joined with a neighbor in a "breaking team," contracting to plow a hundred acres of tough sod with the simple implement of the period drawn by three yoke of oxen. Somewhat later, while he was operating his own farm, he had as a sideline sold farm equipment for a Beloit company. All of these experiences with pre-Civil War machinery were to be of far-reaching importance to Johnson in the business enterprise into which he now threw his energies.

Fuller and Williams had national connections. The company was general agent for the Walter A. Wood Mowing and Reaping Machine Company of Hoosick Falls, New York, a firm that had branch offices in Chicago, St. Louis, San Francisco, and even in London. For twenty years Fuller and Williams made spectacular sales records for the parent company in the area to the west served by Madison, Wisconsin. Wood's self-raking reaper had earned international renown in 1867 by winning two medals in Paris. It had also placed first in a reaper competition at Rochester, New York, and had captured top honors in an exhibit sponsored by the Minnesota State Agricultural Association. By 1869, when Johnson took to the road for his company, this implement had made a name for itself throughout the Midwest.[3]

Advertising campaigns of Fuller and Williams made good use of the fact that their new salesman was a Norwegian: a booklet extolling the special virtues of the company's machinery was printed in both English and Norwegian. The pamphlet introduced "J. A. Johnson" as a reliable agent, so well known that he needed no recommendation. It stated that he would gladly answer all questions, asked in either language, regarding the firm's products.

The fact that in the early 1870's Johnson was a part owner of *Skandinaven*, the Norwegian-language newspaper published in Chicago, greatly facilitated his first years as a salesman. The paper was a prime medium for the best advertising effort of Fuller and Williams. Week after week, a

[3] *Farm Implement News* (Chicago), June, 1891.

half-page or page advertisement set forth the merits of the Wood reaper and other machinery sold by the Madison firm. These notices stressed that the reaper was economical: it saved the work of two men; one team of horses could pull it. When Walter A. Wood developed the self-binder using wire for tying the bundles of grain, Fuller and Williams sold it, later adding the new Wood mower and other farm machinery. Great improvements over the old hand methods, all these implements sold well.[4]

Over all the eastern United States and particularly in the Middle West, the time was ripe for a boom in the sale of improved farm machinery—especially of the reaper. Between 1851 and 1876, the United States granted nearly 3,000 patents for reapers and their attachments. In 1868 Fuller and Williams sold 1,400 reapers and mowers in Wisconsin, Iowa, and Minnesota. The market moved steadily westward. In the decade of the 1870's—when Johnson was most active as a salesman in the area—the population of the north central section of the United States, the grain belt, grew 34 per cent. This was a peak period of immigration from northern Europe: the Germans were coming to Wisconsin and the Scandinavians to Minnesota and Dakota Territory. The immigration agent at Madison, Wisconsin, recorded that in 14 days in July, 1868, a thousand European land seekers had arrived in Madison on their way to Iowa and Minnesota. Two thirds of them were Norwegians. And it was said of the present area of North Dakota that anyone speaking Norwegian could find companionship sooner than one using only English.[5]

Fuller and Williams followed the settlers, sending their agents into all areas of the developing empire. As early as 1869 John A. Johnson and L. W. Hoyt were selling Wood's machinery for the Madison company in southern Iowa, Dakota Territory, Colorado, and Nevada. M. E. Fuller had an agency covering Wisconsin, northern Iowa, and Minnesota. At one time or another, Johnson, who enjoyed a decided advantage in dealing with his Norwegian countrymen, sold farm implements in all these states. In 1870 Fuller and Williams marketed 7,500 reapers. Believing strongly in the power of the printed word, the new salesman reported glowingly to his newspaper in Chicago. Jokingly, the editor of *Skandinaven* declared that, if all the testimonials in praise of the reaper which

[4] *Skandinaven*, February 6, 13, 20, March 5, 19, 26, May 14, June 16, 1868, February 22, 1876.

[5] Edward H. Knight, "Agricultural Implements," in *The First Century of the Republic*, 48 (New York, 1876); *Skandinaven*, May 26, 1869.

Johnson relayed to him were printed, there would be room in the paper for nothing else.[6]

Johnson also sent to *Skandinaven* interesting personal impressions of conditions as he observed them in his travels. From Nebraska in 1871, he reported that the part of the state lying from a hundred to two hundred miles west of the Missouri River was unusually fruitful. The soil was rich. There were no forests, but the cottonwoods and soft maples "grew unbelievably fast." The absence of hardwood for fuel would soon make it necessary to ship in coal as the area became populated. He added, however, that coal was available in both Iowa and Wyoming. In the Black Hills of the Dakota country, wood and coal, as well as gold, were to be found. "But that region," he wrote, "is still in the possession of the Indians. They will have to be moved before these natural resources can be developed."[7]

From Kansas the observant Johnson reported that he was in the land of the buffalo; he had seen herds of thousands. Some fifty miles south of Emporia, he visited a Norwegian settlement, where the plain seemed to stretch endlessly to the horizon. "Nowhere in the world," he reported, "does corn grow as it does in parts of Kansas." Near Eureka he was delighted to find several pioneer families who had moved from his own home community of Koshkonong. Wisely they had chosen good land along a river, where there were trees and water. Hopefully, a railroad would soon reach them. Johnson also added a word of caution: Kansas was a land of uncertain rainfall. People should investigate carefully before locating in that state, for dry years could easily consume what the good years had accumulated. In much of the region, he advised, cattle raising was safer than the planting of wheat.[8]

Although selling farm machinery was his main business, Johnson—remembering his own early years in a strange land—felt a deep concern for the welfare of the immigrant families he met. As he traveled in newly settled areas, he took careful note of the lay of the land and of its resources, of transportation, markets, and the problems peculiar to a given region. Not all immigrant settlers were successful. To help them and their compatriots in the East and in Europe, he sent back to his newspaper detailed factual articles calculated to inform people who were thinking of starting life

[6] *Skandinaven,* May 18, August 31, 1870. Many of these testimonial letters were printed in a circular and distributed by Fuller and Williams.

[7] *Skandinaven,* June 14, 1871.

[8] *Skandinaven,* June 17, 24, 1873. Johnson included in his letters the names and addresses of persons who could give help to anyone planning to go to Kansas.

over in the Middle West. He made it clear that in his judgment an immigrant would be better off to establish himself in one of the more settled states until he had sufficient funds with which to battle the rigors of the Western frontier. Parcels of land could still be bought in Iowa and Minnesota, where a small-scale farming operation, with dairy cattle, could prosper to a modest degree. Homestead land could also be found in these states. But the western edge of the frontier was different. Johnson had seen enough deserted, weed-grown fields and abandoned sod houses to have any illusions on one point: No immigrant without sound financial backing should take a chance on the frontier.[9]

In 1876 Johnson was in southwestern Minnesota at a time just after the area had been devastated by grasshoppers. He traveled in Nobles, Cottonwood, Watonwan, and Jackson counties. He drove with horses the 30 miles from Worthington to Luverne and saw the complete ruin caused by the insect plague. There would be no crops; selling farm machinery that year was out of the question. Nevertheless, he saw beyond the present crippling loss. "In spite of the destruction," he declared, "one could see that this was wonderful prairie land, rolling but not hilly." [10]

Experience in the field made Johnson a keen judge of the farm machinery market; the knowledge he was accumulating was preparing him for larger responsibilities with his own company later on. His sales record was excellent. He sent messages about his work from Omaha, Nebraska, Clinton, Iowa, from Mankato and New Ulm in Minnesota – and from a variety of other places in the states west of the Mississippi. In August, 1874, he wrote to a friend in Madison: "I have been out in the field trying the self-binder and exhibiting it – a decided success." A year later he sent a similar report to *Skandinaven* from Mankato: "I am extremely busy and will be for 3 or 4 weeks. I started a binder yesterday, went well. Is not that good news?" [11]

The time was now approaching when Fuller and Williams would consider offering their most successful salesman a greater opportunity in the company. The first years of Johnson's association with the firm had coincided with a favorable time for agriculture in the Middle West. Abundant wheat crops had brought from $1.00 to $1.50 a bushel, an extremely

[9] *Skandinaven,* June 14, 1871.

[10] *Skandinaven,* June 6, 1876.

[11] Johnson to Rasmus B. Anderson, August 8, 1874; a copy of the letter is in the Rasmus B. Anderson Papers at the State Historical Society of Wisconsin, Madison.

good price at the time. With the expansion of wheat farming, the demand for reapers provided a burgeoning market—and farmers had money to pay promptly for implements purchased. The good years had given Johnson a running start in the business and had won for him a secure relationship with his employers. Though there were hard times resulting from the panic of 1873, the Madison firm, with his help, had built a solid foundation which would enable it not only to survive but actually to expand its trade territory and its sales of farm machinery.[12]

On September 17, 1873, John A. Johnson, then aged forty-one, took a step which was to have an important bearing on the future course of his life: He affixed his signature to articles of copartnership with the firm of Fuller and Williams in an affiliated business enterprise to be known as Johnson, Fuller and Company. The four partners representing the original Madison firm were M. E. Fuller, E. M. Fuller, Chauncey C. L. Williams, and George Gernon. With these men he was to be associated for many years—and, building on their foundation, he was to be the moving force in establishing a business that would grow in extent and influence far beyond its relatively modest beginnings.[13]

The first corporate move of Johnson, Fuller and Company was to establish a branch in St. Paul, which would have the exclusive sale of the Walter A. Wood mowing and reaping machines throughout an expanded territory in Minnesota and Wisconsin. Johnson was designated the managing partner of the new enterprise, which set up its headquarters at 42 Sibley Street. Specifically, he was made responsible for sales in all of Minnesota with the exception of the southeastern section of the state: Goodhue, Wabasha, and Houston counties and the eastern half of Fillmore County. In Wisconsin his territory included St. Croix, Polk, and Barron counties and the northern portion of Pierce County. The original partners, having seen what Johnson could do singly as a salesman, had chosen him as the best man in their organization to develop a promising virgin area into a valuable addition to their trade territory.

Fuller and Williams furnished $25,000 for the business and agreed to bear all expenses, including the salaries of assistants. Johnson, whose

[12] World conditions favored the economic development of the American Middle West after the Civil War: The industrial revolution was well on its way in the United States, and the Franco-Prussian War also had a part in stimulating the growth of the economy. See Johnson, "Memoirs."

[13] The original contract between John A. Johnson and Fuller and Williams is in the possession of the Gisholt Machine Company, Madison, Wisconsin. Two copies are in the Johnson Papers.

salary was set at $2,000 a year, was not required to furnish any capital, but was to give his full time to the business. He was to serve as general manager of the St. Paul office, reporting annually to the parent company on the financial condition of the branch. It was understood that he would consult regularly with his partners concerning the progress of the business, and that his records would at all times be open for inspection by officers of Fuller and Williams. According to the contract, Johnson was to have one-fourth interest in the profits of the new concern, with three fourths accruing to the company in Madison.[14]

Although he spent considerable time in St. Paul, Johnson, by choice, continued to make his home in Madison. At this period of his life, his household consisted of his wife and two older sons, then youngsters in the local schools. With his strong personal and family attachment for the Wisconsin capital, it is not surprising that he did not move to Minnesota. He had an excellent assistant in the St. Paul headquarters in the person of Oliver H. Swerig, to whom he could delegate a great many matters of routine responsibility.[15]

As the years passed, the Walter A. Wood Company became well aware of the record Johnson, Fuller and Company were making in sales of their reaping and mowing machines. The manufacturers were especially pleased with the businesslike management of the St. Paul branch, and Edward H. Valentine, manager of Wood's Chicago office, wrote Johnson in a personal complimentary vein: "I hope you will continue to be the man at the helm in the management of your territory. . . . You and you alone are the only man in your firm or out of it to handle it as it should be done. I am free to say that I am personally desirous as well for myself as also the interests of this company to have you continue your connection with the sale of the Wood machines, and, I hope to see you connected with this business as long as I may be connected with it." [16]

Valentine referred in this letter to Johnson's contact with Oliver Dalrymple, a wheat grower reported to own at that time a bonanza farm of 75,000 acres of land in the famous Red River Valley. "I most earnestly hope," the Chicago manager wrote, "that you will succeed in holding

[14] The letterhead of the St. Paul branch carried the name of Johnson, Fuller & Company. The sales territory of the new office was to be gradually enlarged as the Northwest became more fully settled.

[15] Numerous letters from Swerig in St. Paul to Johnson in Madison, all dealing with business matters, are in the Johnson Papers.

[16] Edward H. Valentine to Johnson, September 21, 1878.

Dalrymple exclusively." There was good reason for Valentine's solicitude. In 1876 Dalrymple had used 10 Wood self-binders in harvesting his wheat. The next year he employed 41 of the machines – and in 1878 he bought 35 more. Johnson, Fuller and Company, whose territory by 1878 had extended to the northwest far beyond earlier expectations, had handled the sale and delivery of all these machines.[17]

Coincidentally with his increasingly successful career in marketing farm machinery, Johnson took a leading part in establishing the Hekla Fire Insurance Company. In 1871 a group of prominent Scandinavians, mainly Norwegians living in Wisconsin, promoted the new venture in spite of opposition from old and well-established companies in the state. No legal barriers were raised, however, and both houses of the Wisconsin legislature approved the necessary charter. The company was capitalized at $100,000, with the possible future limit set at $500,000. Of the original sum, $10,000 was deposited with the Wisconsin state treasurer as protection for the insured prior to the issuance of any policies. With these particulars attended to, the Hekla Fire Insurance Company adopted a constitution on March 25, 1871, and began operation on June 1 of that year.[18]

Officers and directors of the company were men well known in business and public life in Wisconsin and Minnesota. Mons Anderson, a well-to-do merchant in La Crosse, was elected the first president; John A. Johnson became the first vice-president. Halle Steensland, a successful Madison businessman, was chosen secretary and treasurer. Among Johnson's friends and associates who joined him as stockholders and directors of the new organization were his brother, Oliver Johnson of Pleasant Springs, Rasmus B. Anderson, at the time a member of the faculty of the University of Wisconsin, O. B. Dahle of Perry, Wisconsin, and Harald Thorson of Northfield, Minnesota.[19]

The early years of the Hekla Fire Insurance Company were successful. By May 24, 1871, the capital stock of $100,000 had nearly all been subscribed; most stockholders were from Wisconsin, but some Norwegians

[17] Valentine to Johnson, September 21, 1878. On April 30, 1878, *Skandinaven* had printed a full page of testimonials for "Walter A. Wood's Self-binding Harvester." Later, when Johnson became a manufacturer of farm implements, he continued to hold the Dalrymple market.

[18] *Skandinaven*, March 29, 1871. The constitution was printed in both Norwegian and English. A copy in Norwegian is in the C. J. Sjolander Papers in the archives of the Norwegian-American Historical Association, Northfield, Minnesota.

[19] *Skandinaven*, July 19, 1871.

in Iowa, Illinois, and Minnesota invested in the enterprise. At the annual meeting held in December, 1872, with Vice-president John A. Johnson presiding, the financial report revealed that the "newborn child" was making startling growth. Its assets had reached $67,393.36, a figure nearly double that of a year earlier. The company continued its favorable progress: At the fifth annual meeting in 1875, Treasurer Halle Steensland reported that net worth had increased to $143,509.02. Claims for fire losses had been satisfactorily adjusted and promptly paid, and the orderly conduct of the business as a whole received a vote of confidence from the stockholders.[20]

John A. Johnson as president and Halle Steensland as treasurer guided Hekla carefully through the years, including the panic of 1873.[21] Despite adverse conditions, the company paid annual dividends of 10 per cent and strengthened its reserves by substantial amounts each year. This was a period when other financial institutions were failing, and Hekla's record attracted favorable attention. In a letter published in *Skandinaven* on December 9, 1879, a correspondent calling himself "Racine" indulged in a glowing but accurate simile: "It [*Hekla*] stands like a green oasis in the dry desert."

By January, 1880, when the ninth annual meeting was held, assets had reached $289,209.22. The firm seemed solidly established and secure with leaders of recognized ability at the helm. A contemporary local newspaper view of Hekla as it neared the end of its first decade was highly complimentary to its management: "The well-known financial standing and business integrity of the company's directors and officers is a guarantee that it is sound to the core." This editorial judgment was seemingly confirmed by wide public acceptance of Hekla as a successful and valuable Wisconsin institution.[22]

Halle Steensland succeeded John A. Johnson as president in the late 1880's; he also continued to hold his original position as treasurer. Johnson assumed his former office of vice-president, and W. R. Freeman was elected secretary. Now for the first time differences apparently arose between the two major stockholders and ranking officers. What caused the

[20] *Skandinaven*, April 12, May 24, 1871, January 21, 1873, April 25, 1876; *Wisconsin State Journal* (Madison), January 10, 1876.

[21] Johnson served as president of the company through most of the 1870's and early 1880's, during which time Steensland continued as secretary and treasurer. The two men were the largest stockholders in the company.

[22] *Skandinaven*, February 3, 1880; *Wisconsin State Journal*, January 19, 1880.

resulting dissension is not wholly clear. A large part of it certainly stemmed from the conflicting views of the two men concerning the new secretary. Johnson supported Freeman, considering him to be an able insurance executive; Steensland felt that his old friend more readily accepted Freeman's judgment than his own on important matters. The friction extended to the stockholders, who unwisely took sides.[23]

What followed was a dramatic surprise to citizens of Madison, who knew Johnson and Steensland well. On February 12, 1890, Albert Scheffer, president of the St. Paul German Fire Insurance Company, offered to buy the Hekla stock. The next day Hekla stockholders voted to announce that their company would retire from business in Madison and that, as of February, 1890, its risks were being insured in the St. Paul German Company. Some of the assets of the Madison firm were assumed by a new company, also called the Hekla Fire Insurance Company, originally incorporated in 1871 in Wisconsin and reorganized in St. Paul in 1890. In this institution, Johnson became a stockholder. The next year, when Hekla of St. Paul merged its capital and business with the original St. Paul company, he exchanged his Hekla shares for holdings in the St. Paul German Fire Insurance Company.[24]

After nineteen years of successful operation, the Hekla Fire Insurance Company — still in sound financial condition — had come to an end as a business institution in Wisconsin. There were regrets, not the least centering about the unfortunate clash of personalities which had prompted the breakup of the business and of long-time friendships. Mons Anderson, first president of Hekla and a director for all of the company's Madison years, wrote to Johnson, his words no doubt expressing accurately the thoughts of others close to the situation: "I regret very much that there seems to be so much difference of opinion among you gentlemen at Madison. I was in hopes that the Company might have been spared from its being wound up so hastily on account of its being an organization originated by us Norwegians. I had a certain amount of pride that prompted these

[23] Halle Steensland to Johnson, February 25, March 12, 1889; *Skandinaven*, January 22, 1890.

[24] *Skandinaven*, February 12, 1890; *Cyclopedia of Insurance in the United States 1890* (New York, 1891); Hugo Schlenk to Johnson, October 4, 1890; Albert Scheffer to Johnson, November 16, 27, 1891. The St. Paul German Fire Insurance Company was a relatively new concern that had been organized in April, 1889, with a capital of $300,000. In addition to the Hekla assets sold to the St. Paul German Company, in February, 1890, some assets were sold to the Union Trust Company of Madison.

feelings. I very much would like to see the Company go on and continue to do business just for the reason above given."[25]

In 1872, John A. Johnson extended his business activities by engaging in a Chicago journalistic enterprise. Joining with Knud Langeland, former editor of *Skandinaven*, and Iver Lawson, he formed a partnership for publishing a Norwegian-language newspaper called *Amerika*. When Iver Lawson died in the fall of 1872, *Amerika* was merged with *Skandinaven*, and early the next year the consolidated journal began publication as *Skandinaven og Amerika*. Its publishers were John A. Johnson, John Anderson, the owner of *Skandinaven*, and Victor Lawson, the son of Iver Lawson, who had become a member of the firm upon the death of his father. After 1873 the owners dropped the name *Amerika*, and *Skandinaven* again became the official title.[26]

The articles of copartnership specified that the firm would publish newspapers and books and do job printing, and that the partners had an equal interest in the business. Editorial offices were located in a building belonging to the Iver Lawson estate at 123 Fifth Avenue, Chicago. For a time the owners of *Skandinaven* printed the *Chicago Daily News* on their presses; later Victor Lawson became the owner of that well-known Chicago newspaper.[27]

The editorial policy of *Skandinaven* reflected the joint thinking of John A. Johnson and Knud Langeland, its editor until 1881. The two men held similar views on many of the issues of the day. They had opposed slavery; both had supported the public schools. They valued the democratizing function of these schools, their indirect teaching of religious tolerance, and their promotion of respect for the United States as a great country. They especially admired the emphasis which American education at all levels focused on the principles of freedom and equality. Neither man, however, felt any constraint in offering constructive criticism of American institutions. Both Johnson and Langeland, though they sensed the danger

[25] Mons Anderson to Johnson, January 10, 1890.

[26] "The Story of *Skandinaven*, 1866–1916," a 16-page booklet containing excerpts from an article appearing in the jubilee issue of *Skandinaven*, May 1, 1916, at the time the paper celebrated the fiftieth anniversary of its founding. A copy is in the Johnson Papers.

[27] A copy of the articles of copartnership is in the Johnson Papers. Melville Stone, later manager of the Associated Press, was publisher of the *Chicago Daily News* at the time it was being printed on *Skandinaven's* presses.

of immigrant provincialism, wished to retain what was of value in their Norwegian cultural and religious heritage.[28]

As their key principle, the publishers of *Skandinaven* adhered to a spirit of editorial independence. They believed that a paper with a sound financial basis need never cater to any group; thus its editors would be left free to present the cause of the generality of people and to choose high ethical ground freely and without fear. This approach proved well suited to the times and to the clientele the paper served. In spite of its sometimes prickly independence, *Skandinaven's* subscription list grew steadily – an indication that most Norwegian Americans found in its columns what they wanted to read.[29]

In helping to make his paper a strong influence in immigrant life, Johnson had not been seeking a lucrative business investment. His interest lay rather in an ambition to advance his countrymen in their efforts to achieve the best type of American citizenship. In seeking this goal, he was most fortunate in his associates: Their aims were the same as his, and he gave each of them high praise for his abilities and spirit.

Considered one of the ablest printers in Chicago, John Anderson had left a fine position on the staff of the *Chicago Tribune* to engage in the relatively insecure enterprise of a paper for Norwegian immigrants. Knud Langeland had a rare insight into the problems of these people who, like himself, had chosen America over the Old World. With great felicity of expression in his writing, this open-minded editor quickly attracted the attention of the public. Johnson wrote of him that his efforts would remain a living memory in the minds of his grateful readers. The remarkable talents of Victor Lawson were soon to establish him as one of the country's outstanding journalists. There was a special quality to the man as well: Devoted to his church, his humanitarian spirit led to regular visits to the sick in Chicago hospitals and to a lifelong interest in the improvement of American schools. With such leadership, it is not surprising that *Skandinaven* made a name for itself of which Johnson was extremely proud.

In addition to the financial assistance that Johnson gave *Skandinaven*, he also wrote articles for the paper and gave its editors his wholehearted moral support. Later, as the enterprise gained momentum and stability, he felt free to withdraw from his active connection to give full attention to

[28] Arlow W. Andersen, "Knud Langeland: Pioneer Editor," in *Norwegian-American Studies and Records*, 14:134 (Northfield, Minnesota, 1944).

[29] *Skandinaven*, May 9, 1876.

his own business. In 1876 he retired as part-owner, but he continued to be a contributor, particularly of articles espousing the cause of the common school, which to the end of his life he believed to be the great safeguard of democracy in America.[30]

Skandinaven continued publication from its beginning in 1866 for nearly three quarters of a century. During almost all of this time, it served its intended purpose: to help the Norwegian immigrant, in a period of cultural transition, to learn about contemporary America in a language he could understand. When the children of foreign-born parents had universally gained facility in reading American newspapers, *Skandinaven* – its main mission accomplished – could cease publication. It was absorbed by *Decorah-Posten* in 1940, having by that time continued publication a great many years longer than had been prophesied by its most optimistic supporters.

His versatility made Johnson a marked man in Wisconsin politics in the turbulent years following the Civil War. Always actively interested in public affairs but not by nature an avid office-seeker, he nevertheless found himself frequently pushed forward as a candidate by friends who admired his character and abilities. He had run for the lower house of the Wisconsin legislature in 1868, but in this race he had been defeated. In November, 1872, however, he had been willing to enter a contest for a seat in the state senate – and this time he had been elected as a Republican to represent the seventh district, which included the city of Madison.[31]

Soon he found himself immersed in an extremely crowded Wisconsin legislative calendar. The Granger movement, born of an agrarian revolt of the late 1860's, had become a major political factor in the Middle West. The bubble of prosperity following the Civil War had burst, and farm prices had seriously declined. Ambitious new western railroads were accused of allowing secret rebates and practicing discrimination in rates and services in favor of big shippers, and angry small farmers discovered in the Grange a chance to "right nearly all wrongs at the ballot box." The panic of 1873 followed, and legislatures in agricultural states like Wiscon-

[30] Andersen, "Knud Langeland: Pioneer Editor," in *Norwegian-American Studies and Records*, 14: 131–138. In appreciation of the support Langeland and *Skandinaven* had given the common school, the board of education in Chicago in 1884 named a new elementary school building for the editor.

[31] *Legislative Manual of Wisconsin, 1873*, 457.

sin found themselves deeply embroiled in a bitter battle involving railroad legislation. Into this struggle John A. Johnson vigorously threw himself.[32]

In the session of 1873, the problem of how to regulate the railroads loomed large before the Wisconsin lawmakers. The issue was double-edged. The state badly needed the railroads to develop its economy; on the other hand, supervisory legal restrictions seemed necessary to prevent the railroad interests from making their own rules at the expense of everybody else – particularly the farmers. Governor C. C. Washburn, a Republican pledged to support railroad legislation, recommended the organization of a state board of railroad commissioners.[33]

The issue was not new to Senator Johnson. Sixteen years earlier, as a member of the Wisconsin assembly, he had recognized the urgent need for bringing railroad service to the people of the state. At that time, before the Civil War, control of the new roads was not an important factor. They were essential to the state's progress, and he had moved with other legislators to encourage the two companies laying rails westward from Lake Michigan to the Mississippi. It had also been imperative to extend the railroads into the northern forested areas and into the mining region of the Southwest. Now, however, in the 1870's, the railroad companies were becoming strongly entrenched, and – as in other Western states – a cry had gone up for regulation of their operations. The issue was a complicated one, but Johnson had no difficulty in making what was for him a natural, even inevitable, choice: The common people of Wisconsin must be protected against any aggregate of political power assumed by the railroads or other business institutions serving the public.[34]

The senate had been in session only a week when John A. Johnson introduced a set of resolutions. He urged that the committee on railroads study the advisability of enacting a law providing for the appointment of a board of railroad commissioners. This body should be empowered to examine the operating conditions of all state railroads, to determine the amount of capital stock and indebtedness of each, to look into salaries and watered stock, and to inquire into the reasonableness of freight and passenger rates. The three-man commission, as proposed by Senator Johnson, was required to have an engineer as one of its members; in addition

[32] Henrietta M. Larson, *The Wheat Market and the Farmer in Minnesota, 1858–1900*, 106 (New York, 1926).

[33] *Wisconsin State Journal*, January 7, 9, February 5, 1873.

[34] Appendix to the Wisconsin *Assembly Journal, 1857*, 16; *Assembly Journal, 1857*, 919.

it was to make its report at a specified time. The bill requested that the senate's railroad committee be instructed to present its opinions of the resolutions by February 5, 1873.[35]

Johnson's resolutions – a direct challenge to the committee on railroads – produced no constructive results. On February 4, a day before the deadline, the senate committee replied that action on his Resolution No. 9 S had been indefinitely postponed. It chose a cautious course, arguing that it was not prudent to adopt crippling restrictions and regulatory legislation at a time when the state was still desperately in need of extending its railroads to all productive areas within its boundaries. It was clear that the pledge of Governor Washburn and the Republican party could not be validated and that the 1873 legislature would make no progress in settling the issue.[36]

Balked in his plans for railroad legislation in this session, Johnson turned to other matters that concerned him. In a month's time he introduced two major bills. On January 27, he proposed that legislative manuals be distributed throughout the state by way of information to normal schools, the library of the University of Wisconsin, the state supreme court, and the library of the state historical society. This bill was passed in January, 1873. Johnson also put his progressive thinking regarding women's rights into Bill No. 131 S, which provided that married women be enabled to transact business, make contracts, sue, and be sued. This legislation, which clarified the liabilities of husbands and wives, was passed in 1874 and enacted into law. A bill to "enable poor persons to obtain justice freely" also had his active support. Altogether, during the session of 1873, he introduced 10 resolutions and bills.[37]

The Republican party convention in August, 1873, nominated Governor Washburn for re-election, and in its platform reiterated its stand on railroad legislation, stating unequivocally that the legislature had the constitutional right to regulate the railroads within the state. With this burning question the major issue in the election, Washburn was defeated and William R. Taylor and the entire slate of Reform candidates were swept

[35] "Resolution No. 9 S," Wisconsin *Senate Journal*, January 17, 1873, 39. The "S" in the designation of this and other bills stands for "Senate." Johnson was a member of two senate committees during the 1873 sessions: on federal relations and on printing.

[36] *Senate Journal*, February 7, 1873, 116.

[37] *Senate Journal*, January 27, 67; January 30, 84; February 5, 125; February 6, 1873, 145.

into office. In the new assembly, Republicans were in the minority; their majority in the senate was cut to one. As the 1874 legislative session opened, Johnson and his fellow Republicans found themselves with their backs to the wall in the battle over railroad legislation. Nevertheless, they stubbornly prepared to renew the fight.[38]

John A. Johnson, one of fifteen senators holding over from the year before, was a staunch Republican around whom advocates of state supervision of railroad operations quickly rallied. On this question his position in the previous legislature was well known. Strengthening his leadership was the fact that in the new legislative setup he had been named as one of the nine members of the railroad committee. This appointment seemed at first to be of strategic advantage, for it was clear to everyone that the all-important committee of the senate could not sidetrack the issue as it had done in 1873. Public opinion had been aroused throughout the state, and arguments pro and con appeared in various newspapers. A prominent Milwaukee journal came to the point bluntly: "For twenty years," its editor wrote, "the railroads have established the rates; now let us try something else." [39]

Two days after the 1874 session began, Senator Johnson presented Bill No. 2 S, a proposal to establish a board of railroad commissioners and to define their duties and powers. It was only one of many attempts to solve the pressing problem. Other railroad bills came thick and fast, clogging the legislative machinery and creating a stalemate between the two houses. The assembly and the senate could not agree on an acceptable bill. Finally, on February 5, 1874, the senate in despair voted to refer the bothersome matter to a joint select committee on tariff and taxation of railroads. Johnson was strongly opposed to this tactic, which he considered dilatory, and voted against it, but the senate approved the motion by a disappointing 18 to 11 majority. [40]

[38] The Wisconsin legislature of 1874 has since been known as the "Reform Legislature." See William L. Burton, "Wisconsin's First Railroad Commission: A Case Study in Apostasy," in *Wisconsin Magazine of History*, 45: 190–198 (Spring, 1962); Graham A. Cosmas, "The Democracy in Search of Issues: The Wisconsin Reform Party, 1873–1877," in *Wisconsin Magazine of History*, 46:93–108 (Winter, 1962–1963); *Milwaukee Daily Sentinel*, November 6, 1873; *Madison Daily Democrat*, November 5, 1873.

[39] *Senate Journal*, January 15, 1874, 10; *Milwaukee Daily Sentinel*, February 18, 1874. In addition to his membership on the railroad committee, Johnson served as chairman of the three-member committee on state affairs during the 1874 session of the legislature.

[40] *Senate Journal*, January 16, 18; February 5, 1874, 188; *Madison Daily Democrat*, January 17, 1874; *Wisconsin State Journal*, February 5, 1874.

Soon thereafter, Senator Robert L. D. Potter introduced a bill (No. 132 S), a plan of regulation classifying Wisconsin railroads into three groups. For each class the bill established specific passenger and freight rates. It empowered justices of the peace to impose fines on violators of the law, and it further provided for a commission of three men who were to inquire into railroad construction costs and to report in detail concerning each railway in the state.[41]

Meanwhile the assembly had passed a hybrid railroad bill, tacking the regulation of express and telegraph companies onto the earlier plan of supervising railroads only. This bill (No. 466 A), the product of the joint select committee, had survived inspection by the assembly, but the senate made short work of removing from it all references to express and telegraph companies. In essence, what remained was the Potter proposal — and on this amended version the senate voted favorably 26 to 5 — with John A. Johnson included in the small minority. Returned to the assembly, the bill was soon passed by a large majority.[42]

On March 9, the *Milwaukee Daily Sentinel* carried the headline: "Potter Railroad Bill Goes to the Governor for Approval." Two days later Governor Taylor signed it into law, and on April 28, 1874, it was formally published under its original but inaccurate title, "An Act relating to railroads, express and telegraph companies in the State of Wisconsin." The bill as law no longer included any statement regulating express and telegraph companies. In spite of the erroneous title, the *Wisconsin State Journal* of March 21, 1874, referred to the legislation as "The Potter Railway Act" — its common name since the year of its enactment. Disregarding the confusion between text and title, both parties in both houses had contributed heavily to the vote favoring its passage.[43]

In view of Senator Johnson's earlier advocacy of railroad legislation, why had he voted "nay" on the Potter bill? In a prepared published statement defending his unwillingness to approve the bill, he presented two main arguments: (1) The specific proposal to lower existing railroad rates by 20% was not based upon careful research; it was guesswork that

[41] *Senate Journal*, February 7, 1874, 218; *Milwaukee Daily Sentinel*, February 12, 1874.

[42] *Senate Journal*, March 2, 505; March 5, 1874, 559–560; *Madison Daily Democrat*, March 5, 1874; *Wisconsin State Journal*, March 26, 1874; *Manuscript Bill 466 A*, Division of Archives and Manuscripts, State Historical Society of Wisconsin, Madison.

[43] *Laws of Wisconsin, 1874*, 599–605; Emanuel L. Philipp, *Political Reform in Wisconsin*, 202 (Milwaukee, 1910).

might do irreparable damage to the railroads, the most important means of communication the state possessed. (2) By passing hasty and unjustly restrictive laws, the state would frighten capital away from investing in Wisconsin, thus depriving the people of opportunities for economic development that should rightfully be theirs. Johnson, as a businessman, was well aware that the railroads had taken advantage of the people. He had expected to vote for curtailing any dishonest excesses that might be investigated and proved. But he felt just as strongly that the financial stability of the railroads must be considered in drawing up legislation to regulate them. His was the long view, and he could not accept a hastily drawn makeshift scheme instead of a permanent solution to a complex economic problem affecting every citizen of the state.[44]

Johnson's own bill to establish a board of railroad commissioners had been more carefully prepared than the Potter Act that superseded it. No. 2 S contained eight precisely written sections stressing the need for the commissioners to secure detailed sworn financial and operating statements from the railroad companies *before* formulating state laws governing them. With extreme thoroughness and fairness, Johnson, in the seventh section of his bill, had listed 44 subdivisions setting forth the data needed by the commissioners to enable them to make considered judgments in recommending legislation. In Johnson's view, as stated in his article on the Potter act in *Skandinaven*, "a fundamental and comprehensive investigation" was a vital necessity in drafting a law for so important an institution as the railroads.[45]

It was characteristic of Johnson that he took meticulous pains in preparing himself to write his railroad bill. He read widely — local papers, the *Chicago Tribune*, the *Springfield Republican*, the *Nation*. He knew the Wisconsin situation at first hand, but to broaden his knowledge he investigated the railroad problem in the neighboring state of Illinois. He studied resolutions adopted by the State Farmers Association of Illinois at their convention held at Bloomington in January, 1873. This vigorous

[44] "Wisconsin Legislature," in *Skandinaven*, March 3, 1874. The article, written in Norwegian, is signed with the initial "J," which Johnson regularly used in his articles sent to this newspaper. An excerpt from the statement regarding his vote on the Potter railroad bill is given in English in the Appendix, p. 283.

[45] A ragged, worn copy of Bill 2 S, the only one in existence, is in the Johnson Papers. Across the back of the last page, in Johnson's handwriting, are the words: "No. 2 S, a bill to establish a Board of Railroad Commissioners and to establish their powers and duties." The introductory paragraph of the seventh section — the most comprehensive of this bill — is in the Appendix, p. 284.

organization, defending the agricultural interests of the state against the encroachments of the railroads, had been successful in shaping public opinion, and the legislature was being forced to take notice of an impending issue.

Johnson may well have been directly influenced in his thinking by an act passed by the Illinois legislature, effective on July 1, 1873. This law set up a commission empowered, after investigation, to prepare schedules of railroad rates and to supervise the general financial and operational management of the state's lines. The Illinois Railroad Law did not survive without effort, but it has stood the test of time. By contrast, the Potter Law was short-lived; Wisconsin, through changing political adjustments, had to wait until 1905 for a reasonably satisfactory solution of its problems with railway regulation.[46]

Concerned as he was over the pressing problem of the railroads, Senator Johnson interested himself personally in sponsoring other legislation that he felt would benefit the people of his state. Ethical and religious considerations always interested him. Early in the 1874 session, he submitted a resolution urging that the president of the senate be requested to invite the clergy of Madison to open daily meetings with prayer. The proposal was quickly adopted; later the legislature passed a bill introduced by Johnson providing for payment of these chaplains. Continuing his lifelong aversion to any excess in the use of alcohol, he remonstrated on the floor of the senate against the proposed repeal of the Graham Law, enacted in 1872 to establish responsibility in the sale of liquor.[47]

The panic of 1873 brought bank failures and heartbreaking loss of lifetime savings to many Wisconsin families. Such financial disruptions proved that the banking laws of the state were clearly outmoded, no longer suitable to the institutions of the day. Existing statutes provided depositors with no protection against loss either from bank failures or from dishonest dealings by trusted bank officers. To Johnson this intolerable sit-

[46] S. M. Smith, secretary of the State Farmers Association of Illinois, to Johnson, January 29, 1873. See also Solon J. Buck, *The Granger Movement: A Study of Agricultural Organization and Its Political, Economic and Social Manifestations, 1870–1880*, 147–149, 158 (Cambridge, Massachusetts, 1913), and Robert S. Maxwell, *La Follette and the Rise of the Progressives in Wisconsin*, 75–80 (Madison, Wisconsin, 1956). The Wisconsin Railroad Law of 1905 was similar in general character to Johnson's 1873 "Resolutions," to his 1874 Bill No. 2 S, and to the 1873 Illinois Railroad Law.

[47] *Senate Journal, 1874*, 8, 17, 468, 471; *Madison Daily Democrat*, January 23, February 25, 1874.

uation cried out for immediate reform — and he set forth his thinking on the problem in a resolution designed to establish a law protecting the investor. He urged (1) that private business firms and banks receiving money on deposit be required to make semiannual statements to the state treasurer, and (2) that bank examiners should inspect semiannual statements of banks as a protection to depositors. The senate voted to submit the resolution to the committee on banks and banking for further study. Although no law was enacted in 1874, Johnson's main ideas were later incorporated in Wisconsin's banking statutes.[48]

Johnson also initiated a move to correct what he considered to be abuses in the sale of state lands. On February 5, 1874, he introduced a resolution (No. 24 S) stating that land owned by Wisconsin was being sold at a very low price and that speculators were getting their hands on far too much of it. Johnson pointed out two aspects of the issue: (1) at the present low price only negligible financial returns could be realized by state trust funds; and (2) the individual citizen interested in establishing a new farm home had to pay the unregulated speculator's price. School land in Wisconsin had sold at an average of $2.00 per acre; at the same time other states had received $6.00 an acre. To remedy the situation, Johnson urged that amounts of land on sale be limited to 160 acres per purchaser and that actual settlers should have preference.

The committee on public lands, at the senator's request, made a study of the resolution and finally came to the conclusion that it was unwise to change the existing land policy. In reporting on No. 24 S, the committee stated that in its original grant the federal government had given over 7,000,000 acres to the state of Wisconsin. Of this grant, more than 5,000,000 acres had been sold, leaving a remainder of slightly less than 2,000,000 acres. If the lands had been properly graded when first put on sale, a much larger monetary return would have been realized. By 1874 most of the valuable state land had been disposed of, and the committee argued that what was left was selling so slowly that nothing of a constructive nature could be done to save the situation.[49]

John A. Johnson's career as a member of the Wisconsin senate ended

[48] *Senate Journal, 1874*, 36; *Madison Daily Democrat*, January 23, 1874. During his term of service in the Wisconsin senate in the 1870's, Johnson was a stockholder in the First National Bank of Madison, an institution that successfully weathered the panic. See also N. B. Van Slyke, president of the bank, to Johnson, December 31, 1870, and Wayne Ramsay, cashier, to Johnson, January 5, 1871.

[49] *Senate Journal, 1874*, 186, 187, 200, 480; *Wisconsin State Journal*, February 6, 1874.

with the close of the session of 1874. He was not, however, out of politics. The next summer, prior to the Republican state convention of July 7, 1875, friends advanced his name as a candidate for nomination as secretary of state of Wisconsin. *Skandinaven* rejoiced at the suggestion, declaring that if there was to be a Scandinavian candidate for the high state office, there was "none better than Johnson" — a man who had an understanding of the Norwegian people and who was at the same time an American who had served in important positions with great honor to himself and to both immigrant and native-born citizens.[50]

Opposing former Senator Johnson in the race for the Republican nomination was Hans B. Warner, who had come to America in 1849. He had enlisted as a private in the Civil War and had been captured by the Confederates and imprisoned for the duration of the conflict in Danville and Libby prisons. In 1868 he had been elected county clerk of Pierce County, his only experience in public office. Supporters of Johnson felt that their man was far better prepared for the position in the state government. Through the broadening education in political leadership he had received as county clerk of populous Dane County and in both the assembly and the senate, Johnson knew at first hand about the issues that the secretary of state would have to meet. In his campaign, he never questioned Warner's integrity, yet he let it be known that he doubted his opponent's capacity for understanding and solving the complex problems and intrigue that the successful candidate would inevitably face.

The Wisconsin Republican convention in July, 1875, chose Hans B. Warner over John A. Johnson as its nominee for secretary of state. Such a result apparently arose out of a complex tangle of cross-purposes which influenced the vote. *Skandinaven* from faraway Chicago had enthusiastically backed Johnson, but inside Wisconsin, the *Daily Republican and Leader* of La Crosse was in violent opposition. This newspaper singled out and unified disgruntled anti-Johnson groups that had not favored his position on state lands and railroad legislation. Land speculators were well aware of Johnson's attack on them in the senate, and one of their attorneys was a leader of vocal opposition to the former senator. As a result, in some of its arguments, the *Daily Republican and Leader* seemed to be giving support to the speculators. In similar fashion, Johnson's opponents won over the farmers who could not understand his vote against the Potter railroad bill. Other offended groups carried into the convention

[50] *Skandinaven,* June 22, 1875.

grievances against his forthright actions of an earlier day, including his stand on the slavery question and the common school. The sum of all this discontent, fostered by a politically powerful state newspaper, undoubtedly cost Johnson the nomination — and probable election — to an office for which he seemed to have the highest qualifications.[51]

In spite of other opportunities, John A. Johnson now seemed unwilling to trust himself to the vagaries of a rough-and-tumble campaign for elective office. He told a persistent committee of backers in 1877 that he did not wish to run for the office of vice-governor of Wisconsin. Pressure upon him was heavy, for the group urging him to become a candidate included the most prominent men in the state Republican party: C. C. Washburn, former governor, United States Senator Angus Cameron of La Crosse, J. B. Cassoday of Janesville, speaker of the assembly in the previous session, and David Atwood, editor of the *Wisconsin State Journal.* Because of urgent business commitments in St. Paul, Johnson did not attend the Republican state convention held in Madison on September 11. Instead, he sent word to his sponsors to withhold his name — a request which they reluctantly honored. At the age of forty-five, he had made a decision to turn from hazardous competitions for political office to devote full time to his increasing responsibilities in business. Later he did accept important appointive offices in his home state of Wisconsin.[52]

Meanwhile he continued to have a strong interest in public affairs. Through his writings in local and more distant papers, he made his position known on such matters as the public school and the University of Wisconsin. Having himself missed the opportunity for a formal education, he had been untiring in his personal efforts to improve himself — an attitude which made him sympathetic to young people of ability who lacked funds to obtain a higher education. He and Mrs. Johnson gave several such young men a home in Madison while they attended the university. Soon he took a more important step by setting up an endowment fund to aid needy students.

In a letter to the board of regents of the University of Wisconsin dated February 12, 1876, he stated that he was donating to the university the amount of $5,000 as a perpetual fund, the annual income of which was to

[51] *Skandinaven*, September 14, 1875. In the fall election of 1875, Hans B. Warner was elected secretary of state.

[52] *Skandinaven*, July 31, 1877. In 1878 he accepted appointment as a member of the board of trustees of the Wisconsin State Hospital for the Insane.

be allocated to students in need of financial help. President John Bascom in his next annual report acknowledged the handsome gift in these words: "The present year has been marked by the bestowment of the first scholarships. Hon. John A. Johnson, of Madison, has established ten annual scholarships of $50, each, under conditions elsewhere given. We express our thanks for this donation. The value of these scholarships, and the need of additional ones, will be more and more apparent as the University advances." Since the awarding of the first Johnson scholarship for the academic year 1876–1877, generation after generation of students who otherwise might have been forced to forgo a university course have been encouraged by timely help from this source to continue their education.[53]

In forwarding his scholarship fund to President Bascom, Johnson outlined the main criteria to be used in selecting recipients of the scholarships. In several particulars, his thinking was far in advance of commonly held attitudes of the time. He himself felt greatly indebted to the common school, in his view the basis of a democratic attitude in society. For this reason, he specified that students to qualify for a scholarship must have attended the common school for at least one year before reaching the age of fifteen. Recipients of assistance from the endowment had to present evidence of talent for learning and of ability to apply themselves. They must have a record of good conduct and establish a real need for financial help. Without doubt the donor was looking back on his own youth thirty years earlier. He knew the anxiety of one who longed for more education but found it just beyond reach—and he must have remembered that *he* could have fulfilled every requirement he was now citing for others.

Johnson, in setting up his scholarship fund, did not forget his immigrant countrymen. He treasured his old-world heritage, believing that, by merging its values with the best in American life, Scandinavians could become more useful citizens of their adopted country. But education was vital to this process. To encourage the children of immigrants to attend the University of Wisconsin, he made a special suggestion regarding the use of his gift: An otherwise qualified applicant for help who could read or speak reasonably well either Norwegian, Danish, Swedish, or Icelandic should be given preference in the selection of Johnson scholars until the year 1900. He gave it as his opinion that by that time students of Scandi-

[53] *Annual Report of the Board of Regents of the University of Wisconsin, 1876*, 29; Reuben Gold Thwaites, ed., *The University of Wisconsin, Its History and Its Alumni*, 110–112 (Madison, 1900).

navian descent would be indistinguishable in the stream of American life and should take their place in competition with others.[54]

In his statement to the president of the university regarding administration of the scholarships, Johnson also included what was at the time a most unusual guideline: "No distinction as to sex shall be made by the committee in giving aid." The thought was unique in the 1870's, when universities were still questioning the capabilities of women as students and there were few of them at the University of Wisconsin. But Johnson had always believed in equality of opportunity for the sexes. "Your daughters," he wrote elsewhere, "deserve as thorough an education as your sons."

In addition to his forward-looking step in supporting higher education for women, the donor also introduced another pioneering principle — now common in collegiate aid programs. He felt that the scholarships should be regarded as loans rather than as outright grants. As a businessman, he had observed that a loan would stimulate energy and self-reliance, whereas a gift often had a contrary effect. Accordingly, it was his stated wish that students receiving aid should be encouraged to pay back the money, and that this should be added to the original fund — "as soon as they may be fairly and reasonably able to do so." No interest would be charged, and no time limit was to be set.[55]

The suggestion was a wise one. In the years since the fund was established, many students have returned their loans — often with additional gifts of their own, adding significantly to the original principal. According to administrators of the University of Wisconsin aid program, as of the fiscal year 1962, Johnson's gift of $5,000 had increased almost twentyfold to nearly $96,000. In that year, 88 men and 12 women received loans from the John A. Johnson Aid Fund.

Another important institution benefited from Johnson's continuous loyal support. Lyman Draper of the state historical society wrote to his friend on December 27, 1876: "I shall feel thankful if you will give me leave to submit your name for membership at our business meeting Saturday evening of this week. We want men of your stamp to join us. You did

[54] *Annual Report of the Board of Regents, 1876*, 25. For terms governing the selection of students for the Johnson scholarships, as outlined in the report of the regents, see the Appendix, p. 284–285.

[55] Johnson to John Bascom, February 12, 1876. The letter is included in the *Annual Report of the Board of Regents, 1876*, 27. See also Johnson, *Fingerpeg*, 103, for his views on women.

us good service while in the Senate and we shall be glad to have your continued good will and efforts." The historical society was, in Johnson's mind, a most worthy organization devoted to promoting the interests of his home state, and he was quick to accept Draper's invitation. Three days later he received word from the State Historical Society of Wisconsin that he had been "unanimously elected an active member." For the rest of his life he devoted himself vigorously to advancing all phases of the Society's program. He served as curator and member of the Society's executive committee from 1877 to 1901, and on the standing committees for contributions and endowment and for the museum.[56]

The 1870's was a decisive decade in the life of John A. Johnson – a period roughly covering his forties. Choosing business as his major occupation, he had had the good fortune at first to enter an expanding market and to score a notable success. Soon, however, the adversities of a national panic had threatened. But in bad times as in good, his knowledge and judgment in financial affairs had carried him through successfully. In an elective legislative position, against odds, he had given expression to a sensitive perception of social and political realities and a concern for the rights and needs of individuals in the society of his time, particularly in his own Middle West. Expediency had meant little to him – so little that finally he had given up all thought of political preferment and had turned his energies into other channels. Like a thread running through this period of his life was his dedication to cultural achievements, to education, to whatever contributed most to a better social order. Here his Norwegian heritage was a strong influence. To assist his fellow immigrants in making an effective adjustment to American life became an abiding passion lasting as long as he lived.

[56] The official notification, dated December 30, 1876, is in the Johnson Papers. See "Death of John A. Johnson," in State Historical Society of Wisconsin, *Proceedings*, 20–22 (Madison, 1902).

CHAPTER V

Merging Two Cultures

By the time he had reached his fiftieth year, John A. Johnson had fully developed his attitude toward the country he now regarded as his homeland. Early in 1883, he epitomized a feeling that had been growing since his first days in the New World: "We have chosen to live with a people and only through cooperation can we become a part of the adopted country." He was addressing his fellow immigrants and their children, growing up as young Americans. As a cardinal tenet in his thinking, he held that both generations should learn English. To become a part of the living culture of the new land, immigrants must learn to express themselves freely in the common language. Unless they did so, he believed, they would have to be satisfied to exist as an isolated people in a still-strange environment.[1]

Language was indeed the key. Johnson was ambitious that some of his countrymen should enter public life. As a means of fitting themselves for positions of leadership, he urged preparation and practice in speaking and writing the common tongue. No one could serve adequately whose command of English could be called into question. Knowledge of American history followed as a corollary. In fact, Johnson believed that every good citizen – whether in public life or not – should know the history of his new homeland. He favored the reading of American newspapers in which day-to-day history was being unfolded. To be sure, there were the papers pub-

[1] John A. Johnson, "How Rapidly Shall We Be Americanized?" in *Skandinaven*, January 16, 1883.

lished in the language of the immigrant, but he recognized their limitations and with keen foresight realized that the passage of time would inevitably reduce their number and influence.

Johnson was not satisfied with a slapdash combination of Norwegian and English. He aimed considerably higher. What he strove for – and advocated for others – was proficiency in the language used in America as well as in the one they had brought from the homeland. In truth, he was bilingual: he had no intention of giving up his Norwegian for English. All languages interested him, and he saw the value of familiarity with German and other European tongues. Despite deficiencies in his formal education, his approach was that of a literate man who made no effort to conceal his admiration for the broad and scholarly view.

Because of this attitude toward language, some Norwegians distrusted Johnson's ideas for the Americanization of immigrants, and accused him of being disloyal to their interests. In their view, he seemed to be deserting his own people when, in the late 1860's, he joined the Madison business firm of the Fullers – established "Yankee" families. So it came about that certain of his immigrant countrymen helped defeat him in 1868 in his candidacy for the assembly on the Republican ticket. Svein Nilsson, editor of *Billed-Magazin*, a Norwegian publication in Madison, would not support him, saying – prematurely, as it turned out – "J. A. Johnson's political career is at an end." He declared that Johnson had some prestige among Americans, but that he was not in good standing among Scandinavians. Later political campaigns seemed, partially at least, to bear out this judgment, indicating a bias and a narrowness that helped finally to drive Johnson out of politics. In perspective it is clear that he paid the penalty of being misunderstood because he was, in both cultural and political matters, ahead of his time.[2]

It would be unfair and inaccurate to imply that Johnson was ready to discard the influence of his Norwegian heritage and his associations in the New World. Quite the contrary, as all contemporary evidence reveals. He had early been a stockholder in *Emigranten*, he had helped found *Amerika* in Chicago, he had been a part-owner and sometime editor of *Skandinaven.* To all these journals he had contributed articles in his native language – writings whose tone and content provided a constructive element

[2] Svein Nilsson to Mathias Lindas, May 14, 1869, in *Norwegian-American Studies*, 21: 127 (Northfield, Minnesota, 1962). This letter is one of a series included in an article, "Norwegians Become Americans," translated from the Norwegian and edited by Beulah Folkedahl.

in the life of Norwegian immigrants. He remembered his own late childhood and how he had learned as a young man that he "straddled two cultures" and that "in the new land a tug of war between his old and his new self was going on." Now in middle life he looked to the future of his people in America and saw more clearly than most the part they were to play in the developing society of the new country.[3]

In his advocacy of the English language, Johnson directly opposed the leaders of the Norwegian Synod, many of whom had received their theological training in Norway and were well prepared in Greek, Hebrew, and German in addition to Norwegian. Strongly devoted to their religious mission in a new country, the pastors felt themselves to be custodians of the culture of their homeland. English was a foreign tongue which seemed to stand between them and the program of their church. As a result, they took action at a Synod meeting at Muskego, Wisconsin, in 1852, ruling that immigrant children should not begin the study of English until they were twelve years old. At that time a child would have the Norwegian language well in hand and would be solidly grounded in Lutheran teachings. Johnson's views on this touchy subject undoubtedly stemmed from his own experience. Soon after coming to America, he had found himself eligible under Synod precepts to attend common school. He had rejoiced in the opportunity, but was troubled later on when he saw children being denied the privilege which had meant so much to him. In spite of criticism, he continued to urge a liberalization of the strict position of the Synod.

Fortunately Johnson did not stand alone. There had been a few forward-looking ministers who, even earlier, had been aware that at some later time English would replace Norwegian for immigrants who would make America their permanent home. Elling Eielsen, who had come from Norway in 1839, recommended in 1846 that children should be trained in both languages. Five years earlier he had translated Luther's *Smaller Catechism* into English, and soon he was urging that children should attend the district schools. The Reverend J. W. C. Dietrichson of Muskego, who served the home congregation of the Skibsnæs family at Heart Prairie, organized a district school open to all children – where English was taught. Young John A. Johnson lived for a time in Dietrichson's home, working for his keep, while he was preparing for confirmation. There he no doubt learned to admire the broad-minded pastor's philosophy of ed-

[3] Einar Haugen, "Language and Immigration," in *Norwegian-American Studies and Records*, 10:1 (1938).

ucation and absorbed ideas which directed his own thinking into similar channels.[4]

It is not surprising that the first generation of immigrant families fresh from the Old World were slow to adapt themselves to a new language, particularly in the church. Since childhood they had been trained in Norwegian translations of the Bible and Luther's *Catechism.* Accustomed to the ritual and theological language of the Norwegian Lutheran Church, they found comfort in continuing their familiar religious life in a land where all else was strange. It was natural that Norwegian parents should speak their native tongue at home, particularly in rural areas, where all neighbors did the same. In the cities, the problem was more complicated: there most associates of the second generation used the language of the New World. Typically, the children of John and Kaia Johnson, growing up in Madison, spoke English — actually they were forbidden to speak Norwegian at home.

For the immigrant, using the English language and attending the common school were but two facets of the same problem. Thoughtful men like John A. Johnson found no real issue. The district school was a peculiarly American development paralleling the rise of the common man; manhood suffrage had demanded education for all citizens. Johnson saw these relationships early in life and enthusiastically embraced the American philosophy of education developed by such men as Horace Mann. He believed that the roots of democracy lay in schoolrooms where all children had the same opportunity to learn — and he gave these institutions his ardent support. He rejoiced that European class distinctions had no place in America, where ideally all belonged to one class. The home, the Sunday school, the parochial school should provide religious instruction. The tax-supported common school, however, had an important, separate function: to prepare its students for citizenship. It was a parent's first duty to support the development of a progressive system of public education.[5]

In addition, Johnson favored the establishment of academies where

[4] Theodore C. Blegen, *Norwegian Migration to America: The American Transition,* 244–246 (Northfield, Minnesota, 1940); J. Magnus Rohne, *Norwegian American Lutheranism up to 1872,* 89–93 (New York, 1926). Dietrichson, Johnson's pastor and teacher, also established a parochial school where religion in the Lutheran tradition was taught.

[5] Carl R. Fish, *The Rise of the Common Man, 1830–1850,* 200–203 (New York, 1927); Merle Curti, "Education and Social Reform: Horace Mann," in *Social Ideas of American Educators,* 101–138 (New York, 1935); *Skandinaven,* September 4, 1877.

young people could have access to better educational facilities and make the acquaintance of good teachers. He also saw a place for special schools where a vocation might be learned. Academies, he believed, should use English, but he advocated the teaching of Norwegian along with German and other languages. Albion Academy, located in the village of the same name in Dane County, was, in his view, a school with a promising future. In the very heart of a large Norwegian community, the academy seemed an ideal place, and Johnson urged parents to send their children there. He supported this advice with two arguments: Albion was quiet and peaceful – it had neither saloons nor gambling houses – and on its faculty was his friend Rasmus B. Anderson, instructor in Norwegian and a teacher who would give special attention to Scandinavian students.[6]

The foundations of the Wisconsin public school system had been laid in 1848 amid the limitations of a raw frontier society. The federal government had set aside land in every township to provide funds for education, but the earliest schools – often housed in log cabins – were humble and crude. There was no assurance at the beginning that strong and viable schools would ever rise. Upon this shaky base, the state began in slow and fumbling fashion to build. There were no well-trained teachers, though talented individuals exerted a stimulating influence, long remembered by their students. Their pay was meager; the profession was not respected. A few parents could afford to send their children to private schools in the East, but the average man on the Wisconsin frontier found this move an utter impossibility. John A. Johnson, growing up in Walworth County in the 1840's and 1850's, realized that illiteracy would be the fate of the masses unless better schools that everyone could attend were provided.[7]

The quarter century following the end of the Civil War – a period in which the Wisconsin public schools made notable progress – witnessed a damaging controversy between the clergy of the Norwegian Synod and advocates of the district school, many of whom were themselves well-known Norwegians and Lutherans. As a prominent layman who championed the public schools, Johnson soon became deeply involved in the differences

[6] Albion Academy at the time was owned by the Seventh Day Baptists. Johnson to the editor of *Emigranten*, October 2, 1865. See also Johnson, "Albion Akademi," in *Skandinaven*, August 22, 1867.

[7] Victor Lawson, one of Johnson's associates in the publication of *Skandinaven*, went to Phillips Andover Academy in Massachusetts in 1869 to prepare for Harvard. See Charles H. Dennis, *Victor Lawson: His Time and His Work*, 24 (Chicago, 1935).

growing up to plague the Synod. On certain issues, he emerged as a leader of the liberal laymen arrayed against the conservative clergy. Specifically, the debate raged over the church's policy regarding public and parochial schools.

The clergy were critical of the common school and jealous of its progress and influence. In Norway they had represented a city culture and had belonged as a rule to the official and professional classes. Many had been teachers in the schools of Norway where, as members of a highly regarded profession, they had taught the doctrines of the state Lutheran church. Hence it was difficult for upper-class clergymen, reared in the atmosphere of the Norwegian school system, to accept the district school in America. To them the public school was irreligious. It did not indoctrinate students with positive Christian beliefs; the United States had no state church.[8]

Leaders of the Synod were apprehensive lest fostering the common school and its emphasis on English should break the solidarity of the Norwegian-American people and their relation to the Lutheran church. In spite of their unhappy experience of 1861 over the issue of slavery and secession, several of the clergy in the Norwegian Synod still regarded the Missouri Synod as a model for religious organization. They were particularly interested in the extensive parochial school system which the Missouri leaders had developed. Soon they were pondering the establishment of a similar program in Wisconsin. It followed as a corollary that the pastors active in planning the new move were at the same time increasing their agitation against the public school.

The overt act which was to precipitate the long and debilitating controversy within the Lutheran church came in 1866. At Manitowoc, Wisconsin, the Synod adopted a policy establishing a number of parochial schools that would offer not only religious instruction in Norwegian, but would also teach other subjects generally regarded as the province of the district school. The church body recognized that its members would have to pay taxes for the state's program of public education. But the Synod leaders would not entrust their children to the common school.[9]

[8] Arthur C. Paulson and Kenneth O. Bjork, tr. and ed., "A School and Language Controversy in 1858: A Documentary Study," in *Norwegian-American Studies and Records*, 10:78 (1938).

[9] Laurence M. Larson, *The Changing West and Other Essays*, 122–126 (Northfield, Minnesota, 1937). The Reverend A. C. Preus defended the position of the Synod in an article in *Skandinaven*, September 27, 1866. In editorials on April 21 and May 26, 1869, *Skandinaven* presented its position in favor of the common school.

Now the real issues were in the open and the debate between proponents of "public schools" and "parochial schools" began in earnest. Knud Langeland, editor of *Skandinaven,* with the strong support of his colleague John A. Johnson, entered into the exchange of ideas with a vigorous defense of the common school – although in fairness he regularly printed letters from the opposition. *Fædrelandet og Emigranten* was more cautious, generally leaning toward the viewpoint of the clergy favoring parochial schools. Vigorous Rasmus B. Anderson, widely known among Wisconsin Norwegians as a crusading editor, is supposed to have emblazoned on his letterhead the words: "Opposition to the American Common School is treason to our country." Pastors like C. L. Clausen and S. M. Krogness of the liberal group in the Synod joined Langeland and Johnson in championing public education. All these men, however, believed that religious teaching must not be neglected – provision for that important phase of education must be made.[10]

The unhappy quarrel continued into the 1870's, with public school officers heightening the feeling by directing charges against the Scandinavian clergy. H. B. Wilson, superintendent of schools in Goodhue County, Minnesota, in his annual report for 1869, wrote that in his area Lutheran pastors were hostile to the American schools and had even called them "heathen" institutions. The Reverend Bernt Julius Muus, whose home parish was Holden in Goodhue County, a vigorous leader in church education and a man of strong will, reacted at once in an article entitled "Schools and a Good School," published in *Fædrelandet og Emigranten* on March 10, 1870.[11]

The common school had no place in Pastor Muus's program. He was firm in his conviction that it was not advancing the Kingdom of God. In words that struck a fateful note, he declared: "In these schools pupils perhaps may read some romance or other entitled history of the United States." Knud Langeland, editor of *Skandinaven,* could not brook this kind of attack on American education. In his editorials, he pointed out that Lutherans were also citizens. They should remember that the first amendment to the constitution contained a message for them: "Congress

[10] Blegen, *Norwegian Migration to America: The American Transition,* 271–273. See also letters written by the Reverend C. M. Hvistendahl, who defended the parochial school, and the Reverend S. M. Krogness, who took the opposite side, in *Skandinaven,* April 14, 28, 1869. On May 6, 12, 1869, *Fædrelandet og Emigranten* included articles dealing with the same debate.

[11] Blegen, *Norwegian Migration to America: The American Transition,* 264.

shall make no law respecting an establishment of religion, or prohibiting the free exercise thereof." The Lutheran clergy could hardly expect the United States government to adopt the Augsburg Confession as the state religion and prohibit all other denominations by law. For *Skandinaven*, Langeland promised to continue support of Americanization for Norwegian immigrants and "to oppose and to obstruct any system of education, the aim of which is to keep our people in an alien state or condition."[12]

The interchange between Muus and Langeland brought Johnson into the debate to second what his friend had written. Wasting no time, he replied directly to Muus, citing logical and practical arguments countering the pastor's intemperate attack on American public schools. The smaller communities, he wrote, could not support parochial schools and at the same time pay taxes to develop good public schools. Johnson did not accept Muus's claim that the teachings of the district school in any way hindered the advancement of God's Kingdom on earth. Was it a sin to teach English, geography, history? He thought not. Looking back on his own experience, he recalled that he and his friend Knute Nelson, later to be a United States senator, had both begun their education in the "English schools" of Walworth County, Wisconsin. Both would now give testimony that some of their teachers had inspired two boys, who knew hardly a word of English, to strive to improve themselves to the full extent of their abilities. Johnson found it significant that both men had later become teachers in just such schools. It was the American way.[13]

Other defenders of the common school arose to encourage Johnson in his stand. In Madison his friend Halle Steensland, an influential member of the Norwegian Synod, gave the cause his support. From St. Paul, Hans Mattson, secretary of state of Minnesota, sent a letter warm with approval of Johnson's article on the controversial issue then troubling residents of his state. He wrote that he respected the Reverend Mr. Muus as a minister but disagreed with him on the school question. He could not resist writing, "to bring forth my respect and gratitude to you for your position concerning our American common school. . . . It pleased me to read your reply to Muus. The tone of your article was so clear and honest, your

[12] Larson, *The Changing West,* 132; Arlow W. Andersen, "Knud Langeland: Pioneer Editor," in *Norwegian-American Studies and Records*, 14:129 (1944).

[13] Johnson, in *Skandinaven*, April 30, May 4, 1870; Johnson, in *Fædrelandet og Emigranten*, April 21, 1870; Larson, *The Changing West*, 132; Martin W. Odland, *The Life of Knute Nelson*, 12–16 (Minneapolis, 1926).

arguments so convincing that it seemed to me that there was nothing more to say." [14]

A confrontation between the two leading debaters occurred at the 1874 convention of the Norwegian Synod held at Holden in Goodhue County, Minnesota, the home parish of the Reverend B. J. Muus. Johnson was in attendance, as a representative of *Skandinaven*, to report the proceedings of the meeting to his paper. Sharp differences of opinion developed among Synod delegates. Pastor Muus gave it as his view that religion was the end to be sought in education and that any program that did not aim at this goal was a failure. He was supported by the Reverend H. A. Preus. Both clergymen insisted that parents should refuse to abide by the laws of the state if they came in conflict in matters of religion with what the parents wanted taught to their children in the schools. Not all Synod leaders could support so drastic a line of argument. The Reverend U. V. Koren and Professor F. A. Schmidt of Luther College, neither in sympathy with the common school, objected. They declared that parents could not choose what laws they would obey.

An interesting personal sidelight to the stern clash of ideologies took place at this Synod convention when Pastor Muus objected to Johnson's presence and sought to have him barred. The minister protested that *Skandinaven*, in its defense of the common school, had been "hostile to the Christian religion"; hence the newspaper should not be allowed a reporter at the meetings. This repressive proposal was voted down, and Johnson remained. The Synod went on to mull over the school question, but the moderates would not accept the program of action advocated by Muus and Preus. Finally nothing was settled, and the whole issue continued to be a matter of debate.[15]

Johnson believed that the layman had a place in determining the policies of his church, and that the congregation was more than a "will-less mass in the pastor's hand." Holding that in a democracy the individual man had a part to play, he could not be at ease as a mere cog in a machine

[14] Hans Mattson, who had been born in Sweden and reared in the Vasa settlement near Red Wing in Goodhue County, was a leader among Scandinavians in Minnesota. In 1868 he had been sent to Sweden to interest more of his people in emigrating to Minnesota. His letter, dated May 14, 1870, and written in Swedish, is in the Johnson Papers. See also Theodore C. Blegen, *Building Minnesota*, 172, 207, 232 (New York, 1938).

[15] John A. Johnson, in *Skandinaven*, December 15, 1874; Blegen, *Norwegian Migration to America: The American Transition*, 269; Larson, *The Changing West*, 135; L. J. Erdall, "An Answer to Johnson," in the *Madison Daily Democrat*, September 4, 1877.

directed by his superiors. It was in this spirit that he dared to take issue with the clergy. Though he had respect for their learning, he could remember that *he* also had been vested with public authority and had been active in areas where he had taken upon himself responsibilities for others. His very prominence, however, made him a target for the clergy who differed with him. Bitterness developed and backbiting remarks were made about him. One Synod pastor, writing in *Skandinaven*, quoted an old adage advising him to "mind his own business." But Johnson was not deterred. Pastors and professors, he replied, apparently had the right to criticize. Though they implied that laymen had no such privilege, he insisted that when the occasion arose, he would claim the same right for himself.[16]

By 1870 Johnson's relations with the Synod had been strained to the breaking point. He had been a Lutheran since his confirmation in the Heart Prairie church in 1848. In Dane County, he had belonged to the West Koshkonong church and had continued his membership in that congregation during his early years in Madison. In 1861, when he sold his farm and moved to the capital city to make his permanent home, he had applied for membership in the Norwegian Synod church in that community. The time had proved inopportune for him: At the moment of his application he was engaged in the Civil War agitation against the Synod clergy for their position on slavery. There had followed his championship of the common school and the use of the English language. All this may have had some bearing on what came to pass: the Synod in all the intervening years never acknowledged his application for membership. Apparently the church leaders whom he had opposed in these matters had written him off as a rebel.

There were other prominent Lutherans who had become disaffected with Synod leadership, and in 1870 they joined forces to form a new Lutheran church body. This organization took the formal name of the Norwegian-Danish Evangelical Lutheran Church in America—commonly called the Conference. A strong leader in the dissenting group was the Reverend C. L. Clausen, Johnson's ally in the antislavery struggle and in

[16] *Skandinaven*, August 17, December 7, 1870. In the middle of the controversy, Johnson read these words in his own newspaper: "Skomager bliv ved din Læst" (Shoemaker, stick to your last). See also Nelson and Fevold, *The Lutheran Church among Norwegian-Americans*, 1:250, and Frederick Jackson Turner, *The Frontier in American History*, 355–359 (New York, 1920).

the movements supporting the common school and the use of English. Another advocate of withdrawal from the Norwegian Synod to form a freer church conference was August Weenaas, a theologian educated in Norway, who was soon to become Johnson's close friend. Weenaas at the time was professor of theology at the seminary of the Conference at Marshall, Wisconsin.

Influenced by Clausen and Weenaas, Johnson made an important decision: he would leave the Synod and join the Conference. The shift of church allegiance was not hastily made, for he had deep roots in the older church body. In an article written in the spring of 1870, Johnson revealed that the wrench of parting was painful to him. He believed that the Synod had done much that was good – organizing congregations, furnishing pastors, building schools, publishing books. In spite of his frequent differences with some of the ministers, he wrote, "My sympathies are there." He pointed out that he had been reared and confirmed in the original church body which had become the Synod, and that he had been a member of the board of trustees of one of the oldest Norwegian Lutheran congregations in America. He "had the same faith," and admitted that separation would cause him great grief.[17]

Having cast his lot with the Conference, Johnson moved at once to help establish an affiliated congregation in Madison. A group of five men met at his house on July 26, 1870, and voted to form a new church, which took the name of the Evangelical Lutheran Immanuel Church. Johnson was elected chairman of the founding committee, which included his friend Professor Rasmus B. Anderson of the University of Wisconsin. At this first meeting, the men voted to send a letter to the Reverend C. L. Clausen calling him to become their pastor.

Johnson took a leading part in the development of Immanuel Church. His wife Kaia soon became a member, and both she and her husband were steadfast workers in the church's program. On December 18, 1870, Johnson was elected a deacon, and he served a few weeks later as a delegate to the Conference meeting held in Madison, on January 3, 1871. Pastor Clausen remained as minister only a short time. He was succeeded by the Reverend August Weenaas. Later pastors were the Reverend M. Falk Gjertsen and the Reverend T. H. Dahl. All were able preachers and leaders in the new Conference organization in its early years.

From 1873 to 1876, Johnson was a trustee of Immanuel Church. His

[17] John A. Johnson, "Is Unity Possible?" in *Skandinaven*, May 4, 1870.

financial contributions were generous: When the congregation was raising money for a church building, he subscribed the largest amount, and he was a member of the committee planning the new edifice. In 1885 he was behind the drive soliciting funds for a church organ. Members of Immanuel joined with other similar Norwegian Lutheran groups in 1890 to form the Bethel congregation in Madison, a liberal church which in that year—no doubt to Johnson's immense satisfaction—began the use of English in its Sunday school.[18]

In the Conference Johnson found congenial and sympathetic friends. The leading pastors in the organization were at his side in favoring the common school and in desiring a freer hand for laymen in church affairs than the Synod had ever permitted. Two who gave him courageous support in these matters were new teachers at Augsburg Seminary. Sven Oftedal and Georg Sverdrup, born and educated in Norway, were recognized as children of the liberal political movement in that country. Oftedal had joined the Augsburg faculty in 1873, Sverdrup, a year later. Another firm friend of a few years' longer standing was Pastor August Weenaas, who had given Augsburg enlightened leadership since 1869, when he served as its first presiding officer in Marshall, Wisconsin. In the 1870's he, like Oftedal and Sverdrup, drew Johnson's interest and support to the developing seminary.[19]

Early in the year 1871, when discussions were held concerning the moving of the seminary, the Conference committee studying the matter was instructed to locate the school near a state university. Arguments for both Madison and Minneapolis were heard, but the choice, logically enough, fell on the Minnesota metropolis. The city lay directly in the path of the northwestward push of Norwegian migration. Minneapolis was a Scandinavian center. There were other practical considerations favoring it—substantial gifts of money and building materials offered by generous and interested citizens and a building site just across the Mississippi River from the campus of the University of Minnesota. President William Watts Folwell agreed that Norwegian students at Augsburg could enroll in

[18] The Bethel Lutheran Church in Madison is at present located at Wisconsin Avenue and West Gorham Street. For further details, see "Forhandling protokol," the secretarial record of the church. An anniversary brochure published in 1945 gives a historical account of the congregations which had joined ranks to form Bethel Lutheran.

[19] Nelson and Fevold, *The Lutheran Church among Norwegian-Americans,* 1:295; Blegen, *Norwegian Migration to America: The American Transition,* 270.

courses in English at the university, with no tuition fee. Altogether the attractions of Minneapolis outranked those of Madison, and Augsburg Seminary left Wisconsin permanently in 1872. Men like John A. Johnson and Rasmus B. Anderson undoubtedly had hoped that Madison would be the choice — but both quickly transferred their interest in the Conference seminary to its new location in Minnesota.

When the first building on the new Augsburg campus in Minneapolis was dedicated on October 27, 1872, "the Honorable J. A. Johnson" of Madison addressed the audience in Norwegian on the topic "The Relationship between the Theological Seminary and the University." There were several other addresses by Conference pastors, but it is significant that a layman had so prominent a part in an event of such historic importance. In its way it was a symbol of the liberalizing influence beginning to creep into organized Lutheran religious thinking — and it was an unusual personal tribute to Johnson by the leadership of his church. Less than three years later, Augsburg held another "festive occasion" when it dedicated an addition to the campus. Professor Georg Sverdrup gave the main address, and Johnson, representing *Skandinaven*, filed an enthusiastic report. "It was wonderful," he wrote, "to hear Christianity defended so eloquently. . . . May the institution light the way for us."[20]

Johnson's interest in education had begun with his championship of the common school. Now in the late 1870's and early 1880's, he wrote and worked to relieve Augsburg of the heavy debt that hampered its development. The income upon which the seminary relied came from individual congregations, a year-by-year source of support that condemned the school to a hand-to-mouth existence. The institution had no financial security in the present and none in prospect. In his newspaper articles, Johnson wrote that the salaries of the professors were meager and often in arrears. He felt that the teachers, in order to give top service, must be freed from concern for their livelihood. He knew them; they were able, conscientious men with strong qualities. They were already making sacrifices. Was it not more reasonable, he asked, to establish an endowment fund that would assure a definite income? He stated an axiom: good teachers and good libraries can be had only if there is money to pay for them. He declared with considerable feeling that justice to faculty and students de-

[20] Andreas Helland, *Augsburg Seminary gjennem femti aar, 1869–1919*, 86 (Minneapolis, 1920); *Skandinaven*, June 22, 1875; Nelson and Fevold, *The Lutheran Church among Norwegian-Americans*, 1:227.

manded such a fund as a sound financial basis for the seminary. Otherwise Augsburg would fail in its mission.[21]

Professor Sven Oftedal assumed leadership of the drive to raise an endowment fund of $50,000 for the seminary. College campaigns for financial support in the 1880's were not as well organized and supported as they are today, and there was considerable opposition to be overcome. Here Johnson's letters and well-reasoned articles in the newspapers were a key factor. In 1882 the "Augsburg Seminary Endowment Fund" reached its goal of $50,000. Johnson had made a substantial financial contribution, and his advice had been sought and followed throughout the fund-raising effort. At his suggestion, a committee of five men with a treasurer was designated to invest and manage the fund, thus insuring a businesslike future handling of the precious first endowment.[22]

In spite of his steady support of the common school and the use of English, Johnson never for a moment lost his love for Norwegian. He believed that his native language should remain a part of the cultural heritage of his people in their new American environment. To this end, he began to advocate that the Scandinavian languages should be taught in high schools and colleges on the same basis as German. He felt it particularly important that the University of Wisconsin should include the Northern languages in its course of study. Interest in this proposal was to come to a head in a convention of the "Scandinavian Lutheran Education Society" to be held in Madison in the late winter of 1868–1869; supporters of secular public education were sure that they would meet opposition then from leaders of the Norwegian Synod.

A few days prior to the convention, Johnson wrote a letter to President P. A. Chadbourne of the university. He made no mention of the church controversy about languages; he did, however, suggest the advantages of having courses in Scandinavian taught at the state university of a commonwealth in which so many citizens were of Scandinavian descent. With both personal and professional interests in mind, he hinted that his friend Rasmus B. Anderson of Albion Academy might be the man to fill the post

[21] See O. Nilson, "Scrapbook, 1871–1872," in the archives of the Norwegian-American Historical Association, Northfield, Minnesota. This scrapbook has a number of miscellaneous, undated newspaper clippings of articles signed by John A. Johnson.

[22] Nelson and Fevold, *The Lutheran Church among Norwegian-Americans*, 1: 232.

of professor of Northern languages at the university. The seed thus planted would mature later on. In a few days President Chadbourne replied quite favorably for both himself and the regents. Yes, he believed that university authorities would seriously consider creating a chair of Scandinavian languages. He let Johnson know that he had himself traveled in the Northern countries and that he held membership in the Royal Antiquarian Society of Copenhagen.[23]

With Chadbourne's letter in hand, Johnson could bring the good news to the convention scheduled to assemble on March 4, 1869. He took satisfaction in doing so, for he regarded this as a service to his countrymen that he felt sure would lead them to a better understanding of American institutions, and at the same time would foster ties with the older culture cherished by all.

The theme of the convention of the Scandinavian Lutheran Education Society was the support of public education — a topic that sounded innocent enough. The well-advertised meeting was attended by three hundred people, including both friends and foes of public educational institutions. The Reverend C. L. Clausen was elected president and John A. Johnson, vice-president. Supporting their liberal views were others who believed in the public schools and the universities: Rasmus B. Anderson, Knud Langeland, and the Reverend S. M. Krogness. Arrayed against them were some of the leading clergy of the Norwegian Synod. The Synod president, the Reverend H. A. Preus, led the opposition with familiar arguments against the dangers of secularizing education. Even on Johnson's pet project, the training of Scandinavian teachers for university positions, a deadlock developed. Nothing could be accomplished, and Johnson's group withdrew from the convention. It was clear that the controversy would now spread to a much wider field. Time was on the side of those who wished to liberalize the attitude of the immigrants toward the whole system of American education.[24]

The congregations of the Norwegian Synod gradually came to realize that it was usually beyond their means to support both a common school

[23] John A. Johnson to P. A. Chadbourne, February 20, 1869; Chadbourne to Johnson, February 26, 1869. Copies of these letters are in the Johnson Papers. For an excerpt from Johnson's letter, see the Appendix, p. 285–286.

[24] John A. Johnson, in *Skandinaven*, March 17, 1869, an editorial reviewing the Madison meeting of March 4, 1869. See also Larson, *The Changing West*, 128–131; Blegen, *Norwegian Migration to America: The American Transition*, 258–262; B. H. Narveson, "The Norwegian Lutheran Academies," in *Norwegian-American Studies and Records*, 14: 192 (1944).

and a parochial school. A shortage of teachers who were prepared to present both religious and secular subjects developed in the parochial schools, and at the same time the public schools steadily improved. The gifts of American institutions were at hand for immigrant children to receive. Johnson and others worked unceasingly to bring to their Norwegian countrymen a realization of what they stood to gain by merging the best of the old and the new cultures.[25]

All his life, Johnson recognized in himself a regret that he had missed a liberal education. This may partially explain the joy he experienced in helping worthy young people to go on to college. He helped them with money and with advice; his papers are full of requests for both. His letters reveal his concern for even the humblest of petitions and are a record of the many benevolences he extended to students needing assistance.

One of Johnson's protégés was Rasmus B. Anderson, fourteen years his junior, but of such individuality and drive that in the middle life of both men he was to be a partner in many concerns of common interest. Johnson helped and advised Rasmus when the latter was floundering to find himself. The younger man was the son of immigrant parents, settlers in the Koshkonong area, whose father had died when he was four years old. Helped by such pastors as A. C. Preus and J. A. Ottesen, he had entered Luther College, only to be expelled for insubordination in his senior year. Characteristically he had recovered quickly from this seemingly disastrous setback and was soon — at the age of twenty — a "professor" at Albion Academy.

Ambitious to attract Scandinavian backing for Albion, the young teacher approached Johnson in his office of Dane County clerk in nearby Madison. Both Rasmus personally and the possibilities at the academy appealed at once to the older man. Johnson quickly developed admiration for Rasmus' intellectual ability and dynamism, and began at once to urge his Norwegian countrymen to send their children to Albion. In 1867 he became a member of the board of trustees of the academy and continued as a patron of the school until it closed. His personal interest is evidenced by a letter he wrote to Anderson in the spring of his first year on the board — about a young girl who had been helping Mrs. Johnson with the care of the children. "At the academy," he wrote, "she can study both

[25] Joseph Schafer, "Immigrants and Social Amelioration," in *Norwegian-American Studies and Records*, 4: 61 (1929); *Skandinaven*, August 7, 1870.

English and Norwegian. I should wish to get a place for her to board in some good family that would see to her as she is young, 14." [26]

Johnson, out of his own experience and his developing philosophy of education, encouraged Rasmus Anderson to continue in teaching and offered him valuable advice. "In that field," he maintained, "a good and faithful laborer can accomplish more good than in any other. Let a man with good natural abilities well developed by a good education, of a sterling upright character and exemplary habits, labor in the field earnestly and faithfully and generations will bless him. . . . An intelligent person may not have a more intense religious feeling, yet as faith is based upon conviction he is more firm. Such a person will influence his family as well as elsewhere; therefore it is a duty to God to obtain an education. Parents should be made to understand how impressionable children are." [27]

Although Johnson thought attendance at academies like Albion to be a valuable step upward in education, he was turning his attention more and more to institutions on the university level. In 1868 he addressed Anderson at Albion in that vein: "Albion is a good school," he wrote, "but not just the place for a classical education." He believed that there should be a professor of Scandinavian languages at institutions like the university for "the purpose of drawing our youth there for a classical education." Coincidentally, at about this time, Rasmus Anderson was angling for an appointment as a member of the University of Wisconsin faculty, and the support of his highly-regarded older friend was valuable. And it is quite likely that Johnson was already visualizing the stimulating Albion teacher as a future professor in the classrooms of the state university.[28]

In another area the budding virtuosity of Rasmus Anderson attracted Johnson's favorable interest. While still a fledgling teacher at Albion, Anderson read Snorre's *Heimskringla*, the sagas of the Norwegian kings, and was fascinated by the lore of the Northern countries. He found references to the discovery of America by the Norsemen in the tenth century.

[26] *Life Story of Rasmus B. Anderson*, 85 (Madison, Wisconsin, 1915). See also *Skandinaven,* August 22, 1867, and Paul Knaplund, "Rasmus B. Anderson: Pioneer and Crusader," in *Norwegian-American Studies and Records*, 18: 29 (1954); John A. Johnson to Rasmus B. Anderson, April 16, 1867. This letter is in the Rasmus Bjørn Anderson Papers, State Historical Society of Wisconsin, Madison. For a full treatment of the career of Rasmus B. Anderson, see Lloyd Hustvedt, *Rasmus Bjørn Anderson: Pioneer Scholar* (Northfield, Minnesota, 1966).

[27] John A. Johnson to Rasmus B. Anderson, November 11, 1866. The letter is in the Anderson Papers.

[28] John A. Johnson to Rasmus B. Anderson, May 11, 1868. The letter is in the Anderson Papers.

His curiosity aroused, he discovered at the state historical society more exciting materials published by the Royal Antiquarian Society of Copenhagen. His imagination was fired by what he read, and he prepared a lecture on "The Norse Discovery of America Five Centuries before Columbus." On this theme Anderson lectured widely throughout Wisconsin from his base at Albion. Understandably, Johnson realized how this particular thesis would appeal to immigrants who remembered the thrilling old tales. As a result, he engaged the courtroom in Madison and advertised the coming of Professor Rasmus B. Anderson of Albion Academy. And in May, 1868, the twenty-two-year-old speaker delivered in the capital city an eloquent lecture on "The Discovery of America."

As it turned out, Johnson was to play an important role in the successive steps which led to Anderson's career as a professor at the University of Wisconsin. The young teacher and lecturer was attracting attention at Albion, and there was a question whether he could be released to accept President Chadbourne's offer, tendered on two different occasions, to teach at the university. Determined to keep their popular instructor, officials at Albion refused to accept Anderson's resignation. Misunderstandings arose, and to resolve the matter the board of trustees of the academy invited Knute Nelson, an Albion graduate and at the time a Dane County lawyer, and John A. Johnson, as a board member, to advise on the proper procedure to follow. Whatever influence the two men may have had in the decision, Anderson did accept an appointment to the teaching staff at the University of Wisconsin to begin in the fall of 1869.[29]

In the meantime, during the spring quarter of 1869, Rasmus Anderson was registered as a student at the university. It was a low point in his life. He had broken off relations with Albion Academy, but he was not yet a university instructor. He had no savings to tide him over until the salary for his first teaching would begin. At this juncture, Johnson came forward to offer much-needed help. It was decided that Mrs. Anderson, who had been living with her parents in Cambridge, Wisconsin, should continue her residence there. Until he could make more permanent arrangements, Rasmus, upon the invitation of "my good friend, John A. Johnson," moved into the Johnson house. There, in return for services like sawing wood and taking care of the family's small daughter, Ida, he earned his board and

[29] In later years Knute Nelson moved to Minnesota, where he served as congressman, governor, and United States senator. Many of his letters from Minnesota to his friend John A. Johnson in Madison are in the Johnson Papers.

room. Later in the year he rented a small cottage opposite the Johnson residence and transferred his family to Madison.[30]

Johnson faithfully continued to serve as friend and sponsor of Rasmus' budding career at the university. Much to Anderson's disappointment, his first assignment did not include any teaching of Scandinavian languages. Both he and Johnson were disturbed over this turn of affairs. In the second term of the 1869–1870 academic year, however, he made history by being the first instructor to teach Norwegian in an institution of higher learning in the United States. Since that time courses in Norwegian have been a regular part of the curriculum at the University of Wisconsin. Johnson had been working toward this day, and naturally he was pleased that his native language had won its place at an American university. In an article in his newspaper, he reported that he had favored Rasmus Anderson for this service both to Norwegians in Wisconsin and to the progress of higher education throughout the country. He intimated that Anderson's ability might soon entitle him to a full professorship.[31]

In spite of Johnson's backing, promotion of his friend within the university faculty came grudgingly. President Chadbourne, who had been helpful to a fledgling instructor not yet secure in his position, retired in 1870. The change of administration at the end of only one year was a sharp blow. Rasmus was still a comparative stranger, known to very few influential people among either the faculty or the regents. In his *Life Story* written many years later, he recalled that at the time he had had two friends in Madison. Now only John A. Johnson remained. But *he* was a rock of strength to the worried younger man. Johnson had a wide acquaintance with state officials, including members of the board of regents. His recommendations carried weight: "He knew how to approach the people in authority in my behalf and in the interests of the cause." [32]

One of the ways in which Johnson came to the aid of the struggling young teacher was in helping to stock the university library with books in the Scandinavian languages. Out of a limited budget, officials granted Anderson almost no funds to build up his department. Determined to do something to improve matters, he approached Ole Bull, the renowned Norwegian violinist, who at the time was living in Madison.[33] Would he

[30] Anderson, *Life Story*, 135.

[31] John A. Johnson, in *Skandinaven*, March 23, 1870.

[32] Anderson, *Life Story*, 143.

[33] Ole Bull had married Sara Thorpe, member of a prominent Madison family, and considered the Wisconsin capital his home in America.

give a benefit concert to raise money to buy Norwegian books? Bull had taken a liking to the vigorous instructor and stood ready to assist him in a project that would help to make the music of Norway known in America. Yes, he would give the concert. So it was arranged. Both Anderson and Johnson were delighted, and the latter used his influence to engage the assembly chamber of the capitol and to advertise the concert widely in Wisconsin and Illinois.

On Norway's Independence Day, May 17, 1872, a large audience, including delegations from La Crosse and Chicago, assembled to hear Ole Bull. The concert was a signal success, both musically and financially. With an added gift from Iver Lawson, Johnson's associate in publishing *Skandinaven*, a net profit of $534.60 was realized – soon to be turned into books forming the nucleus of the Norwegian section of the University of Wisconsin library. A reception, at which President John H. Twombly of the university presided, followed the concert. Governor Lucius Fairchild, John A. Johnson, Ole Bull, and Rasmus B. Anderson shared the speech making. It was an evening of great enthusiasm and of pride for Norwegian Americans, who could feel that they had brought to their fellow citizens a greater appreciation of the culture of their native land.[34]

Johnson kept a watchful eye on his protégé at the university. He was pleased when President John Bascom, assuming office in 1874, took an interest in Anderson's research and writing in the field of Scandinavian mythology. Availing himself of this development, Johnson arranged an early interview with the new president at which the future of the department of Scandinavian languages and its teacher was the main topic of discussion. In a letter to his friend, Johnson analyzed the situation. Bascom had expressed himself as willing to keep Anderson in his present position, but he could not at the time offer him a professorship. Patience was indicated. "I told him," Johnson said, "that I had thought a great deal of you since boyhood, and should be greatly pleased at your success." [35]

The conference between Johnson and the university president probably was not in vain. In less than a year, Bascom announced that a chair of Scandinavian languages, history, and literature was to be established at the University of Wisconsin. In June, 1875, the regents voted to appoint Rasmus B. Anderson to the position of professor of Scandinavian lan-

[34] Anderson, *Life Story*, 147.

[35] Knaplund, "Rasmus B. Anderson: Pioneer and Crusader," in *Norwegian-American Studies and Records*, 18:32; John A. Johnson to Rasmus B. Anderson, September 7, 1874. This letter is in the Anderson Papers.

guages — the first native-born resident of Wisconsin to hold that rank at the university. Johnson was jubilant. "Glory!" he wrote to Anderson. "What I probably as much as you have wished for has been attained. I have hoped from your first connection with the university that you would be one of the professors." The older man, however, did not withhold a word of caution and advice for the future: "Your impatience has sometimes been dangerous. This I trust I have done something to restrain." [36]

Even in the field of publishing, Anderson, the author, relied on his friend for practical advice. S. C. Griggs, the Chicago publisher who had brought out the professor's *America Not Discovered by Columbus* in 1874, had at first been skeptical about the sale of such a book. Through Johnson's Chicago friend, Victor Lawson, however, an advance order of 500 copies had been pledged for possible sale to readers of *Skandinaven.* Encouraged by this kind of support, Griggs had overcome his doubts and had published the book. It sold well and was considered a success.

Anderson, however, was not quite satisfied. Ambitious to lend prestige to his second book, *Norse Mythology*, he began to think of securing an Eastern publisher. Hjalmar Hjorth Boyesen, another Norwegian-American author, had won a recognized place among writers of the East, particularly in Boston. A publisher whose name was associated with poets, novelists, and philosophers in that mecca of culture would reflect honor on him. He might become the Boyesen of the West.

All this was such heady stuff that Anderson sought out Johnson and unraveled his dreams to his mentor. It would be interesting to know what went on in the older man's mind as he listened to the author's plans and gave his qualified support. Probably he thought it wise to make this a test case. At any rate, Johnson made a contribution of $100 to enable Rasmus to take a trip to Boston. There, with some help from Henry Wadsworth Longfellow, he met the latter's publisher, James R. Osgood. Shortly Anderson returned to Madison with the news that Osgood "would be pleased to publish the work at once." At this stage, there were no written contracts anywhere. On learning that Osgood might steal Anderson away from him, Griggs rushed to Madison, claiming that a prior agreement had been made with him. In his distress, Anderson turned to Johnson as arbiter. The latter could not support the author in his neglect of the Chicago publisher, who had served him well on his first book. Relying on the es-

[36] *Skandinaven*, June 22, 1875; John A. Johnson to Rasmus B. Anderson, June 18, 1875. This letter is in the Anderson Papers.

sential fairness and previous friendship of the two men, Johnson made a firm ruling. Anderson acquiesced, and Griggs became the publisher of *Norse Mythology*. Like its predecessor, the book had a good sale.[37]

In 1883, Professor Rasmus B. Anderson resigned his position at the University of Wisconsin to enter the life insurance business. Johnson's interest in the Scandinavian department, however, continued on much the same basis as before. He was in close touch with the situation and was gratified to know that the class work in the Northern languages, of which he had been sponsor and patron, now had the strong support of the university administration. In a letter written after Anderson's resignation, the president told Johnson that the experience of ten years had convinced everyone that a professorship of Scandinavian languages was desirable both for the university and for the state. The content of the courses in relation to other languages and to the literary and political history of Europe had proved most valuable. Within the state, the professorship had been an important means of attracting to the university students from Scandinavian families, and of assisting them in merging their culture with that of native-born Americans.[38]

It may be guessed that Johnson did not expect his friend Rasmus to remain long an insurance salesman, even though he might be quite successful. However that may be, Johnson soon approached Senator William F. Vilas of Wisconsin with the suggestion that Rasmus B. Anderson would be an excellent man for an appointment in the foreign service of the United States. Earlier Johnson had made unsuccessful attempts to advance men of Norwegian ancestry for state department posts, especially in the Scandinavian countries. Now he had his best candidate — and Senator Vilas, interested in the Wisconsin political backgrounds of such an appointment, immediately used his influence in Washington to bring the matter to the attention of Secretary of State Thomas F. Bayard.

Johnson's original suggestion was to bear fruit. Fortunately for Anderson, he had voted for Grover Cleveland in 1884; hence he was on record as a Democrat. The wheels of patronage ground on, and shortly after the inauguration of Cleveland in 1885, it was announced that Rasmus B. Anderson had been appointed United States minister to Denmark for a four-

[37] Anderson, *Life Story*, 216.

[38] John Bascom to John A. Johnson, June 20, 1883. The letter is in the Johnson Papers.

year term. Both Johnson and the man in whose career he had so personally interested himself were overjoyed at the outcome of their planning. Of all European cities, Copenhagen, then known as the intellectual capital of Scandinavia, would provide exactly the right cultural environment in which to pursue the literary and historical study and writing that always had been close to Anderson's heart.[39]

Friends of the new minister to Denmark gathered for a farewell banquet at the Park Hotel in Madison on April 24, 1885. Ex-Governor Lucius Fairchild, who had himself been minister to Spain, presided. The remarks of two distinguished speakers must have had special significance for thirty-nine-year-old Rasmus Anderson on his day of glory, for *they* had helped him up the long road to the spot he now occupied: John Bascom, president of the University of Wisconsin, and John A. Johnson, a Madison businessman well known to all.[40]

Rasmus B. Anderson went alone to Copenhagen; the new minister did not believe he should spend the money required to take his wife, and, moreover, the Andersons were well settled in Madison in a friendly environment with good schools. Besides – there was their good friend John A. Johnson in whose care Rasmus could place them all during his long absence. Messages from Copenhagen to the family mentor were frequent and detailed. From May 27 to December 26, 1885, every month and sometimes twice a month, letters – never less than four pages – reached the guardian in Madison. The correspondence is a revelation of the divergent personalities of the two men, and a commentary on late nineteenth-century life in a sophisticated European city and on that, by contrast, of a simple middle-class American home in the Middle West.

In his letters, the minister to Denmark – his conscience apparently troubling him a little – begged Johnson to help make clear to his family that he had refrained from taking them to Copenhagen out of concern for *their* future. His friend in Madison reassured him that the Anderson home seemed comfortable and cheerful. (He had even seen to it that the leaky roof had been repaired.) "It is lonesome without you," he wrote in an early letter, "yet it would be selfish to hope for your speedy return. Your boys are doing nicely and Letta [*the daughter*] is a perfect lady with the sense of one twice her years. . . . Everything seems to run smoothly at

[39] Knaplund, "Rasmus B. Anderson: Pioneer and Crusader," in *Norwegian-American Studies and Records*, 18: 35.

[40] *Wisconsin State Journal*, April 24, 25, 1885.

your house. Nothing but the senior partner of the firm is wanting to make a perfect alcove of happiness. There is no disguising the fact that Mrs. A. longs for you very much." Mrs. Anderson did finally go to Europe. In a letter of May 12, 1886, Johnson added that by that time, he hoped, she was safely in Denmark. But she could stay only a short while.[41]

Anderson, from his base abroad, called on Johnson to manage all his financial affairs, a process that included looking after the needs of the family. The minister had instructed his wife to draw on their guardian for what money she might require, adding that he would settle the account. "My life insurance premium will be due in April," he explained to Johnson, "and if she [*Mrs. Anderson*] needs money I trust she may come to you for it." On August 6, 1887, Anderson sent a draft for $2,000 "which I hope you will invest for me as well as you can." After tending to all details with care, Johnson appended a revealing hint to one of his replies dealing with financial matters: "I shall pay the Barfield note [of $500] as you requested and do anything else to accommodate you, but I am opposed to all kinds of speculation." [42]

Questions and answers regarding affairs at the university and about political trends crossed the Atlantic. Johnson relayed information concerning Rasmus' brother-in-law, Professor Julius Olson, his successor in the Scandinavian department – particularly that Olson was establishing a favorable reputation and was to receive a substantial increase in salary. The minister queried his friend about free trade, a subject on which the correspondents disagreed. Anderson believed in such a policy, but Johnson could not accept it. He wrote convincingly that free trade must come gradually; as industries in the United States developed and could compete in the world market, protective laws would become "superfluous and inoperative." He thought the issue was a serious matter, for free trade might come with the Democrats in power.

President Cleveland, Johnson believed, was doing very well and would be re-elected if elections were held in June, 1886. Congress, on the other hand, was doing very little, and every step was taken with party advantage in mind. Anderson, in a letter from Copenhagen late in his tenure there as minister, complimented his friend on an article about the United States navy and American commerce which Johnson had written for the *Madi-*

[41] This and other letters written from Madison are in the Anderson Papers. Letters written by Anderson from Copenhagen are in the Johnson Papers.

[42] Rasmus B. Anderson to John A. Johnson, December 7, 1887, February 3, 1888; John A. Johnson to Rasmus B. Anderson, July 19, 1886.

son Daily Democrat. The minister had sent a copy of the article to the state department in Washington as representing the views "of a man who has given much thought to the subject." [43]

Since Johnson was a Republican, Anderson importuned his friend to intercede for him in Washington when Benjamin Harrison won the election of 1888 over Grover Cleveland. In a letter concerning his possible reappointment, Anderson wrote: "I know you cannot find another person in all America more suitable than I am. It seems to me that you have the best opportunity that you will ever have to show that you have any influence in the [Republican] party to which you have returned by having me retained here at least for a year or two." [44]

Loyally, Johnson took immediate steps to smooth the way for his friend to stay at his post in Denmark. Wisconsin's Senator John C. Spooner also did what he could. After Harrison's election, he reported to Johnson from Washington: "I have your favor of the 11th recommending the retention of Professor Anderson. Of course your recommendation on the subject is entitled to, and will receive, great weight both with Senator [Philetus] Sawyer and myself. I expect to be in Madison one day during the holidays, although I do not wish it generally known, and will call upon you for a talk upon the subject." All was, however, in vain. In spite of the efforts made in Anderson's behalf, the new administration had its own plans, including the appointment of a new minister to Denmark. After four years in the congenial atmosphere of Copenhagen, in the spring of 1889 Rasmus returned to Madison to take up again his life as a private citizen.[45]

When Anderson returned from Europe, John A. Johnson was in his late fifties. Perhaps his ideas and attitudes were becoming more firmly fixed and his patience was growing a little thin — particularly with a mercurial personality like Rasmus. However that may be, the two men, though remaining friends, had many sharp differences in outlook. Johnson could be goaded to desperation and on such occasions he did not spare the rod. In 1899 Anderson published in his Madison newspaper *Amerika* a spiteful denunciation of Julius Olson as "an enemy of Christianity" because in his classes at the university the professor had praised the writings

[43] Rasmus B. Anderson to John A. Johnson, December 7, 1887.

[44] Rasmus B. Anderson to John A. Johnson, November 24, 1888. Johnson had voted for Cleveland in 1884, but in 1888 he had rejoined the Republican party and had voted for Harrison.

[45] John C. Spooner to John A. Johnson, December 17, 1888. This letter is in the Johnson Papers.

of such prominent Norwegian authors as Henrik Ibsen, Bjørnstjerne Bjørnson, and Arne Garborg. This was too much for Johnson, who dispatched to the editor from Berlin a nine-page letter in a tone of firm dissent and displeasure. He declared that he knew of no man to whom he would sooner entrust the moral guidance of his children than to Professor Olson. An attack on this good man was an attack on the university, for parents would hesitate to send their children to be trained by a man considered to be an enemy of Christianity. Johnson urged Rasmus to go to Olson to make the matter right.[46]

In a second letter a few months later, Johnson, now old and infirm, again wrote to Anderson of the distress he felt over the editor's criticism of Olson. His words conveyed the bitterness that he felt: "This attack I deemed grossly unjust, in fact unjust is no name for it. It is a serious matter to attack an educator of our youth for what is certainly one of the gravest of offenses, when such an attack is without foundation. The attack becomes grotesque when as in this case it was for recommending the works of the most prominent Scandinavian authors." [47]

On another occasion, Anderson in his newspaper denounced Storm Bull, another university professor, who was a candidate for mayor of Madison. Johnson was vigorously supporting Bull as the best man for the position. Political arguments – from university policies to sponsorship of Norwegian interests in Wisconsin to sound money and free silver in the national arena – drew the two old friends into a battle of polemics which at times descended to spiteful personalities. Probably because of Johnson's support, Storm Bull was elected mayor of Madison in the spring of 1901. By this time, John A. Johnson and Rasmus B. Anderson, sadly enough, had drifted into an impasse of permanent estrangement. Their last letters were exchanged during the final week of December, 1900.[48]

Many years later, in mellowed retrospect, Rasmus B. Anderson set down in his autobiography a kindly judgment of his friend and mentor. "There was much of the milk of human kindness in Mr. Johnson's heart," he recalled. "When I was in Madison, I walked daily in and out of Johnson's home. When I was troubled, time and again I laid the matter before

[46] John A. Johnson to Rasmus B. Anderson, June 22, 1899.

[47] John A. Johnson to Rasmus B. Anderson, December 28, 1900. On a later occasion, Johnson did not hesitate to castigate Rasmus for the latter's distorted and illiberal attack in *Amerika* on Prince Peter Kropotkin, who had been invited to lecture at the University of Wisconsin; *Wisconsin State Journal*, May 7, 1901.

[48] O. N. Nelson, ed., "Storm Bull," in *History of the Scandinavians and Successful Scandinavians in the United States*, 2: 331 (Minneapolis, 1897).

him." Although Johnson left no such written appraisal at the end of his life, it is certain that his fair-mindedness encompassed Rasmus' good qualities as well as his irritating faults. He always believed that Anderson had sterling abilities which, rightly guided, could be put to notable service. They stood together in contributing significantly toward making the Norwegian cultural heritage known and admired throughout the American Middle West.[49]

Another young man whom John A. Johnson helped at a critical time in his life was Gjermund Hoyme. He had come to America from Norway in 1851, at the age of four, with his parents and eleven brothers and sisters. The prolonged illness of his father during the boy's childhood plunged the family heavily into debt; their home was mortgaged. In Springfield, Iowa, near Decorah, Gjermund attended common and religious school, recognized wherever he went by his teachers and pastors for his unusual abilities as a student. As he grew older, he had a strong yearning for a college education and a career in the church. In 1869, at the age of twenty-two, he arrived at Marshall, Wisconsin, to attend Augsburg Seminary.

The Reverend August Weenaas, headmaster at the seminary, soon realized that his new student possessed great natural talents and the gift of leadership. Hoyme's aim was to study theology, a course requiring knowledge of Greek, Latin, German, and English. These subjects were not being taught at Marshall, and Weenaas advised the young man to transfer to the University of Wisconsin, where he could continue his language studies. Hoyme was eager to go, but without funds the move seemed to him to be impossible. At this point, Weenaas appealed to his friend John A. Johnson—with the result that a door was unlocked for Gjermund Hoyme, opening the way to his highly significant later career as a brilliant pulpit orator and church leader.[50]

A biographer of the Lutheran church leader wrote many years later: "Hoyme still remembers with gratitude how Hon. J. A. Johnson met him at the depot, took him to his home, and kindly assisted him in many ways." For two years the young theologian had a home in Madison while he attended the university. In the midst of their own growing family, John and Kaia regarded Gjermund as their oldest son: his board and room were

[49] Anderson, *Life Story*, 294.

[50] A. Sophie Boe, in "The Story of Father's Life, the Reverend N. E. Boe," a manuscript in the archives of the Norwegian-American Historical Association.

free. As it had been with Rasmus Anderson, only shortly before, he found "heart room" in the Johnson household.[51]

The unfolding career of the Reverend Gjermund Hoyme was to give his sponsor great satisfaction over the years. The university student grew to be a man of striking appearance, tall and straight with black hair and beard. He came to be regarded as the most eloquent preacher among Norwegian-American Lutherans. Of him one biographer wrote: "[We admired his] towering personality, the thunder of his voice, the scintillating epigrams, the musical alliterations, and the irresistible logic of his arguments." Hoyme was president of the Conference from 1886 until that church body in 1890 joined with two other Norwegian Lutheran groups to form the United Norwegian Lutheran Church in America. He then became president of this enlarged church organization, a position which he filled with distinction until his death in 1902.[52]

In later years, Hoyme has come to be regarded as the chief early exponent of union among Lutheran churchmen. One of his most famous sermons, delivered in 1887, was a dramatic plea for the unity of his fellow Lutherans. As a parliamentarian and presiding officer, he was said to have no equal among the Scandinavian clergy of the United States. He was a distinguished leader in developing higher education within the United Norwegian Lutheran Church. When St. Olaf College affiliated itself with this church body, Hoyme assumed the chairmanship of the committee established to raise funds for the building program of the college.[53]

A great variety of letters in the Johnson Papers testify to the wave of appreciation that flooded in to Johnson as a result of his favors to people in all walks of life. One such communication invited him to be the speaker at a Seventeenth of May celebration at Madison, Minnesota, in 1890. "We will guarantee you a splendid audience. You may not remember this,"

[51] Nelson, "Gjermund Hoyme," in *History of the Scandinavians and Successful Scandinavians in the United States*, 2: 382. See also Gjermund Hoyme to N. E. Anderson (Boe), December 1, 1871, in the archives of the Norwegian-American Historical Association. There is an old Norwegian proverb: "Where there is heart room there is always house room."

[52] N. N. Rønning, "The Reverend Gjermund Hoyme," in *Lutheran Herald* (Minneapolis) 27: 84–86 (January 26, 1943).

[53] Nelson and Fevold, *The Lutheran Church among Norwegian-Americans*, 1: 328. Hoyme's sermon urging union is found in J. A. Bergh, *Den norske lutherske kirkes historie i Amerika*, 327–340 (Minneapolis, 1914). See also E. G. Lund, "Mindeskrift over formand G. Hoyme," in *Kort utsigt over formand Hoymes liv og virksomhed*, 41 (Minneapolis, 1902); William C. Benson, *High on Manitou: A History of St. Olaf College, 1874–1949*, 111 (Northfield, Minnesota, 1949).

the writer added, "but you helped me to get the night watchship in the House during the Legislature when I studied at Madison." [54]

Johnson had sent a man a check helping to pay for artificial limbs. A plaintive letter acknowledged the gift of friendship in these words: "For all your past kindness to me, accept my grateful thanks. May you prosper as you deserve and when you have time please write me, nothing cheers like hearing from friends." A Chicago bookbinder confided to Johnson that his business was not successful enough to enable him to support his family. Therefore he must seek other means of making a living. "In anticipation of your Philantropy [*sic*]," he wrote, "I would most respectfully solicitate [*sic*] your influence, if within your reach to obtain a clerkship in one or another business." This particular type of appeal was a common one, for it was known that Johnson had influence in recommending clerks for state and federal offices, to stores in Madison, and particularly for his own expanding business operations in St. Paul and Madison. On quite a different level, there were — besides Rasmus B. Anderson — a number of other ambitious friends who bespoke Johnson's aid in securing posts as United States representatives abroad or as immigration agents in various American cities.

At least once, Johnson's swift reply to a cry for immediate help resulted in fame and fortune for a young friend. Victor Lawson, at the time aged twenty-seven, on June 18, 1878, wrote to Johnson with whom he had been associated earlier in the publication of *Skandinaven.* Lawson explained that he had had a sudden opportunity to buy out a competing Chicago newspaper to the great advantage of his own youthful *Chicago Daily News.* The price made the other paper an unusual bargain, but after exhausting all his resources, he lacked $6,000. It looked as if a fine chance to forge ahead would go by the board. In haste, he had appealed to his friend. "I don't suppose it is such security as banks in general would accept," he explained, "but you, knowing and understanding the nature of the security, know that it is worth a good deal more than $6,000. Can you help me out? Please oblige with an immediate answer, as this whole matter is at its culmination."

The $6,000 arrived almost by return mail. With it Lawson strengthened his position in the evening newspaper field in Chicago and went on to build his *Daily News* into "the most prominent evening newspaper in the

[54] K. O. Jcrde to John A. Johnson, March 21, 1890.

United States . . . [and] one of the most honest and finest organs of news and opinion in the world." [55]

With the Reverend C. L. Clausen, Johnson's friendship was not that of patron and protégé, for Clausen was the older man and had been Johnson's spiritual adviser in his youth. Equally liberal in spirit, the two men had seen eye to eye on current controversial issues of the day in church, school, and state. Johnson never ceased to admire the simple and sincere way in which Clausen preached to his people. He believed that *he* would have done much the same had he been a minister.[56]

In 1884, at the age of sixty-four, while serving as pastor at Blooming Prairie, Minnesota, Clausen suffered a crippling stroke forcing him to give up the active ministry. At once, Johnson moved to help his long-time friend. In an article in *Skandinaven*, he proposed raising a fund to provide for the minister's needs. He believed that Clausen's congregation would not let him "suffer want," but his aim was to solicit gifts from a larger circle. "What do you say, good friends?" he wrote. "Let us make our old friend happy in his old age and during his suffering." [57]

Clausen's last congregation and others from distant places responded in a spirit of love and appreciation for his forty-two years in the Lutheran ministry. A substantial sum was pledged. Johnson became treasurer of the project, which he continued to manage with the assistance of a committee of seven from the Blooming Prairie church. With additional help from his sons and from his Civil War pension, the stricken pastor was enabled to live in comparative comfort in Austin, Minnesota, for the last eight years of his life. When he died in 1892, the Reverend Gjermund Hoyme preached the funeral sermon. In a published tribute, John A. Johnson summed up his personal judgment of the man who had meant so much in his own life: "His influence on his countrymen was both great and constructive. No one came in touch with him without being moved to a better life." [58]

Norwegian immigrants in Wisconsin regularly looked to Johnson to support a variety of projects of particular importance to them. To such

[55] Charles H. Dennis, *Victor Lawson*, 48, 450. The quotation is from a statement by Gerald Barry, editor of the *London Saturday Review*.

[56] H. Fred Swansen, *The Founder of St. Ansgar: The Life Story of Claus Laurits Clausen*, 227 (Blair, Nebraska, 1949).

[57] *Skandinaven*, February 5, 1884.

[58] *Skandinaven*, March 18, 1884, March 30, 1892.

requests he responded generously with his time and hard work, eager as he was to foster a wider appreciation of the contributions of Norway and of Norwegians. He was pleased by the interest in Leif Ericson stirred up in 1874 by the publication of Rasmus B. Anderson's *America Not Discovered by Columbus* – a wave of sentiment finally resulting in a drive for funds to erect a monument to the Norse explorer. Johnson joined with Anderson and Ole Bull in a committee – of which Bull was chairman, Rasmus secretary, and Johnson treasurer. The project was soon vigorously under way, with the three Madison Norsemen behind the planning and organization to finance an American statue of Leif Ericson.

Raising money for such an ambitious undertaking among the rank and file of Norwegians took time and energy. Most contributions were in such small amounts that the fund grew slowly. Again Ole Bull and his violin came to the rescue. With his wife Sara Thorpe Bull as accompanist and Rasmus Anderson as master of ceremonies, the Norwegian musician gave a series of benefit concerts in Wisconsin and Iowa. The entertainers were greeted by enthusiastic audiences; Johnson, as treasurer, received about $2,500 from Bull's tour. When the violinist returned to Norway, he presented another series of concerts there, the proceeds adding substantially to the American Leif Ericson fund.

Recognizing the wave of interest in the early Norse discoveries that the writings of Longfellow and others had aroused in the East, Ole Bull took pains to solicit the help of interested persons there in putting the project on a national basis. Distinguished Easterners rallied to support his plans. Thomas G. Appleton, of a prominent Boston family, assumed the chairmanship of a committee formed to sponsor the completion of the undertaking, a group that included Henry Wadsworth Longfellow, President Charles W. Eliot of Harvard, and Edward Everett Hale. Johnson sent the contributions he collected to Nathan Appleton, treasurer of the fund in New England. Acknowledgments from the latter included a letter explaining the importance the Leif Ericson monument had assumed in the East. "I cannot tell you," Nathan Appleton said, "how much pleasure the receipt of this money has given my half-brother, Mr. T. G. Appleton, and myself. We have no doubt but that it will result in a beautiful statue and fountain for Boston, the capital of New England. Though erected here it will be seen, appreciated and owned by the whole country." [59]

[59] Nathan Appleton to John A. Johnson, April 5, 1879. There are in the Johnson Papers a number of letters containing names and amounts of money for the Leif Ericson monument from communities in the Middle West.

There can be no question that Johnson and Anderson had been working directly toward a specific goal: that the monument should be erected on the campus of the University of Wisconsin. Unfortunately this was not to be — and the disappointment of the original sponsors can be imagined. The Ericson statue by a recognized sculptress, Anne Whitney, with a Viking ship as a pedestal, was unveiled in 1887 on Commonwealth Avenue overlooking Boston's Back Bay. It was the first monument of the Norse seafarer on American soil. The inception of the idea and the early initiative had come from the three friends in Madison. Not one of them, however, could be present at the dedication ceremony. Minister Rasmus B. Anderson was in Copenhagen, and Ole Bull had died before the statue was finished. John A. Johnson remained in Madison, where, as treasurer in the West, he was completing the solicitation and collection of money for the monument fund.[60]

During the period while John A. Johnson was living in Madison, the community, widely known as the home of a cultured Norwegian group, was frequently visited by notable personages from Norway, including such artists as Ole Bull and Bjørnstjerne Bjørnson. On such occasions, Johnson was usually on the welcoming committee. In the winter of 1867–1868, when Ole Bull made an American concert tour from the Atlantic to the Pacific, the Wisconsin capital was an important stopover. Johnson and several others greeted Bull on the train at Milton Junction and traveled with him to the Madison station. There a large Norwegian delegation met the famous musician and, with a traditional torchlight parade, escorted him to his hotel. Johnson delivered an address of welcome to which Ole Bull responded. Later at an official banquet, the mayor of Madison gave an address and Johnson, speaking in Norwegian, expressed the pleasure of his immigrant countrymen that one of their great artists could be among them.

Some years later, a memorable incident — in which Johnson, Rasmus Anderson, and Ole Bull played leading parts — took place at Moscow, a country town in southwestern Wisconsin. This community was widely known for its promotion of Norwegian cultural interests: It was the home of a unique circulating library association, and in addition was locally famous for its sponsorship of Seventeenth of May celebrations. In 1873 it had secured Anderson as speaker for a program which — as it turned out — was to be long remembered. Ole Bull was in Madison at the time, and it

[60] Anderson, *Life Story*, 207.

was arranged — to the great joy of the Moscow Seventeenth of May committee — that he should accompany the speaker. No railroad served the town, and so it came about that Senator John A. Johnson, as coachman with his carriage and pair, set out on May 16, 1873, to drive the invited guests to the scene of the next day's celebration. In a newspaper account a few days later, Johnson wrote that it was a beautiful day for a ride in the country. The cold spring weather had given way to the May sun, and the greening fields and budding trees added beauty to the landscape.[61]

That Seventeenth of May was Moscow's greatest day. A brass band and a delegation of celebrators met the trio's carriage outside the village. C. L. Holland, member of a family with marked literary inclinations, presided. The band played the Norwegian national anthem and Professor Rasmus B. Anderson gave the oration of the day. Senator John A. Johnson also delighted his hearers by speaking with equal facility in English and Norwegian. Ole Bull was asked to play, but he had not dared to risk his delicate instrument on the cross-country jaunt from Madison. However, a violin was produced by an immigrant who had made it himself. Then Ole Bull played for his countrymen the old melodies they had cherished in days gone by. To such men as John A. Johnson and Rasmus B. Anderson the occasion must have seemed the culmination of their dreams.[62]

In the 1870's the fame of Bjørnstjerne Bjørnson, Norwegian novelist, poet, and dramatist, began to have a marked impact upon his countrymen in America. Among them, Johnson, who followed closely political and cultural changes in his native Norway, particularly relished the great writer's liberal views. Bjørnson was a leader in the Young Left movement, which was urging his country toward a national democracy. In such stories as *En glad gut* (A Happy Boy), he pictured the peasant in a new light. Johnson read his works, and like many other immigrants, could identify with their old-world characters. "Bjørnson's stories," he declared, "brought out the good and the beautiful in the peasant." [63]

Attracted by the poet's great appeal to readers in America, Johnson

[61] *Skandinaven*, May 27, 1873. The travelers were royally entertained overnight at the home of O. B. Dahle in Perry.

[62] See Bjorn Holland, *et al., History of the Town of Moscow from 1848 to 1919*, 66–70, 128 (Hollandale, Wisconsin, 1919). Peter Holte, who owned the violin, had come from Norway in 1866. The instrument played by Ole Bull is still in the possession of the Holte family.

[63] *A Happy Boy* was published as a serial in *Emigranten* in 1861. Copies of Bjørnson's books were sold by Fleischer's Book Shop in Madison and by J. T. Relling and Company in Chicago.

and Knud Langeland arranged with Bjørnson to write for *Skandinaven* a series of letters from Norway. When these appeared in 1873–1874, the editors took great pride in presenting to their readers as a correspondent this champion of the common people of Norway. The letters made lively reading, dealing as they did with the small farmers, the labor class, the low-church element supporting the liberal political party, and the burning question of suffrage. All these topics had special appeal for folk not long removed from personal participation in events involving the common man in the Old World. Bjørnson's approach pleased native Americans as well, for his theme was faith in the very democratic principles upon which they hoped to build the future greatness of their own country.[64]

Johnson had hoped that Bjørnson would visit America, but it was not until 1880 that the latter could be persuaded to cross the ocean. A few days before Christmas, Johnson was in a group that gathered at the Palmer House in Chicago to greet the distinguished guest from Norway. Later he introduced Bjørnson when the novelist spoke in Madison. After the Norwegian writer had lectured widely in the Middle West, a wave of disappointment arose in many minds over his critical views concerning their religious beliefs. Johnson recognized the force of this change of feeling toward a great artist, but his personal views remained the same. He was attracted to Bjørnson's political thinking and, to the end, he believed that the poet's greatest service had been in advancing democracy in his own country.[65]

The famous visitors from Norway offered festive interludes. Johnson was anxious that they should be well received, and he took pride in their artistic accomplishments. He never wavered, however, from his main purpose: to help his immigrant countrymen to advance themselves in all ways and become assimilated in the main stream of American life. Men like Ole Bull and Bjørnson of course dramatized this goal, but Johnson — both before and after their visits — worked and spoke and wrote to the major end that he kept constantly in view. He contributed a series of articles to *Billed-Magazin*, published in Madison and widely read by Norwegians on

[64] Arthur C. Paulson, *The Norwegian-American Reaction to Ibsen and Bjørnson, 1850–1900* (Northfield, Minnesota, 1937), a printed summary of a doctoral thesis submitted to the department of English at the State University of Iowa, 1933. See also articles in *Skandinaven* in 1873 and 1874.

[65] *Skandinaven*, December 28, 1880; Arthur C. Paulson, "Bjørnson and the Norwegian Americans, 1880–81," in *Norwegian-American Studies and Records*, 5: 84–109 (1930); Karen Larsen, *A History of Norway*, 454–483 (New York, 1948).

both sides of the Atlantic. Particularly he answered questions that people in Norway were sure to be pondering when they gave serious consideration to emigrating to the United States.

Johnson explained to them the problems and opportunities that America presented, but he did not urge them to come. He made it clear that work was the basis for success in the New World. Industrious, decent folk would find a good future here, for America offered unusual possibilities for advancement. But he often returned to this theme: real progress could not be won without effort. The poor who had no future in Norway could look forward to a better day in the United States. Trained seamen were in demand on the Great Lakes; wages would range from $70 to $80 a month for three quarters of the year. Dependable Norwegian maidservants could readily find work in American homes. Artisans – carpenters, blacksmiths, masons, mechanics – were badly needed. Loggers would be welcomed in the woods and clerks in the stores in Wisconsin communities.[66]

America also needed professional men and would greet doctors in particular with open arms. But Johnson set down a word of warning: Immigrants must understand that Americans did not confer upon men in the professions the same high social distinction bestowed upon such people in Norway. Pharmacists with some knowledge of English would have no difficulty finding suitable positions, for Americans, Johnson confided, were great users of "pills, powders, and drops." Ministers here had to work too hard; many more were needed from Norway to serve their countrymen on this side of the water. Congregations treated their pastors generously. People in immigrant communities were eager to buy land and to build churches and parsonages. America offered a great opportunity for a minister, Johnson explained, adding (with tongue-in-cheek irony) that he would find reaching the position of archbishop a slow process.[67]

How should immigrants coming to America prepare for the journey? Drawing no doubt upon his childhood experiences twenty-five years earlier on the "Salvator," Johnson had ready answers. He urged the travelers to pack their possessions in strong, locked boxes, ironbound at the corners, of a weight that two men could handle. Food that had lasting qualities and could be eaten without further cooking would be best on the ocean voyage. Warm everyday clothes, bedding, and knives and forks should be

[66] John A. Johnson Skibsnæs, "Om udvandringen," in *Billed-Magazin* (Madison, Wisconsin), no. 8, p. 58 (January 23, 1869), no. 9, p. 66 (January 30, 1869).

[67] John A. Johnson Skibsnæs, in *Billed-Magazin*, no. 11, p. 86–89 (February 13, 1869).

provided. The trip by sea would be monotonous; so he recommended bringing books and particularly maps of the United States and of the state to which a person might be going. Travel on a sailing ship took more time than on a steam vessel, but it was less expensive. Two children under fourteen years of age required only one ticket, and a babe in arms needed none at all. As a final bit of advice, Johnson urged immigrants on shipboard to conduct morning and evening prayers and to attend worship on Sundays. Such observances would strengthen them in the midst of new and trying experiences.[68]

Johnson could offer help to newcomers in his official capacity as a member of the immigration commission of Wisconsin and as a sponsor of the immigrant aid society. He urged people who had come earlier and were now settled to remember their own first days in this country. They could be of immense help to those who had just arrived. Johnson published articles in *Skandinaven* in which he pointed out that 1868 was bringing the greatest influx of immigrants from Norway ever to come to the United States.[69]

Johnson constantly expressed concern for the poor among the waves of newcomers. Some of these people even lacked money to reach their destination. High prices in America would increase their difficulties. "Our Christian love," he reasoned, "induces us to open hand and heart. A gift to this cause is a gift of gratitude for our success. We can help if the will to do so is there." The immigrant aid society would publish the list of gifts. He explained where money could be sent in Chicago, Madison, and La Crosse. Work must be found for men who had to earn money immediately. Johnson suggested that if fifteen farmers each would employ one man, the needy in a number of families would be cared for. Farmers in the West were also his special concern, for he had seen at first hand how a drought year had reduced Norwegians there to actual want.[70]

Immigrants to the American Middle West found farming methods of the 1880's far different from those they had been accustomed to in Norway. Realizing this fact from his own wide experience, Johnson took it upon himself to help them adjust quickly to agricultural conditions in a strange environment. In a guidebook published in 1884, he encouraged

[68] John A. Johnson Skibsnæs, in *Billed-Magazin*, no. 15, p. 114 (March 13, 1869).

[69] John A. Johnson, in *Skandinaven*, June 4, 10, 1868.

[70] John A. Johnson, in *Skandinaven*, June 10, 1868; *Emigranten*, August 2, 1861. In 1861 Johnson was a member of a committee in Madison gathering money and food for destitute farmers in Kansas.

Norwegians in this country to make farming a commercial enterprise rather than a temporary, hand-to-mouth way of life. Something of a physiocrat, Johnson believed that agriculture was the cornerstone of a people's economy. He urged farmers to improve their methods by learning what progressive tillers of the soil were doing. Parents should teach farm children to work with their hands; the resulting skills would help them later to be sympathetic to the laboring classes. At all times he preached thrift and sternly admonished against the evil of greed.[71]

Johnson had observed the hazards of one-crop farming. The answer, he was sure, was a program of diversification. Too many men had turned to growing wheat or tobacco to the exclusion of all else. If one of these crops was lost in a given season, a complete failure resulted. The same product planted year after year exhausted the soil. Farmers should realize that the good earth must be replenished. In Dane County, Johnson wrote, tobacco was a popular crop, but it took so much out of the soil that it was necessary to use a fertilizer each season. He cited colonial Virginia, where reliance on tobacco alone had played havoc with the state's economy. "Mixed farming with cattle is safest," he advised. To go with this type of management, he encouraged farmers to develop methods of preparing and storing silage, then a new idea in American agriculture.[72]

A diversified farming economy, of which Johnson was an early advocate, required a knowledge of farm animals — the various types and the best ways to manage them. He especially liked the Morgan horse, a beautiful animal ideally suited for draft purposes. He pointed out the values of two kinds of cattle: those yielding the most milk and those raised for beef. For high milk production, he favored Holsteins from Holland; Shorthorns and Herefords had placed first among beef cattle at the Chicago stock show in 1882. Johnson believed that a progressive farmer should keep all kinds of animals: pigs, sheep, chickens. Even a swarm of bees would pay for itself — and sweeten the housewife's table besides.[73]

The economic side of running a farm appealed particularly to a businessman like Johnson. It resembled storekeeping or banking. Records should be kept of amounts of produce raised, money received and expended, and net income. He gave examples of such records. Farmers ought to study markets, for buyers would respect a man who was informed

[71] John A. Johnson, *Fingerpeg for farmere og andre* (Hints for Farmers and Others), 5–8 (Chicago, 1884).

[72] Johnson, *Fingerpeg*, 8, 42–44.

[73] Johnson, *Fingerpeg*, 28–31.

about prices — a fact which would protect them from being cheated by sharpers. When marketing his produce, a farmer should be scrupulous to present what he had to sell in a true light; in this way, one would establish a valuable reputation as an honest man.[74]

Johnson emphasized that buying land was a serious matter. He explained the various government land acts with care. In addition, he dealt with a number of other practical details of farm management: deep plowing, drainage, irrigation, fertilizers, fencing, and buildings. Norwegian immigrants were not familiar with American farm machinery — an area in which Johnson had become expert. To help newcomers with the complex new machines, he explained the workings of such implements as the seeder, the reaper, and the binder — all unknown on the small farms in Norway. He advised immigrants to study the operation and maintenance of these advanced Yankee machines. There were small tricks to be learned. For example, a man must choose his plow with an eye to the type of soil he had to work. Properly managed and maintained, all the various implements needed on a farm in the Middle West should last for many years.[75]

Letters of appreciation came to Johnson from farmers who had found *Fingerpeg* a valuable aid in the early days of their transition to American-type agriculture. An attorney in western Minnesota declared that the manual filled a long-felt need: "Every Scandinavian in the West knows you and will read your book with interest. It is clear and concise and in every point is worthy of the good will of all the farmers who read it." A letter in Norwegian testified that Johnson had written an excellent book providing solutions to many problems faced by immigrants as they moved onto their American farms and began to learn all over again how to till the soil.[76]

In his later years, the clarity and vigor of Johnson's writings earned him a reputation among influential friends. Not realizing, perhaps, how engrossed he was in business, they turned to him with proposals of larger literary projects. One of these suggestions was that he assume responsibility for the compilation of a history of the Norwegian people in America.

[74] Johnson, *Fingerpeg*, 84–87, 157–159.

[75] Johnson, *Fingerpeg*, 54–57, 75–84. In addition to giving immigrant farmers sound, practical advice, Johnson's manual served as a valuable advertising medium for the farm machinery sold by Fuller and Johnson.

[76] Kris Jerde to John A. Johnson, October 19, 1885; K. S. Knudtson to John A. Johnson, March 16, 1885.

The Reverend S. M. Krogness of Chicago, in an article in *Skandinaven*, made a public appeal to "Honorable J. A. Johnson" to undertake the project. Earlier, Knud Langeland had written Johnson urging him to consider the matter of collecting material for a "Scandinavian History of Immigration." Langeland went beyond this point to suggest that he seek the help of his brother, Ole C. Johnson, and Rasmus B. Anderson as possible collaborators. As it turned out, Johnson could not find the time to engage in so exacting a literary enterprise.[77]

Of all the men Johnson worked with toward the full cultural development of Norwegian immigrants, he felt that Knud Langeland had given him the steadiest support. The two men had met not long after 1850, when Langeland was approaching forty and Johnson was a young man half his age. They had fought side by side as liberals on all controversial issues; each had had the courage to stand and be counted for what he believed in. Their association in the launching of *Skandinaven* in the early 1870's had drawn them together even more intimately. Their friendship ripened in the later years of Langeland's life. Its character speaks from the lines of a letter which he addressed in his seventieth year to his younger friend. "I have very few friends that care anything about me now that I am old and useless," Langeland explained. "I feel therefore the more thankful that you should have thought of me and especially for your kind invitation to make your house my home while in Madison. Nothing would please me better than once more to see you in your happy family circle, but unfortunately it cannot be this time." He revealed to Johnson that he was suffering from rheumatism and that it was advisable for him to stay at home – and he placed in his friend's hands a matter of business which he asked Johnson to take care of.[78]

When Langeland died in 1888, his son, James Langeland of Milwaukee, sent Johnson a letter in which he closed the chapter: "May I express my deep appreciation as well as that of my family for your sympathy and kind words about my father." [79]

John A. Johnson's life epitomizes the struggle of Norwegian immigrants to adapt themselves to life in America. In him the European back-

[77] S. M. Krogness, in *Skandinaven*, January 15, 1884; Knud Langeland to John A. Johnson, December 29, 1883. Rasmus B. Anderson in 1895 published in Madison his book, *The First Chapter of Norwegian Immigration (1821–1840): Its Causes and Results*.

[78] Knud Langeland to John A. Johnson, December 29, 1883.

[79] James Langeland to John A. Johnson, February 16, 1888.

ground and the American environment sought to merge as the two cultures did for each newcomer who gave up the Old World for the New. A natural democrat, Johnson found in America a democratic principle to which it was easy to give allegiance. Fortunately he drew around him in the days at *Skandinaven* a cordon of like-minded spirits—John Anderson, Iver Lawson, and Knud Langeland. All had sprung from the common people of Norway.

For his old-world heritage Johnson had great respect; he gave it generous support. But he was essentially an American. He was critical of the professional and official class from Norway, of men who were ambitious to advance a point of view neither democratic nor American. For this attitude he was sometimes accused of being disloyal to things Norwegian. This judgment did not change him; he remained convinced that, in order to become good citizens of their new country, immigrants must sense the values of its democratic principles, must incorporate these principles in their way of life. He believed with all his heart that here in the United States a great experiment was being tried—such an experiment as the world had never before witnessed. He was proud to be a part of it.

CHAPTER VI

The Fuller and Johnson Company

John A. Johnson had grown to manhood at a time when farming was done with hand tools and crude machines usually fashioned in a country blacksmith shop. With a wooden plow strengthened by strips of iron, he had broken virgin sod laced with tough, leathery grass roots. He knew the rhythm of the scythe, the cradle, the hoe, the hand rake, the pitchfork. He had scattered seed over the fields and had flailed the harvested grain. With a hoe he had covered the kernels of seeded corn in May; cornknife in hand, he had cut the dry stalks after the September frosts. He had husked the ears in the biting fall winds and had shelled them by hand. He had experienced the physical cost and frustrations of all such primitive labor. And even as a youth, he had dreamed of the day when better tools and machines would – in Henry Ward Beecher's prophetic words – "augment the power of man and the well-being of mankind."

What Johnson had learned early in the fields and had later often turned over in his mind was destined to be a major part of the capital he brought in his mature years to the Fuller and Johnson Manufacturing Company. The development of the new firm in the 1880's and 1890's – the last twenty years of his life – included the design, manufacture, and marketing of farm machinery which would have an important part in revolutionizing agricultural methods the world over. The story of his emergence as a manufacturer and business leader reveals his sensitivity to the close relation between building a successful industrial enterprise and improving the lot of the American farmer.

Between the end of the Civil War and the beginning of the twentieth century, agriculture in the United States underwent a tremendous expansion. The great plains were being settled at the same time that the industrial revolution made possible the mechanization of the main processes of farming previously accomplished by muscle power. Agricultural and industrial revolutions stimulated each other: The products of the farm — cereals, cotton, wool, livestock — were the raw materials for burgeoning industries of all kinds. In approximately forty years, major areas of the states west of the Mississippi and east of the Rocky Mountains came under cultivation. In the last three decades of the nineteenth century, 430,000,000 acres in the West were settled and 225,000,000 were plowed. Homesteading reached its high point in the 1880's in the Dakotas, Nebraska, Kansas, and Colorado.

Railroads pushed westward from metropolitan centers, contributing to the rapid development of new settlements, new products, and new markets. The Illinois Central reached Sioux City, Iowa, in 1868. The Chicago and North Western extended its lines to Watertown in eastern Dakota Territory in 1873, and westward to the Missouri River in the center of what is now South Dakota in 1880. The grain trade through Duluth, Minnesota, to markets in the East dates from 1870, when the Northern Pacific connected that Great Lakes port with the fertile regions of the Red River Valley to the west. The Minneapolis, St. Paul and Manitoba Railway reached Devils Lake in what is now North Dakota in 1883. This railroad was merged with the Great Northern in 1890, and the enlarged system built feeder branches, laid out model farms, and engaged in a colonization program which induced thousands of settlers — many of them European immigrants — to come to western Minnesota and the eastern and northern sections of Dakota Territory.[1]

Conditions peculiar to the various regions in the Middle West dictated the special role that each would play in agricultural production. Iowa became the leading corn state; hard winter wheat grew best in Kansas. A new chapter in the development of the West began when it was discovered that hard red spring wheat would flourish in Minnesota and the Dakotas. Invention added to nature's bounty. New, lower-cost milling processes developed finer flour with better lasting qualities, enhancing the value of

[1] Henrietta M. Larson, *The Wheat Market and the Farmer in Minnesota*, 68 (New York, 1926).

hard spring wheat. In 1860 Minnesota ground 30,000 barrels of flour; in 1885 it produced more than 5,000,000 barrels.[2]

Cultivation of the vast reaches of the western plains created a pressing need for farm machinery. The demand could now be met, for low-cost steel – the basic material in the manufacture of agricultural implements – was available in quantity. A fortuitous combination of events had occurred. The Bessemer process wrought a marked improvement in steelmaking in the 1860's. Rich deposits of ore were discovered in 1880 in northern Minnesota, conveniently located for Great Lakes shipping headed eastward. An abundance of Pennsylvania coal was ready to feed the furnaces of Pittsburgh and other industrial centers.

The agricultural implement firm of Fuller and Williams, which John A. Johnson had joined in 1869, was a Madison jobbing concern selling what others manufactured. As a salesman for this company and later as a member of the affiliated Johnson, Fuller and Company, he had traveled widely in the Middle West. As a result, he knew intimately its regions, its changing landscape, and its people. His overview enabled him to understand its potential as a territory for a Midwestern company making farm implements. Its factory should be based close to the market, and Madison seemed an ideal spot for the new venture. With these thoughts in mind, Johnson and his old associates launched a manufacturing business of their own.[3]

In the year 1880, John A. Johnson, M. E. Fuller, and several others formed a corporation and purchased the business of Firmin, Billings and Company, a small firm which had been making plows and some other farm implements in Madison since 1846. Chartered on January 14, 1880, Johnson's new business – known at first as the Madison Plow Company – listed its capital stock at $35,000. Almost at once this figure was increased to $100,000, its thousand shares selling at $100 each. The company was to include in its corporate structure nine directors, three officers, and a superintendent.

John A. Johnson and M. E. Fuller were elected directors late in 1881, and at a formal organizational meeting of the board of directors on January 19, 1882, Johnson was unanimously chosen president; serving with him as first officers were Walter C. Noe, secretary, and Edward M. Fuller,

[2] C. B. Kuhlmann, *The Development of the Flour Milling Industry in the United States*, 77, 115–122 (Boston and New York, 1929); Larson, *The Wheat Market*, 127.

[3] *Farm Implement News* (Chicago), June, 1891, March 17, 1898.

treasurer. Six months later, the corporate name of the firm was changed to the Fuller and Johnson Manufacturing Company. The articles of incorporation, with the amended name, were filed with the Wisconsin secretary of state on June 16, 1882.[4]

With the official incorporation of the new company, further increases in capital stock followed quickly – in 1882 to $200,000 and two years later to $300,000, with 3,000 shares valued at $100 each. In 1884, the word *Limited* was attached to the company name, but after two years it was dropped. In this early period, George H. Bartlett became superintendent of the shop and John Lamont was named superintendent of agencies.[5]

John A. Johnson knew that his fledgling manufacturing business would immediately face strong competition, but he did not fear it. He believed that if a man did not have the courage to meet it head on, he should not go into the business at all. In the years after the Civil War, Wisconsin and Illinois, in the heart of the agricultural area, became a kind of mecca for shrewd businessmen who could see the immense potential in the production of agricultural implements. Expansion in this field was reaching tremendous proportions: in 1850 the value of manufactured farm machinery was $7,000,000; in 1870, only two decades later, the figure stood at $50,000,000. Johnson knew that he was plunging into the center of this industrial surge. But his eyes were open. He realized that only superior factory methods and the most astute financial management could insure success. In these areas he felt most confident.[6]

There were certainly reasons for optimism. Johnson, of course, was right in believing that at this time the Middle West was the dynamic region of America. In his lifetime, he was to see farming change from a self-sufficing, primitive operation to a commercial, somewhat scientific business. No longer would the farmer be "an economic microcosm." The plains were being transformed into a great agricultural empire. The most significant developments in farming methods in history were taking place during the second half of the nineteeth century. Liberal government land policies aided greatly in opening the prairies to settlers, but individual initiative in the invention of improved farm machinery and the resulting introduction of better farming methods were the great spurs to progress. Here John-

[4] "Articles of Incorporation, Fuller and Johnson Manufacturing Company," in State Historical Society of Wisconsin, Madison.

[5] "Articles of Incorporation, Fuller and Johnson Manufacturing Company."

[6] Edward H. Knight, "Agricultural Implements," in *The First Century of the Republic*, 175 (New York, 1876).

son contributed materially. In advising farmers, he had always stressed the potential of commercial agriculture. Now he was to take the lead in creating, manufacturing, and distributing advanced labor-saving machines — the new tools which would ease the physical strain of the farmer's life and increase the financial returns rewarding his hard work.[7]

The Fuller and Johnson Manufacturing Company moved into production of a varied line of agricultural implements in 1883. Three types of plows, five kinds of cultivators, harrows, mowers, and sulky rakes made up the bulk of the heavy, horse-drawn machines produced in the first year. To these were added in some quantity such hand implements as corn cutters and tobacco hoes. The beginning was full of promise, with production and sales both increasing as the company assembled its "Statement of Business for the year ending Dec., 1883, Fuller and Johnson Manufacturing Company." [8]

Johnson's years of experience as a salesman of farm machinery throughout the Middle West enabled his new factory to make a running start in the company's first year. Sales in 1883 totaled close to $200,000. The expense involved in selling that amount was equal to 3.86 per cent of sales. In addition, orders to be delivered in 1884, already on the books in 1883, amounted to $114,000. Second-year sales increased to over $230,000, and in 1885 the total reached approximately $240,000. To produce such dollar returns in the 1880's of course required the sale of a large number of implements.[9]

Sales for 1883 indicated that plows, harrows, and cultivators were the backbone of the company's business. They were what the farmer needed first: to turn over the virgin sod, to prepare it to receive the seed, to conquer the marching army of weeds threatening to choke the growing crops. These were the days before electric power saved human muscle in the factories — a time when blacksmiths with strength and driving energy were

[7] L. B. Schmidt, "The Agricultural Revolution in the Prairies and the Great Plains of the United States," in *Agricultural History*, 8: 169–195 (Baltimore, October, 1934); *Farm Implement News*, April, 1887.

[8] See Table 1, "Manufacture of Agricultural Implements, 1883, Fuller and Johnson Manufacturing Company," in the Appendix, p. 286.

[9] "Statement of Business for year ending Dec., 1883, Fuller and Johnson Manufacturing Company," and similar statements for 1884 and 1885, in Division of Archives and Manuscripts, State Historical Society of Wisconsin. See also Table 2, "Wholesale Prices of Implements, 1883, Fuller and Johnson Manufacturing Company," in the Appendix, p. 286–287.

still the key force in making machines to be used on lonely farms a thousand miles from their forges.

The times demanded innovations in the manufacture of agricultural farm implements. Special conditions in various areas called for new patterns and new dies. Johnson moved vigorously ahead with original ideas in both design and factory production. He pioneered in improving plows, mowers, rakes, planters, and cultivators. He did not need to create new types of machinery; rather he geared his factory to adapt to new farming needs the machines already in use. He made special-purpose plows and other implements and sold each unit to a buyer who knew the kind best suited to the soil and crops in his particular region. To insure the preeminence of his product, Johnson insisted on taking the time required to design and manufacture each machine carefully and to test it thoroughly before putting it on the market. It did not deter him that his conscientious attitude sometimes delayed the release of some promising new device for a year or two. Always the perfectionist, he was also endowed with the saving grace of patience.

Specialized machinery benefited every phase of agriculture by increasing production. This was the economic key. The enlarged volume of farm produce proved a boon to railroads and markets. The resultant improvement in the marketing system assured the farmer a larger percentage of the price of his grain. Elevators dotted the landscape, and mills to process the yield of the farms — especially wheat farms — grew in number. The consumer in turn profited as more and better grain and fiber products reached the markets. With the use of improved machinery and new methods, the farmer — also a consumer — became more enterprising and successful: his income increased and he moved up in the social scale. Johnson could take pride in all this changing agricultural structure. As an inventor and manufacturer of farm implements, he was adding to the general well-being of all who lived in areas depending on a farm economy.

The pressing need for plows to break the prairie sod provided the first challenge to Johnson and his mechanics. The old iron plow with its wooden moldboard had been used in the sandy, stony soil of the East, but it did not work well in the rich vegetable mold of the western plains. The share clogged and failed to scour. To turn a clean furrow in a particular soil, a special plow had to be designed. Other factors, too, had to be considered. Was the field to be plowed sod or stubble? Sand or clay? Moist or dry? There were areas in which one or two of these characteristics predominated. Each needed a plow that would perform at maximum efficiency.

Fuller and Johnson soon built a reputation as manufacturers resourceful enough to make any special-purpose plow that might be needed. Their Bonanza Prairie Breaker was constructed to master the tough virgin sod of the plains. For soil already tilled, the improved stubble plow met a widespread need. Its moldboard had a patented steel facing giving the front a sturdy thickness. The hardened steel, capable of enduring any strain, guaranteed this implement added years of service. Although the use of expensive tempered steel increased the plow's cost, in the end it was the best buy for hard, year-after-year use. Two of the company's widely used plows – the Columbian, a three-wheeled gang plow, and Young America, a one-horse implement light enough for a boy to guide – became so popular that the factory worked overtime to keep pace with orders for them.[10]

To meet the needs of stony land, Fuller and Johnson designed the Eclipse Stone Dodger and advertised it with a guarantee – "no more stopping for stones." Testimonial letters confirmed its success. One farmer wrote with enthusiasm on March 30, 1898: "This day bought one of your Stone Dodger Sulky Plows and I must say it does the most perfect work of anything I ever saw. It passes over the stones without jarring and rides as easy as a buggy." The Eclipse was ingeniously designed with a spring-trip device which allowed it to elevate itself over any obstacle without stopping the horses. Its special construction prevented damage to the plow and injury to the driver.[11]

The great virtue of Fuller and Johnson sulky plows lay in the fact that they lightened the farmer's work. No longer was the plowman forced to trudge all day over soft, uneven ground. Now he rode. Johnson improved his sulkies with a patented design of his own which introduced a rigid frame with side pieces. He added thills with holes, which allowed them to be adjusted securely to the crosspiece. The company put a premium on ingenious new ideas. Built into all its farm machinery were innovations –

[10] In 1888, Johnson, who had made a special study of moldboards, was granted a patent on the steel-faced moldboard used on his stubble plows. See also *Farm Implement News*, March 17, 1892, for material quoted from the Fuller and Johnson catalogue of 1892; United States Patent Office, *Official Gazette*, October 2, 1888; *Farm Implement News*, November, 1888, January 19, 1893, November 2, 1893.

[11] Letters from satisfied owners of the Eclipse Stone Dodger were published in full-page advertisements in *Farm Implement News*, July 14, 21, 28, 1898. See also *Farm Implement News*, March 17, 1898, July 5, 1900.

the invention either of Johnson himself or of mechanics employed to create and develop practical changes in design, materials, and manufacture.[12]

Sturdy patented wheels were a feature of all implements sent out by the Fuller and Johnson factory. Uniformly they were strong and durable, having replaceable boxings and long bearings. In addition, they were so constructed that any blacksmith could quickly replace broken spokes. Company mechanics also invented and installed the Patented Reversible Heel on Landslide, one of the stubble plows. Secured by one bolt, this steel plate could be turned around when the lower side became worn. A simple device, it doubled the life of the plow. In his advertising, Johnson always stressed the durability of his machinery. He stated as a principle that his plows were expensive, but he was able to demonstrate repeatedly that the good materials used guaranteed that they would outlast any others.[13]

Through personal experience, Johnson could give his customers practical hints on plows and plowing. He advised farmers to do their deep plowing in the fall. Contact with the atmosphere during the winter, he believed, enriched the exposed subsoil and helped it to resist drought. He advocated going as deeply as possible, as the rich earth under the surface held its moisture longer. To get maximum depth, he told farmers to lengthen harness tugs and never to let plowshares get dull.[14]

The day of scattering seed by hand over a limited farm area had come to an end. Improved plows were turning a large acreage of prairie sod, but this great step forward would have little value unless it was followed at once by complementing advances in mechanized methods of sowing and cultivating. To Fuller and Johnson, the opportunity for rapid agricultural expansion offered a challenge.

In many states of the Middle West — including particularly Wisconsin, Illinois, Minnesota, and Iowa — corn was replacing wheat as a staple crop. Properly planted and cultivated, it grew luxuriantly, providing food for farm families as well as for their livestock. But the time-honored method of planting corn — the hoe making the hole, the farmer dropping kernels by hand and covering them by foot, hill after hill, row upon row — was

[12] United States Patent Office, *Official Gazette*, June 2, 1885.

[13] United States Patent Office, *Official Gazette*, vol. 48, has an excellent description of the Johnson patented wheels. See *Farmers' Pocket Companion* (Madison, Wisconsin, 1890), a pamphlet distributed to customers of the Fuller and Johnson Company. A copy is in the Johnson Papers. See also John A. Johnson, *Fingerpeg for farmere og andre* (Chicago, 1884).

[14] *Farmers' Pocket Companion.*

hopelessly slow and inefficient. Scarcely better was the back-breaking labor required to operate the plunger hand planters which had appeared in the late 1850's. What was needed was a revolution in sowing technique. Thousands of acres of plowed land were ready to be turned into waving cornfields once an efficient machine for rapidly dropping the seed kernels could be manufactured in quantity.[15]

The need was soon met by the construction of a horse-drawn implement capable of planting twenty acres of corn a day. Fuller and Johnson mechanics played a leading role in the early development of this machine by adding an invention of their own known as Starks Combined Force-Drop Planter and Check-Rower. The Starks attachment soon earned a recognized place in the market as an improvement over the old check-rower which only marked the place where the seed should fall. The force-drop device saved time and labor: it indicated the place and planted the seed at the same time. The kernels did not scatter as they were dropped, and the efficient spacing mechanism made it possible later on to cultivate the growing corn two ways. Concerning this valuable selling point, Johnson stressed in his advertisements that his improved corn planter "would save its purchase price for every 100 acres planted by not having corn destroyed while cultivating."[16]

The force-drop principle – which in the hands of Fuller and Johnson was to make such an important contribution to the development of mechanical corn planters – was the invention of a country schoolteacher. On October 25, 1878, Nils O. Starks, then an instructor in the village school at Nora in Dane County, Wisconsin, made application to the United States Patent Office stating that he had "invented certain new and useful Improvements on Corn Planters."

It is likely that Starks had consulted Johnson in nearby Madison, for the inventor's patent dated February 25, 1879, was secured in Washington by the patent solicitors who had handled Johnson's earlier patent business. However that may be, Starks on the day of issuance of his patent assigned "one third his right to John A. Johnson of Madison, Wisconsin." From that date, the two men were to be closely associated in the manufacture of a new and mutually profitable piece of farm machinery.[17]

[15] Other sections in which corn became one of the major crops were the older farm areas of Ohio and Indiana and the newly opened prairies of Nebraska, Missouri, and Kansas.

[16] Johnson, *Fingerpeg*, 82; *Farmers' Pocket Companion.*

[17] A copy of Starks's patent is in the Johnson Papers.

Starks wrote Johnson on March 7, 1879, asking whether the latter's company would be willing to risk a part of the expense of putting the new attachment on the market. The answer was in the affirmative, and the inventor was soon engaged in testing his mechanism on the farm of John A. Johnson's brother Oliver. On August 14, 1879, he wrote to Johnson that the new device "worked nicely." Starks straightway gave up schoolteaching to become an employee of Fuller and Johnson, a move which soon resulted in his promotion to the position of shop superintendent.[18]

The force-drop planter was a popular addition to the Fuller and Johnson line. In 1888 the firm sold every corn planter it had in stock, and as a result had to borrow from dealers to have available machines to exhibit at fairs. Exclamation points featured the half-page advertisements in the trade journal: "Force Drop! Wrought metal wheels! Iron seed boxes! Center lock lever! Very light draft!" Johnson did not hesitate to show his pride by proclaiming his implement "the best planter and check-rower on earth." Dealers added their highest point of praise, "It's a money maker," and farmers provided the clincher, "It's a money saver." [19]

The boom in plows and corn planters was soon to produce a pressing need for cultivators. On thousands of acres, young green-growing shoots of corn were fighting a life-and-death battle with grass and stubborn weeds. Machines must be hurried to the farms to loosen the soil and to keep the corn rows clean. Anticipating just this situation, Johnson and his mechanics had invented, patented, and manufactured their Bonanza Riding Corn Cultivator, destined to become one of the leading implements of its class on the market. It had practical features designed to help the farmer, including four reversible shovels controlled by a foot pedal — an important device because it left the hands of the driver free to manage his horses. Its axle was adjustable to differences in width between the rows, and the whippletrees, to which the tugs were fastened, also could be shortened or lengthened according to the height of the corn. Johnson did not hide his implement under a bushel: in his advertisements he referred to the Bonanza as "the only perfect gang cultivator on earth." [20]

Situated in the tobacco-growing region of southern Wisconsin, Fuller and Johnson took the lead in developing machinery to replace the slow

[18] Starks's letters, unless otherwise indicated, are in the Johnson Papers.

[19] *Farm Implement News*, January, 1888, August, 1888, October, 1890, September, 1891.

[20] *Farm Implement News*, March, 1889. Fuller and Johnson also manufactured two other well-known cultivators: the Tip Top and the Victor.

hand method of transplanting tobacco shoots. As with the Starks corn planter, Johnson was alert to secure the most promising device available in a new field. On March 18, 1890, Frank A. Bemis of Lodi, Wisconsin, was granted a patent on a tobacco transplanting machine – and on July 28 of the same year he contracted, for a stipulated sum, to grant to Fuller and Johnson the exclusive license to manufacture and sell the Bemis Tobacco Transplanter throughout the United States. He also assigned to the company any later patents he might obtain for improvements on his original invention. The machine soon earned for itself wide recognition as the most efficient device for resetting growing tobacco plants in the soil. The inventor became a member of the company's sales staff to assist in advertising and marketing the new implement.[21]

The transplanter had a wooden frame resting on three wheels – one in front and two behind. Made of pressed steel with concave outer rims, the wheels had wooden guards and metal scrapers. The water reservoir rode on the front of the frame. Released by a brass valve and a hose arrangement, the water trickled down to the shoe where the tobacco plants were to be placed by hand. The machine was drawn by a two-horse team driven by a man seated on the water barrel. Cut into this cast-iron seat was the inscription "F. & J. Mfg. Co." To the rear, only a little above the ground, were suspended two other seats for the "operators," who took each shoot from a "flat" of tobacco plants in front of them and placed it behind the shoe. As the shoe dug a hole, the plant was reset in it and watered in the same process. Interestingly enough, children, as partners in the family business, often were called upon to ride the transplanter as operators.

What the Starks force-drop planter did for corn, the Bemis transplanter did for tobacco. The implement sold widely and proved to be an important factor in developing the growing of tobacco into a successful business. It had its largest market in Wisconsin, Ohio, and New York, where the transplanter is in use to the present time. A small company in Verona, Wisconsin, still manufactures the Bemis machine. Iron and steel have replaced wooden parts, and tractors rather than horses furnish its motive power. But its basic construction is the same today as it was when it was first made in the 1890's by Fuller and Johnson.

Trouble developed over the Bemis patent, and late in 1894 Fuller and Johnson, as plaintiff, brought court action to establish the company's ex-

[21] The Bemis machine could also be used for transplanting tomatoes and cabbages. See *Farm Implement News,* July 20, 1893.

clusive right to the Bemis name. The complicated litigation arose because Thomas Lormer and Jacob Wettelson, copartners, of Stoughton, Wisconsin, had begun marketing a machine called the New Bemis Automatic Transplanter. The implement thus advertised and sold was being made by the Stoddard Manufacturing Company of Dayton, Ohio. The suit brought by Fuller and Johnson was entered in the circuit court in Madison on November 18, 1894.[22]

Evidence in the trial established that, through its contract with Frank A. Bemis in 1890, Fuller and Johnson had prior right to the use of the Bemis name. To support the defendant's case, Fred H. Bemis, a brother of Frank, testified that he had obtained a patent on what he alleged to be certain improvements on the original invention of Frank A. Bemis. Fred Bemis had been an employee of Fuller and Johnson at the time that he arranged with the Stoddard Company to manufacture a transplanter. The plaintiff charged that Fred H. Bemis and the Stoddard Company had "with fraudulent intent" adopted the trade name used by Fuller and Johnson, thus seeking to derive benefit from the established reputation of the Bemis transplanter as manufactured by the Madison company. On February 18, 1895, the circuit court ruled in favor of John A. Johnson's company and ordered the Stoddard Manufacturing Company to cease using the Bemis name in advertising or selling its tobacco transplanter.

Horse-drawn hay mowers had such obvious superiority over the hand scythe that Fuller and Johnson moved into the field early and with vigor. Drawing upon a wide practical experience with cutting hay, Johnson was able to advise farmers about the advantages of using a mowing machine: to save labor, to shorten the haying season, and to improve the quality of the hay. He advocated keeping the sickle sharp, even if that involved sharpening the knives each day. He felt that the purchaser of a mower should choose one that was simple and strong in construction, easy to operate, and easy to repair. "See to it that it rides well," he advised. "The seat should not shake when the mower is in operation." He strongly urged that good machinery deserved good housing; that was *the* important factor in lengthening its life.[23]

[22] "Fuller and Johnson Manufacturing Company, Plaintiff, *vs.* Thomas Lormer and Jacob Wettelson, Defendants," March 1, 1895, in *Records of the Circuit Court*, Dane County, Madison, in Division of Archives and Manuscripts, State Historical Society of Wisconsin.

[23] Johnson, *Fingerpeg*, 80.

Mowers claimed an important share in the annual sales records of the Fuller and Johnson Company. In 1884 the firm marketed 1,700 of these implements. The next year its mowing machine was further improved when that ingenious mechanic, Nils O. Starks, was granted a patent on a "shoe" — which at once became a standard attachment on all models. Leading all special types of the company's mowers was Red, White, and Blue, concerning whose merits Johnson waxed eloquent. One horse could pull it — the sickle could be lifted by a handle operated from the driver's seat. In keeping with the unrestrained advertising of the time, the "World Beating Red, White, and Blue Mower" was marketed under the sales slogan: "The mower that leads them all." [24]

With thousands of mowers cutting an ever-increasing acreage, farmers raking hay by hand fell far behind, and a demand for a mechanized hay rake drawn by horses developed everywhere. Fuller and Johnson responded by manufacturing a line of such implements, the leading ones being the Bonanza and the Sweep Stakes. Both had tines of the best steel and were marketed at the same price. The Bonanza, light in weight, came equipped with thills so that one horse could be used, or with a tongue for a team. The Sweep Stakes had wheels four inches higher than those of any other rake at the time. A truss under the axle made it possible to control the center tines without moving those on the sides. With the high wheels and axle, the long tines could be utilized to make haycocks, a labor-saving feature that added to the usefulness of the rake.[25]

Near the end of his life, John A. Johnson, looking back on the early years of his company, expressed regret that it had not aggressively engaged in the manufacture of twine grain binders. He had come to feel that definite decisions at the strategic time in the past would have increased greatly the volume of business for Fuller and Johnson. As it had happened, however, a series of minor obstacles had been allowed to block the firm's entry into the lucrative grain binder field.

By 1873, after selling Walter A. Wood reapers for several years, Johnson realized that self-binding machines using wire had seen their day. There were too many objectionable features. The wire found its way into straw fed to cattle, even into the wheat being ground into flour. Wire was

[24] *Farm Implement News and Country Hardware Trade* (Chicago), March 31, July 31, 1884; *Farm Implement News*, June, 1886, July, 1888.

[25] *Farm Implement News*, June, 1891, June 8, 1893. The Johnson self-dump rake was also a popular item in the company's line, which included a lighter, cheaper model carrying the firm's guarantee.

hard on the binder's machinery. Something must replace it — and experiments on a machine utilizing twine seemed to be the answer. Soon inventors in several states were at work on the problem, and machines giving promise of success were being tested in the fields.

Johnson noted the machinists whose ideas for a twine binder seemed most likely to meet the practical needs of farmers. One was J. J. Appleby of Mazomanie, Wisconsin, and another Hector A. Holmes of Owatonna, Minnesota. Both men produced field machines at about the same time; somewhat different in design, each had interesting possibilities. In 1879 Appleby approached Fuller and Johnson, offering the opportunity for an association of interests. But apparently the time was not ripe. M. E. Fuller, the senior partner, did not favor taking the risk involved. Chauncey C. L. Williams, one of the original partners, had died the year before, and his death and the settlement of his estate had created a temporary shortage of capital that no doubt influenced the company's decision. Therefore, instead of plunging into the reaper manufacturing field, Johnson referred Appleby to Walter A. Wood. After building ten experimental binders from Appleby's design, Wood's company backed off and contracted instead to manufacture the twine binder designed by Minnesota's Holmes.[26]

It is known that Holmes as well as Appleby had talked to Johnson about his invention of a twine binder. In 1901 Johnson asserted that a golden opportunity had been missed: "We could have secured both Appleby and Holmes. Had we taken hold and thus controlled the patents on both, the marsh in East Madison might have been covered with shops and ten to twenty thousand men employed therein."[27]

Although Fuller and Johnson machines harvested no wheat, one of them made an important contribution toward bringing in another food crop. As early as 1890, the company was marketing a one-horse corn harvester which could cut from five to seven acres a day. At the time the latest and most improved implement of its type, it was so constructed that several bundles could be cut and accumulated on the machine. Two men could do the work — a driver and a shocker. When enough bundles had been cut to make a sizable shock, the harvester was stopped and the shock was set up.[28]

[26] John A. Johnson, *Manufacturing in the United States: A Retrospect and Forecast*, 8 (Madison, Wisconsin, 1901). This 16-page pamphlet is in the Johnson Papers.
[27] Johnson, *Manufacturing in the United States*, 9.
[28] *Farm Implement News*, June 7, 1894.

In his years as president of the Fuller and Johnson Manufacturing Company, John A. Johnson developed and formulated a personal business credo. He believed that the reputation of a company such as his rested equally upon the creation of a high-quality product and upon the most careful management. The office personnel and sales force were as valuable as the machinists in the shop. Pen and paper were as important as hammer and anvil. All employees must be capable individuals. At the top, the organization must have a leader whose judgment was sound, who possessed common sense in ample measure and the ability to inspire confidence. In a business in which competition was sharp and profit margins small, only a superior over-all performance could insure success.[29]

In Johnson's view, skillful management by the marketing organization of a manufacturing business was vital: the product must be sold if the enterprise was to thrive. Management should aim to create demand by making the purchasing public aware of the nature and quality of the products offered. Successful marketing was complex. It required a field organization consisting of branch offices, an advertising program, a sales and collection force, and dependable transport and delivery of goods as ordered. Having been "through the mill" as a salesman of farm machinery, the president of Fuller and Johnson knew the value of thorough training for men engaged in selling. Everything representing a company must be first-class. The written message was another salesman. "The character of a commercial house," Johnson asserted near the end of his career, "can be judged by its letters." Correspondence should carry the tone that would impress all readers with the excellence of the firm sending it out.[30]

The president and board of directors of Fuller and Johnson were well aware that the agricultural implement industry required relatively larger capital than most other manufacturing enterprises. New machines must be tested in the field for every improvement made; sometimes it took years to perfect them. On the other side of the ledger, the farmer needed long-term credit, particularly when misfortunes like drought, hail, or grasshoppers devastated his crops. The company more than once had to draw on its reserve of capital to tide the farmers in a stricken area over a disastrous year. Only with ample financial resources of its own could such a firm stay in business in both good times and bad.

[29] Johnson, *Manufacturing in the United States*, 5.

[30] Johnson, *Manufacturing in the United States*, 5. Johnson also believed that, whenever feasible, a manufacturer should make an approach to the foreign as well as to the domestic market.

From the early 1880's, when he first engaged in the manufacturing business, Johnson realized that large-scale production and volume sales would be necessary to reduce unit costs. All his planning was directed toward building in this direction — a program of expansion that demanded increasing financial resources. From the $200,000 capital stock with which the company began operations in 1882, the total was gradually increased until in 1890 it stood at $500,000, a goal toward which its officers had been moving. Patient and driving effort had brought about a remarkable advance in less than ten years.

The company remained a Madison institution. In its small number of stockholders, President John A. Johnson was always the largest investor, and M. E. Fuller was a close second. After five years of operation, it was reported at the annual meeting of January 19, 1887, that 2,013 shares of stock were outstanding. Of these Johnson held 709 and Fuller, a director, 669. Vice-president Samuel Higham and another director, B. J. Stevens, each had 100 shares. Fred A. Johnson, son of the president, had 75 shares, Secretary Walter C. Noe, 60, and Nils O. Starks, superintendent of the shop, 50. All these larger stockholders were actively associated in the management of the business.[31]

A special stockholders' meeting held one week later — on January 26, 1887 — voted that persons having shares should accept common stock in lieu of dividends. The directors then declared a 10 per cent dividend on preferred stock and a 6 per cent dividend on common shares, and voted that holders of common stock should accept shares in place of dividends. At the 1888 annual meeting, the officers reported that the increased capital stock then stood at $432,000. And on January 19, 1889, a 6 per cent dividend was voted on both preferred and common shares. As before, the dividends of common stock were to be exchanged for common shares.[32]

With these changes in the amount and ownership of stock, Johnson and his son Fred continued to hold more shares than any other family. In 1891, a group of nineteen stockholders attending the annual meeting controlled 4,664 of the outstanding 5,000 shares. Besides officers and directors, they included the following well-known residents of Madison: W. R. Bagley, R. M. Bashford, Sarah Fuller Bashford, John J. Bayfield, A. Berg, M. J. Cantwell, M. R. Doyon, Wayne Ramsay, Halle Steensland, George

[31] "Record of the Secretary of the Fuller and Johnson Manufacturing Company," in Division of Archives and Manuscripts, State Historical Society of Wisconsin.

[32] "Record of the Secretary of the Fuller and Johnson Manufacturing Company."

B. Tanberg, and C. J. Togstad. From its beginning, the strong home-town concern for the success of Fuller and Johnson was undoubtedly an important factor in the steady growth and solidarity of the firm. In 1899, at the close of the century, forty-one stockholders were listed, the largest number reported up to that time.[33]

Even in times of unstable business conditions, the top management of the company saw to it that capital was well spent and that wise decisions concerning demand, production costs, selling price, assured income, credit, and profits were made year after year. With great steadiness, Johnson led the executive team through panics and depressions and in the face of fierce competition among manufacturers. The institution that emerged claimed a prominent place in the farm implement industry of the United States.[34]

To extend its territory westward and northwestward, the company set up branch houses at strategic distributing points. The first of these was established in Minneapolis, in the heart of the wheat region, where such millers as Pillsbury, Washburn, and Crosby had given the city a reputation. For a time, this important branch served not only Minnesota but also the Dakotas. Others were soon located at Des Moines and Council Bluffs in Iowa, Peoria in Illinois, Mitchell in South Dakota, and Grand Forks and Fargo in North Dakota. Later the push to the west moved them as far from home base as Kansas City, Denver, Helena, Montana, and Los Angeles. The one distributing agency which Johnson and Fuller opened east of Madison was in Grand Rapids, Michigan.[35]

Such a far-flung network of outlets required close co-ordination by a superintendent of agencies in the home office. The earliest occupants of the position were John Lamont and A. E. Proudfit. The latter, who had been the bookkeeper when Fuller and Johnson began their operations in 1882, was soon chosen as head of the agency program, a post which he held until 1890. Later the extension of branch houses in the West made the superintendent one of the key officers in the organization. During this period, covering the late 1890's and the early years of the new century, Charles H. Allyn made a valuable contribution as head of the agency phase of the company's business.

[33] "Record of the Secretary of the Fuller and Johnson Manufacturing Company."

[34] Johnson, *Manufacturing in the United States*, 5–7.

[35] Merrill E. Jarchow, "King Wheat," in *Minnesota History*, 29: 16 (March, 1948); *Farm Implement News*, July 18, 1895. See also *Farmers' Pocket Companion*.

Branch managers also had to be competent men capable of handling complex situations and emergencies. Among the well-known men that the company put in charge of the Minneapolis office in the early 1890's were J. W. Monroe and A. G. Bagley. Later, over a long period of association with the company, Oliver H. Swerig served as manager of the Minneapolis branch and as a successful marketer of Fuller and Johnson implements throughout the Midwest.[36]

Salesmen, valise in hand — the roving messengers who called on local implement dealers — were vital links in the chain of agents bringing Fuller and Johnson implements to distant farms. Johnson himself had done this work and now he coached his men carefully. They must know the complexities of the goods they sold and must shrewdly evaluate the financial position and reliability of the dealers. In the areas they visited, they must assess and forecast the sales possibilities for their firm. Back to the home office from these newsmen must flow a stream of detailed information concerning market conditions on the periphery of the trade territory. The travelers were Johnson's pets. He advised young men in his firm to begin at the bottom as salesmen. If they succeeded in that basic training, he held out to them the promise of promotion in the hierarchy of the business.

Local implement dealers, the company's direct contact with the individual purchaser, were also important representatives of the manufacturer. Standing between the Fuller and Johnson salesman and the farmer in the field, they took orders and delivered the machines. They were the judges of what credit could be allowed buyers. They also made collections, an important function because the financial life of the company depended on this final step. If crops were good, collecting contracted payments presented no problem. When crops failed, however, and personal misfortunes piled up on a struggling farmer, the whole matter became painful to both the dealer and his neighbor, now a delinquent debtor.

Under such circumstances, the company relied on other collection agents, officers of banks or professional collectors. Upon such men fell the difficult decision whether the customer should be given an extension of time or whether legal steps should be taken. Patience or pressure — which should be applied? The president of Fuller and Johnson chose his collection agents with care; when cases became seriously involved, he urged them to come to him for advice. Johnson was long-suffering, with little natural inclination to go to court. But a debtor who showed indif-

[36] *Farm Implement News*, February 17, 1898.

ference to his obligations over a period of time could expect no coddling. In October, 1885, Johnson sent a series of notes for collection to an agent, adding these words: "Please collect these promptly, and remit as usual. I do not propose to grant *any* extension, crops and prices are fair and they *must pay*."

In the fall of each year, Johnson addressed letters to his salesmen and dealers advising them to lay plans for the coming spring. He urged them to "size up" their needs early, so that shipments could be on the way in good season. Orders coming to the factory by January 1, he pointed out, would give six-weeks' leeway and prevent a spring rush. Dealers were encouraged to place large orders all at one time to reduce shipping cost per unit. Care in checking contracts would eliminate misunderstandings concerning details later on. Always a believer in learning by reading, Johnson sought to influence his salesmen in the field to keep up with trade journals and to pass them on to dealers. At times his circular letters specified certain articles as required reading. And he regularly solicited suggestions to be filed with the home office. "Such suggestions," he advised on one occasion, "will receive prompt attention." [37]

Beginning in 1883, sales of Fuller and Johnson increased each year until 1888. Then, in certain prairie states, drought or grasshoppers or both took a disastrous toll, and there was little opportunity to sell farm equipment. Sales in that ill-fated season fell to $170,000. The company was also discovering other reasons for fluctuations in its sales charts. Some salesmen performed better than others, and shifting trends in different territories caused ups and downs in market volume. Old established farming communities proved to be steadier and more predictable than those lately settled on the true frontier. The company, however, surmounted all obstacles and moved steadily ahead.[38]

As the frontier pushed westward, the Red River Valley became a flourishing market for the Fuller and Johnson line. Late in 1883, J. T. Odegaard, from his branch office in Fargo, North Dakota, sent a carload order to Madison. "Fill the car as follows," he stipulated to Johnson: "60 Harrows, 5 16-inch Bonanza Breakers, 5 14-inch Bonanza Breakers, 4 12-

[37] Copies of such letters are in the Johnson Papers. The one quoted here, dated October 11, 1897, is in Johnson's original longhand. Copies were sent to all members of the sales force.

[38] Sales made at the Madison office, as well as those at distant outlets, are included in the 1888 total given above. For a breakdown of sales by individual salesmen, see Table 3 in the Appendix, p. 287.

inch Bonanza Breakers, 1 Mower, 1 Bonanza Sulky Rake. Fill car with Casaday Sulkies." [39]

The next spring, Odegaard, after ranging up and down the valley of the Red River, sent in a detailed topographical report – and incidentally another sizable order. Between Wahpeton and Fargo, he wrote, lay high-quality land, well timbered and watered. No better soil for bountiful crops existed anywhere Odegaard had ever traveled. He found particularly choice acreage around Fort Abercrombie, where in early June, 1884, he had sold twenty crossplows, four Bonanza rakes, and four mowers. Hallam Brothers, large-scale farmers in the area, had placed the new order and would pay in cash in the fall. In all the region, the Fargo agent concluded, farmers were prospering – there were few unpaid notes.[40]

In the same month as the Hallam Brothers order, R. K. Kingslee, a dealer in Portland, North Dakota, in a section of the Red River Valley north of Fargo, requested delivery of fifty-five plows. The next winter one of the implements in this shipment produced a follow-up letter to Johnson. A farmer near Mayville, North Dakota, who had bought a Fuller and Johnson plow from Kingslee in the fall of 1884, was well pleased! "It is an excellent plow. It does good work." [41]

Now Johnson was benefiting from his experiences in the 1870's selling Walter A. Wood implements for use on the famous farms of the Red River country. He knew the land and he had valuable contacts with prominent people. He was well acquainted with the Grandin Brothers, bankers from Pennsylvania who had exchanged their depreciated Northern Pacific Railway bonds for large tracts of land in the fruitful valley. In 1877, when he had traveled in Dakota Territory, the Grandins owned 46,000 acres in Traill County about thirty-five miles north of Fargo. In the same year, he had sold Wood implements to the great Dalrymple farm, where ten to twenty gang plows were working over 600 acres a day.[42]

Dalrymple was a synonym for bonanza farming in the Northwest. Such a customer was important. The confidence that Johnson had built up a decade earlier now stood him in good stead. As a prominent manufacturer of farm machinery, he continued to do business with some of the same men he had dealt with a dozen years before. In 1889 Odegaard sent a message to Johnson from his Fargo branch office: "I have seen your old

[39] J. T. Odegaard to John A. Johnson, December 26, 1883.
[40] J. T. Odegaard to John A. Johnson, June 10, 1884.
[41] Andrew A. Skarperud to John A. Johnson, January 12, 1885.
[42] Reynold N. Wik, *Steam Power on American Farms*, 49 (Philadelphia, 1953).

friend Dalrymple. I told him that you were perfecting a new gang plow and that when you thought you had it right you would like to send him one to try." [43]

Fuller and Johnson had signal success in developing their market in the Northwest, first in one region and then in another, moving from Minnesota into the eastern Dakotas. Early company records and correspondence indicate how the foundations were laid. In 1883, the first year in the sales field, Odegaard sent $50,000 to the home office in Madison from Fargo; other Red River Valley agencies remitted $25,000. Considering the low prices for wheat, the North Dakota agent felt that collections had been good. Oliver H. Swerig, at the end of 1885, reported that on his most recent sales trip to western Minnesota and eastern South Dakota he had had encouraging success: "I sold goods for over $7,000. My trip this time has not been bad." [44]

Many letters to the company president revealed the importance of the fact that he was a native of Norway who had shared the common experience of immigrants in the United States. Clannishness still persisted and national origins extended their influence into business relations to the advantage of his firm. In 1885 Odegaard sent Johnson a list of Norwegians in North Dakota, particularly in the area of Colfax and Dwight. The men Odegaard mentioned had all used Fuller and Johnson implements. "All of them think well of your machines," he reported, "and every one of them would be willing to act as a dealer for the company. I suggest that you write each one a personal letter about the matter." [45]

From other areas of the expanding frontier came a stream of inquiries to the Madison office. By this time everyone knew from the immigrant newspapers that Johnson could carry on a correspondence in Norwegian. In Wisconsin and nearby Iowa and in distant western Minnesota and the Dakotas, farmers had been attracted to Fuller and Johnson advertisements in *Skandinaven* (Chicago), *Decorah-Posten* (Iowa), and *Folkebladet* (Minneapolis). In their letters to the president of the company, they referred to particular farm implements that had been advertised. They probed and asked questions. Johnson built up a widening circle of friends for his business by answering in Norwegian. A letter from a farmer in Woodbury County, Iowa, wanted details about a corn planter

[43] J. T. Odegaard to John A. Johnson, October 24, 1889.
[44] Oliver H. Swerig to John A. Johnson, December 18, 1885.
[45] J. T. Odegaard to John A. Johnson, May 30, 1885.

he had read about in *Skandinaven.* Similar letters filtered in from faraway Texas, where Norwegian farmers had heard of the good machines being manufactured in Wisconsin by the Fuller and Johnson people.[46]

"As you are one of our countrymen," a Wisconsin man explained to Johnson, "all the Norwegians in my area prefer to buy from you." The theme was familiar, and in this instance it meant considerable business. The writer had been named purchasing agent for an association of like-minded farmers. Another long-time friend in Goodhue County, Minnesota, dispatched a letter to Johnson asking for a copy of *Fingerpeg,* "as advertised in *Skandinaven.*" He added that he had been using machinery sold by Johnson for twenty years. In 1888 from Medicine Bow, Montana, on the edge of the frontier, came an order for a mower. In a friendly tone, the farmer told of coming to the United States from Norway in 1864. He mentioned Johnson's "fair proposition" regarding the mowing machine, for which he enclosed payment. He had seen the company's advertisement in *Decorah-Posten.* His letter closed on a note pleasing to the manufacturer: "If the machine is satisfactory," he promised, "I will do all I can to open up a trade for you in this vicinity." [47]

Even the distant Pacific coast, now reached by dependable transcontinental railroad lines, revealed interested awareness of the manufacturing reputation of the Fuller and Johnson Company. The president of an implement firm in Portland, Oregon, addressed a message to Johnson in 1884: "We have sold most of your mowers, and the purchasers have found them satisfactory in every respect." Even better news was to come back over the mountains. A carload of Fuller and Johnson implements reached California in 1888 — an event of historic importance. The *San Francisco Examiner* noted its arrival in a story that must have pleased Johnson and his associates: "The first special through train of agricultural implements that has ever crossed the continent arrived here yesterday for the Bull and Grant Implement Company, making the unusual quick time of nine days from Madison, Wisconsin, by way of the Chicago, Milwaukee and St. Paul and the Union and Central Pacific Railroads. This trainload consisting of twelve cars, of Red, White and Blue mowers and Bonanza and Star Sulky hay rakes, is valued at $48,000 and is said to be the largest single purchase and shipment ever made by any one importing house on

[46] Edwin Swenson to John A. Johnson, March 2, 1885; Thor G. Odland to John A. Johnson, April 20, 1885; H. Olsen to John A. Johnson, October 8, 1883.

[47] Martin O. Wrolstad to John A. Johnson, October 8, 1883; Halvor Voxland to John A. Johnson, January 4, 1885; A. G. Hansen to John A. Johnson, July 14, 1885.

the Pacific Coast." The next year the Madison manufacturers shipped three complete trainloads of their farm machinery to California, Oregon, and Washington.[48]

Johnson firmly believed in advertising. In the days before public relations agencies spent millions of dollars for their business clients to sell products and to create a corporate image, he shrewdly developed for his company a soundly conceived and varied program to acquaint potential customers with the virtues of his machinery. He wrote his own copy, created his own slogans, and chose his own media. Even more important, he built public confidence by making direct personal contact with the men who controlled his market and by insisting on a follow-through of high-grade performance for every machine that bore the company's label. The program created its own image.

Fuller and Johnson made wide and continued use of advertising in newspapers and magazines in the Middle West. It distributed catalogues generously and was especially successful in displaying prize-winning implements at fairs, great and small. In modern terms, the company's advertising budget seems very limited. In 1889, Johnson spent approximately $2,800 in the total program. In the panic years that followed, the figure dropped, but in 1898, as recovery from the bad years began, the authorized budget reached to almost $3,400 — and in 1900 $5,000 went into advertising.[49]

Catalogues and newspaper advertisements of the company, in both Norwegian and English, were noted for eye-catching pictures. Detailed descriptions of implements left the reader with a fund of accurate information to turn over in his mind. Slogans and testimonials made up a conspicuous part of many advertisements, but price lists were not hidden in small type. Johnson consistently told the public that he did not presume to have the lowest prices. Instead, high quality and durability were the objectives in every machine he offered for sale. The slogans, couched in the flamboyant language of the time, now seem rather too extravagantly phrased to be convincing, but the testimonials must have won many a

[48] C. P. Frank to John A. Johnson, August 9, 1884. *Farm Implement News* in March, 1888, reprinted the story of the first transcontinental train of agricultural implements from the *San Francisco Examiner*. See also *Farm Implement News*, January, 1889.

[49] Financial statements of Fuller and Johnson Manufacturing Company for the years 1889–1900, in Division of Archives and Manuscripts, State Historical Society of Wisconsin.

buyer. With thousands of unsolicited testimonials to choose from, Johnson wisely selected simple statements, obviously from the heart. One writer praised his Fuller and Johnson mower: "It speaks for itself—just try it." Another owner reported that he had tested his Red, White and Blue mower alongside implements made by other firms. After the trial, he told the company's agent: "Yours is the best. I wouldn't take one of the others even if it were a gift." [50]

The most successful media for the advertisements of Fuller and Johnson were two Chicago publications: the newspaper *Skandinaven* and *Farm Implement News*, a leading trade journal. Johnson continued his earlier personal connection with *Skandinaven*, now enjoying a wide circulation among Norwegian immigrant readers. With an eye to its extensive readership at a distance from his immediate area, he frequently used it for full-page "ads" of his machinery line. In *Farm Implement News*, he inserted advertising each month until November, 1891. At this time the magazine became a weekly, and Johnson changed to a more frequent schedule of notices in each issue. He realized that his firm was getting excellent results for its advertising dollar in this particular medium.

Each message in the trade magazine spoke of pamphlets and price lists. At corn-planting time in 1891, a typical advertisement presented Starks Force-Drop Planter, the Tip Top Tongueless Cultivator, and the Winner Cultivator, in a half page of bold type. In June of the same year, the factory offered a great saving of freight for carload lots. "Write for illustrated circulars of the best line of implements in the world," another ad trumpeted. Better times loomed in late 1898, and in its Christmas number for that year, the trade journal used color for a full-page display pushing the Force-Drop Planter and the Balance Hammock Seat Cultivator. That Johnson was aware of the pulling power of his messages in the farm magazine is evidenced by a letter to its editor in 1892: "We regard the *Farm Implement News* as the very best implement trade journal published." [51]

In the spring of 1898, Fuller and Johnson issued two handsomely printed brochures presenting a full line of their implements. One, as before, described machinery for farm use: walking plows, sulky and gang plows, harrows, cultivators, corn planters, disk harrows, hay rakes, mowers, and a variety of smaller implements. The other publication was some-

[50] Testimonials of Knud Hendersen of Cambridge, Wisconsin, and Seth Bartlett of Madison, in *Fuller and Johnson Katalog*, 21, 22 (Madison, 1884).

[51] *Farm Implement News*, March, April, June, 1891, December 1, 1892.

thing of a departure. It was devoted to surreys, phaetons, buggies, carts, road wagons, farm wagons, and freight wagons. Fuller and Johnson did not manufacture these vehicles; instead, they were jobbers representing the Mandt Wagon Company of Stoughton, Wisconsin, of which Johnson at the time was vice-president.[52]

Exhibits at state and county fairs spread the news that Fuller and Johnson in Madison, Wisconsin, were manufacturing a first-class line of farm machinery. In every region in the Middle West where wheat and corn were staple crops, the company found strategic advantage in showing its wares. In 1891 it exhibited implements at the Minnesota state fair in St. Paul and at similar fairs in Peoria, Illinois, and Lincoln, Nebraska. Four years later, Johnson sent F. D. Waugh, R. R. Waugh, and W. L. Jordan to supervise a display at the Illinois state fair. These men were salesmen of long experience with the firm. From the home office the same year, H. G. Grinder and A. S. Brown managed a showing of the entire Fuller and Johnson line at the Wisconsin state fair in Milwaukee. Here the corn harvester was the focal point of interest. The company, as a Wisconsin institution, took pains to demonstrate the completeness of its line at Milwaukee. Potential customers could examine heavy grub-breaker plows for work in the clearings of the state's wooded northwestern area — as well as steel- and wood-beam walking plows, riding and walking cultivators, disk and spike-tooth lever harrows, and hay rakes.[53]

In the fall of 1900, Nils O. Starks and Charles H. Allyn headed a group of branch managers and salesmen in charge of a Fuller and Johnson display at the Nebraska state fair in Lincoln. Here they exhibited not only their usual variety of plows and harrows but also their grain seeder and the Mandt line of farm wagons and carriages. To the Iowa state fair at Des Moines the same year the firm sent Vice-president Samuel Higham, Charles Allyn, Nils O. Starks, and W. R. Bagley, the company attorney, as leaders of a delegation of approximately a dozen field representatives. To complete the 1900 circuit of the three most important state fairs — in pivotal wheat and corn states where machinery markets were excellent — Johnson selected another group of his best men to supervise the display at the Illinois state fair in Springfield.[54]

Overshadowing all other fairs, however, was the Columbian Exposi-

[52] *Farm Implement News*, April 18, 1898.

[53] *Farm Implement News*, September, 1891.

[54] *Farm Implement News*, August 2, 30, 1900. Fuller and Johnson men at the Nebraska fair included E. S. Clary, G. W. Gibson, Frank Sigafoos, and J. H. Siga-

tion, the world's fair held in Chicago in 1893 – an event of prime importance in the history of the American agricultural implement industry. Trade journals announced in advance that Fuller and Johnson Company, as a leading manufacturer, would have an exhibit at the world's fair. The challenge moved Johnson to prepare an outstanding display of his machinery – one which would be remembered as a symbol of the excellence of his implements and of the success of his business enterprise.[55]

The firm's exhibit at the Columbian Exposition was managed by H. G. Grinder, a company executive. Headlines declared it to be "A Handsome Show," and writers of newspaper reports referred to "an excellent exhibit." Apparently President John A. Johnson felt that this was the place for a little modest elegance in the spirit of the time. An Axminster carpet covered the display platform, which was enclosed by a brass railing. One striking implement was the Bemis Tobacco Planter, finished in polished cherry wood and nickel plate. The famous Starks Force-Drop Corn Planter and Check-Rower stood like a knight of old in a glistening coat of nickel plate, its steel frame revealing its strength and durability. Two famous Fuller and Johnson plows – the Young American Sulky and the appropriately named Columbian Gang Plow – were also dressed in polished nickel. A Sater Stubble Plow had a beautifully carved walnut beam, and the two-horse Winner Steel Beam Cultivator was elegant in black walnut and nickel finish.[56]

The background was resplendent with banners of velvet lettered in gold. Johnson had seen to it that all of his company's latest patented innovations were prominently labeled so that no distinctive feature would be missed. The display, as it turned out, was a popular one. The *Farm Implement News* was especially complimentary. "The policy of this company," the trade journal editorialized, "is and has been to be on the market in advance of others with new and useful improvements by which its agents are enabled to take front selling places always. It is an old and reliable concern with ample means, a first-class plant, and experienced management. They make goods for which a demand is certain, and in such a manner as to increase the demand." [57]

foos. At the Iowa fair, among others representing the company, were E. H. Decker, who had charge of the display, E. S. Clary, and J. W. Monroe.

[55] *Farm Implement News*, July 14, 1892, February 16, 1893.

[56] *Farm Implement News*, July 20, 1893. Hans Sater, a master plowmaker in the Fuller and Johnson shops, gave his name to a well-known stubble plow.

[57] *Farm Implement News*, July 20, 1893.

Johnson's extra efforts to stage an outstanding exhibit at the Chicago fair were rewarded. Firms showing products had to submit full drawings, specifications, and details to the judges in the classes entered. A written statement citing specific points of excellence and significant new ideas accompanied each award. In the sharp competition in all classes of farm implements, the Fuller and Johnson Company won two major and two minor citations. Its Columbian Gang Plow and Young American Sulky each earned the highest medal in its division, and the published prize lists also included the Starks and Bemis planters.[58]

Foreign exhibitors of farm machinery were honored guests at the Columbian Exposition. This courtesy followed naturally the excellent reception American manufacturers had been accorded at the Paris Exposition in 1878. At that international fair, fifteen years earlier, such implements from the United States as the John Deere plow, the Walter A. Wood mower, and Cyrus McCormick's reaper-binder had taken top prizes. Even earlier, Wood and McCormick products had won acclaim for Yankee ingenuity at the International Exhibition in London in 1862 and at the Paris Exposition in 1867. Now at Chicago in 1893, the displays of foreign exhibitors were a source of interest and pride to the managers of the first great American fair.[59]

A banquet was tendered to guests from other countries by prominent members of the American agricultural implement industry. In the planning of this event, the Fuller and Johnson Manufacturing Company was represented by H. G. Grinder of the Madison office. The gathering was a distinguished one. William I. Buchanan, chief of the agricultural department of the world's fair, as master of ceremonies, welcomed the representatives of several countries widely scattered over the world: Great Britain, France, Russia, Sweden, Italy, Canada, Argentina, Chile, Colombia, Algeria, the Orange Free State, Turkey, and the Malay Peninsula.[60]

In spite of tremendous development in both industry and agriculture between the Civil War and the end of the century, the United States expe-

[58] *Farm Implement News,* July 20, October 26, November 2, 1893. In the issue of July 20, 1893, this journal printed a picture of the Fuller and Johnson display at the Columbian Exposition. A copy is in the McCormick Collection, State Historical Society of Wisconsin.

[59] Dwight W. Morrow, Jr., "The Impact of American Agricultural Machinery on France, 1851–1914," a dissertation presented in partial fulfillment of the requirements for the degree of doctor of philosophy, Harvard University, 1957.

[60] *Farm Implement News,* July 20, 1893.

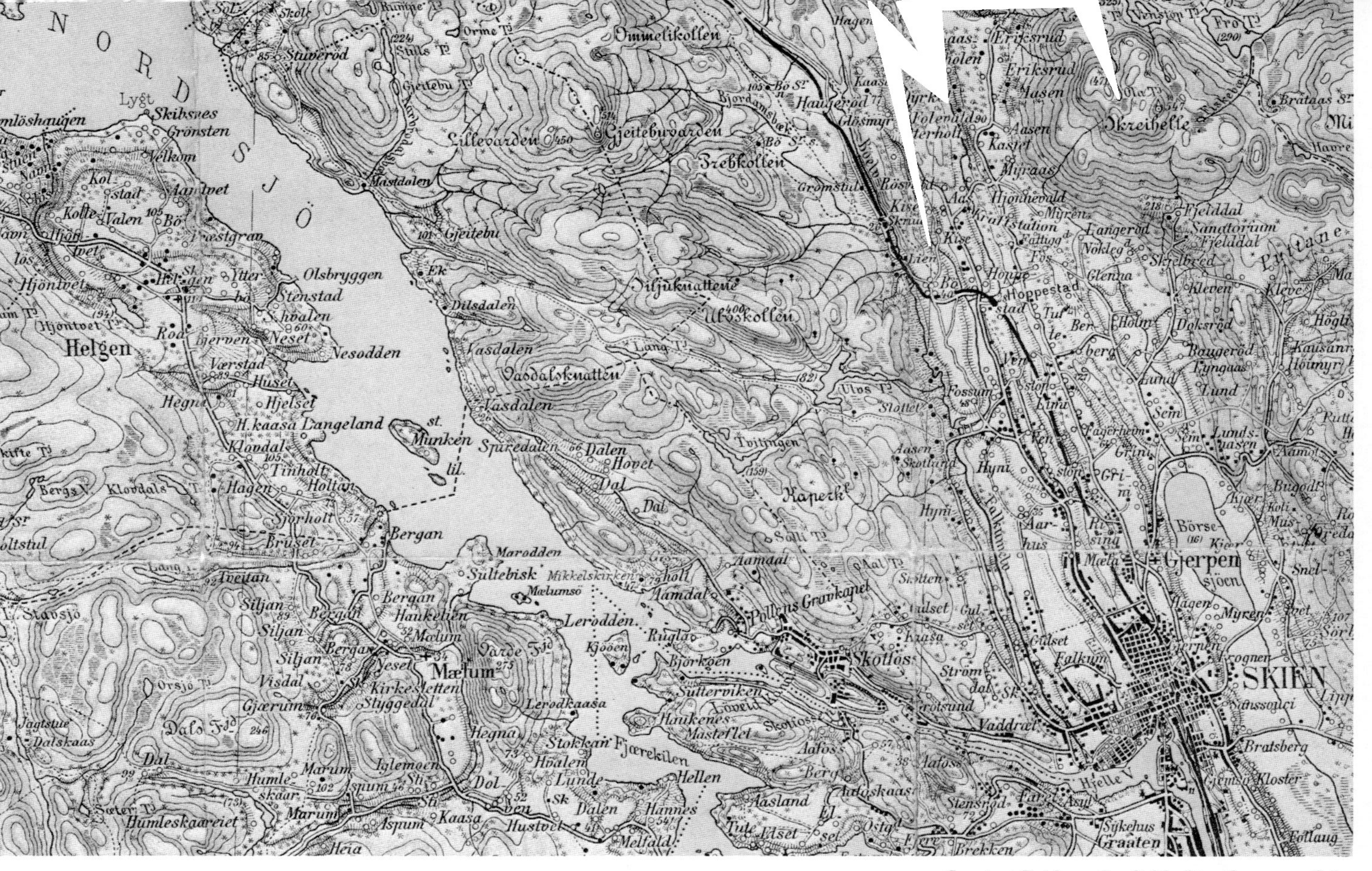

Courtesy Brødrene Sundt Machine Company, Oslo

John A. Johnson's Boyhood Environs

The Gisholt Farm, Norway, in Recent Times

Courtesy Clarence B. Hagen

The Heart Prairie Church, Near Whitewater

Colonel Ole C. Johnson

FULLER & JOHNSON,
MADISON, WISCONSIN. Oct 30 1884

DICTATED TO STENOGRAPHER.

Ole K. Hauge Esq
Pennington, Minnehaha Co Dak

Dear Sir.

Your favor of 11th has not been answered earlier on account of absence. Your model is here. It is certain it will do what you claim, unless it should ~~no~~ work hard when the horses are drawing. I was at Sioux Falls this week and intend ~~to~~ be there again on Thursday next week, and I would like to have you meet me there and then have one of the attachments with you so I can see a full sized one. I suppose you have had yours made of wrought iron. Of course they will be cheaper of malleable iron.

The drawback is of course the cost and the weight. There will be a few pounds more for the horses to haul. But I would give it a good fair trial, and if the farmers want it then I would push it strongly.

I do not know how often you have mail but trust that you will get this in ample time so as to meet me.

I shall stop at the Cataract House in Sioux Falls.

Yours truly
J. A. Johnson

Courtesy Norwegian-American Historical Association

A Typical Johnson Business Letter

Casaday
SULKY PLOW.

Denne Sulky Ploug har vundet Anerkjendelse for at være bedre end nogen anden Sort.

Udførlig Beskrivelse vil blive sendt paa Forlangende.

From John A. Johnson's Fingerpeg

A Successful Fuller and Johnson Plow

A Fuller and Johnson Riding Cultivator

George E. Gernon with 1889 Model Turret Lathe

Hobart and Carl Learning the Business

The Long-Time Johnson Residence in Madison

Kaia Johnson

Ida Johnson Fisk

The Fuller and Johnson Company Buildings Today

George H. Johnson

The Gisholt Library Auditorium

Foreground: The Gisholt Machine Company Plant in Present-Day Madison

rienced periods of deep financial insecurity. Deflation had followed the war, and the panic of 1873 put severe pressure on both farmers and manufacturers. Canada, Argentina, Russia, and Australia were developing as great wheat-growing areas, their output adversely affecting the world market at a time when American farmers were themselves indulging in overproduction. Natural disasters — infestations of grasshoppers, frost, and drought — also took their toll. And, as a corollary, when the farmer's income fell off, the manufacturer of farm machinery soon felt the pinch of hard times. He had to have capital or dependable credit to carry his customers and his own business until the economic pressure eased.

From 1890 to 1895 the financial situation was particularly precarious in the Middle West. A drought lasting several years had struck the wheat areas of a number of states. Untimely frosts had ruined crops in other sections. Farmers were heavily in debt for buildings, horses, and machinery — and interest rates on chattel mortgages ranged from 10 to 12 per cent. The market for new farm machinery dropped to almost nothing in the regions hardest hit. In the states that escaped the dry years, wheat prices sank so low that a farmer with a reasonably good crop found himself almost as badly off as his counterpart whose fields had been parched by continued drought. In the middle of this five-year period, the country was convulsed by the panic of 1893.

Correspondence that crossed Johnson's desk between 1885 and 1897 clearly reveals the problem he had to face. "Collections are hard this fall," reported P. L. Norman in 1885 from Montevideo, Minnesota, where he was a dealer. He went on to say that many farms were mortgaged and that their owners had no money — and he pointedly asked Johnson whether he thought it best to grant extensions of time in preference to suing debtors. Three years later, J. T. Odegaard, then an officer of the Griggs County Bank, Cooperstown, Dakota Territory, addressed an almost despairing letter to the Madison office: "Our community was seriously hurt by frost. I thought you should be advised of this as it will no doubt affect your collection very materially and you will no doubt take it into consideration in the shipping of goods." Another communication referring to the same area revealed the disheartening news that a carload order had been countermanded at Grafton because "the wheat was badly damaged . . . the main money producing crop." [61]

[61] P. L. Norman to John A. Johnson, December 5, 1885; J. T. Odegaard to John A. Johnson, August 24, 1888; T. C. Mandt to John A. Johnson, August 27, 1888.

Crop failures were repeated in 1890 and 1891, and purchasers of machinery could not pay their debts. From a South Dakota farmer came this plea: "I went to Watertown yesterday and payed $55.00 on my note. My crop this year was so light that it is hard for me to live through the winter. My wheat only went five bushels to the acre. Now will you be kind enough to carry me till next fall on the balance of my note. It would help me very much." A collector for Fuller and Johnson in North Dakota sent word that a certain client could not pay even a note for $25. His entire wheat crop was only fifty bushels; there was a question how he was to provide food for his family. Again a familiar question was raised by the company's agent: Would Johnson take another note on this man's crop for the next summer? [62]

Johnson's company fared well until the panic of the 1890's was well under way, in spite of the earlier crop failures and the resulting loss of income from once-prosperous areas. Profits were good until 1890. Then came the first serious drop. Profits of that year declined $36,000 from the previous year and a worrisome $47,000 from the totals of 1887. Not one to be easily discouraged, Johnson nevertheless wrote to his partner, M. E. Fuller, late in the summer of 1890, the bad year: "We have absolutely made no money this year, hardly held our own." [63]

This was a time of great stress for the Fuller and Johnson Company. In his letters of the late summer of 1890, Johnson noted both gains and losses. New and improved plows, promising well for future sales, were in production, but new plant equipment—furnaces and dies—had caused heavy expense. The tobacco transplanter had held its own, but all materials used in the manufacture of implements had gone up in cost. Unfortunately, the prices of farm machinery generally had gone down. For the first time there was a suggestion that Johnson was considering retrenchment. On one occasion he indicated that he favored working off the agricultural stock gradually and utilizing the shops for making tools. He added, however, as if to reassure himself: "Our goods and their reputation are in better shape than ever before by a good deal."

Yet, admittedly, the over-all financial situation was serious, and other officers—including Vice-president Samuel Higham and M. E. Fuller, an original partner—were deeply concerned. In a letter to Fuller, Johnson

[62] J. N. Long to John A. Johnson, November 14, 1890; John R. Aaness to John A. Johnson, February 19, 1891.

[63] John A. Johnson to M. E. Fuller, October 18, 1890.

went so far as to discuss the need to raise $200,000 for additions to the capital stock if they were to remain in Madison. At this particular juncture, the president seemed to feel that he and his associates had undertaken too much for their available capital.[64]

If they were to remain in Madison! The depth of the pressures Johnson faced can be measured by the fact that he would even consider the possibility that some other city might offer superior advantages. He had always been intensely loyal to Madison; it was his home and the company's home, and he would make no quick decision. He had had, however, a letter from C. C. Rogers, secretary-manager of the Association for the Advancement of Milwaukee, which said: "If you are interested in moving your factory to Milwaukee, we can find a very desirable location for you. Please advise in detail if you are interested." [65]

A few weeks after receiving Rogers' letter, Johnson wrote to M. E. Fuller: "If we go to Milwaukee it is on the strength of the Fuller and Johnson Company. . . . If we go to Milwaukee both companies will go. [But] all the Milwaukee capital will go to the Fuller and Johnson Company." In a later letter to Fuller, he revealed that a representative from Milwaukee had been in Madison to discuss with him the matter of moving the firm. It is clear that the Milwaukee association was offering strong inducements to influence an important new business to relocate in its city.[66]

Word that Johnson and Fuller might leave Madison seems to have been rather widely circulated. A responsible firm in New York urged Johnson to locate his business near Knoxville, Tennessee, where coal and iron were close at hand. And soon a letter came from the East Tennessee Land Company, Harriman, Tennessee, containing an intriguing proposal: "The matter of your removal to Harriman will be considered by our Board on Tuesday next at New York City, and you can expect to hear from us at once with something definite. Meantime we trust that you will not close with any other town until after our Board meeting." [67]

Whatever the inducements to move, the company decided to remain in

[64] John A. Johnson to M. E. Fuller, September 22, 1890.

[65] C. C. Rogers to John A. Johnson, August 8, 1890. There is nothing in the Johnson Papers to indicate that Johnson had previously made contact with Rogers in any way.

[66] John A. Johnson to M. E. Fuller, September 22, October 18, 1890. The reference to both companies implies the Fuller and Johnson Manufacturing Company and the Gisholt Machine Company. Johnson was president of both.

[67] J. D. Wolstenhowe to John A. Johnson, September 27, 1890.

Madison – probably mainly through Johnson's personal influence. He had always been sensitive to the advantages of the Wisconsin capital. Of first importance were the practical factors. Though it lacked the favorable situation of a port on Lake Michigan, the city was an excellent distributing point, with important railroad connections. Of nine roads entering Madison, the Illinois Central, the Chicago and North Western, and the Chicago, Milwaukee and St. Paul had extended their lines into the distant agricultural areas of the West. These railway systems had ample yard facilities for handling large orders of farm machinery. And they possessed the huge flatcars and boxcars needed to transport heavy implements across the great rivers, over the sweeping prairies – even over the distant mountains to the Pacific coast. Madison pointed westward and so did Johnson's business enterprise. No other city could serve him better.[68]

Equally compelling were the social and cultural factors. Johnson recognized that Madison was a good city in which to live – a community where people could own their own homes and live in comfort without economic strain. He relished the atmosphere of concern for the people of the state that centered about the capitol and its lawmakers. Situated among a chain of lakes, the town had an attractive setting. Its cultural advantages stemmed naturally from the University of Wisconsin, which Johnson supported generously and where he sent his five children. The atmosphere of a university town appealed to the scholarly side of Johnson's nature – as it had since the day he had passed through the city as a boy forty-five years earlier. It is not surprising that late in life he was loath to break the ties binding him to the home town to which he felt himself so well suited.

In making his decision to stay in Madison, the president of Fuller and Johnson must have considered the excellent employee relations he had always had with the men who worked for him. The year the company produced its first farm implements, fifty men in the shops had done the manufacturing. As the organization grew, workers were steadily added, until at the end of the century four hundred men were making machines and tools in the Madison factory complex. Employees were recruited locally – from Madison, from nearby towns, and from the countryside. Many tilled their farms in the summer and "made plows" in the winter. They were a steady, dependable crew, some of whom worked for John A. Johnson and his sons for over fifty years. In the days when a hundred-pound sack of oat-

[68] *Farm Implement News,* June 21, 1894.

meal cost $1.25, Johnson's men earned that wage for a ten-hour day. Working six days a week, the Fuller and Johnson labor force were happy with their economic lot. There were no strikes.

This was a time when there were few vocational schools. To fill their place, the Johnson and Fuller factory became a training ground where a man might earn a living and at the same time learn a trade. Johnson, remembering his own youth, encouraged boys in their teens to prepare themselves for useful work in industry by serving as apprentices in his plant. Coming as raw recruits, they wore a distinguishing kind of cap and sat on a bench waiting for a bell to ring to call them to action. The youngest workers began by running errands – jumping up to make a trip to the "tool crib" to get a needed hammer or wrench for a skilled worker. Their beginning pay was no more than fifty cents a day.

These were the days before aptitude tests, but *aptitude* and *opportunity* were the key words. As a bright and willing apprentice matured and proved himself, he was assigned to some special mechanical task for which he seemed to have the requisite abilities. He might have shown interest or demonstrated skill in tool designing, pattern making, or foundry work. Or he might have the qualities of a salesman. His future lay with him and with the way he developed: If he made a noticeable success of his early opportunities, the company had a permanent place for him somewhere in its organization.

Johnson had the good will of his workmen. As he moved through the shop, he carried a walking stick fitted with a crosspiece on which he sat when he stopped to talk. Often during the lunch hour also, he visited with the men, not limiting his conversation merely to "shop talk." His interests ranged widely, and his discussions with the workers might turn to politics, the tariff, foreign trade, the Boer War, or the acquisition of the Philippines. He found some of the men interested in these subjects and ready to draw upon his facts and opinions for ideas of their own. It was one of his ways of earning the friendship and respect of the artisans who made his machines.

On more than one occasion, Johnson merged his humanitarian interest with his business. Some of the apprentices who got their training in his plant came from the Homme Orphans Home in Wittenberg, Wisconsin. He had supported the institution, which had been started in 1882 by the Reverend E. J. Homme, a Lutheran clergyman. The first boy from the home to become old enough for self-supporting employment was Soren

Olson. On March 26, 1891, Soren came to Madison as an apprentice under Johnson's sponsorship. Later others from the home also profited from the same opportunity to earn their livelihood and prepare for a vocation.

Beyond question, the company's most famous apprentice was Ole Evinrude, "the world genius of the outboard motor." Like Johnson, Ole had come from Norway as a small child and had grown up on a Dane County farm. Endowed with unusual manual skills and a keen, imaginative mind, he had given up farming to try to make his way in the world as a machinist. In the early 1890's, at the age of sixteen, he had walked twenty miles to Madison to become an apprentice in the Fuller and Johnson factory. At the time, he had had barely three years of schooling, but the steel lathes in the shop delighted him. Everything in the factory kindled his interest in technical education, and he fell to studying books on algebra, calculus, trigonometry, and engineering. When he left the company, Ole was considered a crack mechanic. Always interested in boats and motors, he pioneered in putting the two together in the perfection of the outboard motor. In 1909 he began to produce his outboard motor in a Milwaukee shop. The small Evinrude Motor Company later developed into the Outboard Motors Company and ultimately into the Outboard Marine and Manufacturing Company — today the largest concern in the boating industry. Looking back in later years, Ole Evinrude must have been grateful for the opportunity he had enjoyed on the apprentice bench in John A. Johnson's factory. It had been just the place for him.[69]

Throughout the history of the company, Fuller and Johnson stockholders gave evidence of their confidence in the leadership of the organization. This meant that they explicitly trusted John A. Johnson's guidance. Year after year they unanimously elected him their chief executive; there was never another nominee. A number of times they willingly voted to pass dividends in order — on the president's advice — to "plow back" profits into the treasury. In 1891, when the financial condition of the firm was a topic of serious discussion, the loyalty of the rank and file was severely tested as the result of Johnson's decision that the company should issue bonds sufficient to take up the floating indebtedness. His strong recommendation to take this step came at the annual meeting on January 19 of

[69] Gordon MacQuarrie, *Ole Evinrude and the Old Fellows* (Milwaukee, 1947, by Gordon MacQuarrie); Kenneth O. Bjork, "Ole Evinrude and the Outboard Motor," in *Norwegian-American Studies and Records*, 12: 167–177 (Northfield, Minnesota, 1941).

that year. He was the largest stockholder; moreover, the Fuller and Johnson Manufacturing Company had obligated itself to him for a personal loan of $70,000. Though he thus had much to lose if a mistake were to be made, he argued that the firm was in no position to pay its debt without reducing the value of the stock and damaging its over-all financial position. For that reason, he advocated that bonds in the amount of $200,000 be issued.[70]

On the motion of B. J. Stevens, the resolution embodying the president's proposal was unanimously adopted by the stockholders. They voted to empower the directors to issue 400 coupon bonds of $500 each, bearing 7 per cent interest and payable within ten years. An added provision allowed the company the right to redeem them at par after five years. The bonds were to be secured by a mortgage against all the company's property, rights, and interests, the trustees to be William F. Vilas, lawyer, and Wayne Ramsay, banker, prominent residents of Madison. At the same meeting, it was suggested that the treasurer be authorized to set aside each year net profits to the extent of 4 per cent of the capital stock to create a sinking fund for the redemption of the bonds. The directors met immediately after adjournment of the stockholders' meeting to implement the resolution just adopted. The trust deed was prepared and drawn between the Fuller and Johnson Manufacturing Company and the trustees. The document was signed by John A. Johnson, as president, and Walter C. Noe, as secretary, and also by Vilas and Ramsay. Members of the directors' executive committee – Vice-president Samuel Higham, Treasurer Edward M. Fuller, and Robert M. Bashford – also affixed their signatures to the document.[71]

Work in the Fuller and Johnson shops did not stop during the panic years. In spite of declining sales, new implements were perfected. In the bad year of 1891, the Columbian gang plow and the Young American sulky plow reached the market, together with a new disk frame harrow. At the same time, Johnson and T. C. Mandt of Stoughton, Wisconsin, patented a vehicle axle. Nils O. Starks and Johnson, a little over two years later, were granted a patent on a corn harvester. By 1896, through Johnson's connection with the Mandt Wagon Company, the Madison firm announced that it could supply a whole line of vehicles – including a low-

[70] For an excerpt from the minutes of the meeting of January 19, 1891, explaining Johnson's proposal in detail, see the Appendix, p. 288–289.

[71] "Record of the Secretary of the Fuller and Johnson Manufacturing Company."

priced road wagon and a steel-gear wagon with Savern wheels designed especially for heavy farm use. It was not Johnson's philosophy to give up hope and slow down; instead he kept his machinists busy in the shops in expectation that an economic upturn was sure to come. More and more patents followed: In the years 1889 through 1899, the government granted thirty-two patents for inventions by Johnson and his employees.[72]

The work had gone on in the face of continued discouragements in the market. Crops in 1891 were good and hopes were high for 1892. The company's sales in that fiscal year did creep above those of the previous twelve months, but farmers in large numbers were asking for extensions on the payment of their bills. On August 31, 1892, Fuller and Johnson reported something over $500,000 in accounts receivable. The next year the Columbian Exposition gave the firm a great psychological lift and some minor improvement in business, but 1894 began as another slow year—promising decline rather than advance. There was only the wishful thought that *if* the crops were good and *if* the tariff question could be fairly settled, then there should be a gradual swing upward.[73]

Official figures proved the hope a vain one, for the company's gross sales for 1894 fell off to about $320,000, the lowest in all the panic years. In February, 1895, news from Madison indicated unusual activity in manufacturing; it was hinted that there might even be a shortage of finished farm implements. Once more the optimistic forecast was proved unjustified by events: the summer again brought drought to parts of the stricken West. The end of the year found prices for farm products at a low ebb. Wheat was selling at 63.3 cents a bushel, a ruinous decline from the price of $1.04 a bushel twenty-five years earlier. Collections were almost at a standstill, and the number of business failures was larger than in 1894. The name of Fuller and Johnson, however, was not in the list of failures. It was by no means a happy year for the company's leaders, but they had stayed above board and—although their notes and accounts receivable were the largest in the firm's experience—they had not lost their faith in the future.[74]

[72] United States Patent Office, *Official Gazette*, October 6, 1891, March 13, 1894; *Farm Implement News*, March 29, June 7, 1894, March 5, 1896.

[73] "Record of the Secretary of the Fuller and Johnson Manufacturing Company"; *Farm Implement News*, April 19, 1894.

[74] *Farm Implement News*, February 28, 1895; John D. Hicks, *The Populist Revolt: A History of the Farmers' Alliance and the People's Party*, 56 (Minneapolis, 1931). For a detailed statement of the financial condition of the Fuller and Johnson Manufacturing Company in 1895, see Table 4 in the Appendix, p. 287–288.

Fortunately 1896 brought the long awaited upturn, and Fuller and Johnson announced the good news that their factory was "running full force and full time with marked improvements in business prospects." Orders were accumulating and plant capacity was larger than ever before. The next year *Bradstreet's Commercial Reports* listed the firm as worth between $500,000 and $1,000,000 and gave it an "A" rating. Johnson wrote to his salesmen in his old optimistic vein on October 11, 1897: "We may fairly hope for a reasonably prosperous year. . . . Trade for 1898 will double that of 1897." The trend continued. On August 31, 1899, at the end of the fiscal year, company officers reported to the trustees of the bondholders that gross sales were substantially over the million dollar mark. The depression years were over, and the beginning of better days was already at hand.[75]

Over the years the physical plant of the Fuller and Johnson Manufacturing Company had a steady growth. In its first year of actual production, a new high-pressure steam engine, built especially for the factory, was set in place. For its time, this was a giant installation capable of delivering up to 200 horsepower. At first it served to propel the extensive machinery of all the company's shops. But in 1884 — to meet the demands of the growing business — a 225-horsepower gasoline engine was added to the plant's facilities. By this time the shops had been extended in size; one had a line shaft 160 feet long, with machines powered by a single-cylinder engine. A warehouse 50 feet by 300 feet was built. Even in the depressed period of 1892, the company enlarged its factory by adding floor space measuring 50 feet by 230 feet, thus increasing plant capacity by approximately one third.[76]

The turn of the century found the Madison factory one of the best equipped and most modern for the manufacture of agricultural implements. Its plant in 1898 had a floor space area of well over 200,000 square feet. The complex of shops, yards, and grounds covered about fifteen acres and included sidetracks and platforms extensive enough to permit loading fifteen freight cars at once. These served the three main railroad lines used by Johnson's firm for shipments to dealers in their western territory. The official business address of the company was 1400 East Washington Avenue, a location at the corner of East Washington Avenue and North Dickinson Street. As the plant grew in size, it even-

[75] *Farm Implement News,* March 5, 1896.

[76] *Madison Daily Democrat,* November 7, 1882, April 18, 1883; *Farm Implement News and Country Hardware Trade,* January 28, 1884, January 19, 1893.

tually reached the corner of Dickinson and Dayton, a block behind East Washington. The front entrance continued to be on Washington, but the rear of the enlarged area faced Dayton Street.[77]

In his fifties and sixties, John A. Johnson became a leader in the organization and development of a number of trade associations of manufacturers in the farm implement industry. He found these contacts interesting and valuable to him in planning his own business. His first connection of this kind stemmed from attendance as an active member of the Northern Plow and Cultivator Association at annual meetings held in Chicago in 1884, 1885, and 1886. On the agenda at these conventions, topics for discussion included raw materials, prices, and the possible limitation in the production of plows.[78]

Johnson and his son, Carl A. Johnson, soon to be twenty-three years old, were instrumental in organizing the Madison Implement and Vehicle Association in March, 1893. The president of the Fuller and Johnson Manufacturing Company — "one of the oldest machine men in the Northwest" — was a natural choice as speaker at the meeting launching the organization. The following year, on March 7, 1894, one hundred fifty persons attended a banquet of the new local association of implement manufacturers. John A. Johnson gave the principal address, in which he advised his audience to save money for a rainy day even if it involved a great effort. In addition to thrift, he stressed integrity as an essential factor in the machine business. "Always stick strictly to the truth," he said. "Be the farmer's counselor and do not sell him an implement he does not need." He urged young men wishing to enter the farm implement field to serve an apprenticeship under a good dealer in order to learn the whole machinery business before striking out for themselves.[79]

By far the most significant of Johnson's relations with the trade associations began in February, 1894, with his participation in the founding of the National Association of Agricultural Implement and Vehicle Manufacturers of the United States of America. The next October, at the first annual meeting of the Association in Chicago, Johnson gave an address

[77] *Farm Implement News,* March 17, 1898.

[78] *Farm Implement News,* January, 1886, August 18, 1892. Representatives of Fuller and Johnson also attended the meeting of the Northwestern Plow and Cultivator Association at the Grand Pacific Hotel in Chicago in 1892.

[79] *Farm Implement News,* March 23, 1893, March 15, 1894. At the time of the 1893 meeting, Carl A. Johnson was in business with his father.

on "Credit." In developing his theme, the president of Fuller and Johnson drew upon his company's experience in this field. "Upon a firm and rational basis, credit means prosperity, thrift, and advancement," he said. "It is a part of our responsibility to enhance its usefulness in all honorable business ventures." He believed that short-term credit—because it resulted in fewer losses—was better than long-term. Referring to his personal involvement in credit problems, he added with wry humor: "During the drastic grasshopper plagues, we made no effort to collect. We let matters rest and when the situation had improved and farmers were in a position to pay, we suffered no serious losses on our 'grasshopper accounts.'" He left one further thought with his hearers. If salesmen and their supervisors were carefully trained to inspire confidence, few mistakes in judging a customer's willingness and ability to pay his just debts need be made.[80]

In the same address, Johnson suggested that careful thought be given to a new bankruptcy law. He believed that a debtor should be released from his debt upon honestly surrendering his assets. Then he could begin again, to become in time a solvent consumer of the agricultural implements needed to build himself up as a successful producer. Johnson urged the establishment of conciliation courts to deal with unavoidable debt. As things stood, farm implement men, manufacturers, and dealers preferred losing money rather than risking the high costs of court action. At this Association meeting, Johnson, always well informed on national issues, took an active part in discussions of the tariff and other political issues. Backing up his convictions, he contributed to a special fund designed to bring the position of the farm implement group to the early attention of congress.[81]

As a member of the Association's executive committee, Johnson was named in 1896 to represent his organization in a delegation of the all-embracing National Association of Manufacturers created to visit South America in the interests of international trade. The next year, he was further honored by being elected to the presidency of the farm implement association.

[80] During the months just preceding the 1894 annual meeting, Johnson had served as a member of the Association's committee on credit.

[81] *Farm Implement News*, October 18, 1894; National Association of Agricultural Implement and Vehicle Manufacturers, *Official Report*, October 10–12, 1894. This report is in the Baker Library, Harvard University. Following the business meeting, 200 members of the Association attended a banquet at which John A. Johnson was one of several responding with toasts.

The officers of this association — president, vice-president, treasurer, and secretary — were nominated by a special committee elected by vote of the representatives at the annual meeting. All officers served a one-year term. Each company paid an annual membership fee based on its capital; the range ran from $10 for a firm having stock not exceeding $200,000 to $20 for a corporation whose capital was more than $1,000,-000. The objectives of the organization, as outlined in its constitution, were stated as follows: "[To take] suitable and timely notice of, and act upon, matters of legislation, national and state, matters of educational interest pertaining to agriculture, matters concerning freight and transportation, and all those matters attention to which, and action upon which, will protect or promote the interest of the members, and to foster and promote the interests of American agriculture and agriculturalists." [82]

It was a propitious time for the well-known president of Fuller and Johnson to head his national trade association. The panic was slipping into the past; the future was promising. In his formal call to the members for the fourth annual meeting in Detroit, on October 5-7, 1897, Johnson did not need to restrain his optimism. "We are on the threshold of a great expansion of our industries," he wrote to his colleagues. "We must realize that this Association can do much to encourage and promote the prosperity that seems to be at hand." He went on to affirm his belief that Americans were destined to become the greatest manufacturing people in history. To clinch his point, he cited the immense natural resources, particularly minerals, which the United States possessed, and the potential foreign markets opening for the country's manufactured products. "Come to Detroit with your advice and encouragement," he urged. "Our Association must not lag in its onward march." [83]

As president, John A. Johnson gave the opening address at the Hotel Cadillac, Detroit, on October 5. Sixty-five years old at the time — with a rich personal and business experience and a lifetime of thought and study behind him — he made this public statement one of the most eloquent and

[82] The constitution and by-laws of the Association were adopted on October 11, 1894. Copies of these documents are in the Johnson Papers.

[83] The *Farm Implement News* of September 30, 1897, published the call of the Association president to the meeting. Johnson knew that labor costs in America were higher than in Europe, but — like Henry Ford not many years later — he reasoned that high wages for laborers would be a great boon to the over-all economy of the nation.

significant of his career. What he said to the convention delegates was widely reported and quoted. The *Farm Implement News* devoted four pages to publishing the complete address.[84]

In the main part of his address, Johnson turned to a number of problems of interest to American manufacturers in general and pointedly to those in the farm machinery business. He advocated improving foreign trade by correcting a current deficiency in American ocean shipping. The United States, he said, paid at least $200,000,000 per year for ocean carriage of our exports and imports; of this huge traffic, only 10 per cent went to American shipowners. In earlier days, our vessels carried nearly 90 per cent of such business. He urged that the government should extend aid to our maritime industry in order to recapture the strong position it once held in a service so basic to all the country's manufactures.

England, Johnson continued, owned 56 per cent of the world's ocean-going tonnage. How had she acquired such a commanding position of leadership? The answer lay in the extension of government aid and encouragement in the form of bounties and subsidies. He pointed out that the British at one time had excluded foreign vessels from their coastal and colonial trade and had imposed duties favoring their own country's shipping. England, of course, had abandoned some of these restrictive practices, but, along with France and Germany, she still included in her maritime policy the granting of subsidies to her shipping industry. The United States would do well to meet foreign competition by adopting the same measures.

There were concrete evidences in his address that Johnson was looking ahead almost prophetically. He reminded his audience that a merchant marine would be of immense service to the United States in time of war. A canal across the isthmus connecting North and South America would greatly increase trade between the two continents. He referred to the French company then working on a canal in Panama. Should they fail, he argued, Americans should construct a canal across Nicaragua in the near future. In urging the granting of subsidies to shipping interests, he proposed supplying such help to all steamship lines carrying mail — a policy only feebly supported at the time. He further recommended that a small tonnage bounty also be paid to freight lines. Johnson believed that such subsidies would not stir up international animosity toward the United

[84] For an excerpt of several paragraphs from the introductory portion of Johnson's address at the national convention, see the Appendix, p. 289–290.

States—and on the positive side would give impetus to the shipbuilding industry and thus furnish employment to skilled laborers and seamen.

One other phase of our foreign trade which Johnson touched upon in his Detroit address revealed his ingrained belief in education as the key to progress. He suggested the establishment of schools where young men could prepare themselves for careers as salesmen of American products in foreign lands. Such men must learn new languages—must study the history, resources, and development of the countries to which they were to go. To create and maintain a market abroad for what United States manufacturers had to offer, such trade ambassadors must be well trained and backed up by a carefully planned organization at home. The rewards of such a program would be such as to compensate richly for any effort it might be necessary to make to put it in operation.

Near the end of his life, Johnson accepted the chairmanship of a group of manufacturers and jobbers of agricultural implements that met in Madison on April 6 and 7, 1899, to discuss such vital subjects as prices and railroad rates. The president of Fuller and Johnson spoke of his long and intimate interest in these matters. The question was raised whether the firms represented should agree on charging the same price for machinery to every buyer. Johnson's decision was firm: there should be one price for all—no discrimination. No doubt going back to his early political involvement in railroad legislation, he emphasized the same point of view he had advocated over a quarter of a century before. On principle, he could not accept discrimination of any kind.

With the years of recovery in the late 1890's, the Fuller and Johnson Manufacturing Company was in excellent position to enter the new century with zest and energy. As reported to the stockholders for the fiscal year ending August 31, 1900, the resources of the firm were listed as well over $1,500,000. In 1901 the firm changed its fiscal year to end on June 30 instead of August 31, at which time, only ten months after the previous report, a substantially larger figure for total assets appeared in the new financial statement. The gain in resources was being matched by the company in the extension of its markets all over the world. In Europe there were outlets in England, Germany, France, Austria, Russia, and the Scandinavian countries. The Fuller and Johnson trademark was on farm machinery used in Canada, in several South American countries, and even in faraway Australia.[85]

[85] "Record of the Secretary of the Fuller and Johnson Manufacturing Company";

At the annual meeting on January 19, 1900, President Johnson strongly recommended to the directors that a 12 per cent dividend be granted to holders of preferred stock. During the panic years, no such dividends had been possible. Now times were better, and, inasmuch as net earnings for the past fiscal year had been high, he urged that consideration must be given to those who had stood firm in a time of financial crisis.[86]

Johnson's proposal at the meeting in 1900 was the last official act of service he could render to his associates. When the stockholders and directors gathered in January, 1901, they found Vice-president Samuel Higham presiding. For the first time since the founding of the company, John A. Johnson was not present. Too ill to attend, he had sent his son, Carl A. Johnson, to serve as his proxy. From this point on, his three sons – Frederik, Carl, and Hobart – represented their father at meetings called during the remaining months of 1901. Before the year ended, John A. Johnson had died, closing a career which lacked only a few days of twenty years in service as executive head of the Fuller and Johnson Company.[87]

Two months later, at the annual meeting of the firm on January 19, 1902, B. J. Stevens moved the adoption of the following resolution: "Resolved, That in the death of our late President, Honorable John A. Johnson, this company has sustained an irreparable loss, and be it further resolved that directors R. M. Bashford and Secretary W. C. Noe are hereby appointed a committee to prepare and cause to be recorded as a part of the proceedings of this meeting, a suitable memorial. Honorable John A. Johnson having departed this life on the 10th day of November 1901, and having served continuously as a director of this company from the 30th day of November 1881 and as President thereof from the 19th day of January 1882. Resolved, That we here record our appreciation of his worth as a man, of his kindness and consideration to his associates and employees, of his faithful and efficient service on behalf of the corporation and of our deep sense of the loss occasioned by his death not only to his family and business associates but to the entire community."

When John A. Johnson became president of a small manufacturing company in 1882, he had had limited capital and a group of employees small in number and with little actual factory experience. At the time of

Amerika (Madison), April 5, 1899. For the company's balance statement of June 30, 1901, see Table 5 in the Appendix, p. 290.

[86] "Record of the Secretary of the Fuller and Johnson Manufacturing Company."

[87] "Record of the Secretary of the Fuller and Johnson Manufacturing Company."

his death, both the firm's assets and the size of its labor force had increased approximately eight fold. In the beginning year, capital stock had stood at $200,000. Twenty years later, the company was paying its workers each year more than its total original capital. Here was an American success story bound up in the life of one man.[88]

During the serious illness of John A. Johnson and after his death, directors of the corporation gave considerable thought to its future. They debated selling the business, but did not do so. Mrs. John A. Johnson and her children continued for some time to hold a large block of the capital stock. At the 1902 annual meeting, Carl A. Johnson was elected a director for a term of three years, and Samuel Higham was elevated from his position as vice-president to the office of president. Edward M. Fuller, formerly treasurer, became vice-president, W. C. Noe was re-elected secretary, and Carl A. Johnson was chosen the new treasurer. President Higham reported at the time of the reorganization meeting that the business was "in a prosperous condition." [89]

The company continued to do well. During the month of February, 1902, shipments of Fuller and Johnson machinery were the largest for any corresponding month in the history of the firm. At a meeting on March 2 of the same year, the directors announced the startling news that a farm pump powered by a gasoline engine had been perfected by the Gisholt Machine Company and the Maurice I. Johnson Company, firms at the time wholly owned by members of the Johnson family. The new device provided a labor-saving system of pumping water by use of a gasoline engine. Carl A. Johnson, realizing that the power pump would be sold chiefly to farmers and implement dealers, proposed that marketing should be placed in the hands of Fuller and Johnson. At a later meeting, the directors confirmed the arrangement, and soon the new pumps were put on the domestic market. Later they were sold around the world – in Canada, South America, Asia, Malaysia, and Australia.[90]

As time passed, the Gisholt Machine Company, for which John A. Johnson in his later years had laid the foundation, developed into an institution demanding increasing attention from members of the Johnson fami-

[88] "Record of the Secretary of the Fuller and Johnson Manufacturing Company"; *News Crib*, March, 1947, a publication of the Gisholt Machine Company; David Atwood, ed., *Madison Past and Present, Wisconsin State Journal Semi-Centennial*, 158 (1902).

[89] "Record of the Secretary of the Fuller and Johnson Manufacturing Company."

[90] "Record of the Secretary of the Fuller and Johnson Manufacturing Company."

ly. Gradually and coincidentally, the Fuller and Johnson Company commanded less of their interest — and the Gisholt Company more. By 1925 the Fuller and Johnson Company had passed entirely into other hands.

In 1901 John A. Johnson speculated: "How much more may grow out of what we have is uncertain, but it is easier to start other undertakings as we have shop tools, and skilled labor to facilitate further developments. I can say now that there is an enterprise in embryo that in time may develop into far greater proportions than we have yet attained." His prophecy was accurate: the embryo of which he wrote was to grow into full strength. Under the guidance of his descendants — sons, grandsons, and great-grandsons — the Gisholt Company was to move into the twentieth century with an impetus that would write another success story far surpassing the excellent record of its nineteenth-century parent.

CHAPTER VII

The Gisholt Machine Company

As early as 1885, John A. Johnson began to consider the possibility of manufacturing machine tools. Always alert to new ideas that might increase production and sales, he could see direct advantages in an expansion into the new field. Machine tools could be used immediately by Fuller and Johnson; eventually they might be placed on the market. There was an added personal consideration: expanding the firm's operations would in a few years make places for his four sons. Frederik, the oldest, had been active in the company since its organization in 1882. Carl and Hobart, still in high school, were soon to enter the University of Wisconsin, where their major field of study would be mechanical engineering. With his eye on the future, the father was already dreaming of a project in which the sons could use their training — one that conceivably they might develop into a business of their own.[1]

With a clear eye and a realistic view of manufacturing trends, Johnson could see limitations to the future development of the Fuller and Johnson Company. He was well aware of the intense competition in the farm implement field; he knew that some small companies had been forced into bankruptcy. He did not fear that contingency; his firm had already won an established place in supplying the expanding needs of farmers in the Middle West. But a bigger question — a strong reservation — kept coming back into his mind: Could his company achieve the notable success he had dreamed of in competition with the big-name manufacturers who were

[1] Maurice, the youngest son, was only nine years old in 1885.

making their new mechanical harvester the all-important leader in the farm implement field?

The immediate reason for Johnson's concern was the rumor that two well-known Illinois manufacturers—Cyrus McCormick and William Deering—were considering a merger. The rumor proved to be well founded. Just such a combination, consolidating several leading manufacturers of farm implements who were making binders, was incorporated in 1890. Led by McCormick and Deering, the American Harvester Company included such manufacturers as Walter A. Wood, A. S. Bushnell, and A. L. Conger. Unable to secure adequate financial backing at the time, the combine soon fell apart, but the idea of a super-concern persisted—ultimately to be realized in 1902 with the organization of the International Harvester Company.[2]

The fact that Johnson's firm was not invited to join the combination of 1890 indicates that his uneasiness over rising competition was justified. There is, indeed, some evidence that the Fuller and Johnson Company had not been included in plans for the merger because it did not manufacture a harvester, and hence was not considered a competitor. The idea that the Madison firm would join the large Illinois corporation stirred many minds, however, and letters reached Johnson's desk with questions about the possibility. One writer from Hoosick Falls, New York (home of the Walter A. Wood Company), inquired whether "the new combine have bought out your plant or not and [whether] they are negotiating for it or no."[3]

The threat in the late 1880's that others were forming a manufacturing complex that would dominate the farm implement business undoubtedly quickened Johnson's interest in shifting gradually to the making of machine tools. He reviewed the subject in a letter to his inactive partner, Morris E. Fuller. In the previous year, he had advanced several proposals: He would erect a shop in which to make tools on the grounds of the company—or he would install a few tool-making machines in the Fuller and Johnson plant until the firm needed the space. He had offered to pay rent, to reimburse the company for the necessary power, and to carry all expenses during the experimental period. If tool making proved successful, it might eventually replace the manufacture of farm implements. Innately

[2] Cyrus McCormick, *The Century of the Reaper*, 107 (Boston, 1931); *Farm Implement News*, December, 1890.

[3] McCormick, *The Century of the Reaper*, 111; Walter Scott to John A. Johnson, December 15, 1890.

conservative, Fuller, apparently after some consideration, had refused to support any part of the plan.

Johnson had tried hard to persuade his partner to make what seemed to him a necessary change of direction. He had specifically informed Fuller that he preferred to have the tool business "tied up" with the Fuller and Johnson Company. "We have in my judgment," he wrote, "an opportunity that does not often present itself and will probably not present itself to us again. I care for no interest that is not also yours. . . . We missed a golden opportunity by not entering the twine binder business. I do not wish to throw aside this opportunity without a little investigation." He added that their present company could well afford to assist him in developing a machine-tool branch of the business. It would involve no loss to the firm — and might indeed be a big step forward.[4]

In his letter to Fuller, Johnson revealed that he had already made progress in his study of the feasibility of entering the tool-making business. He had talked to machinists outside his own company, and what he had learned from them had encouraged him to go ahead. Since 1885, tinkering with such tools had been going on in the Fuller and Johnson shop. In January, 1886, Johnson had made his first investment in the venture: a small milling machine purchased from Brown and Sharpe of Providence, Rhode Island, for $660. The next year he made a definite move to carry out his plans by hiring C. M. Conradson, a Milwaukee mechanical engineer, who had already demonstrated inventive skill and initiative in the designing of machine tools.

Johnson had known Conradson since 1881, when the young inventor was a student at the University of Wisconsin. Equipped with both a bachelor's and a master's degree in mechanical engineering from the university, he had embarked on a career as an engineer with the E. P. Allis Company in Milwaukee. Johnson had followed his progress, and in 1885, with others, he had helped the inventor to finance experiments with a typesetting machine. In a contract dated November 27 of that year, Conradson — in return for $900 to be furnished by Johnson and five associates — agreed to assign to the subscribers one-third interest in any future royalties from his typesetting and type-distributing devices.[5]

[4] John A. Johnson to Morris E. Fuller, dated January 22; the probable year is 1889. A copy of the letter is in the Johnson Papers.

[5] Agreements and receipts, dated in 1884 and 1885, reveal the progress of Johnson's association with Conradson's typesetting venture. Apparently nothing came of it.

On July 18, 1887, Conradson wrote indicating the terms on which he would accept a position to work for Johnson. He requested a salary of $2,500 per year for three years, and further stipulated that he and Johnson should "divide the profits if any." On these terms, Conradson became part of the machine-tool venture. Johnson was now able to arrange for limited space in the Fuller and Johnson shop to carry on the new work. Equipment in Madison proved inadequate for making parts required for the heavy machines that the two men had planned. Much of the work, therefore, had to be done in Milwaukee at excessive cost and with great inconvenience. To oversee details, Conradson spent much of his time in 1887, 1888, and 1889 in Milwaukee, where he still had connections with the Allis Company. Working in the shops of this firm, he conceived the idea of building a heavy-duty turret lathe capable of shaping the parts of large machines.

From Milwaukee, early in 1888, Conradson wrote enthusiastically about the prospects of the venture he and Johnson had embarked on: "As soon as we get a plant, we can begin to take special jobs . . . and there will be an endless amount of [them]. Bullard's man was here today and wanted me to send a plan of an improved turret machine to them. It is a machine that we could build and will be a standard tool in five years from now." Later in the same year, Conradson informed Johnson that he could sell an 18-inch turret lathe "if we can supply it by January, 1889." He could get $1,700 for this lathe, he went on, and $2,200 for a 24-inch model. Drawings could be finished and work could be started on the smaller machine in ten days. "The prices may seem rather high," Conradson added, "but the machines are enough better to make them cheap at such figures. The market is ready for the machines. All the large concerns are going in for the best tools available." [6]

In the early years of their association, actual sales of tools designed by Conradson and manufactured and marketed under Johnson's supervision were small. They were encouraging enough, however, to justify further plans to expand the business. In a report made in July, 1888, the sale of two tool grinders was recorded, along with charges from Fuller and Johnson against the cost of their manufacture. Up to the end of 1888, approximately $1,100 had been received in payment for tools sold.[7]

[6] C. M. Conradson to John A. Johnson, March 16, August 30, 1888. In an earlier letter, the young man thanked Johnson for the "beautiful watch which you sent me."

[7] Fred W. Coombs, "Memorandum Re Gisholt Machine Company" (Madison, 1907). A typescript copy of the memorandum is in the Johnson Papers.

Late in the summer of 1888, Johnson made the decision to form a separate company to manufacture machine tools. This concern, entirely independent of Fuller and Johnson, was organized on September 10 of that year; its legal entity dates from January 22, 1889, when articles of incorporation were filed with the Wisconsin department of state. John A. Johnson, C. M. Conradson, and Frederik A. Johnson signed the original document, which stated that the corporation intended to engage in the business of "manufacturing and selling tools and machinery." The authorized capital stock was set at $40,000 – in 400 shares valued at $100 each. Management of the business was to be in the hands of three directors, a president, a vice-president, and a secretary and treasurer.[8]

On the very day that the new enterprise was incorporated, Johnson explained in a letter to M. E. Fuller why he had formed the separate company. So that there might be no misunderstanding as to his position or intention, he also informed his partner that in case of failure in the toolmaking experiment, he would be willing to leave whatever new machinery had been acquired to Fuller and Johnson. Apparently the original company at one stage had considered taking the project under its own control, but difficulties had arisen, and Johnson eventually had been forced to go on alone. He concluded his letter to Fuller with the following remarks: "It did seem to me that the Fuller & Johnson Company might well have offered me what facilities they could when there would be no loss to them, but I cheerfully acquiesce in the decision and will make the trial in some other way."

The name chosen for the new firm – essentially Johnson's own enterprise – was the Gisholt Machine Company. It was derived from the farm in Norway that had a special place in Johnson's memories of his childhood. The Gisholt farm was situated on lovely Lake Norsjø, in a picturesque valley with a backdrop of mountains. There the founder of the new American company had spent many happy days with his paternal aunt and her husband. Now, after fifty years, the name of Gisholt was to make itself known throughout the manufacturing world.

The company needed a building. There was no longer any thought of finding adequate space in Johnson's original plant for the necessary toolmaking machinery. Actually two buildings were soon constructed on property at the corner of North Dickinson and Dayton streets, across

[8] A copy of the original articles of incorporation, together with all amendments to September 19, 1940, is in the Johnson Papers.

from Fuller and Johnson. First came a shop, a structure 80 feet by 100 feet, on which Johnson's three older sons — ranging in age from sixteen to twenty-six — served as construction workers. A modest office building, only twelve feet square, was erected on Dickinson Street next to the new shop. At this stage, Johnson had no intention of spending money on frills — there was no plush. He and his men made the office chairs, with wooden legs attached to metal seats similar to those standard on Fuller and Johnson corn planters.[9]

Financial responsibility for the new enterprise rested squarely on Johnson's shoulders. On September 27, 1890, Conradson subscribed for 200 shares and Johnson took the remaining 200 for himself, his wife Kaia, and their three oldest children — Frederik, Ida, and Carl. But he also paid for Conradson's shares. In all, as of September 1, 1890, he had furnished the venture $41,030 in cash, not counting unpaid interest. It is clear that no one else had provided any funds up to this time, and that Johnson had advanced what was needed to cover the erection of new buildings, additional equipment, and other expenses attendant on the formation of the Gisholt Company.[10]

When the corporate organization of the firm was formalized, John A. Johnson became its first president — at the same time continuing in his similar position with Fuller and Johnson across the street from the Gisholt office. C. M. Conradson was named vice-president and superintendent of the shop, and Frederik A. Johnson assumed duties as secretary and treasurer. He doubled also as office manager and as the paymaster who handed the employees their wages on the tenth of each month. In fact, he helped wherever he was needed. The crew that moved into the new shop building in 1890 consisted of only a handful of men. But by this time the project was fairly launched; on all sides there was a firm belief that the business would grow and prosper.

Conradson continued to make preliminary drawings for the big turret lathes, sketching them full size on a large board propped up against the wall. His assistant was F. D. Winkler, later known as the inventor of the Alemite car-greasing technique. Carl A. Johnson, aged twenty, while attending the university, also worked in the drafting room. In time a small frame building to house lathe patterns was erected close to the shop,

[9] *Wisconsin State Journal* (Madison), New Year's Edition, 1930.
[10] Coombs, "Memorandum Re Gisholt Machine Company."

whence their keeper, Chris Hagen, could provide them on short notice. R. W. Hargrave was head man of the engine room, and E. O. Brown was an early supervisor of the tool room. He later became the first of the original crew to travel for the Gisholt Company. Certain machine operators remained for many years with the firm, and some were promoted to larger responsibilities as foremen of various phases of the shop work.

By the time the Gisholt Machine Company moved into its own quarters, its draftsmen had made real progress in designing machine tools. Conradson's first successful invention was a tool grinder for lathes and planer tools. So sound was his design that it remained the basic one until 1939. By far the most important contribution of the Gisholt inventor, however, was his turret lathe – a machine equipped to do work with heavy castings and to shape large machine parts. Lathes for light work were at the time in common use, but Conradson's was the first heavy turret lathe to be manufactured. This tool, made in 1889, eventually came to be known in the trade as a "gisholt." It was the foundation on which John A. Johnson's company was built. In later years, although it went through various alterations, this distinctive machine has remained an important component of the whole success story of the firm.[11]

Five sizes of turret lathes – known as G, H, I, J, and K – were designed in the Gisholt shop in 1891. These machines were the first to have the headstock cast solid with the bed – and also the first to have a square tool post with a slot around the four sides for carrying tools. A special screw machine was built in the same year. It is believed to have been the first turret lathe to have a revolving stop bar with six stop blocks rotating in unison with the turret head.[12]

In the early years, marketing of the finished product went slowly. The basic idea was new, and it proved difficult to convince potential buyers that the heavy type of turret lathe had practical value. The first machines were sold to the Pawling and Harnischfeger Company, a Milwaukee firm dealing in heavy machinery. Soon thereafter, the Fraser and Chalmers Company of Chicago bought a large lathe. This machine gave considerable trouble, but it did serve to demonstrate that Conradson's engineering principle was sound, and that his lathe's ability to handle heavy work was

[11] Louis Bagger and Company, solicitors of patents, Washington, D.C., to John A. Johnson, June 9, 1890. See also in the Johnson Papers a memorandum entitled "Gisholt Firsts" by Al Ebel. This memorandum, dated October 11, 1940, covers the years 1889 to 1928.

[12] *News Crib*, February, 1948, a publication of the Gisholt Machine Company.

a promising advance. Although several substantial payments for machines came to the Gisholt Company in 1891, expenditures in that year exceeded receipts by approximately $17,000.[13]

With the growth of his new business, Johnson found that securing qualified personnel for supervisory positions would be a pressing problem. He especially needed talented, responsible people – trained machinists and pattern makers – who could take charge of various phases of shop work. It was easier to find unskilled men, but they, too, must be ambitious and ready to work hard. Early Gisholt employees came mainly from Madison and its environs; such workers often helped as unofficial recruiters, encouraging their friends to "come down to Gisholt and get a job." Although at first unfamiliar with shop work, the best of them under proper direction could be taught skills that would ensure them promotions and permanent places in the organization.

It soon became necessary, however, to send out a call for both skilled workers and beginners. As early as 1889, Johnson advertised in newspapers in Norway and Germany, urging experienced workmen to come to Madison. A number of skilled Swiss machinists joined the Gisholt staff. The company also utilized the American press, especially the Norwegian-American and German-American newspapers, in its search for talent. On January 9, 1891, an advertisement in the *Wisconsin State Journal* carried a typical message: "Wanted: a bright active young man to act as time keeper and to learn drafting. No drones need apply. Gisholt Machine Company." Seated on a corn-planter-seat chair, Conradson interviewed the thirty-one young men who hurried to reply to this ad. William L. Millar, who got the job, was paid fifty cents a day.[14]

In a sense, Gisholt became a trade school, not only serving the interests of the company but benefiting its younger workers as well. Johnson took more boys into his shops for training than he could use for operations. Those who qualified got regular jobs; others had training that would aid them elsewhere. The president of the company took a close personal interest in the worthiest of his trainees. Late in 1891, he gave each of the five

[13] Fred W. Coombs, "The Gisholt Company: Fifty-Four Years of Pleasant Progress with C. W. Burton, Griffiths and Company," a typed manuscript now in the Johnson Papers. See also Coombs, "Memorandum Re Gisholt Machine Company."

[14] George J. Weber, "The Gisholt Machine Company," a typewritten manuscript in the Johnson Papers.

apprentices in the Gisholt establishment a Christmas bonus, ranging according to length of service from $7.50 to $12.50.[15]

The Gisholt organization in the 1890's was kept simple and informal. Men often shifted from one task to another as the changing circumstances demanded: The secretary might leave letters unanswered in the office while he rolled up his sleeves and unloaded heavy castings. Humorous incidents now and then occurred. On one occasion, two representatives from manufacturers in the East came to the plant to discuss price quotations on machines that interested them. In top hats and frock coats – rather pompous in demeanor – they were shown to the office and settled on the corn-planter seats. After some time, the office boy stuck his head in the door to say that he would take care of them as soon as he washed up. The young handy man who represented the Gisholt firm that day was Carl A. Johnson – later to become president of the company.

Costs of production had to be considered in the years of deficit operation, and certain primitive methods prevailed until the company could afford better things. These even involved utilizing the power of the older company. Although Gisholt in 1890 was a separate enterprise in its own building, it transmitted power for all its machines from the Fuller and Johnson plant across Mifflin Street, using a rope belt running above the thoroughfare. This makeshift arrangement worked well enough in dry weather. Even a brief shower, however, might shrink the rope to the breaking point – and an all-day rain meant not only a holiday in the Gisholt shop but an upset in production schedules as well.

Despite the need for economy, Johnson did not spare capital in securing tools and equipment for producing high-quality machines. As soon as feasible, he replaced manual operations with power cranes and other labor-saving devices. He invested in jigs, tools, and fixtures that could improve any phase of the shop work. On the other hand, Johnson was always critical of waste. Employees remembered for years his oft-repeated slogan for the daily routine of their work: "Produce true work in an economical manner." [16]

In 1892 the *American Machinist* requested from prominent establishments in the American machine industry a somewhat detailed statement

[15] John A. Johnson, *Manufacturing in the United States: A Retrospect and Forecast*, 6 (Madison, 1901); "Early Days at Gisholt," in *News Crib*, May, 1947.

[16] Peter J. Connor, "A Review of Fourteen Years with The Gisholt Machine Company, 1897–1911." This typewritten manuscript, dated May 11, 1911, is now in the Johnson Papers.

telling what each was producing. In answer, John A. Johnson prepared a careful summary of the Gisholt production program. In his introduction, he described his company as manufacturers of turret lathes, universal tool grinders, and special iron-working machinery. In addition, he listed other machine tools manufactured by the firm, pointing out their variety, adaptability, and cost-saving features.[17]

At the same time, Johnson made a decision destined to have important consequences: He would prepare a Gisholt exhibit for the Columbian Exposition to be held in Chicago in 1893. His enterprise at the time was young and comparatively unknown, but he realized that a great international fair offered a rare opportunity to make the Gisholt name and products known to the world. The company had fairly good equipment, enabling it to build complete machines in its own shop. It took considerable courage to engage in face-to-face competition with well-established manufacturers, but Johnson did not hesitate to accept a challenge in which the stakes were so high.

The carefully prepared Gisholt exhibit included four machine tools, and Johnson had his men working on them during the summer and fall of 1892, well in advance of their actual showing. From the drafting of the patterns to the last polishing of the finished product, everything was done in the company's own shops. It was important to demonstrate the latest designs and innovations; here was the big opportunity to score firsts, no matter what the competition. Some of the lathes were equipped for work with cast iron; others had automatic chucks. One machine featured "the first headstock cast integral with feed bed." The display was ready when the fair opened. By then its importance to company fortunes had grown to crucial proportions: the financial report for 1892 revealed a total deficit of over $53,000. What happened at the Columbian Exposition might well determine the fate of the enterprise.[18]

At the fair, the company's exhibit was housed in Machinery Hall, alongside those of such well-known firms as the Pratt and Whitney Company of Hartford, Connecticut, the Brown and Sharpe Manufacturing Company of Providence, Rhode Island, and the Lodge and Davis Machine Tool

[17] *American Machinist* (New York), January 5, 1893. For an excerpt from the Gisholt statement, see the Appendix, p. 290–291.

[18] Coombs, "Memorandum Re Gisholt Machine Company." At the same time, Johnson was sponsoring the successful exhibit of Fuller and Johnson in the field of agricultural implements.

Company of Cincinnati, Ohio.[19] Twenty-year-old Hobart S. Johnson, the third son in the family, was placed in charge of the Gisholt display—a responsible assignment indeed for a university junior, who had to face up to distinguished engineers from both Europe and America in explaining the merits of his father's machines.

The very favorable notices that the *American Machinist* gave to John A. Johnson's exhibit proved of vital importance to his company. Early in the summer of 1893, the national trade journal carried a picture of machinery exhibits at the Exposition, with the Gisholt display in prominent juxtaposition with those of other companies. Later on, the magazine singled out the firm for a special article illustrated by two pages of diagrams. "The Gisholt Machine Company of Madison, Wisconsin," the *Machinist* stated, "have some of the most novel machine tools to be seen here. Among them is the universal tool grinder which was illustrated in these columns June 4, 1891, since which it has been improved, though retaining its main features as at that time." The novel construction of the Gisholt machines on display, the article concluded, revealed their variety and adaptability to a wide range of work.[20]

The success of the Gisholt Company at the Columbian Exposition provided a strong psychological lift to those responsible for the firm's future development. Although its only prize was a bronze medal, there were other tangible results of even more immediate importance. Exposure at the fair and the national coverage in a leading trade journal presented the company's tools and machines in a most favorable light to a wide audience. It would never again be a small, unknown concern hidden away in the Middle West. From the clientele newly created for its products, orders and sales were to follow with surprising speed.

The first order came from the representative of Ernest Kirchner and Company of Leipzig, Germany. On October 14, 1893, this firm, manufacturers of wood-working machinery, authorized their agent at the fair to contract for four machines to cost $5,100. On the same date, another contract of far-reaching importance was signed by John A. Johnson and Ernest Kirchner of the German company. Under its terms, Kirchner agreed to sell Gisholt lathes through his agencies in Europe for a period of five years beginning on December 1, 1893. This was a windfall indeed—an

[19] *American Machinist*, June 15, 1893.

[20] *American Machinist*, June 15, August 17, 1893.

entry into the desirable foreign market. The German concern contracted to pay for advertising and to introduce the machines with full instructions for their proper care and use. They also assumed responsibility for payment. For this service, Kirchner was to receive a commission of 10 per cent of the invoice price.[21]

The panic of 1893 caused a serious interruption in new sales by the Gisholt Company. Some machines that already had been contracted for occupied the shops for a time, but there followed a few months when only a dozen employees remained on active duty. Despite its difficulties, the firm added equipment and set its designers to drafting a new line of machines, including a hydraulic lathe which was operated outside the shop behind a high board fence. Retrenchment was necessary, but there was no thought of closing the business – in spite of a deficit of $66,000 at the end of the fiscal year.[22]

A Gisholt catalogue issued in 1894 addressed to manufacturers a statement listing the features of the machines being built in the shops and explaining the company's aims: "The Gisholt Machine Company was organized for the purpose of building extra heavy and powerful Turret Machines, and such other machines and tools required. Our machines have entirely new designs and we believe [they are] better adapted for heavy work than any yet built. We are prepared to build lathes for finishing Corliss engine bonnet glands, pistons . . . pins, and key heads. Cone pulleys, friction clutches, gear wheels, valves and valve chambers can be finished on powerful Turret Lathes, for a fraction of the cost on ordinary lathes. The Universal Tool Grinding Machine was the outgrowth of our own wants for a systematic and business like method of shaping and sharpening lathe and planer tools. It is our intention to build machinery of Best Quality only, as we are convinced that such machinery is more efficient and economical in use than cheap defective tools." The catalogue also reported for the first time the establishment of Gisholt agencies in the East. There were offices at 125 Milk Street in Boston and at 138 Liberty Street in New York City. The Baird Manufacturing Company of Pitts-

[21] The order agreement for the four machines was signed by Ernest Kirchner and C. M. Conradson. Half of the sales price was to be paid when the machines were delivered on board ship in New York, and the remainder in three equal payments over nine months. Copies of the order agreement and of the European sales-agency contract are in the Johnson Papers.

[22] Coombs, "Memorandum Re Gisholt Machine Company"; Johnson, *Manufacturing in the United States*, 6; "Early Days at Gisholt," in *News Crib*, May, 1947.

burgh was agent for the Wisconsin firm's products in western Pennsylvania, West Virginia, and eastern Ohio.[23]

Gisholt shipped its first machines to Germany in 1894 – an encouraging event, lightening the gloom of the depression. The four lathes ordered by Kirchner of Leipzig were principally the work of two Johnson sons: Carl, then twenty-four, and Hobart, just turned twenty-one. Trained in the mechanical engineering course at the University of Wisconsin, they had done the drawings, had made the component parts in the shop, and had successfully tested the assembled machines. Preparation for shipment overseas was no simple matter. The brothers covered the big shipping boxes with white lead and tallow to protect the metal from the salty ocean air. This was a dirty, odorous business, but, in keeping with company policy, the sons of the president rated no favors. What if their work clothes reeked with the smell of white lead and tallow? It was important to learn the business from the bottom up.

In spite of a natural feeling of encouragement that followed the completion of the first European order, 1894 was a slack year. The Gisholt shops in twelve months made and shipped fifty lathes and approximately sixty tool grinders. Losses instead of profits continued, but the company never failed its employees on pay day. The accumulated deficit, as reported for the fiscal year, amounted to almost $79,000.[24]

The financial difficulties of the Gisholt Machine Company were compounded in the middle 1890's by C. M. Conradson's failure to perform in a responsible manner as a ranking officer and superintendent of the shop. In spite of his virtuosity as a draftsman and inventor, he had begun to reveal serious weaknesses as a businessman. He had lost interest in turret lathes – the current lifeblood of the enterprise – and had turned to electric motors. Johnson had agreed to Conradson's experiments with motors, on assurance that the personal diversion would in no way interfere with the main Gisholt operations. Soon, however, it became apparent that the company was suffering from the superintendent's neglect. Johnson, already hard pressed financially, became concerned. He had advanced large personal loans to his young protégé over the years. Now, having made similar loans in large amounts to keep Gisholt going, the president had almost reached the limit of his resources. In all this time, Conradson, regularly

[23] A copy of this catalogue is in the Johnson Papers.

[24] Johnson, *Manufacturing in the United States*, 6; Coombs, "The Gisholt Company" and "Memorandum Re Gisholt Machine Company."

receiving a salary, had made no capital investment to help in carrying the company.[25]

In 1894, when the situation had deteriorated greatly, Johnson called Conradson in for a conference in an attempt to remedy matters. In reply to the president's suggestions for change, the vice-president asserted that *he* expected to make the decisions in the shop and did not welcome outside advice. At the time, Johnson let the matter pass, hoping that there would be a turn for the better. Instead things continued to get worse. Conradson was not only spending company time on his own interests and neglecting the shop for his work on electric motors; he was also using needed operating space, company machines, and employees on Gisholt's payroll. He had divided the shop into two sections: one for the firm's manufacturing operations, the other for his own personal project. Johnson could not help observing that the vice-president and shop superintendent had conscripted for his work experienced men who should have been busy on company orders.

The result was that operations at Gisholt were slowed down, quality standards were not maintained, and deliveries at times were months late. New products were sent out without proper testing. In one case, several expensive new-type machines were completed all at once, contrary to the conservative company practice of making one pilot model to be thoroughly tested and accepted as 100 per cent satisfactory before more were put on the shop schedule. Customers complained, and some canceled orders. Again going against previous policy, Conradson contracted for work with other concerns, a practice which Johnson had always frowned upon because of the inherent risks of high costs and uncertain quality.

A particularly flagrant instance of mismanagement in the shop—costing the company more than $2,000 and considerable good will—finally brought matters to a head. A European concern had ordered a lathe of the type that the firm had exhibited at the international fair in Chicago. Conradson had later designed and tested a similar one and insisted that his newer device be shipped to the foreign buyer. An internal debate ensued, involving three Gisholt foremen—G. L. Crook, E. O. Brown, and George A. Steinle. These able machinists gave Johnson a unanimous opinion: the new product would never be successful. Conradson pressed his views, however, and offered to go to Europe to put the screw machine into

[25] John A. Johnson to C. M. Conradson, March 28, 1895, June 29, 1899. Copies of these letters are in the Johnson Papers.

operation. While the shipment was in transit, he reneged on his offer and refused to go. This was embarrassing enough, but more trouble developed when the customer could not make the machine work properly. Conradson still refused to go, and finally Carl A. Johnson was sent in his place. He found the product faulty and ordered it returned to Gisholt and the original order canceled. Johnson, not at all used to such dealings, was deeply disturbed.

Obviously no company could afford such a state of affairs. When Johnson finally took the position that he would close the shop unless conditions improved, Conradson expressed a desire to sever his connection with the business. This move involved complex negotiations. Johnson, who had covered the company's losses from his own resources, would now (with his family) become sole owner and would assume full managerial responsibility. Conradson, on his part, would be freed from his original agreement to share profits or losses equally.

To clarify details for both parties, Conradson submitted a long and careful letter to the Gisholt president, stating the conditions on which he would withdraw from the company. He would transfer to Johnson his 200 shares of stock for which the latter had originally advanced $20,000 and for which the retiring vice-president had not paid either principal or interest. In return, Conradson was to be released from all obligations. This agreement included the surrender of the $20,000 note which Conradson had given Johnson to cover his half-interest stock purchase. "Neither you nor said company," Conradson wrote in this section of his letter, "is to have any claim against me arising prior to January 1, 1895."

Ownership of Conradson's patents was a matter of major importance to which he devoted another section of his letter to the Gisholt Company: "I further propose to transfer to you the United States and other patents that were obtained by me, prior to January 1st, 1895, on tool grinders for lathe and planer tools, and on turret lathes and on appliances in connection with said machines; and, if desired by you, will, during a period of three years from January 1, 1895, sign applications for you for United States patents on such machines and appliances only, and will transfer to you the United States patents that may be obtained on such applications."

Conradson further promised not to enter into the manufacture of turret lathes or tool grinders in the United States for three years after January 1, 1895. He wished, however, to reserve the right to design and build, or to have built for him, during the three years, such turret lathes as he might use in his own shop. Other manufacturers on contract to him, or for whom he might be working, were also to be free to make lathes from his designs for his use or for use in their plants on their work for him. In addition, he offered to act as consulting engineer for the Gisholt Company for three years, beginning January 1, 1895. Such services were to take only a small fraction of his time, and for them he was to be paid $5,000 for the three years. "[It is] understood," he stipulated, "that the compensation hereinafter named is to be chiefly for agreeing not to enter into the manufacture of turret lathes and tool grinders. . . . At the expiration of three years after January 1, 1895, I am to be entirely free from all obligations."

Johnson on his part was to agree for the same three-year period not to make or sell any electric motors or dynamos. This provision would not preclude Gisholt's manufacturing them for others under existing contracts. "[It is] understood," Conradson recorded, "that you agree not to infringe [my] patents and designs in any way or degree." Finally, the vice-president requested from the Gisholt Company a written contract embodying and accepting the proposals outlined in his letter, for the carrying out of which the president of the company would hold himself personally responsible.[26]

Johnson accepted Conradson's proposals, and on February 15, 1895, the latter assigned to Gisholt twenty patents, dated during the period from April 14, 1891, to July 24, 1894. The departing superintendent reserved for himself the right to make in his own shop the hydraulic lathe he had patented in 1893. The patents assigned to Johnson's company included those for the universal tool grinder, improvements on the grinder and lathes, an automatic chuck, a rod-feeding device, two designs for lathe beds, and an arrangement for varying the speed of machinery.[27]

Although Conradson prophesied that the Gisholt Company would not survive his departure more than six months, the separation was generally an amicable one. Johnson wrote to his erstwhile partner a few weeks after the settlement: "I hope your business will prosper. We certainly shall do nothing against you. As to the Gisholt business, time only will tell. I only hope that we shall be able to make such changes as will make our business

[26] A copy of Conradson's letter stating his terms for withdrawal from the company is in the Johnson Papers. On its last page is the statement: "Feb. 12, 1895. Agreed to by J. A. Johnson."

[27] The document assigning the patents is in the Johnson Papers. Affixed to it is the receipt of the United States commissioner of patents, dated October 15, 1897, recording the official transfer of the patents. With the assignment is an undated, unsigned contract defining the terms on which Conradson left the Gisholt Company.

prosperous." A third-generation president of the company, reflecting many years later on Conradson's contribution to the machine-tool industry, rated the inventor as one of the six mechanical geniuses of his time. It must have been temporarily irritating to Johnson that Conradson took with him to work in his turret lathe enterprises certain trusted employees from the shop. Eventually, however, all who were lured away returned to Madison to work for their old company.[28]

The dark future that Conradson predicted for the Gisholt Machine Company seemed to follow him instead. He had an inventive mind but seemingly lacked responsibility and the sense of loyalty essential in working effectively with others. After he left Gisholt, he flitted from one venture to another. He first became associated with several Madison men in organizing the Northern Electrical Manufacturing Company. In less than three years, however, he left Wisconsin behind to work briefly in Cincinnati before going to Chambersburg, Pennsylvania; there he engaged in building lathes. Differences arose with his associates, work was suspended, and a sheriff's sale disposed of what had been made. Next Conradson joined J. Morton Poole and Company in Wilmington, Delaware, where for a time the manufacture of lathes seemed to point to a successful future. Soon he was moving on, however, to serve as a consulting engineer to a New York shipbuilding firm. In another shift to Warren, Pennsylvania, he engaged – again unsuccessfully – in building lathes. Ironically enough, Gisholt in 1905 became owner of this Pennsylvania concern.[29]

Reorganization followed Conradson's departure, and during 1895 new names were added to the roster of officers and shop managers. John A. Johnson, president, and Frederik A. Johnson, secretary, continued in their positions. Carl A. Johnson, his course in mechanical engineering at the University of Wisconsin behind him, became vice-president and general manager. The position of treasurer and superintendent was filled by Hobart S. Johnson, who had completed his junior year in mechanical engineering at the university. A letterhead of late 1895 carries all these names and positions. Significantly there is one additional name: C. M. Conradson, consulting engineer.[30]

[28] John A. Johnson to C. M. Conradson, March 28, 1895. A copy of this letter is in the Johnson Papers. See also a typescript copy of a paper entitled "Seventeen Years Turret Lathe Experience," by W. L. Millar. This paper, dated March 20, 1908, is also in the Johnson Papers.

[29] W. L. Millar, "Seventeen Years Turret Lathe Experience."

[30] In 1895, John A. Johnson was sixty-three, Frederik thirty-two, Carl twenty-five, and Hobart twenty-two.

At this period of important reorganization, Johnson put in operation at Gisholt a plan of profit sharing in which shop supervisors could participate. For a family-owned-and-officered business, this was a shrewd and farsighted move. It gave recognition and motivation to loyal and able men in the all-important managerial positions. At a time when the recent trouble had shaken morale, it had psychological and strategic importance. On March 19, 1895, articles of agreement, retroactive to January 1 of the same year, were drawn up between "the Gisholt Machine Company of Madison, Wisconsin, party of the first part, and E. O. Brown, G. L. Crook, G. A. Steinle, J. A. Johnson, F. A. Johnson, C. A. Johnson, and Hobart S. Johnson, parties of the second part." [31]

First in the agreement came a statement of what the company would pay each officer and plant supervisor. Brown, Crook, and Steinle, as co-equals, were each to receive $2.50 per day. President John A. Johnson would draw no salary. Fred and Carl were each to have $100 per month. Hobart was judiciously provided for, his relative youth and inexperience being taken into account. He was to receive "such amount per day as he learns the business and as he is actually and fairly worth, it being understood that he is now learning the trade of machinist." All parties were to pledge themselves to give their "best services" to the firm under the direction of its superintendent.

The company agreed to make a public statement of its assets and liabilities once each year. It is significant that due allowance was made for depreciation. If the annual reckoning indicated the accumulation of "net gains or profits," the plan of sharing them — as outlined in the articles of agreement — would be put into operation. First, 7 per cent would be paid to Gisholt stockholders. Second, profits above 7 per cent would be divided into two equal parts. One part would be apportioned to the stockholders "in like manner as the aforesaid seven per cent." The other part would be divided equally among "the said [7] parties of the second part." The contract also stated that John A. Johnson might transfer his interest in the profits to some other person who might in the future become an employee of the company.

It was further agreed that each year, in addition to salaries, the four Johnsons would deliver to the other three parties of the second part — Brown, Crook, and Steinle — half as many dollars in stock as the number of days these foremen individually had worked in the preceding year. The

[31] A copy of this agreement is in the Johnson Papers.

president reserved the right to delay this stock distribution until the termination of the agreement; but, in the event of such a postponement, each supervisor would receive his share of dividends just as if the stock had actually been delivered to him.[32]

The capital stock on which the profit sharing was based was set at $120,000. At the time the agreement was made, capitalization was still only $40,000. John A. Johnson, however, agreed to accept stock at par of $100 per share for $80,000 he had loaned the company. Thus the total capital was increased to $120,000. The original profit-sharing agreement was planned to be effective for five years, but it was hoped that all parties would find the system so satisfactory that an equitable profit-sharing arrangement would be continued. It was agreed that any party of the second part could withdraw at any time. One proviso, however, was added: Anyone who withdrew at any time other than the expiration date of the fiscal year would forfeit his right to a share of the profits for any part of that year.

Despite internal problems, the Gisholt Company staked its recovery on a vigorous campaign to expand its sales. This meant sending out agents as widely as possible, both in the United States and in Europe. Early in 1895, Carl A. Johnson, in his new capacity as general manager, gave earnest in his first sales forays in the Midwest that he could be counted on as a bulwark in the future growth of the enterprise. The company also took steps, in the summer of the reorganization year, to secure an eastern representative. Walter H. Foster of Boston agreed to serve as Gisholt's agent in New England, New York, New Jersey, eastern Pennsylvania, and all coastal states southward, including Georgia. In this large, virgin territory, he was to sell turret lathes, screw machines, universal tool grinders, and other machine tools on a commission of 10 per cent on gross sales.[33]

Turning to Europe, Johnson in the late spring of 1895 signed a two-year contract with Schuchardt and Schutte of Berlin to handle the sale and

[32] According to E. O. Brown's signed receipt, dated January 4, 1896, he received settlement for the year 1895 in stock to the amount of $150, that is, for one half as many dollars as the 300 days he had worked. This share of the preceding year's profit was in addition to his regular pay. The *Wisconsin State Journal* of December 30, 1895, complimented John A. Johnson on the first payments to company personnel under the profit-sharing plan: "The Madison Gisholt experiment reflects great credit on the generous man who conceived it and all wish the plan the largest success."

[33] A copy of the agreement, signed by Foster on July 1, 1895, is in the Johnson Papers.

delivery of grinding machines. Under mutually exclusive terms, the German firm agreed not to handle similar tools made by other American companies, and Johnson gave the Berlin agency exclusive sales rights in Europe – except in Great Britain and France. The Germans were to pay Gisholt its price plus the expense of boxing and transportation to the port of shipment.[34]

In the midst of carrying a heavy burden of debt, the Gisholt Company's leaders were heartened by a relatively successful year in 1895. Profits were large enough to permit the distribution of modest amounts to the men participating in the profit-sharing plan. Business had been brisk. A letter dated October 21, 1895, from the Madison office to E. O. Brown on the road reported that Foster had taken an order in the East for two lathes and two tool grinders. An order for a lathe had come from Moline, Illinois, and another Midwest shop wanted a 24-inch lathe, if it could be delivered promptly. All this was promising. There was enough work to keep a sizable force of men busy. In the interest of economy and quality production, the company was changing some of its earlier practices: It ceased contracting work to other companies, it specialized in a few standard machines rather than in a large variety, and it now built all machines with general attachments instead of making the purchase of extra parts optional.

The company's first complete balance sheet, dated December 31, 1895, showed improvement in its over-all financial condition. It was possible to distribute profits to the supervisors. But the report also revealed a substantial indebtedness. Net assets were valued at $152,000, and notes from accounts payable totaled $72,000 – leaving a net valuation of $80,000 against a capital stock of $120,000. There is no record of current assets in the form of accounts receivable.[35]

When business slackened in 1896, Johnson countered by sending a man to Europe. Results were quick and surprisingly good. A number of orders came in from England and one from a large Berlin electrical company. The favorable impact that Gisholt products had made on foreign representatives at the Columbian Exposition continued to spur sales abroad. During 1896 orders from England and Germany represented 23

[34] A copy of the contract, signed by Schuchardt and Schutte on May 31, 1895, is in the Johnson Papers.

[35] Coombs, "The Gisholt Company" and "Memorandum Re Gisholt Machine Company." See also the balance sheet of the Gisholt Machine Company, December 31, 1895, in the Johnson Papers.

per cent of the company's total business. The next year sales fairly boomed in Europe, and Gisholt again sent a man to England and the Continent. The firm also had some business at home—but for the time being it exploited its success across the Atlantic. With burgeoning sales in that particular area, the company received so many orders in all that the shop personnel had to strain to keep up with them.[36]

At this time, Gisholt established agency relations with two important European concerns. Johnson arranged with C. W. Burton, Griffiths and Company of London to act as sales agents in Great Britain on a discount and commission basis. The American company agreed to dispatch experts from its Madison plant to help in the servicing of highly specialized machines. In Germany, a relationship was established with the Cologne branch of Schuchardt and Schutte. This firm placed an initial order for ten machines with the understanding that Gisholt would furnish a resident machinist for a few months to assist in the process of selling and installing the new equipment.[37]

The next step was to establish a branch office in Europe. Encouraged by the growth of the foreign business, Johnson late in 1897 sent his son Frederik abroad to "get the ear" of important manufacturers in England, Germany, and other European countries. For this task, Frederik was well suited by his experience in both manufacturing and selling. As a very young man, he had begun at the bottom with Fuller and Johnson as a common laborer, and had sold farm machinery in the developing Middle West for that company. In 1889 he had become secretary and treasurer of Gisholt at the time the company had been established. His valuable practical experience included designing and building the firm's machines, and preparing them for shipment overseas. Now at the age of thirty-four he was being entrusted with the responsible assignment of promoting Gisholt's foreign sales effort.

John A. Johnson made a tour of Europe in 1899, during which he took particular pride in visiting his company's branch office in Berlin. In a letter written at this time from Bad Hamburg, Germany, where he had gone to take the baths, he expressed great satisfaction with Frederik's progress as head of Gisholt's foreign office: "Fred speaks, reads, and writes German well, so that he readily does business in German. He is an excellent

[36] Coombs, "The Gisholt Company."

[37] Coombs, "The Gisholt Company." See also his typed manuscript now in the Johnson Papers, entitled "Fifty-Four Years of Pleasant Progress with C. W. Burton, Griffiths and Company and Gisholt Machine Company."

business man and is very successful. He travels in Germany, England, and France, and somewhat in Russia, Austria, and Italy." Frederik had now been living abroad a year and a half; with his wife and two children he had established a home in Berlin, where he was to remain for some years.[38]

The growth of the European business confirmed the belief of Gisholt executives that they had, indeed, the nucleus for a thriving, permanent manufacturing enterprise. Acting upon this premise, they began to consider plans for a larger factory. Although two extensive additions to the original building had been constructed between 1895 and 1898, the firm found itself severely cramped for space. In 1899, to meet pressing needs in all departments, a modern factory was built on East Washington Avenue, at a cost of $75,000 – and in the fall of that year the company moved in. The new facility was much more than merely a building. Into it went high-grade machinery entirely operated by electricity. Hand-operated cranes gave way to electric ones capable of carrying heavy machines to freight cars waiting on a spur of track behind the plant. With excellent lighting and ventilation, the factory, at the turn of the century, was a model of its kind.[39]

Although electrical power had replaced muscle power in his new plant, Johnson realized that working in the Gisholt factory was no easy job. The workday was ten hours long – from 7:00 in the morning to 5:00 p.m., with thirty minutes for lunch. The workweek lasted from Monday morning through Saturday afternoon. To help his men adjust to the rugged schedule, the company president took pains to give them the advantage of working under foremen who had had experience in various branches of the operations – and who had sympathetic appreciation of what it meant to be "on the line." Important also was the opportunity for advancement that Gisholt gave men with little or no previous training. The atmosphere of the plant was co-operative and friendly from top to bottom. A much-appreciated innovation in communication was introduced when Johnson encouraged his workers to try out a policy of making written suggestions to the management.

Now that his company had definitely turned the corner financially, Johnson felt able to realize some other ideas having to do with the crea-

[38] John A. Johnson to his sister, Mrs. Caroline Johnson Stuverud, May 30, 1899.

[39] "Early Days at Gisholt," in *News Crib*, July, 1947; Coombs, "The Gisholt Company." See also *Madison, Past and Present*, a semicentennial publication of the *Wisconsin State Journal* in 1902.

tion of an effective and loyal corps of employees. He had always felt that a worker was not merely a number, not just a pair of hands, but a human being deserving fair, considerate treatment. No doubt his motives were practical as well as altruistic: he believed that a pleasant environment made for contented workers and ensured superior workmanship. With a labor force of some two hundred men, the time had come to provide special facilities not needed for the smaller crew of an earlier period. Moving toward realization of his dream of an ideal owner-employee relationship, Johnson just at the beginning of the new century completed plans for a center for Gisholt workers.

The new brick building was in no sense a part of the factory. Its purpose was to provide facilities for the comfort and convenience of the workers. On the ground floor were located lavatories with hot and cold running water, and there also each man had a locker for which he carried his own key. Rooms where employees could relax and eat their lunches occupied the main floor above. Here too was the most unusual feature of the building — a large room known as the Gisholt Library. It was, indeed, a library, which the company had stocked with books of fiction and general interest, along with those that suited special tastes. The year the building opened the men could choose from among many periodicals lying ready at hand. Later a traveling library also made its books available. Reflecting a touch of nostalgic sentiment in Johnson's make-up, oil paintings of scenes on the Gisholt farm in Norway had been hung on the walls — along with copies of works by famous artists. The large library room had a stage for various kinds of entertainment; seats could be made available for five hundred people.

On January 8, 1900, the Gisholt Library Club was organized by the employees, with G. A. Steinle serving as temporary chairman. Eighty-three members enrolled and agreed to pay dues of ten cents a month. Four officers were elected: E. E. Hart, president, Ed Hall, vice-president, Hobart S. Johnson, treasurer, and E. C. Smelzkopf, secretary. Quite appropriately, John A. Johnson was elected an honorary member.[40]

Versatile members of the club provided talent for programs ranging from educational projects to classical and popular music to slapstick comedy. A committee on athletics took over the management of both indoor and outdoor sports teams. At least three musical organizations — a glee club, a brass band, and an orchestra — gave evening entertainments

[40] The minutes of the Gisholt Library Club are in the Johnson Papers.

on special occasions. The always popular Gisholt minstrels, well supplied with tambourines and burnt cork, could be relied upon to enliven their large audiences and to "send them away laughing."[41]

The first major program of the Gisholt Library Club was staged on the evening of February 5, 1900 — apparently a typical potpourri of music, readings, and oratory. A Madison paper reported the occasion the next day under a flamboyant headline on page one: "Gisholt Library — An Exquisite Concert Given in the New Hall before 500 People — Happy Company of Employees." Gisholt men furnished music and renditions of poetry. A Madison orchestra played an appropriate number entitled "Inauguration," a quartette, no doubt recalling the recent war with Spain, sang "Soldier's Farewell," and F. von Teschke read Schiller's poem, "Song of the Bell." There were zither solos, vocal duets, and more readings. Star of the evening was W. Legried, who played the cornet in such masterly fashion that Johnson expressed the fear that "he and other talented performers would drift out of the machine business and onto the musical stage."[42]

What really was a sort of dedicatory address for the new Gisholt building was given by a local editor. He noted the beautiful library room and paid tribute to Johnson. "We honor this man," he said, "for diverting his later years, not by hoarding of more dollars but by devoting his energies and thought to the lives of those whose labor jointly with his own have availed to build up this great industry." Turning in a personal vein to the Johnson family, the speaker concluded: "The good sense displayed by the father in the teaching of the stalwart sons the trades on which the industry is built is a pledge not only of its financial endurance but of good order and brotherly sentiments on the part of all."[43]

At the end of the company's first decade, Johnson could feel that it had survived its struggling early years and was firmly established for the future. Outsiders held the same opinion. The *American Machinist*, in its issue of June 1, 1899, gave the firm special recognition, featuring on its cover in large type the words: "Gisholt Lathe, Gisholt Machine Company, Madison, Wisconsin, U.S.A." The lead article described the lathe as having great driving power, many speeds, and a variety of feeding devices. The tools attached to the machine had a wide range of usefulness and were

[41] "Early Days at Gisholt," in *News Crib*, July, 1947.
[42] *Wisconsin State Journal*, February 6, 1900.
[43] *Wisconsin State Journal*, February 6, 1900.

simple and easily adjusted. One customer had informed the magazine that his firm had just finished a piece of machine work with a Gisholt lathe at a cost of $600; a year earlier, using an ordinary lathe, he had spent $2,100 on the same process. "Hundreds of Gisholt lathes," the article concluded, "are giving as good results as this one." The *Machinist* listed Gisholt's agencies and offices in the eastern United States and abroad, including in the latter group the Cologne, Vienna, and Stockholm branches of the Berlin firm of Schuchardt and Schutte, C. W. Burton, Griffiths and Company of London, and the Fenwick Frères Company in Paris.[44]

The price of holding pre-eminence in the manufacturing field was a program of constant and aggressive improvement. Competition demanded it, but Johnson had always been a leader in pioneering new machines and in studying and upgrading factory techniques. Now from Gisholt he sent out men far and wide to visit other factories and to observe operations in a wide range of plants, and particularly to study the use of Gisholt machines. In 1899 Peter J. Connor of the engineering department spent four weeks on such an expedition; later he wrote an account of his experiences, including specific recommendations for bettering the company's products. Connor in a relatively short period of service had established himself as a valuable addition to the technical staff. After attending Cornell University, he had been employed by the Niles Tool Works of Hamilton, Ohio. Interested in the Gisholt turret lathe, he had successfully applied for a position in Madison and had begun work as a tool designer in 1897.[45]

Connor's trip took him mainly to manufacturing centers in the East. After visiting Chicago and the Ohio cities of Cincinnati, Hamilton, Cleveland, and Cuyahoga, he went on to Philadelphia, Syracuse, and New York City. In Connecticut he observed factory operations in Bridgeport, Hartford, Torrington, and New London. He stopped in Rhode Island at Westerly and Providence before climaxing his tour in Massachusetts—in Boston, Lowell, Worcester, and Springfield. Reporting on his observations and conclusions after visiting a score of factories, Connor wrote:

[44] In a letter to his sister Caroline from Bad Hamburg on May 30, 1899, Johnson expressed pride and satisfaction in the status of the business: "The Gisholt Machine Company is being wholly managed by the boys. It is successful beyond all expectations."

[45] Connor, "A Review of Fourteen Years with The Gisholt Machine Company." This account gives an extensive list of improvements made on Gisholt machines beginning in 1897.

"I saw Gisholt machines at work under very many new conditions, and handled by all classes of operatives, from painstaking and accurate ones to those who were careless and indifferent as to the results accomplished." The next year Connor and George A. Steinle went on a shorter trip "to see what might be of interest in a mechanical way." In this end-of-the-century period, Gisholt engineers also traveled to England, France, Belgium, and Germany on similar missions.[46]

As he was also doing with his farm machinery company, Johnson moved aggressively in all fields to advertise his Gisholt line. He never overlooked an opportunity to show his lathes and other new-type machines at fairs and expositions. Success of his exhibits at the Columbian Exposition in 1893 had led to a similar entry at Brussels, Belgium, where in 1897 Gisholt won a bronze medal. The climax to all these efforts was to come, however, at the International Universal Exposition held in Paris in 1900. Although not one of the giants of American industry even in its own field, the company never questioned whether or not it would "go to Paris." [47]

One hundred forty United States tool companies prepared exhibits for the department of machinery and electricity at the great Paris world's fair. Class 22 in this division included machine tools designed for working in wood and metal. In this category, the Gisholt Machine Company arranged a striking display of motor-driven machines in actual operation – mainly its new turret lathes and tool grinders. An official compliment preceded the Madison company's exhibit in Paris. F. A. Peck, United States commissioner general for the fair, reported to the Exposition authorities: "The Gisholt lathe is unique among turret lathes in point of size and capacity for work." [48]

Hobart S. Johnson and his wife attended the fair, where they were met by the Frederik Johnsons, who had come from Berlin. Peter Connor, who had been on the Continent studying the plants of prominent manufacturing concerns, joined the Johnson brothers at the Exposition. There they examined with interest displays of such famous European firms as Schneider of Le Creusot in France, Krupp of Essen in Germany, Société John Cockerill of Belgium, and Albert Herbert, Ltd., of Coventry in England.

[46] Connor, "A Review of Fourteen Years with The Gisholt Machine Company."

[47] Johnson, *Manufacturing in the United States*, 15.

[48] *Report of the Commissioner General for the United States to the International Universal Exposition, Paris, 1900* (Washington, D.C., 1901).

Altogether the Gisholt trio studied and admired a great many noteworthy examples of engineering skill and enterprise.[49]

The French had arranged a gala day for the presentation of the awards on August 18, 1900. The director of the National Theater in Paris had charge of the scenic effects. Saint-Saëns, the renowned French composer, had written a march for the occasion; an orchestra and chorus presented an impressive program. Ten thousand seats in the Salle des Fêtes were filled to hear President Émile Loubet deliver an address. Cannons announced his departure with his cabinet from L'Elysée; the "Marseillaise" was sung as he arrived at the speaker's stand. The diplomatic corps and commissioners general of the participating nations had favored seats, as the French president welcomed all on this international occasion. "The relations established between our guests and ourselves," the speaker said, "have been strengthened by a confidence founded upon a perfect acquaintance with the merit and value of each people, and upon the apparent necessity that all conform to the ideal of justice and solidarity." [50]

The high point of the occasion was the presentation of the awards — eagerly awaited by Fred and Hobart Johnson and Peter Connor. Besides the American exhibitors, in Class 22 there were scores of entrants from countries around the world. A large number from the United States and Europe were established firms of many years' standing. Yet, despite its youth, the Gisholt Machine Company won the gold medal in its class. It was, indeed, a great day for the company, for John A. Johnson and his sons carrying on for him, and for the workmen who had built their skill and loyalty into the Gisholt machines.[51]

At the time of the Paris Exposition, plans for the further expansion of the Gisholt enterprise were under way — including a blueprint for a badly needed foundry. Successful on a major scale in Europe, company officers now vigorously turned their attention to increasing sales in the United States. In what was to be his last long article for publication, John A. Johnson, now sixty-eight years of age and in failing health, reminisced about the early experiences of his now-flourishing company. "Much experimenting was done at great cost," he wrote in January, 1901, "and a great deal of work thrown away. We had sold a few machines when the

[49] Connor, "A Review of Fourteen Years with The Gisholt Machine Company."

[50] Report of United States Juror-in-Chief J. H. Gore, in the *Report of the Commissioner General for the United States.*

[51] Report of United States Juror-in-Chief J. H. Gore, in the *Report of the Commissioner General for the United States.*

panic [of 1893] struck. Then business in this line in this country was absolutely dead, and we had very little start abroad. We had to operate at heavy loss for years. . . . However, I added to the shop and equipment so as to be ready if the demand should come. . . . The business did finally come, and we were ready to take care of a limited amount of it, so that the company has done moderately well, and what I prize more is that it has given my sons a very good practical training." [52]

While the plans for further expansion were being carried out, John A. Johnson became seriously ill. Before the year 1901 ended, death had closed his career — and the administration of the Gisholt Machine Company had passed into the hands of his sons. The enterprise they inherited was strong. The firm was producing machines favorably known among manufacturers on both sides of the Atlantic. In Madison the company had established an excellent plant stocked with the best modern equipment, and these facilities were being managed by an able operating and administrative organization.

Significantly, the company was financially sound at the time of transfer to new management. The total assets of the Gisholt Company — as shown in its balance statement of January 1, 1901 — came to approximately $445,000. A fraction over 86 per cent of its liabilities consisted of claims of its owners in the form of capital stock, unpaid dividends, and surplus. It had no long-term fixed-interest obligations, and its current obligations represented only about 13 per cent of its total liabilities. And these were slightly less than the amount others currently owed Gisholt in the form of accounts receivable. The company had relatively large investments in plant facilities and machine equipment. Its valuation of patents, patterns, and drawings was conservative; its investments in inventories — materials, completed machines, and machines in process — was extensive.[53]

There is a large mass of evidence, written and spoken, that the esprit de corps of the Gisholt firm, built on the business philosophy of John A. Johnson, was soundly conceived for advancement in the new century. The founder of the company had always believed that a smoothly working organization — consisting of men well qualified for their specific tasks and loyal to the company — was an essential for industrial success. Creating such an organization, in his judgment, was one of the important functions

[52] Johnson, *Manufacturing in the United States*, 6.

[53] For the complete balance statement of the company, dated January 1, 1901, see Table 6 in the Appendix, p. 291.

of the leaders of any business. Of the success of this general policy, Gisholt was a prime example. A core group of its best employees responded to the ideal of corporate unity by dedicating their working careers to the company. Individuals who began with Gisholt when Johnson hired his first crew continued to work for him and his sons — some for well over half a century. A few saw their sons join them in the ranks. Altogether a sizable group of able and loyal men became veterans in the company's service, contributing experience, stability, and leadership on various levels of the total enterprise.

Three such men — among the very earliest to join the company — were Clem Affholder, Alfred G. Hansen, and Alfred L. Tandvig. Originally employed by Fuller and Johnson, Affholder became a charter member of the Gisholt working force in 1889. For more than fifty years he served the firm as a toolmaker and diemaker. In 1890 Hansen joined the shop employees, at a time when the crew included only a dozen men. Developing as an expert machinist, he became so proficient and versatile — particularly in his relations with other people — that the company sent him on many trips throughout the United States and Europe, demonstrating the operation of its machines. At the time of his retirement, he had been on the staff well over half a century.[54] When Tandvig was first employed as an apprentice in 1896, he began by polishing finished machines. He left Gisholt for a few years, but returned in 1901 to add fifty-seven years in various assignments until his retirement.

David Wright and Edward Johnson were other long-time members of the Gisholt group. Wright came to the company in 1899 and served in various capacities in the traffic department for fifty-five years. Edward Johnson, who was born in Norway, became an apprentice in 1899 and continued in the work of assembling machines for fifty years. Two other apprentices — William L. Millar and Ralph H. Miller — left the company temporarily in 1895 to try their luck with Conradson's new lathe manufacturing venture. Both had started with Gisholt in the early 1890's, and both soon returned to be regular employees again for the remainder of their active lives. Millar, whose second career began in 1904, was an engineer with the firm until his retirement in the early 1930's. In all, Ralph Miller was an engineer in the Johnsons' employ for forty-eight years.[55]

Among company executives, Fred W. Coombs and George Gernon

[54] *News Crib,* June, 1947.
[55] *News Crib,* July, 1947, April, 1948.

compiled the longest records of continuous service. Coombs took a position as bookkeeper with the firm in 1899, and advanced by a series of promotions to the rank of senior vice-president, which he held until his retirement in the late 1930's. Gernon, trained in law at the University of Wisconsin, first joined the Gisholt organization as a legal adviser in 1900. Five years later, he became the firm's corporate secretary, to continue in that capacity until he retired in 1954.[56]

On their father's death, the four Johnson sons immediately assumed responsibility for the family business. In a reorganization of the corporate offices, Frederik A. Johnson succeeded to the presidency of the firm, and Carl A. Johnson continued to serve as vice-president and general manager. Hobart S. Johnson, previously general superintendent, now also became corporate secretary, and Maurice I. Johnson was named vice-president and works manager. With the addition of Maurice, aged twenty-five, to the list of major officers, all four of John A. Johnson's sons were for the first time included in the management of the company.

By the time each of the Johnson brothers in turn accepted an official responsibility in the firm, he had been well grounded in his father's philosophy of how a manufacturer should be trained. By precept and example, by spoken and written word, Johnson had put before them his ideal of the corporate executive. "It is self-evident," he had maintained, "that the man who has literary, technical, and practical training, other things being equal, has great advantages in manufacturing over the man who lacks these qualifications." To this he would add a proviso: if only one type of training was within reach, the practical was to be preferred. "The young graduate [of a university] should spare no time," he advised, "in becoming a good practical workman. Only the man who has himself worked knows what is a fair day's work." As responsible leaders in manufacturing, it is clear that all of the sons had the combined literary, technical, and practical education that the father valued so highly. Each had attended the University of Wisconsin; two had specialized in mechanical engineering. Beginning with the humblest jobs, all had had practical shop training. To prepare them specifically for managerial positions, all had worked in both production and marketing, including experience in the United States and abroad.[57]

[56] "Building Good Will," in *News Crib*, March, 1949.
[57] Johnson, *Manufacturing in the United States*, 14.

Sons and grandsons of John A. Johnson were to serve as chief executives of the Gisholt Machine Company for six decades following the death of its founder. Under their leadership, the firm maintained its reputation as an expanding, progressive enterprise, manufacturing machine tools of the highest quality. When he assumed the presidency in 1901, Frederik A. Johnson had worked closely with his father for a score of years – first in the Fuller and Johnson Company and since 1889 as one of the incorporators of the Gisholt enterprise. He had served in the top management of this company, but his special contribution was his leadership in promoting the wide acceptance of his firm's machine tools by European manufacturers. His term as president proved to be relatively short. Continued ill health following a serious illness suffered on a trip to London in 1904 forced his resignation about two years later. He died in 1908 at the age of forty-four.

For a quarter of a century after 1906, major responsibility for the Gisholt Company was in the hands of the founder's second son, Carl A. Johnson. Like his older brother, he had been closely associated with the father during almost all of his business career. He had benefited greatly from the carefully planned training that John A. Johnson projected for each of the four brothers; he had been literally groomed for the presidency from the time of his graduation from the University of Wisconsin. When he assumed the position in 1906, at thirty-six, he had been for eleven years vice-president and general manager. It was fortunate that he had been so directly prepared for the leadership of the firm, for his administration was to include the difficult period of World War I.

During the war years beginning in 1914, Gisholt became a major supplier of machine tools to the Allies. One early order for fifty large lathes was the largest received up to that time. Shortly thereafter, however, it was followed by another emergency request for seventy-five lathes of the same 24-inch type. British manufacturers turned to the American firm in distant Madison, Wisconsin, for simple, single-operation lathes; in the course of the war, the company shipped 1,600 of these machines to England. Following the end of the conflict in 1918, the abnormal volume of wartime orders declined, and it took wise management during the 1920's to adjust to the steadier flow of peacetime business.

Then came the market crash of 1929 and the beginning of a long and punishing depression. Carl A. Johnson, as chief executive of the Gisholt Company, was among business leaders called to Washington by President

Herbert Hoover to consider how to meet the impact of the sinking national economy of the early 1930's. By this time, the president of the Wisconsin company was a nationally known figure and an officer or director of many important industrial, financial, and philanthropic organizations, to which his balanced judgment and capacity for decisive action made notable contributions. In 1931, when he was sixty-one, death closed his long and distinguished career of service.

After his brother's death while still in office, the third son of John A. Johnson became president of the company. Hobart S. Johnson, then fifty-eight years old, had been an officer since 1895, and since 1906 he had held the position of vice-president. His experience in World War I had been noteworthy, as the executive officer of the Northwest Ordnance Plant built in Madison by the United States government in 1917 and operated under Gisholt management. Here were manufactured—along with other military equipment—4.7-inch field guns. President Hobart S. Johnson in the 1930's was called upon to pilot his company through lean depression years. The firm continued to hold its own, serving a variety of manufacturers: makers of automobiles, of heavy equipment for railroads, of large excavating machines, and of machine parts for the drillers of oil wells. Sales were especially large in Great Britain and France. In 1938, products went to twenty countries; in that year 47 per cent of dollar sales were to buyers outside the United States and Canada.

The outbreak of World War II in 1939 signaled another period of unusual increase in the use of Gisholt machines. To meet the sudden new demands, the company undertook a greatly expanded program. In 1940, the number of its employees had to be increased by 50 per cent to a total of 1,600. As this rapid acceleration was being implemented, Hobart S. Johnson, in his late sixties, was forced into retirement because of ill health. For two years prior to his death in 1942, he served as chairman of the board of directors. He was sixty-eight at the time of his death.

Gisholt now turned to a grandson of the founder for its fifth president. On August 22, 1940, George H. Johnson, the eldest son of Hobart S. Johnson, succeeded his father as president of the company. At the same time, his youngest brother, H. Stanley Johnson, was elected vice-president. The new officers took over the leadership at a time when pressing wartime decisions must be made and carried out with firmness and efficiency. The company at this date was in sound financial condition. The annual report of December 31, 1940, showed its net worth to be $3,800,000, and cash assets were sufficient to cover all liabilities.[58]

For the second time in a quarter of a century, the Gisholt Machine Company made the transition from peacetime to wartime operations. In 1941 it invested over $1,000,000 in new buildings and machinery. It was necessary to increase the labor force to 2,700 employees, working on three eight-hour shifts, seven days a week. The shops turned out military equipment on contracts both with other manufacturers and with the United States government. For its success in the war effort, Gisholt in August, 1943, received the Army and Navy "E Award" for its excellent record of production.[59]

George H. Johnson, president of the firm, was appointed late in 1942 as director of the tools division of the War Production Board, an assignment taking him to Washington, D.C. During his absence, Vice-president H. Stanley Johnson directed the company's Madison operations – which in 1942 alone resulted in shipments valued at over $30,500,000. The amazing variety of Gisholt's major wartime products included radar devices used by navy pilots in the Pacific, gun mountings for the 90-millimeter high-velocity guns on the huge Chrysler tanks used in the Battle of the Bulge, and crankcases for the 2,000-horsepower engines of fighter planes.

After the war, the company – as it had done a generation earlier – gradually returned to serving the needs of the normal peacetime market. Deceleration in the 1940's proved to be a huge task, but it was not so difficult as that of the 1920's. Gisholt executives had anticipated the necessary adjustments and were prepared for the change-over. While the guns were still firing, the research staff was at work developing new ideas, drafting new designs. It is clear that this recognition of the need to keep abreast of the most recent movements in its field was a vital factor in Gisholt's steady advance, despite the impact of two wars and a major economic depression.

Shortly before his death, John A. Johnson had prophesied that the Gisholt Machine Company possessed a potential for achieving an eminent place in its field. The founder had not been wrong. In a time marked by

[58] The death of Hobart S. Johnson removed the last of the sons of John A. Johnson from the rolls of the company. The youngest son, Maurice I. Johnson, who had held office as treasurer and vice-president, had died in 1935 at the age of fifty-eight.

[59] Working days were so scheduled that no one was employed more than six days per week.

intense competition and swift change in the machine-tool industry, his small enterprise had become one of the leading concerns in a broadening area of manufacturing. The first to build heavy turret lathes, it had designed a wide range of other lathes as specific needs revealed themselves. It had been a pioneer in making and improving dynamic balancing machines and in perfecting superfinishers. With innovation as his watchward and quality as his principle, Gisholt's founder had laid a broad foundation for the company's administration and growth.[60]

[60] Although an effort was made in 1940 to distribute some shares in the Gisholt Machine Company to the general public, members of the Johnson family owned well over half of the stock in 1965. In 1966 the Gisholt Company became a publicly owned corporation and continues as an autonomous division of Giddings and Lewis, Inc., of Fond du Lac, Wisconsin. Members of the Johnson family are among the large stockholders of the new corporation, and George H. Johnson is a director.

CHAPTER VIII

Concerned Citizen and Leader

John A. Johnson was one of the uncommon men of his generation. Above and beyond the various skills that made him an outstanding man of business lay other qualities. Chief among them was his vigorous interest in things academic and in the pressing political issues of his time. He gave his energy to these interests in such measure as to mark him a leader in public affairs.

As with many self-educated men, his mind was never idle. With a keen power of observation and analysis, he could see beyond the immediate to forecast trends and to evaluate evidence and decisions. Wide reading enabled him to draw upon the past in a way that made him conscious of the continuing process of change. Familiarity with the long history of political and religious controversy that had wracked the world gave him a clear-eyed view of the great issues of his century: slavery, civil war, conditions of the laboring class, educational advancement, religious tolerance, social reform. Throughout his lifetime, he grappled with these compelling issues and left upon them the impress of his thinking and his personality.

Johnson was also especially well equipped by natural endowment to play a leader's role. His influence on contemporary affairs was enhanced by the clarity and force with which he presented his ideas. To begin with, his mind functioned pragmatically. He was a clear thinker, a forceful and orderly writer. The logical organization of his thoughts, his vigor, and his sincerity made him a convincing public speaker. No ghost writer was needed: every word of his writings and speeches was his own.

Some of Johnson's public concerns grew out of his experiences as a businessman, particularly those which involved marketing his firm's products abroad. As he traveled in Europe, it troubled him that the United States had slipped far behind in the race for trade in foreign lands. He concluded that this inferiority stemmed from the fact that America lacked a commercial fleet to carry its manufactures and grain abroad. "The most progressive nation on earth," he maintained, "is practically without any ocean shipping. It is a lamentable fact that the Stars and Stripes are a total stranger on the sea and in foreign waters."

This judgment on the part of an American industrialist accurately reflected the maritime situation toward the end of the nineteenth century. Earlier it had been different. Before the Civil War and for a decade afterward, the United States—with her great forests of live oak, white oak, and white pine—continued her former pre-eminence as a shipbuilding and seafaring nation. Her world-wide trade flourished. Major competitors in Europe had no such natural resources to draw upon, and America's supremacy in shipping seemed secure. That is, until England began to construct iron ships powered by steam. In the 1880's came steel ships. Lighter and with improved engines, these vessels could carry great cargoes. Britain built up her merchant marine rapidly; the United States shortsightedly lagged behind. Johnson now saw clearly the results of these trends. From Copenhagen, near the end of 1887, he wrote stressing the fact that English steamships had transported over 6,500,000 tons of cargo that year, while those of American registry had carried only a fraction over 500,000 tons. The ratio was 13 to 1.[1]

In the 1880's and 1890's, Britain had a distinct competitive advantage over the United States in labor costs, both in shipbuilding and in operations at sea. Translated into monetary terms, the expense of constructing ocean-going vessels and manning them was more than 25 per cent greater on this side of the Atlantic than in the British Isles. Johnson realized with dismay that England's remarkably rapid ascendancy in industry and trade had made her in a single generation the greatest maritime nation of the century—a distinction he coveted for his own country. There was, however, no denying the facts. Many years later a London historian wrote of

[1] John A. Johnson to the editor of the *Madison Daily Democrat*, November 7, 1887. The newspaper published the letter and reprinted it as a pamphlet entitled *Our Navy and Commerce* (Madison, 1887). The letter was later published as a pamphlet by the Society for the Advancement of American Shipping under the title *The Absence of the American Flag in Foreign Waters.*

his country's position in this period: "[She was] the forge of the world, the world's carrier, the world's shipbuilder, the world's banker, and the world's workshop." From London and Liverpool her ships radiated to all parts of the British Empire, uniting it as the transcontinental railroads bound together the distant American states.[2]

Although he believed England to be the most serious competitor of the United States, Johnson knew that other countries – Germany, France, Italy, Japan, and Brazil – also posed a grave threat to the growth of American trade in foreign waters. At the time, United States shipping ranked a poor fourth behind England, France, and Germany, the leading Atlantic powers. On a trip to South America, Johnson gathered statistics in Rio de Janeiro to substantiate his country's low rating. For the year 1893, the great Brazilian port had been visited by 629 British ships. France had sent 161 vessels and Germany 140 into Rio's harbor. During the same period, only 60 ships carrying the American flag had anchored there.[3]

In his vigorous articles on shipping and foreign trade, Johnson referred to what he believed to be the only effective remedy: "the well worn method of subsidies." In using these words, he was on sound historical ground, for Venice and Spain at the close of the fifteenth century and England under the first Elizabeth had built their powerful fleets with direct aid to commercial shipping. Now in the late nineteenth century, the governments of Britain and the other major maritime powers were all giving financial grants to shipping interests performing special services benefiting the nation as a whole. Contract subsidies provided so great an advantage that non-subsidized vessels could not compete successfully. It seems clear from his writings that Johnson had in mind for the United States merchant marine the contract type of subsidy.[4]

Looking abroad, Johnson quickly became aware that in the major Eu-

[2] John G. B. Hutchins, *The American Maritime Industries and Public Policy, 1789–1914*, 520, 579 (Cambridge, Massachusetts, 1941); L. C. A. Knowles, *The Industrial and Commercial Revolutions in Great Britain during the Nineteenth Century*, 162–167, 298–305 (London, 1926). The quotation is from Knowles.

[3] "Foreign Trade in Brazil in 1893," in *A Three Months Trip to Argentina, Uruguay, Brazil, 1896* (National Association of Manufacturers of the United States, Philadelphia, 1896). Johnson compiled an impressive collection of data concerning foreign trade entering the major ports of eastern South America.

[4] Johnson, *Our Navy and Commerce*, 7. In this pamphlet, Johnson wrote as an American citizen engaged in business abroad: "Why can we not carry out at least a portion of our own products to market? . . . We look on and see the trade that naturally and fairly belongs to us go elsewhere. It is not only necessary to produce; the surplus products must find a market." See also Hutchins, *The American Maritime Industries*, 48.

ropean countries subsidizing a merchant marine was closely linked with military defense. He could see that ships were a vital necessity in wartime, and his thoughts moved inevitably to the shortsightedness of the American government in this important area. In his pleas for an aroused public opinion in his own country, he presented forcefully the argument that in time of war there must exist a close relationship between a commercial fleet and the United States navy. Using England as a prime example, he urged that plans must be made at once to create a strong merchant marine, ready if war came to become an essential part of the country's line of defense on the sea.[5]

As our later history proved, Johnson's case for a subsidized merchant marine was a strong one. Trained commercial seamen, he explained, could be ready "at the tap of the drum" to enter service in the navy. Merchant ships could be built under government specifications, with possible use in mind as transports in case of war. Johnson realized that to subsidize a fleet of commercial ships would require heavy expenditures, but he opposed any "niggardly, half-way policy." The government might find that such a fleet would at first operate at a loss; he pointed out that in time, however, the reduced cost of freight — on both what was bought and what was sold in transoceanic trade — would clearly result in an over-all compensating gain. The sale of American products abroad would increase greatly in volume, and the total national income would grow in direct proportion.[6]

The leadership that John A. Johnson took on the merchant marine issue attracted considerable national attention. On October 27, 1889, the *Minneapolis Tribune* complimented him on his stand. In an editorial, the paper pointed out that he was a successful Midwestern manufacturer whose agricultural implements were important commodities in our country's foreign trade. As a result of his connections overseas, Johnson was well qualified, by his personal experience and by his careful study of world economic conditions, to discuss the position of the United States in shipping and in international business. The Minnesota newspaper concluded by declaring that the views of such an authority must carry unusual weight.[7]

[5] John A. Johnson, "Ocean Shipping," in the *Minneapolis Tribune*, October 27, 1889.

[6] Johnson, "Ocean Shipping," in the *Minneapolis Tribune*, October 27, 1889.

[7] Other articles by John A. Johnson on the development of a merchant fleet were circulated throughout the United States in newspapers and by the Society for the Advancement of American Shipping.

By fortunate coincidence, other factors helped to advance American shipbuilding at the very time that Johnson was urging the government to act. The second half of the nineteenth century saw the opening of iron mines in Minnesota, the development of economical shipping on the Great Lakes, and the consequent upsurge in the production of iron and steel in the great foundries of the East. New inventions facilitated the use first of iron, then of steel, in the building of more and larger ocean-going vessels. The time was at last ripe, and the United States government moved – as Johnson had hoped it would – to enact legislation supporting a merchant fleet. In 1891, Congress passed the Merchant Marine Act. "Under this law," a maritime historian pointed out in a later era, "the first effort to develop a system of American contract lines was made." It is interesting to note that a few years after Johnson's ideas had been published, Admiral Alfred Thayer Mahan of the United States navy published his classic book, *The Influence of Sea Power upon History*, in which he declared that in time of war it was imperative that an industrial state keep its lines of seaborne trade open by the use of armed naval power.[8]

The maritime legislation of the 1890's was a necessary beginning, but at best it was dangerously late. Subsequently, in two world wars, the United States was forced to rush the building of ships on round-the-clock schedules and at excessive costs. The failure to take effective and adequate measures at the time when Johnson first sounded an alarm proved to be a mistake that would take years to correct. His early views were later incorporated in national policy, as indicated in the granting of subsidies for building oil tankers adapted to military use just before World War II. During the drastic emergencies of that conflict, the government took over the oil carriers and used them to perform a vital service in refueling the fighting ships of the United States navy.[9]

For both patriotic and personal reasons, Johnson also interested himself in developing foreign markets. In 1889, the Pan-American Congress, meeting in Washington, D.C., made an attempt to arouse the interest of American businessmen in trade with Latin American countries. This was a beginning, but it took the panic of 1893 to drive home the lesson that foreign trade provided the key to American economic revival. With this trend of thinking, Johnson found himself in complete accord. He could

[8] Hutchins, *The American Maritime Industries*, 438, 459, 533.

[9] The United States government granted shipbuilding subsidies under the Merchant Marine Act of 1936. See Hutchins, *The American Maritime Industries*, 522.

see clearly that the United States was geared to produce more goods than it could consume, and that the time had come for the country to establish closer relations with other parts of the globe. From his experience with his own business, he realized that American manufacturers must reach out to the expanding markets of the world. To the development of this program, he was to devote much of his time and energy during the last decade of his life.

Both the government and organized industry in the United States increasingly focused their interest on South America in the 1890's – a trend which Johnson sponsored in every way he could. American representatives to Latin American countries had been agitating for some time for improved commercial relations between the two halves of the western hemisphere. G. W. Fishback, secretary of the United States legation in Buenos Aires, and William I. Buchanan, minister to Argentina, had been strongly promoting a plan for leading businessmen of both North and South America to meet and to study ways of increasing intercontinental trade. As a result of the groundwork laid by these two men, Argentina, Brazil, and Uruguay invited the United States to send representative manufacturers south to confer with industrialists in the three eastern South American countries.[10]

The time was right for such an interchange of ideas and opinions. Accepting the invitation eagerly, the National Association of Manufacturers, established in 1895, moved at once to organize a trade delegation. At its first convention, it made plans for a "Commercial Tour to South America," and set out to select a group representative of the leading manufacturing industries of the United States. In logical sequence, the well-organized National Association of Agricultural Implement and Vehicle Manufacturers was asked to select a member to go on the southern mission – and it forthwith chose Johnson. His responsibilities were indicated in a formal statement: "[Our purpose is not only] to establish more intimate trade relations between the United States and the more important South American nations but also to convey to the people of the United States through the members of this party a more thorough and practicable knowledge of the resources of the countries visited, and to indicate the means by which the trade between the nations visited and our country can be enlarged and extended."

[10] Nelson M. Blake, "Background of Cleveland's Venezuelan Policy," in the *North American Review*, 47: 259–277 (January, 1942).

It would be hard to imagine a more suitable American industrialist for this particular assignment than John A. Johnson. In 1896, at the age of sixty-four, he was the veteran president of two well-known and established manufacturing companies, both at the time competing successfully in foreign markets, especially in Europe. To this record was to be added the reputation he enjoyed as an observer, writer, and speaker in his chosen field. One other asset was clear to all who knew him: he understood and believed in the goals of the venture he was to engage in.

The twelve-man delegation was to sail from New York City on July 1, 1896, on a three-months' tour. Before the departure, the president of the National Association of Manufacturers was host at a banquet at the Waldorf-Astoria Hotel, attended, among others, by the mayors of New York, Brooklyn, and Philadelphia. From Washington, South American diplomats – the ministers of Argentina and Brazil and the consul general of Uruguay – had also come to add an international flavor to the affair. Among the speakers was John A. Johnson, representing the farm machinery segment of American manufacturing.[11]

The next day, guided by G. W. Fishback, who had come up from Buenos Aires to direct the party, the Americans boarded the "St. Paul" bound for London. United States warships fired a salute as the "Continental Tour" got under way through the Narrows of New York harbor. After a week-long crossing and two days in England, the group re-embarked on the "Danube" of the Royal Mail Line. On the return trip across the Atlantic by the southern route, the ship traveled through the Bay of Biscay to Lisbon, and thence by way of the Cape Verde Islands to the South American continent.[12]

The journey over the South Atlantic took approximately three weeks. On July 21 the "Danube" crossed the equator, and on the first day of August it entered the port of Buenos Aires, Argentina, where an enthusiastic reception awaited the visitors. Here in the city which Johnson called the "Palace of the South," the United States delegation established its base of operations. Argentina, Johnson noted as he visited the hinterland, was a country of tremendous extent. The pampas stretched farther than the eye could reach in every direction. This was a great wheat and cattle area, like the American West Johnson knew so well. Its capacity as a meat-

[11] *New York World*, June 29, 1896, in a story forecasting the event.

[12] *A Three Months Trip to Argentina, Uruguay, Brazil, 1896*. At the time, no passenger steamers connected New York with ports in South America.

producing region caused the observer to speculate that the United States – if it was to compete in world markets – must increase and upgrade its meat production. Unlike North America, Argentina lacked lumber, metals, and coal, and it had little heavy industry. As the result of his observations, the North American visitor saw excellent opportunities for marketing manufactured products, which the South American country could use in quantity.

After a time, the delegation moved on to Montevideo, the capital of Uruguay, and thence to Brazil. Well received everywhere, the American industrialists visited a large number of city factories and penetrated far into the interior to study the natural resources of each country. With a keen eye on conditions in each area, Johnson took special notes concerning problems manufacturers of his country would face in pushing their trade efforts into these remote southern regions. He was particularly interested in the question of local and foreign competition and with making a reasoned judgment about what specific products were needed in South America and would find a substantial market there.

Developing his extensive notes, Johnson, while still in the south, sent the *Farm Implement News* in Chicago a digest of his findings in Argentina and Brazil. On October 15, 1896, the trade journal carried an eight-column article in which he discussed what he had learned to date in South America. Later he drew upon his daily jottings for a small book published on December 15, 1896, under the title *South America: Its Resources and Possibilities*. In the first part of the booklet, Johnson described the economic outlook of the countries he had seen. Going further, he proposed plans for more extended commercial relations with the nations of the southern hemisphere.

The problem of direct competition with Argentina and Brazil in world markets occupied the second part of Johnson's study. One could see, he wrote, that these countries were producing in large quantities the agricultural products – beef and wheat – that were the backbone of the farming industry of the United States. The message to northern agriculturalists, millers, and meat packers was clear: they must study and work to improve their marketing position. Concerning all manufactured goods from North American plants, one could say that there was a great opportunity in the south. Favorable markets and extensive sales awaited only the initiative of alert and able manufacturers in the north.

There was competition, too, from across the Atlantic, Johnson reported. All the maritime nations of Europe were carrying on substantial business with Argentina, Uruguay, and Brazil. Even Belgium sold more goods to these countries than did the United States. All had established banks in the leading South American cities — private enterprises of great assistance in fostering international trade. He suggested that American bankers investigate opportunities to the south, going far enough to imply that they had heretofore been too conservative to explore the challenging possibilities. Of the three countries he had visited, he found that the smallest had the most solid banking system. "The plucky little republic of Uruguay," he pointed out, "has been wise enough to establish and adhere to a specie basis, a gold basis at that, and she will doubtless have her reward." Northern nations might learn some banking lessons in the southern hemisphere.

Johnson was critical of the diplomatic service of the United States in South American countries. He urged the appointment of really qualified men and an end to merely political preferment. Representatives of our country to foreign nations, he maintained, should know the language, habits, laws, and customs of the peoples to whom they were assigned. Personal qualities of a high order — such as integrity of purpose, balanced judgment, and a broad knowledge of the purposes, ideals, and resources of the United States — were required of official representatives appointed by our state department. Again the implication was clear: Johnson had been disappointed in the caliber of diplomats he had met in South America. He was willing to extend the point a step further in his own field: If American industrial companies really wished to flourish in the Latin American countries, they, too, must send south only really qualified men of the highest type.

In the concluding paragraph of his *South America*, Johnson paid a tribute to his own country. He had returned from the South American tour, he declared, better satisfied with the United States — its laws, its government, its institutions, its people. He made special mention of the American system of jurisprudence: "We know not what boon the fathers brought with them in the English Common Law. I myself can appreciate the importance of our free press, the palladium of our liberties and the support of an enlightened public opinion, that alone makes a just and stable government possible. We are marvelously favored with a good country. There is none like it on earth."

After the completion of the commercial mission at the end of October,

1896, Johnson continued in public addresses to urge that trade with Latin America be encouraged in every feasible way. At the annual meeting of his own organization, the National Association of Agricultural Implement and Vehicle Manufacturers, in Nashville, Tennessee, in November of the same year, one evening was given over to a report on what he had seen and learned in his visit below the equator. The chairman of the meeting in his introduction of the speaker of the occasion, revealed the high esteem in which his colleagues held their official representative. "Mr. Johnson is the Nestor of our Association," he said, "and without disparagement to any other member of the distinguished body, it may be said that he is one of its most intelligent and observant members." At the conclusion of Johnson's address, he was "enthusiastically applauded." [13]

The South American sojourn gave Johnson an opportunity to widen his acquaintance among American manufacturers in fields outside his own. Particularly on the long sea voyages, he made new personal friends, whom he described interestingly in his letters to his sons, Fred, Carl, and Hobart. One such member of the delegation, who manufactured steam engines and cotton gins, was "a congenial spirit, a man of good principles and decided natural ability. He is a self-made man who began with nothing but who has built his business by ability and energy." Of other delegates, he observed that one lacked "breadth of observation," and another who showed no interest in reading was "not very penetrative." Outstanding in the group, in his estimation, was J. M. Studebaker, vice-president of Studebaker Brothers, makers of carriages and wagons in South Bend, Indiana. "He is a man of strong business sense," Johnson observed, "not well educated, but [he] details his experiences quite well and knows every detail in his great business. The Studebaker brothers are all good workers. . . . Studebaker is quite communicative," he concluded, "and I hope to learn considerable about his methods, have learned considerable already."

Beyond his involvement in matters of trade and shipping, Johnson's interests had always moved naturally into the realm of foreign affairs. His reading had given him insight into the historical contributions and diplomacy of the larger European nations. He greatly admired England, and in all his writings he appears as a true Anglophile. He visited that country whenever he could — which was frequently in his later years, when the Gisholt Machine Company had developed a substantial market there. It

[13] *Daily Sun* (Nashville, Tennessee), November 18, 1896.

pleased him to make these trips abroad, in which he mingled business, family reunions, and an opportunity to indulge his love for historical and cultural observation.

In 1897, he made such a sentimental journey. That year John B. Cassoday, chief justice of the Wisconsin supreme court, whose daughter Carl A. Johnson had married, was in London. With him, Johnson visited the Inns of Court, a memorable experience which he described in a letter to a newspaper in his home community. "These Inns," he explained, "may be said to be the cradle of English statesmanship, English law and English greatness. [The four inns] were really law schools from which every English barrister must get his diploma." The common law, as developed in England through the centuries, he held to be "the greatest bulwark of the innocent subject and citizen and of the rights of property ever devised by man." Unusual knowledge of English history for an American of his time illuminated Johnson's letter. He referred to the wisdom of Queen Elizabeth in consulting with her "faithful commons"; he contrasted her with Charles I, who probably lost his head because he lacked her judgment. In closing, he reminded Americans back home how much the constitution of the United States and the constitutions of the individual states – Wisconsin included – owed to English sources.[14]

Johnson also went to the British Museum and found it of consuming interest. "It is the greatest in the world," he maintained. He was fascinated to see there, among the other historical documents, the Magna Carta with King John's seal. In surveying English history, he most admired that country's contributions in world diplomacy. An honest critic, however, he recorded England's mistakes in foreign relations, citing two in particular: the harsh treatment of the American colonies which brought on the American Revolution – and the behavior of the British government at the time of the Opium War in China. Despite these lapses, Johnson believed that on balance England's virtues far outweighed her faults.

Most Americans favored the inhabitants of the South African Transvaal and Orange Free State in the Boer War involving Great Britain at the turn of the century. Not so Johnson. The decisive campaigns of the struggle included the last two years of his life, at the time his ties with England were the closest. Aware that his countrymen in the United States were calling him a pro-Britisher, he defended his position with an appeal to history

[14] Johnson, in the *Madison Democrat*, August 10, 1897. The letter was written on July 10, 1897, in Carlsbad, Germany.

and a reference to the international contest for world dominion. He knew what the Dutch had done in the cause of human freedom in the wars with Spain in the sixteenth and seventeenth centuries – and he admired their fight for the recognition of their country as a separate nation. Now, however, the Boers fighting the British in Africa did not seem to him to be the liberty-loving Dutchmen who had battled so bravely for the Netherlands against Philip II, the Duke of Alva, and their Spanish legions.

There can be little doubt that the issue of slavery influenced Johnson to favor England in the war in South Africa. The British parliament had abolished slavery throughout the Empire in 1833, and had offered to pay the Dutch settlers of the Transvaal and Orange Free State for their losses in setting their slaves free. But the Boers, long accustomed to enslaving black Africans, resisted the emancipation act. Friction continued through the century, which saw the American Civil War fought over much the same issue. Johnson's strong lifetime feeling that slaves everywhere must be freed overshadowed other considerations, including sympathy for the underdog Boer farmers in their uneven struggle with the mighty British Empire.

There were complex political issues as well, but on these also Johnson accepted the English point of view in South African affairs. Looking about him, he saw in eastern Europe a kind of specter of power kept at bay only by the strength of British arms. In a paper which he wrote at the time, he declared that England was "the only effective barrier to Russian expansion." If the Boers should win the war and break up British South Africa, the effect would be to cut the line of communication between the English colonies in the south and the Sudan and Egypt in the north. In Johnson's view, such an outcome would seriously disturb the balance of power in the world. Both Great Britain and the United States would be menaced by the rising strength of a despotic Russia.[15]

The end of the Spanish-American War had engaged Johnson's close attention when the disposition of the Philippine Islands became a hotly debated issue in 1898 and 1899. To take responsibility for an oriental people in the Far East would be a radical departure from American for-

[15] Johnson is the author of an undated, unpublished typescript nine pages in length, in which he set down his position on the Boer War. He died before the war ended, but, though seriously ill, he continued writing during the winter of 1900–1901. It is probable that he wrote the paper early in 1901, at a time when it was certain that England would win the war. A copy of this article is in the Johnson Papers and an excerpt, giving his views on Great Britain versus Russia, is in the Appendix, p. 292.

eign policy. Yet the relatively helpless Filipinos obviously could not govern themselves, and to return them to Spanish rule was unthinkable. Should America sell the islands or transfer them to some European colonial power like England? For several months after the cessation of actual fighting, the controversy over what to do raged throughout the United States.

To most thinking Americans, the question of the Philippines was important from both diplomatic and moral points of view. While the commissioners of the United States and Spain were meeting in Paris to draw up peace terms, Johnson — as he had done so often in the past — set forth his views in trenchant newspaper articles. "Spain has taken good care not to educate the people [*the Filipinos*]," he argued, "or prepare them for self government. It taxed them to the utmost, but our sense of fairness and judgment will not permit us to tax them to any considerable extent more than sufficient to defray the cost of governing them. . . . It will never do to surrender the Philippines to Spain so as to expose them, again, to the vengeance and tyranny of their old oppressors. It will not comport with our dignity . . . to sell the islands. We are not fighting for money or for dominion. Our sole motive is humanity and justice." [16]

With his admiration for all things British, it is not surprising that Johnson took seriously the remote possibility that England might be persuaded to take over the government of the Philippines. "If the United States should decide to transfer these islands to Great Britain," he wrote, "it should be done without money and without price or conditions, except that she [*Great Britain*] must not dispose of them without our consent." He added as a suggestion, however, that if the islands should go to England, it should be understood that our trade with them should have preferential status. Actually, Johnson was certain that Great Britain — caught up in the intense power struggle in Europe — would prefer that America keep the Philippines. This it soon developed was to be the ultimate solution. On February 6, 1899, the United States senate ratified the peace treaty with Spain. Under its terms, this country took over control of the islands. Two months earlier, Johnson had come around to this resolution of the issue. "If we cannot give them to [some other] wise and capable government,"

[16] John A. Johnson, "What Shall Be Done with the Philippines?" in the *Milwaukee Sentinel*, June 27, 1898. See also Thomas A. Bailey, *A Diplomatic History of the American People*, 511–513 (New York, 1955), and Samuel Flagg Bemis, *A Diplomatic History of the United States*, 463–475 (New York, 1955).

he reasoned, "we shall have to keep them and do the best we can, although we may hold them at a loss." [17]

Johnson had genuine misgivings about the extension of United States sovereignty into the western Pacific. He felt even more strongly that the North American continent—with its islands, among which he included Hawaii—would one day form a great single nation. "This will not come by conquest," he wrote in 1898, "but by fair and honorable means because of the advantages such a grand union has to offer." A few months later, he summarized his credo for his country in terms that fitted well the story of his own life: "Let the United States speak to all the world in language that can neither be misinterpreted nor misunderstood. This we can do if we afford ample educational facilities for the poorest as well as the richest in our land; if we create industrial development so as to enable everyone willing and able to earn a fair livelihood for himself and those dependent on him, and by administering exact and even-handed justice to every citizen alike, to every citizen of whatever station." [18]

The last quarter of the nineteenth century had brought the Monroe Doctrine into new prominence. A succession of international incidents had stirred Americans—Johnson among them—into new and more extensively national interpretations. With no territorial ambitions for his own country, Johnson was adamant in opposition to any encroachment by other powers in the western hemisphere. He particularly resented the fact that Germany had favored Spain in the Spanish-American War, and was personally affronted by Bismarck's slur that the Monroe Doctrine was "a species of arrogance peculiarly American." Reacting to such anti-American attitudes, Johnson rallied to the defense of the doctrine and of other cherished declarations of America's independent position in the New World. His readiness to take up his pen for his country involved him in one newspaper debate that attracted considerable public attention.[19]

Early in 1896, an article by Professor H. E. von Holst, a German-

[17] John A. Johnson, "Give the Philippines to England," in the *Milwaukee Sentinel*, December 4, 1898. Great Britain, although neutral, was the only large European power friendly to the United States in the Spanish-American War. See Bailey, *A Diplomatic History of the American People*, 511–513, and Bemis, *A Diplomatic History of the United States*, 463–475.

[18] See Johnson's articles in the *Milwaukee Sentinel*, June 27, December 4, 1898. The annexation of Hawaii lagged, but on August 12, 1898, by vote of the senate, the islands were formally transferred to the United States with status as a territory.

[19] Bailey, *A Diplomatic History of the American People*, 460–467, 488–492, 512; Bemis, *A Diplomatic History of the United States*, 415–422.

American scholar who was chairman of the department of history at the University of Chicago, appeared in a Chicago newspaper. Its tone was critical of American institutions and policies. Among other strictures, von Holst wrote that the Monroe Doctrine had ceased to be an issue and that the Declaration of Independence no longer was important. In the course of his remarks, the professor disparaged both Thomas Jefferson and James Monroe, two American presidents whom Johnson particularly admired. This was too much, and in less than a week an answer to von Holst was on its way from Madison to the Chicago paper. Using a quotation from a letter Jefferson had written to Monroe in 1823, Johnson reaffirmed the current force of the Monroe Doctrine. That document was indeed—in Jefferson's words—"the compass setting our course through an ocean of time." It would never cease to be an issue in the minds of Americans. Nor was the Declaration of Independence dwindling in importance. "There are principles laid down in the Declaration," Johnson insisted, "that will never cease to be an issue this side of the Millennium." [20]

John A. Johnson's interest in foreign affairs did not detract from his concern for the internal policies of the United States. In fact, he found the two inextricably bound together. During the last two decades of the nineteenth century, he gave particular attention to the tariff. As an exporter, he sensed the importance to foreign trade of legislation in this area. In 1881–1882, a surplus of $100,000,000 in the United States treasury elevated the tariff issue into new prominence. As a result, from that time to the end of the century, Johnson studied the problems involved and made his thinking on them known through newspaper articles and public addresses. His criticism of the tariff policies of President Grover Cleveland brought him wide recognition in a controversy of national importance.

President Chester A. Arthur in 1882 suggested tariff reform designed to reduce the treasury surplus. Five years later, President Cleveland made the matter a party issue by demanding a general tariff reduction. The Mills Bill before congress at that time became a major subject for debate in the presidential campaign of 1888. Johnson regretted the injection of the tariff issue into partisan politics. In 1884 and in 1886, he supported the Democratic party, but by 1888, he could not accept Cleveland's position

[20] H. E. von Holst, in the *Chicago Tribune Herald*, January 19, 1896; John A. Johnson, in the *Chicago Tribune Herald*, January 25, 1896. Professor von Holst had earlier published a book entitled *Constitutional and Political History of the United States*, originally written in German and translated into English.

nor the provisions of the Mills Bill. Instead, he once more espoused the policies of the Republican party; he became an ardent advocate of a protective tariff for young American industries, particularly if they were competing with well-established industries abroad.[21]

In his public statements, Johnson denied that he was a high-tariff man; repeatedly he declared that he was no dyed-in-the-wool protectionist. He held that the tariff should be revised not for revenue only but "with protection of labor and American industries in constant view." He was never a free trader. Although some persons in his home state criticized him for deserting the Democratic party, fair-minded people who knew him respected his commitment to principle. One Wisconsin newspaper editor, who disagreed with him about the tariff, summed up this point of view: "He is a man of strong convictions and speaks his mind with less fear of consequences than do most men. Johnson's opinions, as are most of our opinions, are biased by self-interest. But his writings are a manly and candid discussion of the question. His arguments," the editor concluded, "are presented with courtesy, and any replies to Johnson should be presented in the same way." [22]

Significantly in view of his own business interests, Johnson suggested that congress should remove the tariff on agricultural implements. He maintained that the manufacture of farm machinery had reached an advanced position in the United States. "It is so superior to [that of] foreign manufacturers," he explained in a newspaper article, "that [no farm implements] are being imported." Strengthening his argument at the time was the public statement of a leading trade journal that farm machinery manufactured in the United States represented the first product to establish any credit abroad for America as a manufacturing nation.[23]

Senator John C. Spooner of Wisconsin presented a petition from John A. Johnson to the United States senate on February 2, 1888. The document formally requested that import duties on farm machinery be abol-

[21] *Skandinaven,* August 7, 1883, October 25, 31, 1888; *Madison Democrat,* December 21, 1899; *Farm Implement News,* October, 1891. Johnson believed that the Mills Bill showed favoritism to Southern states. He pointed out that, of the thirteen committee members reporting favorably on the bill, six were from the South and eight were Democrats.

[22] *Milwaukee Sentinel,* November 28, 1888; N. P. Haugen, "The Tariff on Raw Material," a speech in the house of representatives by Congressman N. P. Haugen of Wisconsin, in the *Congressional Record,* August 9, 1888; *Manitowoc Pilot* (Manitowoc, Wisconsin), January 12, 1888. The quotation is from the *Manitowoc Pilot.*

[23] *Springfield Republican* (Massachusetts), February 5, 1888; *Farm Implement News,* October, 1891, February 27, 1896.

ished. In his remarks introducing the request, Senator Spooner said: "I present the petition of John A. Johnson, president of the Fuller and Johnson Manufacturing Company of Madison, Wisconsin. Mr. Johnson is a distinguished citizen of Wisconsin of Scandinavian birth, who has recently published a very able criticism of the message of the President [*Cleveland*] on the subject of the tariff and as the petition is short, I ask that it may be read."

In his request, Johnson advanced three main points: (1) that present import duties on farm implements are superfluous, useless, and even harmful to American producers; (2) that incorrect allegations claiming that the present duties compel the American farmer to pay much higher prices are believed, even though false, and that, as a result, they cause ill feeling toward American manufacturers; (3) that there is in this instance no need to protect American labor against foreign cheap labor, since no implements of foreign manufacture are now being imported. After the reading by Senator Spooner, the communication was published in the *Congressional Record*.[24]

On the subject of tariff revision, Johnson gave a number of addresses, sometimes in support of political candidates whose views were similar to his own. In October, 1888, when he spoke at Winona, Minnesota, Congressman James A. Tawney of the first congressional district of Minnesota, a high-tariff man, was in the large audience. A local newspaper reported that "the visiting speaker gave an eloquent and argumentative speech." Johnson had been in England when Cleveland delivered his address on the tariff in 1887. At that time, he had seen how the English welcomed the American president's policy. The British had no doubt that the United States was now embarking on all-out free trade. At Winona, Johnson pointed out the reasons why this country could not yet adopt such a policy of free trade as England had put into practice.[25]

England had had more than three hundred years of protection for her products, Johnson said, before she adopted a free-trade policy. Only about forty years had passed since the British government removed its protective tariffs in 1846. By that date, Great Britain had established her industries

[24] *Milwaukee Journal*, February 2, 1888; *Congressional Record*, February 3, 1888; *Skandinaven*, February 22, 1888. The petition is in the Appendix, p. 292–293. In his correspondence with Senator Spooner, Johnson explained that he, not his company, was responsible for addressing congress on the matter of import duties.

[25] John A. Johnson, "This Is the Issue," in the *Winona Republican Herald* (Winona, Minnesota), October 20, 1888.

so firmly that she had little fear of serious competition. Furthermore, from her colonial empire, she drew great wealth in raw materials and from expanding markets. The industrial revolution had come early to England, enabling her to establish world markets in weaker countries. Complete mistress of the sea, she could dictate the policies of Egypt, India, and Turkey – to say nothing of lesser countries. "England preaches to us the advantage of free trade," Johnson warned his Winona audience. "To the unsuspecting fly, the spider sings 'Walk into my parlor.' " [26]

What Johnson was stressing grew out of recent experience with his own two still-young business enterprises. He felt that those who referred to an industry as "no longer being an infant after 25 years" had no conception of the tremendous investment required to maintain a business. Manufacturing in the United States called for large amounts of capital, administrative and technical skill, constant attention to new improvements and to the need for extension of markets. "The average man," Johnson observed in a newspaper article, "has little understanding of the cost of converting tons of pig iron into Bessemer steel – or of the difficulty of finding reliable mechanics and of establishing branch houses and markets." [27]

As he naturally did in other areas, Johnson held dynamic rather than static views concerning the impact of tariff policies on labor. He believed that laborers in America must be protected: The worker should be well paid, for he was also the consumer, and the consumer was the wheel that kept industry in motion. Labor in Europe was cheap – a fact that made it possible for European industries to undersell the products of the United States in the world market. He urged the constant upgrading of American workers through training and education. "A trained and intelligent people will produce more and consume more," he maintained, "and thus be better able to develop our resources." [28]

Agriculture also needed a protective tariff. Johnson was concerned with the situation of the farmer engaged in raising raw products. Of special interest to him was the danger to the Wisconsin tobacco economy. With cheap coolie labor, Sumatra was shipping in large consignments of tobacco, providing a new source of serious competition to the American-grown

[26] Johnson, "This Is the Issue," in the *Winona Republican Herald*, October 20, 1888; Johnson, "The Great Issue: The Protectionist Side of the Tariff Question," in the *Milwaukee Sentinel*, January 9, 1888; *Wisconsin State Journal*, January 10, 11, 12, 1888; Knowles, *The Industrial and Commercial Revolutions in Great Britain*, 131–133.

[27] *Madison Daily Democrat*, January 14, 1888.

[28] *Madison Daily Democrat*, January 14, 1888.

leaf. Although United States importers and manufacturers opposed a higher tariff, farmers could not compete with labor paid only a few cents a day. Here was an issue that touched Johnson's home county. Responding to the pleas of the Dane County Tobacco Growers Association, he journeyed to Washington seeking to advance the cause of all American producers. For this effort in behalf of his neighbors, a Madison newspaper publicly thanked Johnson, and complimented him as "a man of high personal character and rare business capacity." [29]

The manufacturer, like the laborer and the farmer, Johnson believed, would soon be in trouble if tariff revision got out of hand. Since 1828, tariffs in the United States had suffered alarming fluctuations. The uncertainty resulting from these unpredictable changes made for insecurity in business. He urged that tariffs should run for specified periods of time, so that manufacturers would know what to expect.

In all that Johnson proposed for the regulation of the tariff, he took as his basis the certain tremendous growth in business and industry that he foresaw for the country. "Give us 20 years," he said on one occasion, "and the financial center of the world will be in the United States." His words had a prophetic ring when he declared that in the event of war Europe would have to come to us for both money and food. As for the United States, this nation would be well prepared for defense if it could develop its manufacturing potential. In his view, tariff policies must assist, not hinder, the full realization of this great promise of the future. "The cloth mill, the blast furnace, the rolling mill, the machine shop are among our very strongest fortifications," he declared, "and the weaver, the iron monger, the shoe maker, the merchant are among our most effective soldiers." [30]

The tariff issue was not settled in Cleveland's first administration. As a result, it passed to the next congress, which enacted legislation known as the McKinley tariff. This law was to be effective to the end of the single presidential term of Benjamin Harrison. With the help of Wisconsin members of congress — Senator John C. Spooner and Congressman Robert M. La Follette — Johnson followed closely the early course of debate over the tariff bill. He found himself critical of provisions in the act that gave higher protection to some products than was necessary. Sugar was a case in point. The new law placed raw sugar on the free list — and thus satisfied

[29] *Wisconsin State Journal*, February 14, 1888.

[30] *Winona Republican Herald*, October 20, 1888; *Milwaukee Sentinel*, January 9, 1888; *Skandinaven*, February 11, 1888; *Wisconsin State Journal*, February 1, 1888.

the sugar refining interests. But it also put refined sugar under a protective tariff – again helping the refiner at the expense of the consumer. The raw sugar provision was so detrimental to the growers of sugar in the United States that Louisiana and Kansas farmers were compensated with a bounty of two cents a pound. Johnson's doubt concerning the constitutionality of this particular provision only confirmed his general dissatisfaction with the tariff policies of President Harrison's administration.

Johnson was in close touch with Senator Spooner and Representative La Follette concerning a proposed change in the federal election law. On this political issue, he addressed the two Wisconsin legislators in Washington urging the enactment of a free-ballot, fair-count bill. As a Republican, he particularly opposed the views of Southern Democrats. Senator Spooner in his reply revealed his doubt that he and other supporters of the election bill like La Follette could muster enough votes to secure its passage.

The McKinley tariff, however, soon developed into the main political issue, as La Follette pointed out in answering Johnson's letter. After thanking him for his "valuable suggestions" on the election bill, the congressman admitted that he was disturbed because the Republicans had a slender, shrinking majority in the house of representatives. Some new states – such as North and South Dakota and Washington – had just been admitted to the Union; their representatives had added strength to the Democrats. In the upcoming election campaign of 1892, the McKinley tariff would be blamed for the rising cost of living. Mainly because of this factor, tariff revision again became the main national issue in the vote that returned Cleveland to the presidency and elected more Democrats to both houses of congress.[31]

With the new Democratic administration came the Wilson-Gorman tariff, enacted into law in 1894 without President Cleveland's signature. As Johnson followed early debate over the new bill, he objected that the replacement of specific duties by ad valorem duties did not have "a single redeeming feature." Moreover, placing raw wool on the free list favored importers of wool for manufacturing purposes, but was bad for American farmers raising sheep. The new tariff simply brought farm managers in the United States into sharp competition with their counterparts in older countries, which had been heavy producers of wool for hundreds of years.

[31] John C. Spooner to John A. Johnson, July 13, 25, 1890; Robert M. La Follette to John A. Johnson, January 13, 1890.

The problem touched Wisconsin directly: a transition in agriculture in the southern part of the state was phasing out wheat farming in favor of sheep raising. Walworth County in the 1880's led its neighbors in the size of its herds; the Dane County animal census of 1880 counted 81,000 sheep. No doubt Johnson's awareness of how the Wilson-Gorman act affected these familiar localities led to his close interest in the problem. His home state, however, never became a great wool-producing area. Yielding to the competition of the immense sheep ranges in the Western states, Wisconsin in time turned to the development of butter and cheese as more dependable products.[32]

In the aftermath of the panic of 1893, the Wilson-Gorman tariff did not wear well. Once again, the American people were ready for a change in Washington, and the election of 1896 brought to the presidency William McKinley, whose name had been on the earlier tariff law. Now, as president, he called congress into special session to revise customs duties according to the proposed Republican pattern. Out of this came the Dingley tariff of 1897 — the highest to that date, with previously free goods now taxed. Johnson seriously questioned raising the tariff on commodities that needed no protection. The new tariff on copper, he thought, was useless: the United States produced two thirds of the world's copper and none had been imported for many years. The same situation existed for farm implements. Previously always on the free list, they were now to be "protected," even though no one was importing them.

Canadian legislation passed in 1894 placed a 35 per cent tariff on agricultural implements, an act that disturbed Johnson. His reaction was to advocate a treaty of reciprocity with our neighbors to the north. When the National Association of Manufacturers of Agricultural Implements met in Chicago on February 13, 1894, members revealed their alarm over the new Canadian tariff. Certainly this important change would influence the market for farm machinery manufactured in the United States. To meet the situation, the Association named John A. Johnson to head a committee to study the problem and make a report. The gist of the resulting recommendation — signed by members of the Association and dispatched to the United States senate — consisted of two parts: (1) no necessity for general tariff protection on agricultural implements existed; (2) there

[32] Joseph Schafer, *A History of Agriculture in Wisconsin*, 103, 107, 113, 124 (Madison, 1922); Joseph Schafer, *The Wisconsin Lead Region*, 267–276 (Madison, 1932).

was a need for protection against unfair trade, by means of a reciprocity treaty with Canada.[33]

Evidence supporting Johnson's views regarding the tariff on farm implements was furnished by a report published in 1895 by the United States treasury department. Exports of farm machinery in 1894, the report revealed, were over $4,700,000; in 1895 they had increased to over $5,300,000 – a healthy gain of well over a half million dollars in one year. At the same time, imports in this category totaled less than $5,000. The *Farm Implement News* echoed Johnson's assertion that there was nothing to fear in the area of agricultural implements from such a tiny trickle of foreign competition. The ratio in favor of exports was overwhelming.[34]

In 1899, near the end of his active career, Johnson declared he had not changed his views concerning the tariff on farm implements. He was by that time also a very successful manufacturer of machine tools, which required large consignments of iron – but he favored "putting them also on the free list." He by no means advocated, however, the removal of all protective restrictions. Instead, he held that tariffs on some commodities could be reduced and, conversely, that increased protection would be profitable for others. "It is my hope," he wrote in a newspaper article, "that the American people will adopt such measures that will best promote the interests of the country and of mankind." Although lumber and iron were staples in his manufacturing business, there is no indication that Johnson ever sought personal advantage by urging that these raw materials be put on the tariff-free list.[35]

In the late 1880's and throughout the 1890's, Johnson's articles on the tariff were widely published in Wisconsin and beyond the borders of the state. Publications supporting his views included in the Midwest the *Milwaukee Sentinel, Minneapolis Tribune, St. Paul Pioneer Press* – and in the East the *Springfield Republican* and the *Nation*. Established Norwegian-language newspapers – *Fædrelandet og Emigranten, Amerika*, and *Skandinaven* – regularly carried Johnson's writings on the tariff and strongly backed his position with their own editorials.

Many editors – not all on his side of the tariff issue – expressed praise

[33] *Farm Implement News*, February 15, 1894. A large number of members – both Democrats and Republicans – signed the document.

[34] "Finance, Commerce and Immigration of the United States," in *United States Treasury Report* (Washington, D.C., 1895). See also "Foreign Trade," in the *Farm Implement News*, February 27, 1896.

[35] *Wisconsin State Journal*, September 9, 1899.

of Johnson's abilities as a thinker and writer on protection versus free trade. "[His articles are] the ablest and most complete reply to fallacies of the free traders," declared the high-tariff editor of the *Wisconsin State Journal*. "[They are] the most logical argument in favor of the Republican protective tariff that has been made by any of the most able political defenders." Papers like the *Madison Daily Democrat* that disagreed with his stand on tariff matters still recognized that Johnson was an unusually well informed and forceful political writer. "His lucid presentation of the subject is better than [that of] Blaine or Sherman," the Democratic editor maintained. "Mr. Johnson's integrity will not be questioned, he is above suspicion in that regard. There is a degree of fairness running through [his] argument seldom found in the writings of the protectionists." [36]

In the presidential election of 1896, Johnson took a firm stand opposing free silver, the all-important issue of the campaign. He was a staunch supporter of McKinley and the gold standard against William Jennings Bryan, the Democratic standard bearer for "16-to-1" bimetallism. For many years, Johnson had been a student of monetary and banking systems. In the Wisconsin state senate in the early 1870's, he had urged banking reforms. As a leading Madison businessman, he had been a stockholder in two local banks and president of one of them. Two panics had taught him the necessity of wise and cautious financial management. Now in his middle sixties, he had a fund of accumulated practical wisdom that gave his writings on financial matters a particular cogency – especially at a time when a new wave of political hysteria was stirring up the country over the silver issue.[37]

Many of Johnson's articles on monetary matters were widely quoted. In them he advocated a national banking system. In favoring this plan, he explained in an article in a local newspaper: "It is far better than European methods because it is divided into comparatively small banks scattered all over the country and largely owned by small holders, while in England, France and Germany they have very large institutions, the failure of any one of which is a national disaster." Although the Bank of England was a private corporation, it worked so closely with the British government that it had the complete confidence of the public. England was

[36] *Wisconsin State Journal*, July 9, September 3, 1888; "Johnson and the President's Message," an editorial in the *Madison Daily Democrat*, January 10, 1888.

[37] N. B. Van Slyke, president of the First National Bank of Madison, to John A. Johnson, December 31, 1870; Wayne Ramsay, cashier of the First National Bank of Madison, to Johnson, January 5, 1871.

often Johnson's model for America, but in this instance he was firm in his support of the individual bank with local management and ownership.

In the same article, however, Johnson pointed out that the national banks should really be national banks: "A depositor in them should be as safe as if he deposited in the national treasury." He advocated that the government guarantee bank deposits; it could tax the banks to provide an insurance fund. Under such a guarantee, there would never be a run on any national bank. This system would force the states to set up a similar method of safeguarding deposits in state-chartered banks. The deposit insurance plans advocated by Johnson proved to be a generation ahead of their time, but they pointed the way to the present system.[38]

Anticipating the debates on currency legislation facing the McKinley administration and congress in the spring of 1897, Johnson set forth his ideas on the issues in a pamphlet. Widely distributed and often quoted by the press, this publication, *What Shall Our Paper Currency Be?* became one of its author's most influential writings. The gist of Johnson's views is simple: The country must have a currency system strongly backed by the federal government. He held that issuing circulating silver and treasury notes or bank bills was not a proper banking function. All such paper should be retired; in its place, he advocated only the use of greenbacks issued by the federal government. Backed by gold and the credit of the United States, this system would provide a sound, freely circulating currency. The secretary of the treasury should be authorized to maintain a reasonable gold reserve by selling gold bonds when necessary. To support his proposals, he called attention to the successful management of such matters in all leading European countries, where uniformly the currency was under the jurisdiction of the government.[39]

Maintaining that a government could not give metal a value by monetizing it, Johnson was strongly opposed to silver coinage. He could see only two possible plans under which it could be allowed. The first might be free coinage of so-called precious metals with the arrangement that every contract should specify whether payment should be in gold or in silver. Prices also would have to be stated in one or the other metal. The second plan might be to allow free coinage of silver with the stipulation that the metal be legal tender according to its current market value. Johnson regarded

[38] *Madison Democrat*, December 22, 1894.

[39] John A. Johnson, *What Shall Our Paper Currency Be? What Shall Be the Solution of the Silver Problem?* (Madison, 1897). A copy of this pamphlet is in the Johnson Papers. See also *Amerika* (Madison), June 2, 1897.

both of these plans as totally impracticable; he could not give his support to either.

In an article in a Chicago newspaper, he stated his belief that a flexible currency would safely adjust to the country's needs: "We hear much talk about making our paper currency elastic. When issued by banks it will never be elastic in times of depression when elasticity is needed. The banks will draw in as much currency as possible. The key to elasticity is confidence. Make bill holders and depositors safe by government guarantee, and we will have all the needed elasticity." He added that $30 per capita in specie and paper currency would be adequate. Germany had only $15, England $18, and France $40. In this country, he noted, more business was done by bank checks than in France, where banks were comparatively few and more money was needed to transact the same amount of business. The United States government could retire some of its currency and dispose of its silver — which had fallen greatly in value — and still retain ample paper money and specie to constitute the $30 per capita necessary to the country's economy.[40]

Johnson never wavered in his faith in the United States government in matters of finance. The currency act of 1900, which legalized the gold standard and enlarged the redemption fund, must have brought him great satisfaction. Only a short time earlier, in one of his last long papers, he had summarized his views on the American monetary situation: "Given a perfectly safe banking and financial system, one in which confidence cannot be shaken any more than confidence in the government can be shaken, and all other branches of business and industry will take care of themselves. Our great need is safe banks and safe currency. Why cannot we have both? Already we excel all competitors in the great channels of production, but as yet we are only on the threshold. Give us good laws and the American people will, in all future time, lead the world in every element that promises the prosperity and happiness of men." [41]

Although Johnson's increasingly successful business enterprises took the major portion of his time and energy, he continued throughout his active life to take a strong interest in national and state politics. For almost all of this period, he was a steadfast member of the Republican party. He

[40] John A. Johnson, "Sound Views on Currency Reform," in the *Chicago Tribune*, November 22, 1897.

[41] This statement came at the end of an undated, nine-page manuscript which Johnson wrote, probably in 1897. A copy is in the Johnson Papers.

voted for Ulysses S. Grant in 1868 and 1872. In the off-year election of 1874, the Democrats captured the house of representatives for the first time since the Civil War. Troubled Republicans, weighing future strategy, had to face charges of corruption in high echelons of the government — a situation which gave the opposition party just the issue it needed to influence wavering voters.

To meet the imminent danger of losing the election, concerned leaders on the Republican side called a conference in New York City in May, 1876, to organize the party's program in the forthcoming campaign. Foremost in everyone's mind was one question: Who should be the candidate? Prominent Republicans throughout the country were invited by personal letter to come to New York for the meeting; Johnson's invitation was signed by Henry Cabot Lodge.[42]

John A. Johnson, well known as a Republican in Wisconsin, was the logical state leader of the party, and it was natural to suppose that he would join the assemblage of the faithful in New York. Rather surprisingly, he sent Mr. Lodge his regrets. "Sympathizing fully with the movement," he explained, "it would be a very great pleasure to me if circumstances would permit me to attend, but I fear they will not." He did not elaborate on the "circumstances," but went on to urge that the Republican party must seek to re-establish its previous reputation for integrity. "I consider the impending presidential election," he wrote, "one of the most important if not the most important ever held. Resolutions and platforms will be of no avail. We shall not be in want of honest professions. But honest acts are what we want and the party that does not in the selection of candidates consider uncompromising honesty as paramount . . . deserves defeat." Johnson had a candidate in mind — the Kentuckian Benjamin H. Bristow. He closed his letter to Lodge by forecasting that the Northwest "will cast its electoral vote as a unit in his [*Bristow's*] favor."[43]

At the time, Bristow was a prominent Republican with interesting qualifications as a potential presidential candidate. He had served on the Union side in the Civil War as colonel of the Eighth Kentucky Cavalry and later had held office as an assistant United States attorney. In 1876,

[42] A copy of Lodge's letter to Johnson, dated April 29, 1876, is in the Johnson Papers.

[43] John A. Johnson to H. C. Lodge, May 2, 1876. The copy of this letter in the Johnson Papers is in longhand and is a rough unsigned draft; lines have been scratched out and words changed. Johnson's name is on the business letterhead used for this draft.

he had been for two years secretary of the treasury in President Grant's cabinet. In that capacity, he had vigorously prosecuted the St. Louis "Whisky Ring," which had been defrauding the United States government of millions of dollars of revenue on distilled whisky. In the political scandal that resulted, Bristow, a man who would make no compromises with dishonesty, had pursued his investigation even though it touched men in high executive positions in the government. As secretary of the treasury, he had advocated the resumption of specie payment and a partial withdrawal of greenbacks. It is not difficult to understand why Johnson should admire the rugged honesty of his candidate and consider him the best man available to put an end to rumors of corruption in the Republican ranks. Bristow was for a time a leading candidate for nomination in 1876, but he finally swung his support to Governor Rutherford B. Hayes of Ohio, who was eventually chosen president.

Until 1884, Johnson continued his active support of the Republican party and its candidates. He voted for Hayes in 1876 and for James A. Garfield in 1880. As a local campaigner, he was particularly effective in areas in which Scandinavians predominated. During the height of the 1880 campaign, the chairman of the Wisconsin state organization begged him for specific help. "At a meeting of our State Committee Thursday last," this harried Republican leader reported, "your name was suggested to speak for us during the present campaign. I shall be in a straight for some one to speak in Norwegian in particular cases and I write to see if you will be kind enough to agree to speak as these occasions call for." Once again Johnson's bilingual talents were revealed, this time in the arena of practical politics. Two years later, the campaign literature of the Wisconsin Republican central committee included an article by Johnson, in which he summarized the position of his party's candidates for voters throughout the state.[44]

In the campaign of 1884, Republicans nominated James G. Blaine as their candidate. Johnson's reaction was immediate and characteristic. He could not accept Blaine, whom he had long regarded as an unscrupulous political adventurer. As a result, in an action unprecedented for him, he left the Republican ranks to support Grover Cleveland, the Democratic presidential nominee. Bolting one's party was the great offense against the American political code, and Johnson knew that his move would call for

[44] R. H. Baker to John A. Johnson, August 7, 1880.

explanation and justification. Having acted on principle, however, he did not waver in revealing his motives for so abrupt an about-face.

For Johnson, honesty in government was by all odds the most important consideration. Because the progress and the success of the country were involved, he was adamant on this issue. "Blaine is an able man," he wrote in a newspaper article, "but not a man of integrity." Specifically, Johnson was deeply disturbed over Blaine's connection with the Little Rock and Fort Smith Railroad, in which he became involved during his service as speaker of the house of representatives. While holding this responsible position in government, he had sold bonds for the land grant railway. Even more serious was the clear evidence brought out in an investigation by the judiciary committee of the house: He had been implicated in giving assistance to the railroad group that would ultimately result in financial gain for himself. This conflict-of-interest charge involving the Little Rock and Fort Smith line had lost Blaine the nomination for the presidency in 1876 and 1880. Now the same charges were revived and the evidence spread broadcast over the country; they were to play no small part in his defeat for the presidency in 1884. Johnson had said in 1876 that he was convinced in his opinion about Blaine. Eight years later, still convinced, he left the Republican party seeking a more acceptable candidate.[45]

In spite of his temporary defection, Johnson took pains to explain that his unwillingness to vote for Blaine by no means implied that he was at odds with the Republican party on basic issues. He prophesied in a newspaper article two weeks before the election: "The conscience of the American people will defeat a candidate for president whose past political horoscope is bad." Cleveland's candidacy had more than ordinary significance: no campaign since the Civil War had played such havoc within either party. Johnson was in good company. Among prominent Republicans who switched political allegiances in 1884 were Carl Schurz, George W. Curtis, Charles Francis Adams, James Russell Lowell, and Henry Ward Beecher. And Republican newspapers and magazines of long standing — including the *New York Times*, the *Springfield Republican*, the *Nation*, and *Harper's Weekly* — swung their support to Cleveland.[46]

Among Johnson's closest friends, there were sharply differing reactions

[45] For information concerning Blaine's connection with the Little Rock and Fort Smith Railroad, see Henrietta M. Larson, *Jay Cooke: Private Banker*, 273–275, 479n (Cambridge, Massachusetts, 1936); *Skandinaven*, September 2, 1884.

[46] John A. Johnson, "Hvorfor jeg ikke stemmer for Blaine" (Why I Am Not Voting for Blaine), in *Skandinaven*, October 21, 1884.

to his decision to support a Democrat. Knud Langeland, editor of *Skandinaven,* who had always voted the Republican ticket, agreed with his friend's position on Blaine. He thought that Johnson might have said even more about the Republican candidate's unsuitability than he had done. Langeland added that the party's national convention had made a grave error in nominating Blaine, for in so doing it had given its approval to corruption in government.[47]

John Anderson, publisher of *Skandinaven,* on the other hand, was stubbornly loyal to all things Republican – even to James G. Blaine. Johnson had sent an article to the Chicago paper supporting Cleveland. Before printing the communication, Anderson wrote to Madison urging his friend not to press his views so strongly in a published statement. The campaign was proving to be an intensely bitter one, with the personal character of each candidate under public attack. With this in mind, the publisher called attention to current charges of scandal in Cleveland's early life. Johnson, however, chose to support a candidate whose transgressions were private rather than to vote for one who had betrayed a public trust.

John Anderson's letter to Johnson in the summer of 1884 is revealed as an epitome of the national furor surrounding the two men fighting tooth and nail for the presidency. "I suppose we would print it [*your contribution*] in 'Skandinaven,'" the publisher conceded, "as we always were glad to get articles from your pen, but at the same time it would hurt me to print it as I considered you too good a man to become a Democrat just because the Republican party nominated a man distasteful to you. . . . Now, Mr. Johnson, I do not think it wise of you to have it published in 'Skandinaven'; I think it will do you more harm than good, and especially when you advise your countrymen to vote for Cleveland, a man that I cannot help . . . pronouncing a Moral Leper, after reading the articles that now appear in print uncontradicted. . . . In my opinion, it would be better for the American people to have a man in the White House who might be a little grabbe [*sic*] than to have a man that is a notorious libertine."[48]

In 1877 John A. Johnson had given everyone to understand that he would never again seek public elective office. At the time, he seemed disillusioned with politics. Quite surprisingly, nine years later at the age of

[47] *Skandinaven,* September 9, 1884. Langeland's way of meeting his personal crisis of party loyalty was to vote the Prohibition ticket.

[48] John Anderson to John A. Johnson, July 31, 1884. Because of Anderson's objections, Johnson withheld this article until later in the campaign.

fifty-four, he ran as a Democratic candidate for the position of state treasurer of Wisconsin. Many individuals of both parties rallied to his support. Because of his known honesty and his business ability, he was widely considered to be "as well fitted for that position as anyone in the state." But in the off-year election of 1886, the cross currents of partisan advantage ran against him. Wisconsin Republicans accused the Democrats of "running him just to bring in votes." Although Johnson received the highest vote of anyone on the Democratic state ticket, he was not elected. His old party swept every place in the state government.[49]

In December, 1887, President Cleveland defied all precedent and startled people the country over by devoting his entire annual message to the tariff. Johnson's allegiance to Cleveland had never been based on the latter's free-trade policies — and now, with a new presidential campaign looming ahead, he returned to the Republican party. "The re-election of Cleveland," he wrote in a newspaper article, "is inimical to the best interests of the country." As in earlier years, he was importuned to speak for local candidates in Wisconsin. In both 1888 and 1890, he took an active part in the Republican campaign, traveling widely over the state to explain the party's position to voters. Governor William D. Hoard solicited his help in 1890. "You can be of great service to us in this campaign," the governor urged, "and I earnestly hope you may be able to devote some time to the campaign." [50]

Letters came from other states asking Johnson to write articles on the tariff issue for local newspapers. From the first congressional district in southeastern Minnesota came an appeal to "take to task some of the papers supporting free trade." The editor of *Decorah-Posten*, a widely circulated Norwegian-language newspaper in northern Iowa, proposed a debate on the tariff in his columns. "To [inform] our readers on so important an issue," he explained to Johnson, "we think of you as able and well equipped, and we are asking you to present the Republican view of the tariff." [51]

[49] *Farm Implement News*, October, 1886; *Norden* (Chicago), September 28, 1886. Sidelights of Johnson's last candidacy for office included statements that the Democrats had offered him his choice of state positions on their ticket, and charges that he had lost because he had not spoken out firmly enough on temperance and the tariff.

[50] *Milwaukee Sentinel*, July 8, 1888; William D. Hoard to John A. Johnson, September 4, 1890.

[51] Edward Johnson to John A. Johnson, October 18, 1890. Edward Johnson of Lanesboro, Minnesota, representing the Republican committee in his congressional district, particularly asked Johnson to write articles for *Decorah-Posten*. See also B.

In his home state, at the request of the Republican central committee, Johnson threw himself actively into the intensive campaign which began on October 6, 1890, and ran until election day. He spoke at Dodgeville and Darlington and at a number of other political gatherings. At each, the committee supplied the speaker with sample ballots and with campaign literature in English, Norwegian, German, and Bohemian. Johnson often spoke in Norwegian, his special topics being tariff and monetary issues. The 1890 campaign proved to be his last vigorous political effort. He did, however, continue his active support of policies and candidates of the Republican party as long as he lived.[52]

The last quarter of the nineteenth century saw a developing interest in labor issues throughout the United States. As an employer, Johnson had always recognized the importance of good relations with employees. His own manufacturing companies, regarded as models in their field, had never had a strike. But, looking about him, he had seen the havoc that strikes could create and how industries employing large numbers of men had been crippled. As he turned the larger issue over in his mind, however, he recognized the plight of the workingmen. He was well acquainted with their needs and with those of their families, and in his writings he expressed the belief that the workers deserved higher wages and better working conditions. And it is clear also that not a little of his personal concern for the laborers stemmed from his observation that Norwegian immigrants were being exploited by greedy employers.

The first strike on which Johnson took a public stand occurred in the sawmills at Eau Claire, Wisconsin, during the summer of 1881. At these mills, two thirds of the workers were of Norwegian descent; many of them were recent immigrants. The mill owners, operating in a flush labor market, could take advantage of such persons who desperately needed any kind of work at any wages offered. In the summer drive to get the maximum return from their capital investment in machinery, the employers had forced the men in the mills to work twelve hours a day, day in and day out, throughout the working season. Some could not stand the pace, but if a worker faltered, another could be hired at once to take his place.

Anundsen to John A. Johnson, May 11, 1890; Anundsen, editor of *Decorah-Posten*, wrote this letter in Norwegian.

[52] Henry C. Payne to John A. Johnson, September 26, October, 14, 17, 31, 1890; John M. Ewing to Johnson, October 24, 1890; C. F. Osborne to Johnson, October 21, 1890. All three men were active members of the Republican central committee in Wisconsin.

The Eau Claire laborers had finally banded together and struck, demanding a ten-hour day at the same pay. The lumbermen had refused the demand—violence had followed, and the governor of the state had sent soldiers to control the angry workmen.

In an article in a Chicago newspaper, Johnson discussed the Eau Claire strike in the light of the broad labor issue which he saw to be involved. Although he recognized the two sides of a troublesome national problem, he defended the laborers in their demand for more humane working conditions. "No one can deny," he declared, "that it is the moral obligation of an employer to be concerned over a workman's welfare." Lumbermen in Eau Claire had become wealthy, he added, and it was their duty to reward their labor force fairly—perhaps through some profit-sharing plan. All employers should realize that the success of industry depended in large measure on the workers, the cornerstone of the country's prosperity. If paid well, a laboring man could support his family in better circumstances; as a consumer, he would stimulate trade and the national economy would flourish.

Assessing the Eau Claire situation, Johnson said that he well knew it was hard to work twelve hours daily in the mills. No one should wonder that the men wished to shorten the day. Yet he was aware that the mill owners needed to operate as much as possible in the summer. If the employers could get replacements to step in at the long hours, they would make no basic change. Johnson saw at this point the inevitability that disadvantaged workers would join together to bargain collectively. Although he deplored walkouts and violence, he defended both the right to organize and the right to strike. "If manufacturers and railroads can meet to determine their prices," he reasoned, "so can labor." Good employer-employee relations, he believed, should rest on both moral and economic foundations.

He was critical of the state government's decision to send soldiers to Eau Claire. The governor should have appealed first to the workers. Johnson held that no such hasty action had been called for and suggested that the state legislature should investigate the whole matter. No fair decision could be made until both sides had had an opportunity to be heard. Though he seemed to favor the principle of profit sharing, the trend of thinking in his article strongly suggests the need for arbitration of labor disputes. He saw clearly that the interest of the public was involved. "The people of the state should be concerned," he wrote in conclusion, "for in the end they are the consumers and will pay for strikes. It should be the wish of every righteous person that the case of the Eau Claire workers can be properly presented."[53]

Several years later, Johnson again presented his views on labor disputes in a newspaper article. He believed that the inventive American mind must concern itself with finding a solution to the problem, for, if the issue were not soon resolved, businessmen would become so wary of trouble with their labor force that they would be unwilling to risk capital by engaging in industry. "It is the duty of society," he pointed out, "if in its power, to enable every willing working man to provide for himself, for his family, and old age." On principle, Johnson was opposed to low-wage labor. In his view, the interests of employer and employed were never divergent. A business in which both were well paid would be the most successful.

This meant profit sharing. Such a plan would guarantee the workingman a just reward when his efforts had been productive. "Let the surplus be divided yearly," Johnson advised, "upon some equitable basis. Under such a system, the laborer would be a partner in the business. Then [he] will do better work for himself and will insist on full performance on the part of others." Johnson's ideas in this area of business management marked him as an industrialist with progressive views. In his own business, he had to wait until recovery from the panic of 1893 made possible, a few years later, a profit-sharing agreement with his own supervisors. At that time, his company was one of the first in the Middle West to adopt such a plan as a permanent policy.[54]

Johnson's concern for the men who worked for him was not merely theoretical. In the days before pensions, unemployment insurance, and social security, his solicitude for their welfare continued beyond their last day's service in the shop or office. For the elderly he saw a need, and he began planning to establish a home for veteran workmen when age made it impracticable for them to continue to be actively employed. For men who had no better place, there had been only the county poor farm. Feel-

[53] John A. Johnson, "Soldiers in Eau Claire," in *Skandinaven*, August 30, 1881.

[54] John A. Johnson, "Can Strikes Be Prevented, If So How?" in the *Madison Daily Democrat*, March 28, 1886; Herbert Feis, *Labor Relations: A Study Made in the Procter and Gamble Company*, 31–52 (New York, 1928); "Profit Sharing," in Bureau of Statistics of Labor, *Seventeenth Annual Report*, March, 1886 (Boston, 1886). When Johnson wrote the article referred to here, the idea of profit sharing had had only limited acceptance in the United States. A Rhode Island firm had begun such a plan in 1878, and in 1886 a similar system had been adopted by the N. O. Nelson Company in St. Louis and by Procter and Gamble in Cincinnati.

ing a strong personal responsibility for those who had helped him build his businesses, Johnson now had in mind a sort of haven of refuge where men advanced in age could live in comfort surrounded by kindness and good will. In his late sixties, Johnson was able to make all necessary arrangements for the center which he named the Gisholt Home for the Aged.[55]

First came the selection of a site, a detail to which Johnson gave his personal attention. On a farm in Dane County's Burke Township, a half dozen miles from Madison, he found exactly what he wanted – a sturdy brick house on a hilltop overlooking the surrounding country. Inside, the large pleasant rooms were nicely finished in birch and oak. From the wide veranda, one could see nearby flourishing farmsteads – and in the distance the state capitol towering over the city of Madison.

To establish the Gisholt Home, Johnson set up a trust fund of $40,000 with directions for the organization of a corporation for its management. The farm of something over three hundred acres was to provide a large share of the income necessary for financing the institution. Johnson's plan stipulated that the board of directors should be chosen by the supreme court of Wisconsin. When this procedure was concluded, the board of six members and its first officers were announced. Judge R. G. Siebecker was named president; Mrs. J. W. Hobbins, vice-president; Mrs. Frederik A. Johnson, a daughter-in-law of John A. Johnson, secretary; and J. W. Hobbins, treasurer. T. C. Richmond and Nils O. Starks were chosen as the other members of the governing board.

It was a cardinal point in Johnson's plan that the home was to be primarily a charitable institution. The admission fee to worthy applicants was to be kept small; it was to be determined on a scale depending on age. If a man was over seventy, he would pay the lowest fee of $300. The highest fee of $800 was to be charged to those in the age group from fifty-five to sixty. If a person had money or property – or if he came into an inheritance of any kind while in the home – such assets were to become the property of the corporation. Need was the principal criterion: the poorest were given the same consideration as those who had some means. Each must pay the initial fee – after that there were no further obligations. The home was to furnish each resident with board, clothing, nursing, and med-

[55] The Norwegian word *gisholt* means a sunny wood, and it pleased Johnson in the last year of his life when people called the home he had founded "Sunny Woods."

ical attention during the remainder of his life. At the time of death, a respectable burial was to be provided.[56]

Persons who wished to enter the Gisholt Home for the Aged, upon request, were sent an application blank by the board of directors. Johnson was mainly concerned with providing a comfortable retirement home for his workmen who would need help in their old age. As long as room was available, however, the home was open to anyone who might be in need, regardless of national origin or religion. The only exceptions were those who had chronic or contagious diseases. To meet this requirement, each applicant was asked to present with his other papers a certificate from a reputable physician.[57]

The establishment of the Gisholt Home served to put Madison and Wisconsin in the forefront of a movement — not yet widely developed — to provide in each community comfortable retirement homes for needy elderly people. In this instance, as in others in several fields, Johnson was ahead of his time, a pioneer in this particular form of charity. His generosity did not go unnoticed: Numerous letters acknowledging both his benevolence and his foresight came to his desk during the last months of his life. The vice-president of the Marine National Bank of Milwaukee sent a typical message. "Please accept my most hearty congratulations on your noble gift for the establishment and maintenance of a Home for the Aged in Dane County. Some men take pleasure in making money for the purpose of hoarding it, others for the purpose of using it in benevolent undertakings; between the two there is an impassable gulf. I am prouder than ever to have known you. Generations yet unborn will rise to call you blessed." [58]

Johnson was not to live to see the home occupied. In 1902, a few months after his death, the first residents moved in; soon the house was filled to capacity. Later on, the directors added a large dormitory to accommodate the increasing number of applicants. The expansion drew heavily on the trust funds, and, with the rising cost of living, financing the home became difficult. The 1913 balance sheet revealed a serious financial situation; as a result, the board of managers voted to accept no more new

[56] A small booklet published by the corporation contains information about the officers and board of managers and gives details concerning the requirements for admission and the services offered by the Gisholt Home. A copy of these regulations is in the Johnson Papers.

[57] *Wisconsin State Journal,* November 19, 1934.

[58] John Johnston to John A. Johnson, November 9, 1900.

residents. But — according to the original rules of the corporation — as long as there were resident life members, the property could not be sold.

In the years that followed, Carl A. Johnson, as manager, and his sister, Mrs. Ida Johnson Fisk, as secretary, directed the affairs of the home with the help of a resident manager. Upon Carl Johnson's death in 1931, Fred W. Coombs of the Gisholt Machine Company staff assumed responsibility for its management. Three years later, with the death of the last contract member, it became possible to sell the assets of the corporation. The future of the Gisholt Home was then brought before the circuit court, where Judge A. C. Hoppmann ordered that the property be sold to settle the indebtedness and to close the trust. This was done in 1935.[59]

Civic problems in his home city of Madison always concerned Johnson. In spite of pressing business and political involvements, he was quick to take a responsible personal stand and to move for needed action. In 1895, a matter of immediate importance to residents of the city arose when the question of the purity of the city's water supply became a matter of public debate. For some fifteen years, Madison had been facing a growing problem in sewage disposal. With the germ theory of disease now firmly established by the studies of Pasteur and Koch, citizens were asking: "Is our water supply safe?" In an article in the *Madison Democrat* on September 4, 1895, Johnson met the issue head on by declaring: "Sewage must not be put any longer in Lake Mendota and Lake Monona."

A chapter of local history lay behind Johnson's statement concerning needed changes in sewage disposal. In 1880, Magnus Swenson, a brilliant senior at the University of Wisconsin, had written an honors thesis on "The Chemical Analysis of Madison Well Waters." At that time, the city had no central water supply or municipal sewage system. Rather serious occurrences of such germ diseases as typhoid fever, scarlet fever, and diphtheria had caused the city health officers to become suspicious of the sources of drinking water throughout the city.

As a result of his research, Magnus Swenson was engaged as an employee of the Madison health department to make a thorough study of the situation. The young scientist found that nearly all the water in the city was polluted by sewage. In the acrimonious city-wide debate that followed over what to do, conservative diehards contended that "sight and taste"

[59] William H. Spohn to George Ekstrom of the Gisholt Machine Company, August 14, 1947.

were sufficient tests to prove whether or not water was fit to drink — and some prominent citizens pooh-poohed the findings of "an outside expert." But Swenson found strong support for his analysis, and Madison later adopted a central water system with deep artesian wells, and also a central sewage system. The epidemics of disease were brought to an end.[60]

Johnson continued to maintain an interest in the sewage problem from the time of Swenson's first reports. As the city grew and more water mains were required, he found further reason for concern. After some years of study of what had been done in other cities — in both America and Europe — he prepared a comprehensive article applying his findings to the local situation. He addressed himself to the condition of the sewer system on Washington Avenue and particularly to the problem that he saw developing in the East Madison marsh near the Fuller and Johnson plant. He feared that it would be difficult — if not impossible — to keep the ground water out of the sewer on Washington Avenue nearest to the factory. "Similar conditions," he observed, "must have been seen elsewhere. It is reasonable to suppose that the city authorities are not experimenting but have precedents in . . . conditions and systems in other cities."

He was favorably disposed toward the installation of a chemical deposit system for Madison. But he realized that this solution would involve costly chemicals and expensive assembling and treatment tanks. "The filtering of the effluent [is necessary]," he warned. "Otherwise half of the sewage will still be in the lakes." He was more favorable, he said in concluding his paper, to the plan of purchasing one hundred acres northeast of Madison, the tract to be developed as an irrigation field into which sewage could be pumped. In Johnson's considered judgment, the water and sewage systems of the city should be subjected to careful study "before any further expense is incurred." [61]

Patient and long-suffering as he was by natural temperament, Johnson could be a formidable opponent if he felt himself to be the victim of unfair treatment. In such cases, he was indefatigable in searching for facts to

[60] Kenneth O. Bjork, *Saga in Steel and Concrete*: *Norwegian Engineers in America*, 429–431 (Northfield, Minnesota, 1947); Olaf Hougen, "Magnus Swenson: Inventor and Chemical Engineer," in *Norwegian-American Studies and Records*, 10: 152–175 (Northfield, Minnesota, 1938). Johnson took great pride in Magnus Swenson, one of his countrymen, whose later career won him wide recognition.

[61] A manuscript dealing with the Madison sewage system is in the Johnson Papers. This article is written in pencil in Johnson's hand. It is undated and has no title.

support his position and in driving the aggressor to cover. If a principle were involved, he hewed to the line with strenuous stubbornness. In 1900, he had an opportunity to prove that old age had not affected his willingness to do battle when he felt a wrong had been done. The issue turned on the corporate taxation of three large Madison companies: the Fuller and Johnson Manufacturing Company, the Gisholt Machine Company, and the Gas and Electric Company.

As president of the first two concerns, Johnson felt compelled to present his position, particularly since Madison papers had given the matter a great deal of space in their columns. He believed that the taxation of corporations was more than a local issue; in his view, it was of state-wide importance. The Madison city assessor had assessed the Gisholt Machine Company $34,000 on real estate and $24,000 on personal property. Johnson regarded these figures as rather high, but he indicated that he believed the officers had conformed as nearly as possible to the law and to their oath in the assessment of all property, the Gisholt holdings included. He accepted their appraisal without question.

There the matter appeared to rest – that is, until D. K. Tenney, a Madison lawyer, injected his personal point of view into the situation by asserting that the assessor's valuation of the Gisholt Company was too low. Under oath, Tenney stated that the Gisholt property was worth $500,000 and should be assessed at that value. The law specified that the assessment on real estate should be based on the selling value of the property. It was at precisely this point that Tenney took it upon himself to put forward an interpretation of doubtful legal validity. "The assessment of the property," he argued, "should not be based on its selling value, as has always been supposed to be the law, but on its value to the owner."

In June, 1900, acting as a private citizen, Tenney appeared before the board of review for city taxes and demanded that the Gisholt assessment be corrected to his figure of $500,000. The board demurred. On July 12, Tenney had a Madison justice of the peace subpoena Johnson to appear before the board of review. At this meeting, Tenney stated that the board had made an off-the-record investigation of the Gisholt Company and had still refused to correct the assessment. Pressing his case almost vindictively, the lawyer obtained from the Dane County circuit court a writ of certiorari against the board of review demanding that they make their findings public. At the same time, an alternative writ of mandamus was issued against Johnson, ordering him to bring all his company records and freely answer all questions on August 21, 1900.[62]

Up to this point, Johnson had wisely allowed his opponent to make all the moves. They amounted to a challenge to a duel—and the Gisholt president now prepared himself for a legal battle. In late summer, before the actual court trial, he presented his case in a vigorous article in a Madison newspaper. He asserted that Tenney was trying to place three leading Madison companies in the class of tax fighters. "He is seeking to label us as men who are shirking our share of public burdens," Johnson wrote with considerable heat. "I deny and resent Mr. Tenney's accusations." [63]

As defendant in this important tax case, Johnson needed no lawyer to present his arguments. Actually, he had had specific training in the laws of taxation over a period of forty years—as township assessor, as clerk of the county board of supervisors, and as the head of two industrial enterprises which for many years had regularly discharged their tax obligations in full compliance with Wisconsin statutes. It would be hard to imagine a man better qualified to point out flaws in Tenney's charges.

In his comprehensive newspaper article, Johnson discussed the law of assessments for both real estate and personal property. "If the Tenney interpretation is to be accepted," he contended, "it must apply to all taxpayers not only in Madison but in the whole state of Wisconsin." He maintained that Tenney's claim urging assessment on the value of the property to the owner did not conform to the law. He added that other municipalities would certainly not uniformly adopt such a plan. If it were to be accepted only in Madison, local property owners would pay far higher taxes than those of other cities. There would be state-wide inequality and confusion. Johnson also objected to the order in the writ of mandamus for him to bring his company records to the public hearing of the board of review. He asserted that the board, of course, had a right to examine his books, but that he was unwilling to open them to the public. "What a situation," he exclaimed, "if at the call of any person, reputable or disreputable, every business man can be compelled to lay bare his books before the public." [64]

[62] *Records of the Circuit Court*, Dane County, Madison, October 27, 1900, in Division of Archives and Manuscripts, State Historical Society of Wisconsin.

[63] John A. Johnson, "Taxation of Manufacturing Property Discussed—Laws and Rules Explained," in the *Madison Democrat*, September 2, 1900. This article was also published in pamphlet form; a copy is in the Johnson Papers.

[64] John A. Johnson, "Taxation of Manufacturing Property Discussed," in the *Madison Democrat*, September 2, 1900.

On September 16, 1900, Johnson made a countermotion in court to quash the alternative writ of mandamus. To support this action, he presented two arguments: "(1) the relator, D. K. Tenney, is not entitled to the relief sought; [and] (2) sufficient facts are not set forth in the writ to entitle the relator to the relief sought." A month later—on October 15, 1900—Johnson's countermotion was sustained. At that day's session of the circuit court, the writ of mandamus was quashed, thus ending the case in favor of the defendant.[65]

Particularly in the later years of his life, Johnson gave support and leadership to all movements designed to advance the best interests of his home city. He was the first president of the Municipal Reform Club, later to be known as the Madison Civic Federation. This organization, through various committees, sought to encourage fidelity on the part of law enforcement officers, to influence constructive municipal legislation, and to aid in the education of citizens in matters of public interest.

Membership in the Reform Club was open to any Madison resident in sympathy with its objectives—and a large number of the most prominent citizens signed its constitution and participated in its program. The early roll included President Charles Kendall Adams of the University of Wisconsin; Edward A. Birge, later to hold the same office; and Richard T. Ely, nationally known author and head of the university's department of political economy. Local clergymen like the Reverend E. G. Updike and the Reverend W. G. Simonds and such physicians as Dr. Charles Sheldon and Dr. Louis R. Head were prominent among professional men who joined in sponsoring the work of the organization. Among prominent businessmen enrolled as members were W. R. Bagley and Wayne Ramsay, both associates of Johnson in the companies of which he was head.[66]

John A. Johnson's strong interest in public education—evidenced in his earliest years in the New World—continued to the end of his life. As time passed and his responsibilities increased, his pride in the democratic nature of the American school system remained firm. In his later years, he advocated the introduction of manual training in the schools of his home city. In Copenhagen, on one of his trips abroad, he had observed

[65] *Records of the Circuit Court*, Dane County, Madison, October 27, 1900, in Division of Archives and Manuscripts, State Historical Society of Wisconsin.

[66] A clipping from an unnamed and undated Madison newspaper refers to the organization of the Reform Club under the heading, "Its Laws Adopted." A copy of the long article is in the Johnson Papers; the probable date is the middle 1890's.

the *sloid* system in operation and had admired the fine cabinet-making and wood-carving produced by Danish students in their class shops. Believing as he did in the dignity of labor, he urged local Wisconsin school authorities to teach the combined skills of mind and hand, which he considered so valuable to a complete education. It is certain that Johnson influenced the early introduction of manual training in Madison and later throughout the United States.[67]

Throughout his life, Johnson held strong views concerning the use of alcohol. As a youth, he had seen men ruined by addiction to a habit they could not break. He had long wished to help such persons, but only during the last few years of his life did he find what he believed to be a helpful solution to the problem of the confirmed alcoholic. Hearing that the Keeley institution offered a treatment to men trying to break off drinking, he wrote for information. Thereafter he encouraged alcoholics to take the Keeley cure. To some he gave financial help enabling them to rehabilitate themselves, a charity that brought him many letters of appreciation. On the political front, he urged people to petition the state legislature to allow each local governing unit—county, township, village, or city—to determine for itself whether it would permit the sale of intoxicating liquor within its limits. So far as is known, Johnson did not affiliate himself with the weak Prohibition party in national politics.[68]

So wide-ranging were John A. Johnson's interests—so capable was his performance in all the fields he entered—that during his later years many asked: Why has such an influential man not been elected to an important public office? They thought that he would have been an admirable governor of his home state or a superb representative in Washington. They saw his obvious competence, but, as he grew older, they found it difficult to persuade him to enter the political lists. After 1886, he would not seek or accept any nomination. The *Milwaukee Sentinel* in the summer of 1894 publicly urged him to be the Republican candidate for representative in congress from the Wisconsin second district. The paper said of him that

[67] In speaking to the Contemporary Club in Madison on one occasion, Johnson epitomized his belief in American schools in these words: "Our free school system was a marvelous leap in the right direction and it has accomplished wonders in educating and elevating the whole people."

[68] Leslie E. Keeley Company to John A. Johnson, August 14, December 24, 1891; T. O. Lund to Johnson, December 24, 1891; *Skandinaven*, February 4, 1889. Letters of appreciation sent to Johnson by alcoholics whom he had befriended are in the Johnson Papers.

he would exercise ripe and intelligent judgment guarded by conscientious motives. The district would make a mistake, the editor declared, if it allowed a Democratic candidate to be chosen when such an able representative could be elected. Johnson, however, then in his sixty-third year, had put politics behind him once and for all — and nothing came of this final attempt to draft him.

It seems clear that he preferred the kind of public service he could perform outside the restrictions of politics. He was a man who would form his own opinions and speak his own mind. Obviously more the studious statesman than the politician, he found that operating on principle cost him votes and elections. This did not induce him to trim his sails for even the fairest winds. In middle life, he definitely chose business as his career and involved himself in it so deeply that he had no time to spare for building up a personal political following.

It undoubtedly hurt him that some of his countrymen — in the formal church organizations and out of them — felt that he had left them behind for an "American" career. Strongly committed as he was to encouraging and helping immigrants to become good citizens of their adopted land, he persevered in this broad aim, even when strong leaders of various factions questioned his actions and his motives. He was wiser than they. Time was on his side as the history of Scandinavians in the United States was to show in the half century after his death. In Madison, a center of Norwegian culture, he was closest to those of his countrymen who were associated with the University of Wisconsin: men like Storm Bull, Magnus Swenson, Julius Olson, and Rasmus B. Anderson, all members of the faculty and all sympathetic to the cultural trends he believed in. If the conservative clergy or political partisans or newspaper editors with axes to grind opposed him, he rather sadly, but quite firmly, went his way without them. For that was the kind of man he had always been and always would remain.

So it came to pass that John A. Johnson, a Norwegian immigrant, became a public leader in the American sense of the word. Remarkably effective in business and in civic affairs — and as a philanthropist — he found that in these fields he could flourish and make the best use of his talents and energy. It is easy today to understand that he lacked political skills and popular appeal. In his heart he perhaps willingly accepted the fact that he was not a more flexible man. He knew that he had other assets, and that they were of a quality higher than those paraded by others to win personal acclaim. These assets carried him to positions of responsibility in which he served in public ways. They maintained him steadfastly in places of trust, and surely they must have satisfied his deepest desire—which was to be of good use to his fellowmen.

CHAPTER IX

Johnson and His Family

Influenced strongly by both old-country tradition and by personal inclination, John A. Johnson's affection for the family home in Pleasant Springs and for his aging parents remained strong to the end of their lives. As his own career developed, he had the satisfaction of knowing that their hopes had been realized. Anders and Aaste Skibsnæs had made the adjustment to life in America; their early difficulties had faded into the past. They had found the better life for their children — the dream that had given them the courage to uproot themselves and to cross the ocean seeking an uncertain future. Like thousands of other immigrants who had conquered a strange environment of prairie and forest, they had found resources to overcome loneliness of mind and spirit until they could help to build a pioneer community in which the old and the new were commingled. In the process of becoming Americans, they had associated themselves with religious and educational institutions that bridged the gaps in language and culture and aided them in finding contentment.

Foremost among these helpful mid-nineteenth-century institutions had been the church. In 1844, their first year in America, Anders and Aaste had joined the newly organized Norwegian Lutheran Church in the Walworth County community in which they settled. They took comfort in hearing its familiar doctrines phrased in their native language. For a time at least, it seemed that they had not left the Old World so far away. Later — throughout the last half of their lives — they found the church an enduring source of strength.

Next came the schools — offering a most important opportunity which the parents eagerly seized upon in turn for each of their children. It did not trouble them that this was the "English school," for neither Anders nor Aaste doubted the principle that young immigrants should learn English and associate with children of various national origins. America, they could see, was indeed a land where many cultures were mingling; from the first they looked upon education and Americanization as the same process and promise for the future. When John immediately revealed his avid interest and superior aptitude for learning, his family — backed by his teachers and his pastor — made every effort within reach of their limited resources to send him on beyond the rural school. It was little enough — a few weeks in a small frontier academy — and then there was no more money and his formal education came to an end.

All of the Skibsnæs children attended the country schools. And, without further learning aside from what their native wits could pick up, five of them carried the family name into these same rural schools as young teachers. John was the first, in Walworth County, at eighteen. After the family move to Koshkonong, it was convenient to teach in Dane County; the first log schoolhouse was located across the road from the farm. John and Ole both taught in the early Pleasant Springs school. Some years later, their sisters, Inger and Caroline, held classes in a new schoolhouse situated in the center of the district, a mile north of the farm, and Hans as a young man had charge of a country school in Dunkirk Township, Dane County. Anders and Aaste must have taken pride in what their children were doing to help spread the boon of education to the frontier. One may guess that letters back to Norway spread the word of the five Skibsnæs teachers, for was not their accomplishment a glowing symbol of what could happen in the New World? [1]

Caroline in one of her letters included a description of the original log schoolhouse at Pleasant Springs. Children sat on wide boards fastened to the wall, with crude desks in front of them. Each morning the teacher started the fire in the wood-burning stove in the center of the room. At one end stood the teacher's desk with a small blackboard behind it. Spelling was an important subject, and contests were held with the best spellers in one school pitted against the champions of another. These exciting diversions attracted audiences; on winter evenings sleighing parties would

[1] Family letters indicate that Caroline was commonly called Karen by her brothers and sisters.

travel for miles to cheer for the contestants. The pupils were not all children. Sometimes middle-aged immigrants came to learn the English language — serious students who often made real progress. Some teachers did not spare the rod on naughty or lazy children. But the most successful — those who won the love and esteem of all — used kind and gentle means to win the pupils' interest in their work.[2]

Like the school, the newspaper played an important role in the education and Americanization of the Skibsnæs family. Anders, a quiet, thoughtful man, was an eager reader. At first he could understand only the Norwegian-language newspapers; in later life, however, he learned to make his way very well in publications written in English. Other members of the family — with John always in the lead — could read American papers surprisingly soon after their arrival in this country. In the home of his parents, John early began his mastery of two languages — so perfected in his maturity that he could write or speak for Norwegians in their own tongue and turn at will to strongly worded articles or addresses in English.

Participation in township affairs gave the Skibsnæs sons in Koshkonong grass-roots training in local government. John and Oliver at one time or another held every office in Pleasant Springs Township. From this springboard, John went on — during his long residence in Madison — to serve the county and state in various public capacities. Oliver also was a member of the Dane County board of supervisors, and Ole, after his Civil War experiences, interested himself in state politics. In these various offices, the brothers learned about the process of government in a democracy and sensed the responsibilities as well as the privileges of the citizen.

The home that Anders and Aaste Skibsnæs made for their children on the Pleasant Springs farm was a modest one so far as worldly goods were concerned, but it was rich in the things of mind and spirit. For John and his brothers and sisters, the parents provided a quiet example of innate goodness and sturdiness of character — traits that were the best gift that immigrants from Norway brought to their adopted country. Their standards were high, and their bequest to those who were to follow was a strong influence toward a life philosophy like their own.

As John's father and mother approached the end of their long lives, he made frequent visits to the farm from nearby Madison. In letters to his

[2] This undated description was written by Mrs. Caroline Johnson Stuverud for her niece, Mrs. Amelia Sønneland of Los Angeles. The old school bell is still in use, now as a dinner bell, calling men from work at a farm home in Koshkonong, Wisconsin.

brothers and sisters living farther away, he wrote of his gratitude to his parents and of his concern for their comfort. When John was forty-eight, in the year 1880, Anders Skibsnæs died at the age of seventy-six. At the time of his death, the Reverend J. P. Gjertsen, a well-known Lutheran pastor in nearby Stoughton, Wisconsin, expressed his high regard for a treasured companion in a memorial poem entitled "Thoughts on the Passing of Anders Johnson Skibsnæs." [3]

John's mother lived thirteen years after her husband's death, remembered in advanced age as "Bestemor Skibsnæs" (Grandmother Skibsnæs), one loved and respected by everyone. On May 13, 1893, then eighty-five years old, Aaste had come from the farm to spend the weekend of Pentecost at the home of Pastor T. H. Dahl in Stoughton. As she stepped from the buggy at his door, the horse started quickly and she was thrown to the ground. In the accident, she suffered a head injury which caused her death six days later. A Stoughton newspaper at the time of her funeral spoke of her as one "whose whole life was an example of usefulness, of love, of charity." In a letter to his sister Caroline, John, then in his sixty-second year, paid his final tribute to his mother: "She not only helped herself, but helped others till the very last." [4]

The Reverend J. A. Ottesen, long a pastor at Koshkonong, sent a letter to John at the time of his mother's death. Her name, he observed, had historical significance and should be commemorated in the family. "Aaste" had meant "love and mercy" from the early days when the name had been immortalized by the mother of Saint Olaf, the king of Norway who had Christianized his country. Because of the fine qualities of the original Mother Aaste, her name has been revered in Norway and bearing it is still regarded as a mark of distinction.[5]

Johnson's parents are buried in Bøvre Gravgaard, a rural cemetery in Pleasant Springs Township in Dane County. Over their graves stands a granite monument with the inscription:

Anders Johnson from Skipnes and Gisholt Norway
born in 1804 died 1880
Aaste, his wife born in 1808 died 1893
Both came to America in 1844

[3] A copy of this poem is in the Johnson Papers.

[4] The quotation is from an undated newspaper clipping which, however, gives the date of Aaste's death as May 19, 1893. The clipping, which is in the Johnson Papers, does not give the full name of the newspaper.

[5] Gerhard Brandt Naeseth, *The Naeseth-Fehn Family History*, 67 (Madison,

Before the death of the parents, the children, with the exception of Oliver, had established homes of their own. John in nearby Madison was always in close personal touch with Oliver, and by letter with the other three. The bond of affection was strong, and it is easily understandable that John became the counselor to whom the others turned for advice. He was the eldest, of course, but perhaps more significant was the implicit trust they placed in his judgment and kindly consideration. Particularly after his father's death, he assumed by common consent the position of head of the family.

John's letters to his sisters are revealing of the relationship he had with each. Inger, a young widow with three children, had married Gunder H. Stuverud in 1867. They had settled in Aspelund Township, Goodhue County, Minnesota. Here the husband was a farmer who also sold farm implements. Later the family moved to a farm in Codington County, South Dakota. From his district in that state, Mr. Stuverud was elected to the legislature in 1893.[6]

Inger and Gunder Stuverud often asked John for advice on family problems. After their retirement, they lived in Watertown, South Dakota. There Inger became seriously ill. When Dr. Knut Hoegh, a St. Paul physician trained in Norway, recommended surgery, a telegram was sent to John begging him to come at once. The brother, who fortunately knew Dr. Hoegh personally, arrived on the first train for a family council. Inger was unquestionably very ill — and, in the crisis, it was John who helped husband and wife make the difficult decision. The operation was successful. Back home again in Madison, John was able to pass on to Caroline the good news that her sister would regain her health. "I shall hear from her every day," he reported. It was after this evidence of close family co-operation and solicitude that Inger expressed her gratitude to John in a letter: "Now dear Brother, you have always been kind to us." [7]

John wrote frequently to his younger sister Caroline, the baby of the

Wisconsin, 1956). None of John A. Johnson's grandchildren or great-grandchildren was named Aaste. A granddaughter of Johnson's sister, Inger Johnson Stuverud, however, is Aaste Irene Stenson Nordbye of Parshall, North Dakota.

[6] One of Inger's children, Oscar Ustrud, carried on an extended correspondence with his Uncle John. Both John and Ole Johnson thought well of this nephew. In a letter to John, dated March 17, 1885, Ole paid the young man a compliment: "Anyone who follows him [*Oscar*] has to stir. He is a good worker and very faithful and reliable."

[7] Naeseth, *The Naeseth-Fehn Family History*, 67; John A. Johnson to Caroline Johnson Stuverud, April, 1893 (date incomplete); Inger Johnson Stuverud to John A. Johnson, n. d.

family and its only member born in America. In 1874, she had married John H. Stuverud, a farmer living in Dodge County, Minnesota. Soon the family moved to the nearby town of Kasson, where Mr. Stuverud sold farm machinery — including the Fuller and Johnson line — and where subsequently he was elected treasurer of the county. The correspondence between the oldest brother and the younger sister — some sixteen years apart in age — is warm with the affection the two held for each other. Caroline, at a distance from home, was solicitous concerning her aging parents, and her letters express to John her gratitude "for your kindness to them." [8]

The successful older brother was generous. In a letter of January 15, 1887, he wrote to Caroline: "I sent you some days since a draft of $500.00 as a Christmas present. I now send you another draft of $500.00 as a New Years present. . . . Since I sent the first draft I have collected money I did not expect. . . . Well, you were always such a good girl." Carefully he made it plain that the money had not been sent because the family was in need: her husband was a man of industry and economy who managed his affairs well. John advised them to live in their old house until they could build a good permanent residence. "I wish you could have a girl [*a housemaid*] to help you," he added in the same letter. Three months later, he sent Caroline and her husband a draft for a loan they had requested. "If you need the money longer," he promised, "of course you can have it." [9]

There was no need to write letters to Oliver, who lived close at hand as a well-established farmer in Pleasant Springs. The owner of two hundred acres in that township, he was a well-informed and public-spirited man, who held a prominent place in his home community. He had married Signe Skaalin of a family well known in Stoughton for their gift to the village of the Skaalin Old Peoples' Home. Two years younger than John, Oliver maintained the family home in which Anders and Aaste spent their old age. The two brothers were frequently together. With others living far away, they shared the care of their parents and saw to their comfort as long as the old people lived.[10]

By natural affinity of tastes and temperament, John was closest to his brilliant brother Ole. The numerous letters that passed between them as long as Ole lived reveal the compatibility of interests and mutual affection

[8] Naeseth, *The Naeseth-Fehn Family History*, 74; Caroline Johnson Stuverud to John A. Johnson, March 20, 1880.

[9] John A. Johnson to Caroline Johnson Stuverud, April 16, 1887.

[10] *Madison Daily Democrat*, April 8, 1882; *History of Dane County, Wisconsin*, 1193 (Chicago, 1880).

that bound the older man to his youngest brother. Both engaged in business and entered politics. In middle life — when the six-year difference in their ages was no longer a factor in their relationship — their common ground was a continuation of their boyhood dreams. Both loved learning and cherished a lifelong admiration for all that education stood for. They had planned that after his graduation from Beloit College, Ole would study law. John realized that his brother had a good mind, energy and ambition, and a genial personality — qualities that would insure a fine future. He had hoped that Ole could have the college education he himself had given up. The guns at Fort Sumter ended all such hopes.

Letters written during Ole's year at Beloit show the bent of their interests at a time when John was nearing thirty and Ole was in his early twenties. They discussed books, in particular those dealing with international problems and pressing national issues. With the shadow of war upon them, they wrote of their beliefs concerning morality and religion. The question of prayer must have come up, for the younger brother, in one of his last letters from college before enlisting, indicated that he accepted the existence of a power beyond himself. "To place ourselves entirely on our own strength in all these matters," he confided, "I think is going too far." [11]

With his arduous Civil War experiences behind him, Ole C. Johnson, at the age of twenty-seven, settled in Beloit. Soon he was engaging vigorously in the activities of the community and state. In 1871, he was elected immigration commissioner for Wisconsin; in this position he served three years. He was also for a time the mayor of Beloit. Ole's business career in Wisconsin centered on his partnership in the Beloit Plow and Wagon Works, a firm which manufactured agricultural implements. John A. Johnson and J. Thompson were partners in this enterprise. Their shop turned out the well-known Beloit Norwegian Plow, which — appropriately enough — Johnson, Fuller and Company sold in their St. Paul agency.[12]

In the early 1880's Ole sold his share in the Beloit company and moved to Watertown in Dakota Territory to engage in banking. At this time, he took for his family the name Shipnes, a variant spelling of his parents' name and of Skibsnæs, his birthplace in Norway. In 1883, the letterhead of the Watertown bank included the name of O. C. J. Shipnes as presi-

[11] It is likely that this letter was written at a time of spiritual turmoil, when Ole was torn between his desire to continue in college and his strong feeling that it was his duty to volunteer for the Civil War.

[12] Ole C. Johnson to John A. Johnson, December 25, 1877; *Skandinaven,* July 14, 1874.

dent. From his base in Watertown, Ole bought several tracts of land in what is now South Dakota. In his letters, he referred specifically to "the Garfield farm" and "the Thorheim farm."[13]

Ole's health had been impaired during his years of war service, but apparently it had not been a major concern until 1883. Then his letters to Madison became more frequent. Their main substance as usual was business, but the older brother, reading between the lines, realized that Ole was seriously ill. Fearing the worst, John went to Watertown to see him. At this time, the brothers decided that Ole must retire from active management of his business interests. Fortunately, he could place his farms in the hands of his capable nephew, Oscar Ustrud.[14]

The Shipnes family soon returned to Beloit, which Ole considered to be his home, and there his son Wilford attended to business matters under his father's direction. John was with his brother at the time of his death on November 4, 1886. Ole was only forty-eight years old, and it seemed to John that his life had been far too short. He felt the loss deeply, for the brother had been a close confidant and treasured companion. He sent a message to one of his sisters on the day their brother died: "I feel very badly, but I am glad his suffering is at an end."

After Ole's death, his widow and the son Wilford turned to John for help in handling the details of settling the estate. The large real estate holdings in Codington and Brookings counties in South Dakota were to be sold, and Wilford asked the advice of his uncle on the price to be charged and the terms of payment. "Of course Mother would not make any proposition," he explained, "without consulting you." John's respect for the judgment of his nephew grew, as the young man gave evidence of intelligence and responsibility. "Wilford is an excellent boy," he told one of his sisters. In the same letter he expressed appreciation for the kindness and care Caroline Shipnes had given his brother Ole during the years of illness. Wilford later studied law and became an attorney in Chicago.[15]

In his own house, John A. Johnson found in the development of his

[13] Ole C. J. Shipnes to John A. Johnson, April 1, 1885. Ole's wife, the former Caroline Bodther, and their only child, Wilford, made up the family at the time of the change of name.

[14] Ole C. J. Shipnes to John A. Johnson, April 7, May 18, 1885.

[15] Wilford Shipnes to John A. Johnson, April 21, 1887, May 29, 1889. See also W. C. Shipnes to O. A. Buslett, October 18, 1893; this letter is in the O. A. Buslett Papers in the archives of the Norwegian-American Historical Association, Northfield, Minnesota.

growing family the central interest of his life. From 1861, for his remaining forty years, he lived in Madison; there his daughter and four sons were born. He was a devoted husband and father. In *Fingerpeg*, published in 1884 when his oldest son was twenty-one and his youngest was eight, he expressed enthusiastically his philosophy as head of a flourishing household: "In the home one finds the greatest good fortune. A good family life is a glorious thing. A family is something to live for, and also to die for."

In this same publication, he stated his oft-expressed belief that women are equal to men, and paid a fine tribute to the part women play in family life — a role particularly applicable to his own experience. His mother, his Aunt Marie, his wife, the mother of his children — all had shaped his life for good. He was especially fortunate in the faithful partner he found in Kaia Kildahl. It was said of Mrs. Johnson: "She had all the domestic virtues in high degree; she was absorbingly devoted to her home, and watched the growth and development of her children with assiduous care." Mrs. Hobart Johnson said of her husband's parents that often in the evening Johnson would be found reading aloud while his wife sat by his side busy with her handwork. But Kaia also found time beyond her household round to help in organized philanthropy and in the parish work of her church.[16]

This was a day when it was somewhat unusual for a married woman to own property and to audit household bills, but Mrs. Johnson accepted all such responsibilities. She owned stock in her husband's business enterprises and handled the management of the family budget. According to records in the Johnson Papers, checks for home expenses were signed by J. A. Johnson payable variously to Mrs. J. A. Johnson, Kaia Johnson, or Mrs. K. N. M. Johnson. From the family records of 1888, an interesting commentary on household expenses of the period is revealed. The accounts show that the year's total was approximately $2,400, an average of about $200 a month. This figure probably covered a family of five, but there is no way of determining just what was considered "household expenses."[17]

Kaia also held bank stock in her own name. On January 2, 1889, the

[16] John A. Johnson, *Fingerpeg for farmere og andre*, 100, 102 (Chicago, 1884); *Wisconsin State Journal*, February 7, 1908.

[17] In 1888 the three younger Johnson children were still living at home, but the expenses of the two older ones may not have been included in the totals. At the time, Frederik was twenty-five and Ida twenty. Mrs. Johnson's full maiden name was Kaia Nicoline Marie Kildahl.

First National Bank of Sioux City, Iowa, sent Mrs. K. N. M. Johnson a check for $80 in payment of a semi-annual dividend on "20 shares of capital stock of the bank now standing in your name on our books." Over two years later, the same bank sent her $120, the semi-annual dividend on forty shares of the same stock. She had other sources of income as indicated by a letter dated December 11, 1890, from the Bank of Madison to John A. Johnson stating that the bank had received from the First National Bank of St. Paul certificates of deposit for $5,000 payable to the order of Mrs. K. N. M. Johnson.[18]

During John A. Johnson's lifetime, the family owned and lived in three houses in Madison. In May, 1864, when Frederik, the eldest son, was less than a year old, Johnson purchased property on West Gorham Street. For this modest house, he paid Simeon and Maria Mills $650. For seven years the family occupied this dwelling, and there Ida and Carl were born. The Johnsons – now a lively group of five – moved in 1871 to a larger lot and house on Broom and Morris streets, which they bought from Sophia and Nelson Chittenden.[19]

The Broom Street house provided a neat and well-kept home for the growing family. The two youngest children, Hobart and Maurice, were born there, and in the late 1870's the children ranged in age between infancy and early adolescence. The new home had its own well and cesspool. In the kitchen stood a hand pump which brought water into a tank and thence by pipes throughout the house. There was no electricity for pumping. As Carl, the second son, grew old enough, his father assigned to him the task of operating the pump. If there was no water in the pipes, Carl was held responsible. In this homely task the future president of the Gisholt Machine Company probably gained his first engineering experience.

The maturing of the children and the increasing financial resources of the head of the family dictated a move to a more ample house. In 1882, Johnson purchased from Edgar Hill the property at 316 Wisconsin Avenue on the corner of that thoroughfare and West Gorham Street. Before the family moved into this house – which was to be their dwellingplace for forty years – the father had an addition built and the whole interior redecorated at a total cost of $3,000. New furniture, ordered from Chi-

[18] O. J. Taylor, president of the First National Bank of Sioux City, Iowa, to Mrs. K. N. M. Johnson, January 14, 1891; C. Q. Chandler, cashier of the same Sioux City bank, to Mrs. Johnson, July 1, 1891.

[19] The warranty deeds for the Gorham Street and Broom Street properties are in the Johnson Papers. Morris Street was later renamed West Main.

cago, included, among other purchases, easy chairs, a marble-topped table, a hat tree, and a French dressing set. Into this livable residence built in the mid-1860's, the Johnson clan settled to begin a particularly happy period of their lives. When he acquired the Wisconsin Avenue house, Johnson was fifty years old, his wife forty-four. In that year, their eldest son was nineteen and the youngest six.[20]

The house was large. There was the front parlor characteristic of the period, a second parlor that served as the family living room, a library, a large dining room, a tearoom, an ample kitchen and pantry, and a number of bedrooms. The house was equipped with what was then modern plumbing. Surrounding the residence was a spacious yard, the delight of the Johnson children. Here the boys of the neighborhood gathered to play baseball. Other attractions pleased the youngsters and their friends – a hammock and a stand of apple trees. There was no loitering for longer playtime, however, when the mother called; this was an orderly home ruled equally by discipline and love.

The oldest of the children, Frederik Adolph (called Fred by the family), was born on September 14, 1863. He attended the Madison public schools and at the age of fifteen was enrolled in the preparatory department at the University of Wisconsin. From officials there, Johnson received Fred's scholastic record for the term ending December 18 of that year. Appended was a pleasing postscript: "The attendance of your son upon the exercises of the term has been entirely satisfactory. His standing as a scholar has been excellent. So far as it has come under our observation his deportment has been *entirely* satisfactory." [21]

Fred's talents and interest, however, turned early to machinery. Eager to enter his father's business, while still in his teens, he began working in the Fuller and Johnson shop. In order to learn all the workings of a manufacturing enterprise, he started in the bottom rank, working side by side with the least skilled laborers. When Fred was twenty-one, Johnson sent him into the field to sell Fuller and Johnson farm implements. His first summer's experience had its ups and downs, but he stuck it out. His letters home – addressed to "Dear Papa," "Dear Pa," and "Dear Mama" and ending "with love and kisses to all" – reveal an appealing mixture of homesickness and a natural aptitude for business. They contain shrewd

[20] Ida Johnson Fisk, in the family scrapbook in the Johnson Papers. A painting of this residence is in a collection of pictures of old Madison houses in the library of the State Historical Society of Wisconsin.

[21] This record is in the Johnson Papers.

appraisals of sales prospects and penetrating judgments of credit risks among the men he approached for the company. He was a personable young man, whose quiet integrity gained and held the confidence of others. Even as a neophyte salesman, Fred's performance foreshadowed his later success in handling executive responsibilities.[22]

In his earliest letters to the family in Madison, Fred was clearly striving hard to be businesslike, even though he missed the security of the home circle. From Ming's Hotel, Marshall, Missouri, on the eve of the Fourth of July, 1884, he sent his father his first "sales report" with a note of nostalgia in it. "Yours rec'd. It always makes me feel better and encourages me to get a letter from you. I know I am not doing as well as I ought. . . . I don't believe anyone could have done much better for I have sold goods everywhere that there was any chance at all. The dealers I have seen have all said it was too early but perhaps that was only an excuse to put me off. I think that if someone goes over this territory again later on they can sell samples to nearly everyone I have seen. Everybody is very much pleased with our goods; with the planter especially for all admit its superiority over the others. . . . You can write me to K. C."

It was a lonely job for the young salesman traveling constantly through Missouri and Kansas. In the small towns, hotel accommodations were wretchedly primitive. The frontier was still rough and the selling assignment not easy, but Fred—learning about business as he went—undoubtedly believed that the training was a valuable experience. A letter from Pool's Hotel, Kirksville, Missouri, dated July 26, indicated that he had thought of giving up and going home. "Dear Pa," he wrote. "You can see how much I have been able to do so far. If you think I had better come home all right. . . . If I had come from two to six weeks ago I could have sold some goods but now everybody says it is altogether too early or too late. . . . The only thing it seems to me I can do is to show up the goods and let people know how they are and that there is such a firm as F. & J. Mfg. Co. . . . Everybody that I have tried to make arrangements with and whose names I have sent in are first class parties in every respect and have good trade. There is a splendid outlook for spring trade if we can get in in time and get them to keep us in mind."

In a message to his mother from Fremont House, Cameron, Missouri, dated August 6, Fred could use a more personal tone. Yet he could not

[22] Fred's letters to his parents during the summer of 1884 may be found in the Johnson Papers.

forget business. "I suppose," he said, "you think I am a nice fellow for not writing you before but I have been so busy that I have not had time to write. I am alright as far as I know although I have not been doing much business. Anyway if I haven't done much I have started a trade so that the next time the ground is gone over some one will reap the benefit after what I have done. If I don't make a success as a salesman it won't be because I haven't tried."

Following in Fred's footsteps, his three considerably younger brothers, under their father's direction, early began preparations for careers in the family business. Carl Albert, the second son, born in 1870, attended the public schools and matriculated at the University of Wisconsin. There he took an active part in student affairs as a member of Phi Upsilon fraternity and a winner of the coveted "W" as a baseball player. He took the full course in mechanical engineering, graduating in 1891. During vacations, he put on overalls and took his place among the laborers in the Gisholt shops learning the ins and outs of machine production. In his early twenties he used his skill and training as a draftsman in perfecting the company's products.

Some eleven years after Fred's dismal experiences in Missouri, twenty-five-year-old Carl also tried his hand as a salesman, not of farm machinery but of lathes and tool grinders. From Fort Wayne, Indiana, he wrote a personal letter home on January 31, 1895, the mature tone of a seasoned businessman contrasting a bit with Fred's brave attempts from the wilds of the West. He enclosed an order for a 24-inch lathe and a tool grinder – and pointedly inquired whether that "wasn't fair for a starter!"

"Dear Folks," Carl wrote, a little breathlessly and with a fine disregard for punctuation: "I called on these people yesterday morning and met two other machine men there not competitors however. The three of us spent our entire day there first one and then the other talking to the president. I left or rather made out a proposition but could not get him to sign it. He invited one of the other men and me to dinner with him last evening and we remained at his house until 10:30 talking machinery a part of the time. When we started to go he asked me if I was going back to Chicago at 3 this morning with the other men. I told him no that I would stay over until to-day to get his order and it came. As you will notice delivery is f. o. b. Ft. Wayne and I have made a very low price on tools but it will be necessary to do this for a time as everyone is selling at a very low price. I think the terms of payment are satisfactory but we will doubtless get the money before the notes fall due. They can be discounted at all events. . . . I called on some other people but could do nothing. You must get the Siemens & Halske machines and also the Stock Company machine ready now as soon as possible. That Stock machine must be in New York by March 15, I think. You therefore have no time to lose. . . . Love to all."

Hobart and Maurice were also heading for positions in their father's business. Hobart Stanley Johnson was born October 7, 1873. His career closely paralleled Carl's: attendance at the Madison public schools and then three years (1890–1893) at the University of Wisconsin, where he specialized in mechanical engineering. At the end of his junior year, he left the university to joint the Gisholt Company as a draftsman and shop superintendent. The education of Johnson's youngest son varied somewhat from the pattern set by his older brothers. Maurice Ingolf, born on July 16, 1876, after completing his secondary-school period was appointed to the United States Military Academy at West Point. There he spent two years (1894–1896), after which he entered the University of Wisconsin as a member of the class of 1898. Like Carl some time earlier, Maurice belonged to Phi Upsilon fraternity and won his "W" in baseball. His taste for engineering and his inventive skill inevitably drew him into the family business in which he gave valuable service for many years. For a time, he headed his own business, the Maurice I. Johnson Company, in Madison.

Ida Estelle Johnson, born August 17, 1868, grew up as the only daughter in a family dominated by her four brothers. Following her father's ideas concerning the education of women, she earned a degree at the University of Wisconsin at a time when such an accomplishment was unusual for a young woman. Later with her parents she traveled extensively, both in this country and abroad. At home her interests turned to community affairs, notably as an effective worker in Madison charities, on a voluntary basis. Her most important contribution was made as a charter member and active lifelong participant in the work for the needy carried on by the well-known Madison organization called the "Attic Angels."

Some time in 1889, Ida and three other young women took upon themselves the project of making clothes for a pair of twins born in a very poor Madison family. At the time, the city lacked functioning social service agencies. Filling a need, the work of the Attic Angels became a pioneering effort destined to go far beyond the original objective and to set deep roots in the community. Soon the four friends enlisted others of their age, the making over of old clothes was expanded to give help to many underprivileged children throughout the community, and the Attic Angels came to be a city-wide charitable society, with an extensive program of activities. Among the benefits to all residents was the sponsorship of a visiting nurse service, one of the earliest in the country.[23]

Ida Johnson continued to be a leader in the group, and in the membership lists other family names occur frequently: her sisters-in-law — Mrs. Carl Johnson, Mrs. Hobart Johnson, and Mrs. Maurice Johnson. As their service broadened, the Attic Angels, having established a trust fund, sponsored the Fair Ball, a fund-raising venture intended to provide a nucleus to encourage other contributions. The ball was destined to become an annual affair of prominence in the community. In 1899 it was held in the gymnasium of the University of Wisconsin. No effort was spared to make this gala event a leading community social highlight — and incidentally a financial success. Mr. and Mrs. John A. Johnson occupied one of the boxes to watch their daughter Ida among the group of sponsors leading the grand march.[24]

In May, 1900, the Attic Angels on two evenings presented an entertainment called a Kermis to raise funds to support their projects. Dozens of children danced on the stage of the Fuller auditorium in honor of the Kermis Queen, Ida Johnson. After many weeks of preparation in which Ida had been the guiding spirit, this artistic event proved to be one of the most colorful and popular occasions in the long history of the Attic Angels. The group continued to grow in numbers; as the years went by, its contribution to Madison became more and more important. In 1941 the society moved into its own headquarters, a new cottage at 415 Mifflin Street. An open house was held on September 14 celebrating the completion of the organization's new home. In the receiving line on this occasion was Mrs. George M. Fisk (Ida Johnson), then in her seventy-third year.[25]

[23] In addition to Ida Johnson, the founding quartet included Flora Mears and two Bryant sisters, all members of well-known Madison families. The "Attic Angels" took their name from the search they made in many an attic for old clothes that could be given to the poor.

[24] *Madison Democrat*, November 12, 1899. There has never been a time when some member of the John A. Johnson family has not been active in the Attic Angels.

[25] Ida Johnson Fisk, family scrapbook. Clippings from unnamed Madison newspapers describing the Kermis are dated May 5 and May 10, 1900. Kermis (literally *Kirkmess*, a church mass) took its name from a celebration held annually for hundreds of years in the Low Countries of Europe on the feast day of the local patron saint. In Madison, as elsewhere in the United States, the spelling Kermis (or Kermess) was used to designate an entertainment or fair for charitable purposes.

The wedding of Ida Estelle Johnson and Professor George Mygatt Fisk at the Johnson home in Madison on June 28, 1902, was a brilliant affair. For the occasion, the family residence had been beautifully decorated with spring flowers, and a gathering of relatives and friends, including representatives of many well-known Madison families, attended the ceremony. As a pleasing touch, Ida's niece, Ruth, the small daughter of Mr. and Mrs. Carl A. Johnson, was a flower girl in the wedding party.

Dr. and Mrs. Fisk first made their home in Champaign, Illinois, where he held the position of dean of the school of commerce at the University of Illinois. In June, 1909, desiring time for research and writing on his projected documentary history of American commerce, Professor Fisk resigned as dean at Illinois, and he and Mrs. Fisk moved to Madison. There, in addition to his scholarly studies at the University of Wisconsin, he took an immediate interest in the beautification of the city, as a member of the board of directors of the Madison Park Association. With others he purchased farm land on the eastern shore of Lake Mendota and projected extensive improvements for the future. His death on April 29, 1910 — less than a year after the move to Madison — cancelled all his plans before more than a beginning had been made. His book was never published. After approximately eight years of marriage, Mrs. Ida Johnson Fisk was left a widow at the age of forty-one.[26]

John and Kaia Johnson took great satisfaction in the homes established by their children. In a letter to his sister Caroline a year and a half before his death, Johnson wrote at length from abroad about his family; his tone was one of evident pride. "Both Fred's wife and Carl's wife," he said, "are excellent women." Fred had married Emma Rosenstengell, daughter of a professor of German at the University of Wisconsin. With their two children, Gertrude and Russell, they made their home in Germany, where they were happy and contented.[27]

Carl's wife was Bertha Cassoday, daughter of John B. Cassoday, chief justice of the Wisconsin supreme court. Their two children were a son,

[26] George M. Fisk was a man of unusual accomplishments. After graduation from the University of Michigan in 1890, he studied abroad; in 1896 he completed his doctorate at the University of Munich. For the next three years (1897–1900), he served as second secretary to the American embassy in Berlin. See also Richard T. Ely, "George Mygatt Fisk," a clipping from a Madison newspaper of May 17, 1910, and Ida Johnson Fisk, family scrapbook.

[27] John A. Johnson to Caroline Johnson Stuverud, May 30, 1899. When Johnson was away from Madison, his letters often expressed his concern for the welfare of his grandchildren and included special greetings for them.

John Cassoday Johnson, and a daughter, Ruth. The latter attended Bryn Mawr College, completed her education at the University of Wisconsin, and later became the wife of Dr. Frank L. Weston, a Madison physician. Carl and Bertha Johnson suffered a grievous loss in the death of their son at the age of twenty: John Cassoday Johnson succumbed to a heart ailment in his freshman year at the University of Wisconsin. During World War I, the hospitable home of Mr. and Mrs. Carl A. Johnson on Gilman Street was thrown open to boys of the Student Army Training Corps, then quartered at the university—and many young men had occasion to remember the generous encouragement given them there on their way to military service.

The wife of Hobart S. Johnson was Elizabeth Hopkins, a New York girl whose parents had roots in Madison. Her father was the son of Judge James Campbell Hopkins, an early resident of the city, and her mother was a daughter of Andrew Proudfit. Elizabeth Hopkins, who attended Bryn Mawr, was a woman of unusual intelligence and public spirit. In a letter to Caroline, John A. Johnson spoke of her as "kindly and lovable." Hobart and Elizabeth Johnson were the parents of two sons: George Hopkins Johnson and Hobart Stanley Johnson, Jr. Like his brother Carl, Hobart was a benefactor to S. A. T. C. cadets in Madison. During the disastrous influenza epidemic of 1918, twenty boys from the university unit were taken in and nursed back to health in the home of Mr. and Mrs. Hobart S. Johnson.

Maurice, the youngest member of the John A. Johnson family, married Eleanor Bardeen, the daughter of Judge C. V. Bardeen of Madison. Their only child, Frances Hyde Johnson, married Joseph W. Vilas. This family continues to make its home in Madison.

In the last ten years of his life, Johnson's frequent trips abroad gave him opportunity to express his affectionate concern for all members of the family. He wrote common letters to Fred, Carl, and Hobart, beginning "Dear Boys" and signing them "Love to all, Papa." When he mentioned their mother, he always called her "Mamma"; in his many letters to Kaia, he addressed her as "Dearest Wife." To Maurice at West Point went messages of encouragement to a homesick son who doubted that he was cut out for the career of a military man.

The long ocean voyage to South America in 1896 afforded Johnson more hours of genuine leisure than he had enjoyed at any time in his busy earlier life. He was in his middle sixties, a time that naturally created in him a mood of fatherly solicitude for his family in their various pursuits. From Southampton, England, as he changed ships for Buenos Aires, he sent home a letter revealing the depth of his feeling: "What a comfort it is, in going on such a journey especially, but at all times for that matter, to think what good children I have. Fortunate the parents that have such good children as I have."

On board ship he directed to Maurice a long letter about the details of the voyage, turning in the end to what no doubt lay closest to his heart. "The next letter I get from you," he counseled, "I presume will tell me that you are very happy and contented, that you love your studies and that you work very hard and are beginning to feel quite soldierlike, not exactly like fighting, yet thinking about what the country may some day require of you. You may not make army life your profession, unless your country calls upon you in time of danger. Then you will promptly respond. . . . You may be sure I will long for home on this trip. God bless and protect you." [28]

Though his letters on his trip to South America usually dealt with business details at Gisholt, there was time for personal jottings, occasionally spiced with humor. He wrote that he would attend the boat races in England. Chauncey Depew, who had sailed from New York on their ship, was arranging for a special train from Southampton to the races. Anyone could go – and Johnson considered the opportunity too good to miss. In another letter he described an elegant banquet which had been tendered the delegation of American industrialists. No detail had been overlooked. "I wish Ida could have been along," he remarked; "she would have enjoyed the evening." He thought also of the youngsters in the family group. Of his grandchildren, his namesake John, Carl's son, seemed his favorite. "I don't suppose John will know me when I return," he added with a touch of nostalgia.

Johnson's letters written on shipboard mingled easygoing accounts of his own daily routine with serious fatherly advice. "I get up at 7 and take my 'bauth,'" he revealed. "We breakfast at nine, lunch at 1, dine at 6:30. I spend my time reading, sleeping, walking, eating, talking and occasionally at cards. Had a fine game of whist last night and was beaten. I am reading books on Argentina and Brazil. I want to familiarize myself with

[28] John A. Johnson to Maurice I. Johnson, July 7, 1896. The father always spelled the name of his son "Morris," but "Maurice" was regularly used by other members of the family and in all official connections.

these countries in order to assess them more accurately when I get there." To his sons on another day, his message was directly personal: "You boys are getting an excellent start early in life. You now have a fair foothold in an unlimited field of activity. You must, of course, make your present business a success. . . . I wish Hobart would study Spanish. Next to German it will doubtless be the most important foreign language for business America. . . . It [*language*] is not only of direct value but develops and cultivates at the same time." [29]

Supervisors and workers in his factory were often on Johnson's mind when he was absent on extended trips. At one time he forwarded to his sons a suggestion for cementing friendlier relations with the men in the shops. "The carryall should have the cover put on," he advised. "It would be nice to occasionally make up a party of 3 or 4 families, a carryall full, and give them a ride. Say the Togstads with Nels Swerry, or Hagen. Let them form their own party. It will do a world of good. We want to use the team to please our workmen, taking out family groups."

At their home in Madison, John and Kaia Johnson welcomed with friendliness and hospitality persons from all stations in life. Of Johnson it was said that he was entirely free from affectation. He could work with his hands in his shops, a comrade with his men; yet he could move with ease and equality of respect among educators, business executives, and leaders in public affairs. Beginning in the earliest days of their married life in Madison, the Johnsons had helped students by giving them a home while they attended the university. For such boys — almost members of the family — the warm interest continued into later life with exchanges of letters extending over many years.[30]

One student who never forgot the warmth and encouragement of the Johnson home during his student days in Madison was Peter L. Norman. When the young man left the university, he established himself in the farm machinery business in Montevideo, Minnesota, where for forty years he sold Fuller and Johnson implements. During all the latter part of John A. Johnson's life, Norman often came to Madison on business — or for a Christmas visit. On such occasions the old friends renewed an association which grew to have a special meaning to both men.[31]

On one visit, Norman met Carl Johnson on the train, was the latter's

[29] John A. Johnson to his sons, Fred, Carl, and Hobart, July 7, 1896.

[30] *Wisconsin State Journal*, November 11, 1901.

[31] Peter L. Norman to John A. Johnson, January 10, 1883. The Norman correspondence is in the Johnson Papers.

guest in the dining car, and stayed as usual at the Johnson house. In a letter to his wife, he revealed how he had been treated as an honored guest: "My room was the guest room, upstairs over the front parlor, beautifully furnished. Every day I went to that great factory in the carriage with Mr. Johnson, the president of both factories and taken home for dinner." [32]

While he was visiting the Johnsons, Norman met Halle Steensland, then Norwegian consul in Madison. On that day Steensland was host at an afternoon party, at his home across the lake, to a group of Scandinavian editors traveling in the United States. John and Kaia Johnson, who were among those attending the gathering, arranged to bring their guest from Minnesota. Norman described the occasion: "We crossed the lake in Maurice Johnson's beautiful launch run by a gasoline engine. It was a lovely party held on the wide spreading lawn with refreshments served at small tables. It seemed strange to have so many friends and to have done so little to deserve them." [33]

Many years later, Peter Norman's daughter, Ruth Ida Norman, of Minneapolis, writing to George Hopkins Johnson, then president of the Gisholt Machine Company, spoke of the close relationship of the two families. "Your Grandfather John A. Johnson," she wrote, "was very kind to my father and my father spoke very kindly of him and his family." She included in her letter excerpts from Peter Norman's autograph book—one of which read: "Rule of Life. Let all our acts be such that God and man should see them. John A. Johnson, March, 1885." [34]

Thrond Bothne, a well-known editor of Norwegian-American newspapers, often enjoyed the hospitality of the Johnson home. At one time a professor at Luther College in Decorah, Iowa, he held in general the same views that Johnson did about the Americanization of the immigrant. The two men often exchanged letters, and their families were intimate. "My son Gisle," the elder Bothne reported on one occasion, "will be in Madison to attend a meeting of the American Language Teachers. I advised him to see you. I hope you can furnish him room for several days." Gisle Bothne also taught at Luther College and later was professor of Scandinavian studies at the University of Minnesota.[35]

The Johnson residence on Wisconsin Avenue was often the scene of parties. In the early fall of 1896, Mrs. Johnson and Ida were hostesses at

[32] Peter L. Norman to his wife, September 16, 1900.
[33] Peter L. Norman to his wife, September 16, 1900.
[34] Ruth Ida Norman to George Hopkins Johnson, April 27, 1962.
[35] Thrond Bothne to John A. Johnson, July 14, 1884.

an "at home" attended by a hundred guests, many of them the wives and daughters of business associates of John A. Johnson and his sons. The rooms of the big house were appropriately decorated with red and white roses, smilax, palms and autumn flowers — yellow asters and goldenrod in the library. Kaia and her daughter were assisted in the receiving line on this well-remembered occasion by Mrs. Frederik A. Johnson, Mrs. George Gernon, Mrs. Burr W. Jones, and Mrs. Frank W. Hoyt.[36]

It is not surprising that for the last third of his life, John A. Johnson was not the robust man he had been in his earlier years. His intense drive had begun to impair his health. He found it hard to relax, and he suffered from a stomach ailment. After frequent bouts with indigestion, in late 1883 he considered going to Tate Springs, a Tennessee mineral watering place promising help for his infirmity. There is no record that he visited Tate Springs. Four years later, however, he went to Europe seeking relief from the same difficulty. Ida accompanied him to Carlsbad, a spa in Bohemia celebrated for the medicinal qualities of its water. When he returned to Madison, he placed orders with a drug firm in Chicago for cases of Carlsbad mineral water, which he continued to use for a period of several years.[37]

In 1899 he went again to Europe for his health. He had had several years of comparative freedom from his malady, but now — in his sixty-eighth year — his illness had taken a bad turn. A Berlin doctor advised him to go to Bad Hamburg, near Frankfurt am Main, to drink the waters and take the baths. At this time, in a letter to his sister Caroline, he admitted that he was lonely at the fashionable German watering place. "There is not a soul here," he confided, "that I ever saw before." He also revealed to Caroline that he was considerably disturbed over the fact that he had lost twelve pounds.[38]

Johnson returned home, no better for his treatment at Bad Hamburg. His illness continuing, he sought the advice of Chicago specialists in internal medicine. These doctors were in agreement: an operation would not help him. On his return to Madison, he reported in letters to Caroline that he went riding every day and walked some, but he was discouraged

[36] Ida Johnson Fisk, family scrapbook. A clipping from an unnamed Madison newspaper, dated September 9, 1896, gives an account of the reception.

[37] Robert Stevenson and Company to John A. Johnson, March 28, 1899, a bill for a case of Carlsbad water.

[38] John A. Johnson to Caroline Johnson Stuverud, May 30, 1899.

because he could not gain weight. A letter written in January, 1901, reported that for several months he had been in bed most of the time. He could sit up and write, but frequently he had to contend with great pain.[39] Here his natural fortitude and calm philosophy of accepting life as it came stood him in good stead. "Mentally I am happy and contented," he told his sister. "You know my religious opinion, that there is a life hereafter where we shall all meet again and all be happy. I believe in a just God, that created all things, and all for the best. I regard death as but stepping through a door to a place where there is no pain. It is the material part that suffers pain."[40]

The late winter and early spring months of 1901 found Johnson confined to his bed. His mind seemed especially keen; it was never idle. He kept busy reading works on history and economics, drafting bills to propose to the legislature, writing articles for newspapers, making plans for the Gisholt Home for the Aged. During this time he sent substantial donations to Luther and St. Olaf colleges. Previously, he had made contributions to Augsburg College. He had felt a strong interest in all these Lutheran institutions. They had been founded by his Norwegian countrymen in the 1860's and 1870's – offshoots of the Lutheran church in which he had held membership for an extended period of his life. For St. Olaf Johnson in his later years had developed a special fondness, through his friend the Reverend Gjermund Hoyme, the church leader whose pioneering efforts in support of the college had been a turning point in its history.

In June, 1901, John A. Johnson went to Rochester, Minnesota, to consult with Dr. William J. Mayo, a specialist in stomach surgery, and with his partner-brother, Dr. Charles H. Mayo. There he decided to submit to an operation to be performed by Dr. William J. Mayo. The day before the operation he addressed a six-page letter to Willet S. Main of Madison, with whom he had enjoyed an uninterrupted friendship for almost half a century. Later Main, in speaking of the letter, said that it contained little reference to Johnson himself or to the seriousness of his illness. Instead it dealt at length with questions of national importance. Main eventually gave the letter to Senator John C. Spooner, another long-time friend, who was always interested in Johnson's views on public matters and wished to have them available for reference in Washington.[41]

[39] John A. Johnson to Caroline Johnson Stuverud, n. d., but probably in late 1900.

[40] John A. Johnson to Caroline Johnson Stuverud, January 23, 1901.

[41] "The Memorial Services for John A. Johnson," in *Wisconsin State Journal*, November 25, 1901.

After his surgery, while he was convalescing in St. Mary's Hospital in Rochester, Johnson wrote to his sister Caroline. Dr. William J. Mayo had paid him a visit, and the two men had had a most interesting conversation. The doctor had said that at times he had had to strike out for himself in medical situations not reported in books. "Dr. Mayo was perfectly candid," Johnson explained, "and not afraid to admit that he had made mistakes. He is a thoroughly honest man as well as I believe the best surgeon in the world especially as to the stomach. It is not only the cases that he treats, but in pointing the way for other surgeons that will do just as good work as he does. The whole science of surgery is being greatly advanced by him."[42]

Johnson reported to Caroline that he was able to sit up for a while each day, but that he could walk very little. "It is a great shock to the system," he admitted to his younger sister, "to take a person's stomach out, repair it and replace it." Frederik was now with him and would stay until he was able to travel to Madison. This plan was carried out; on July 5, 1901, Fred brought his father home.[43]

The sick man now had relief from pain, but his strength did not return. He grew steadily weaker. His mind, on the contrary, continued to be active and vigorous. It soon became apparent, however, that his physical resources would not be equal to the task – that he was losing rather than gaining. On the morning of November 10, 1901, at the age of sixty-nine, John A. Johnson died at his home in the community where he had lived for over forty years.

The city of Madison and the state of Wisconsin had lost a prominent and useful citizen in the death of this uncommon man, whose all-embracing interests had benefited citizens in every walk of life. All mourned his passing. Flags flew at half-mast over the city hall and over the Dane County courthouse on the day of the funeral.

On a sheet of white paper edged in black, the Fuller and Johnson Company issued an announcement of their president's death, with a review of his life and activities. The company officers, who for a generation had

[42] John A. Johnson to Caroline Johnson Stuverud. This letter in longhand is undated, but it was probably written in late June, 1901, from St. Mary's Hospital, Rochester. At that time the Mayo Clinic had not yet been established. The first official use of the term "Mayo Clinic" appeared on the letterhead of the institution in 1914. A copy of the letter from Johnson to his sister is in the files of the Mayo Clinic, Rochester.

[43] John A. Johnson to Caroline Johnson Stuverud, an undated letter written from Rochester during Johnson's convalescence.

worked closely with John A. Johnson, knew at first hand how his qualities of patience, common sense, and firmness had made them feel a part of something bigger than themselves. Now they paid him a glowing tribute: "[We knew him] as a close student, a profound thinker and a fluent writer, a man of fine character, perfect habits and high ideals." Appropriately, from the shop personnel of the two companies Johnson had headed came the six pallbearers who assisted at the funeral service: Michael Nolan, Charles Togstad, John Loyfield, and Charles Hult of the Johnson and Fuller Manufacturing Company — and George Steinle and August Reider of the Gisholt Machine Company.

The funeral, held at the Johnson home at 316 Wisconsin Avenue on November 12, 1901, was conducted by the Reverend F. A. Gilmore of the Unitarian Church, of which Johnson in his later years had been a contributing member. A group of eight well-known men from a variety of professions — including officers of Johnson's two companies — served as honorary pallbearers: Senator Robert M. La Follette, Senator William F. Vilas, Judge J. H. Carpenter, Samuel Higham, Edward M. Fuller, E. W. Keyes, T. C. Richmond, and J. W. Hobbins. A large gathering of townspeople and friends from Chicago, Milwaukee, and other Wisconsin communities were present. Seated in the audience were clergymen from a number of churches. Fuller and Johnson and Gisholt employees attended in a body. As part of the largest funeral procession in Madison's history, they filled five streetcars. Burial was at Forest Hill Cemetery.[44]

The townsfolk of Madison gathered in the Fuller auditorium on Sunday, November 24, 1901, for a memorial service. They had come not so much to express their sorrow that a significant life had ended as to record their appreciation for the "way in which that life had been lived and for the good that was in it." On the stage were personal and business friends: Dr. Edward A. Birge, acting president of the University of Wisconsin, Mayor Storm Bull, himself a professor at the university, with others of the faculty, Madison business and professional men, and members of the administrative staffs of the companies of which John A. Johnson had been president. In front of the rostrum, seated in a large body, were the men who had worked under the president's direction at Fuller and Johnson and at Gisholt. To the left, close to the stage, sat members of the family.[45]

[44] *Wisconsin State Journal*, November 12, 1901. Johnson was listed as a member of the Unitarian Society of Madison in its January, 1898, register now in the State Historical Society of Wisconsin.

[45] *Wisconsin State Journal*, November 25, 1901.

R. M. Bashford, as presiding officer, introduced associates who had known Johnson intimately at various stages of his career. A colleague in the Wisconsin assembly in 1857 when both were young men, General G. E. Bryant, spoke of him as a student of large affairs and an ardent advocate of liberty in the slaveholding days before the Civil War. Willet S. Main called Senator Johnson's arguments in the upper chamber of the Wisconsin legislature "clear, forcible and convincing" and referred to his long-time friend as a man "possessed of a conscience void of offense toward God and man." Johnson's heritage of character, his good mind, his respect for hard work, said Judge E. W. Keyes, had enabled him to rise to a position of influence. "He was great enough and brave enough," declared T. C. Richmond, "to admit that he was deeply obligated to America. He was a trustee who was administering a sacred trust." Mayor Storm Bull, himself of Norwegian birth, in closing the meeting, pointed out that John A. Johnson, although he had never lost his pride in his immigrant countrymen, had become the complete American.[46]

The record of John A. Johnson's life is more than an account of an immigrant who succeeded far beyond the limits of the common American dream. His sensitivity to the potentialities of the new country to which he came as a child was deep and enduring. His awareness of the great issues of the day and his personal involvement in them gave a broad dimension to what might otherwise have been only one more story of success. In a fluid society and in a dynamic country where notable individual achievement was possible, his was more than a personal accomplishment. A constructive leader, he contributed to the weaving of that new design of culture and to the building of that productive economy which characterized the burgeoning America of his time.

[46] *Wisconsin State Journal*, November 25, 1901. R. M. Bashford was a director of the Fuller and Johnson Manufacturing Company; T. C. Richmond was a member of the board of directors of the Gisholt Home for the Aged.

APPENDIXES AND INDEX

Appendixes

A. AN IMMIGRANT'S RECOLLECTION OF HIS EARLY DAYS IN "ENGLISH SCHOOL"

I had lived with an American family a short time the first winter and was sent to the district school a little, and from the summer of 1845 till I was 18. I was nearly all the time living with Americans, working by the month summers and for my board winters, when I also went to school a little. I did not however learn much. I think the teachers were poor, at least I acquired no taste for study till I was 16. In our district we then had a most excellent lady teacher. Before the close of the three months I was among the better pupils. I "ciphered" through Adams arithmetic that winter and became a fair reader and good speller.

The succeeding winter I attended another school where we also had a good teacher. He was particularly proficient in reading and in orthography and orthoepy, and I soon learned of what sounds our spoken language is composed. I again went "through" a written arithmetic, and the teacher laid great stress on mental arithmetic and used Colburn's excellent little work with great benefit to the class. I also procured a higher arithmetic, which I continued the next winter under another teacher and also took up algebra and grammar. After that I attended a little high school in Fort Atkinson a few weeks, my principal studies being algebra and grammar, though I went "through" a second higher arithmetic. This ended my schooling, which all told was only about one year. I was however considered well qualified to teach district school, and did teach five winters after that.

NOTE: John A. Johnson, "Memoirs," in the Johnson Papers.

B. RESOLUTION OF SOUTHEAST DISTRICT REPUBLICAN ASSEMBLY, DANE COUNTY, WISCONSIN, MAY 19, 1856

Whereas the present stirring scenes in the political affairs of our country seem to indicate that a collision between liberty and slavery can no longer be avoided, but that they must come to a deadly struggle speedily, and whereas we firmly believe that the great principles of equal rights to all, which was the foundation of the great struggle of our fathers' liberty, should be maintained at all hazards; therefore

Resolved, That we will oppose with all Constitutional means, the mighty efforts which are being made to nationalize slavery, and therefore make us, the freemen of the North, supporters of that damning wrong.

Resolved, That as lovers of equal rights we deeply sympathize with the freemen of Kansas in their manly struggle against, not only the Border Ruffians of Missouri, but the perverted Executive power of our nation, and that we will labor, with all means in our power, to obtain her admission as a free State.

Resolved, That since our object is to secure equal rights to all, we most emphatically reprobate the principles of the Know Nothing organization, and will neither sympathize nor act with any such organization.

Resolved, That since unity of action is essential to success, and since the approaching Presidential contest gives indications of being a fierce and hard fought battle, we will support cordially the nominees of the Philadelphia Convention, unless they be men opposed to the great principles embraced in the Declaration of Independence.

Resolved, That we behold with feelings of deep regret the persistent efforts, which the general government, backed by the slave power, are making, to destroy the rights of individual states by judicial decisions which aim at the entire subversion of State sovereignty.

Resolved, That we earnestly recommend a thorough organization of the friends of the Republican cause in every school district.

On motion, the minutes were approved, and the clerk instructed to review and send the same to the office of the *Madison Daily State Journal* for publication.

NOTE: *Madison Daily State Journal*, June 6, 1856.

C. RESOLUTION OF COMMITTEE PROPOSING THE ORGANIZATION OF FIFTEENTH WISCONSIN REGIMENT IN THE CIVIL WAR

Madison, Wisconsin
September 25, 1861

To
His Excellency Alexander W. Randall
Governor of the State of Wisconsin

Sir:

The undersigned as a committee, appointed by a meeting of the Scandinavians from different parts of the state, assembled here at Madison today have been assigned the duty of informing your Excellency that said meeting has passed a resolution to raise a Scandinavian Brigade for the war now pending in this our adopted country; and that we recommend the following gentlemen to be appointed as follows:

Honorable Hans C. Heg as Colonel

K. K. Jones as Lieutenant Colonel

Believing that a movement like this for the defense of our Country and our Flag will meet the approbation and support of the Government, we respectfully remain

Your obedient Servants:
Adolph Sorenson
J. A. Johnson
S. Samuelson
C. F. Solberg   Chr. Winge
K. J. Fleischer
B. W. Suckow

NOTE: "Civil War Manuscripts, September–October 1861, Executive Department, State of Wisconsin," in State Historical Society of Wisconsin.

D. AN ACCOUNT OF THE BATTLE OF CHICKAMAUGA

By Colonel Ole C. Johnson

At two o'clock on the afternoon of the first day, September 19, 1863, fighting broke with great fury. The rebels were better prepared for the battle than were the men from the North. As the various divisions of the North were thrown into battle, they stemmed the tide for a while, only to be driven back. Division after division was thrown into battle. Your nearest and dearest friends fell beside you but everyone fought on with a stolid indifference. Oh how welcome is night after such a day as that! You look wistfully at the sun after each impetuous onset and it seems to you that he never moved so slowly before. What would you not give at such a time as this for the power to make the sun, not like Joshua of old stand still, but to move a little faster. But everything on earth has an end, and the sun sinks slowly in the West at last and night, a thousand times welcome night, spreads his sable mantle over the field and you breathe more freely and thank God in your heart that the army is yet safe.

NOTE: From an address delivered at Albion, Wisconsin, some years after the Civil War. The original handwritten copy is the property of Mrs. Bessie Shipnes, Highland Park, Illinois.

E. WAR LETTERS OF LIEUTENANT COLONEL OLE C. JOHNSON

Libby Prison, Richmond, Virginia, December 7, 1863

Dear Brother!

Again I send you a few lines. I am in good health. Have not yet received any letter from you. Our Congress meets today, and I should think it would do something about getting us [prisoners] exchanged. Many have now been here since May, and many more since June and July, and naturally they are eager to be released. We have had the most beautiful weather one can imagine for more than a week. It is almost a Wisconsin May, but I think King Winter will soon come along and claim his own. We expected an engagement in northern Virginia – judging from Meade's movements – but now it appears that he has given that up, and so I think there will be no battle this winter.

I wish that you could provide me with several books on phonography and some easy German readings, in case I write home for another package, as I shall do if we remain here after New Year's. My love to Kaia, Caroline, Julia, and Freddie, and warmest regards to all my friends.

[The lines above were written for inspection by the censor, the following with invisible fluid on the reverse side of the sheet.]

Dr. Hawley of the Thirty-Fifth Illinois Regiment promised me when he left from here to let you know how this writing can be made visible. And so I will send you some lines, even though I do not have anything especially important to write about. On two occasions I have sent you Richmond papers, first by Lieutenant Clement and next by Dr. Hawley, and I hope that you have received them. By Lieutenant Clement I also sent a long letter, which I hope he was able to take out. Yesterday I sent a letter to Caroline, one side written as this is. For lack of anything else, I'll tell a little about my experiences since I fell into the hands of the Rebels. When we were captured, many of us were rounded up and led back to Chickamauga Creek by a captain on General Hindmand's staff, who, as previously stated, was a gentleman. He showed no vindictiveness and did not permit his soldiers to take the canteens and knapsacks from the prisoners – which they tried to do. I gave him my field glass, which I knew I would not be permitted to keep anyway, and could just as well give to one who had the courage to step forward and fight for what he believed to be right, rather than have it taken away by one or another behind-the-lines officer, who is always found far from the field of battle and is especially vindictive toward the Yankees when he has them in his power and can insult and mishandle them without danger to his own precious body. I think you will find that the common judgment of all who have been prisoners is that they have been abused only by those who are left behind in garrison towns and bases and know nothing of the inconveniences and dangers of a soldier's life, and by the home-guard soldier who is so totally despised by every prisoner. If a prisoner is mishandled and robbed on the field, this is generally done by stragglers among the troops at the rear, who in one way or another slip out of ranks in the march to the front. The man who bravely steps forward to battle is never guilty of such a cowardly deed.

From Chickamauga Creek we were taken two-three miles farther to the troops in the rear, where we found the men who had been captured on Saturday, and at four o'clock we were sent on our way to Ringgold [Georgia], a distance of twelve miles, where – we were told – we would stay overnight and get something to eat. A captain of an East Tennessee regiment was in charge of us, and he was by no means a sweet-tempered man in appearance, and it seemed that he would not have many scruples about stealing or plundering his prisoners or anyone else whom he might manage to get in his power. The two lieutenants he had with him were good-natured, gentlemanly officers and treated us with respect.

At nine o'clock in the evening we arrived at Ringgold, tired and hungry, and were told we must go four miles farther before we could receive rations and leave by train for Atlanta. At eleven o'clock we arrived at a railroad station the name of which I have forgotten and were allowed to light fires. But the night was cold and we got little rest and less sleep. The next morning we were given the unwelcome news that we must go another four miles – on foot – before we could get anything to eat. At eight o'clock we were on our way, and we arrived at Tunnel Hill [Georgia] at ten. A detachment was immediately set to work baking some cornbread, but before this was ready, we were put aboard a train and started for Atlanta. Thus for the third time we were disappointed in not receiving anything to eat, and our one hope now was Atlanta. If it had not been for the fact that some of the prisoners had a supply of rations when they were captured – which they willingly shared with me – I surely would have starved, and I know that there were many who suffered the pangs of hunger.

I must stop here, as I can no longer see the lines. I shall write again in a few days. Write to me in a similar manner – with onion juice or with soda dissolved in water – and let me know how things are in Wisconsin. I hope, however, that we will be exchanged before an answer reaches me. There may be many errors in this letter, but I can correct nothing.

Libby Prison, January 26, 1864

I received your letter of January 4 by the last boat, and I can assure you that I was happy to hear from you. I had expected a letter from Sister Caroline too, but there was none. I am glad to see that volunteers come quickly under the banner, even though you do not mention whether or not the Fifteenth is recruiting. I hope that it gets at least a few volunteers. The weather has been lovely the last days; if only we could be out to enjoy it! Our hope of being exchanged seems to be no closer to realization now than when we first came here; that I can see. I suppose we will become accustomed to the fact in a year or two, so it should not worry us too much. I take life as lightly as possible under the circumstances. I have not made great progress in phonography and German, for the simple reason that I am not working steadily on them. I go at them by fits and starts, but soon become tired and, because I do not have any variation in my life or any bodily exercise, I become numb and must have something that can occupy my mind without too much effort. I have read parts of the books you sent me, but not all. I have now been promised Hume's *His-*

tory of England, which will occupy me for some time. When you write, be so good as to give me all the news you can about the regiment. It is rarely that I hear anything about it. My warmest greetings to Kaia and the little ones. Hope to see you all again. Be so kind as to write at the earliest opportunity.

[On the opposite side the following was written in invisible ink.]

First I will explain – before I forget about it – that it is unnecessary for you to write short letters to me. Letters that go from here are carefully scrutinized, and we often hear growls about their length. But with letters that come here, I have reason to believe, they are not so careful, and so you can make them as long as you wish. We are not as well off as before. The authorities hold back our boxes on the pretense, I think, that they are investigating whether or not their own captured officers are receiving their packages. Why this pretense I do not know. I have never heard that our government has refused to provide prisoners with anything that has been sent to them by friends or relatives. In case the truce boat comes soon, perhaps we will receive our boxes; if not we must live without them. All that we have now, apart from the Rebel rations, is coffee, so we are becoming concerned. The last two days fresh meat has been dealt out, but the ten previous days we received no meat of any kind; the only thing we got was cornbread and a little rice. Meat will soon be discontinued entirely; that is quite certain, as the Rebels now cannot provide enough for their army. If we receive our boxes, we will not ask them for anything. But the poor privates, who get nothing but Rebel rations, must certainly suffer. I am told that they have not once been given rice of late; so now a piece of dry cornbread is the only thing they get.

You can imagine how they deteriorate under such circumstances; still our government shows no tendency toward exchanging. In truth, it seems to have turned its back to these men, without wishing to come to their aid. I do not like to think this of our government, but the finger seems to point in that direction. Why was Butler named as exchange commissioner? It really seems that he was put there only to hinder the exchange. The administration was afraid that it would not be able to withstand the pressure of the people in the North who have friends here, and thought – in order in this way to get around it – to quiet the resentment and to get public opinion on its side. If this will succed still remains to be seen. Please note: I don't say this is so, but I do say that it does appear to be, judging from all that I have been in a position to learn of the matter. There can be circumstances that I am unaware of, and as a result I may have an inaccurate picture of it. Of one thing we are quite certain; that is that the Rebels greatly desire the exchange, and that they will certainly arrange for it if they receive any real compensation. If our government has decided not to exchange during the war, why doesn't it come forward and say so and be done with it? But those who are in favor of that system will shrink from informing the country.

How many are here now, do you think, who will never be able to see their homes again if this policy is adopted? How much can men who have suffered as these have done during the winter bear when the warm weather comes? They will fall off like rotten leaves. Contagious diseases have already broken out among them. I will give you only one example: of 89 men of the Eleventh Kentucky who came here last November, 40 are dead. How many of the remaining 49 will be able to hold out the next six months? This is something that demands the immediate attention of the people in the North. If these men are not to be a sacrifice to indifference, they must be set free, and the only way of setting them free is by exchange. No boastful resolution of Congress calling on millions of men can do it, and I am amazed to see that such a senseless step is being taken. This matter should be laid before our legislature, and it should admonish Congress and demand exchange. I wish nothing for myself, but when I came here I had a group of 40-50 men under me, and I should like to save at least a few of them.

You can put this matter before the authorities in Madison and stress its importance. I give no name and use no expression by which I could be recognized if this writing should be discovered by the Rebels here, as I have no special desire to be put in irons and locked in a dark cell for the rest of my imprisonment.

NOTE: These letters are in O. A. Buslett, *Det femtende regiment Wisconsin frivillige*, 219–222, 226–230 (Decorah, Iowa, 1894). The translations were made by the editor.

K. O. B.

F. STATEMENT OF SENATOR JOHN A. JOHNSON'S POSITION IN OPPOSITION TO POTTER RAILROAD BILL

Railroad matters are now under consideration. The Senate has received a bill setting maximum rates for railroads. It is said that these rates shall be about 20 per cent lower than the present charges. It is easy to understand the extreme indefensibility of such lawmaking. I know with certainty that the one who prepared the bill had no reliable basis for his proposal. He took a freight table of the railroad association and reduced it about 20 per cent, and this proposal was accepted for consideration. So blindly to undertake such important legislation, without a fundamental and comprehensive investigation by men of proper qualifications and competence is more than unthinkable. Almost irreparable damage can be done. The state must be just in every situation. If it gets a reputation for making unwise and unjust laws, capital will stay away from it and economic development will to a considerable degree be restricted. At the same time, capital must be held within reasonable bounds so that the rights of citizens are not infringed. Monopolies because of the people's patience have dared raise their heads and have been allowed to go too far, but we must not for this reason go to extremes in punishing them. The railroad is our most important means of communication. The true interests of the people and the railroads are not incapable of uniting. The mighty lords who enrich themselves at the expense of the people are the ones we should seek to restrain by means of appropriate laws.

NOTE: Excerpt from an article entitled "Wisconsin Legislature" published over the initial "J" in *Skandinaven* (Chicago), March 3, 1874.

G. INTRODUCTORY PARAGRAPH OF SECTION 7 OF SENATOR JOHN A. JOHNSON'S BILL TO ESTABLISH A BOARD OF RAILROAD COMMISSIONERS

Every railroad company incorporated or doing business in this state or which shall hereafter become incorporated or do business under any general or specific law of this state shall on or before the first day of October, in the year 1874, and on or before the same day in each year thereafter, make and transmit to the Commissioners appointed by virtue of this act, at their office in Madison, a full and true statement under oath of the proper officer of said corporation, of the affairs of the said corporation, as the same existed on the first day of the preceding July specifying [forty-four subdivisions which commanded the railroad commissioners to make their recommendations on the basis of detailed financial and operating statements].

NOTE: From a copy of Bill 2 S, 1874, in the Johnson Papers.

H. TERMS FOR GRANTING JOHNSON ENDOWMENT SCHOLARSHIPS

Madison, Wisconsin, February 12, 1876

Dr. John Bascom
President of the University of Wisconsin

. . . .

1st. The said sum [*Johnson's gift of $5,000*] will be paid to the Treasurer of the University at the times aforesaid either in money or in interest bearing obligations, and shall be invested in such manner as the Board of Regents of the University may from time to time direct.

2nd. The income from said fund shall annually be used in aiding needy students, at the University, but until the year 1900, such students only as either read or speak (or both) any of the Scandinavian languages, (Norse, Swedish, Danish or Icelandic,) reasonably well, shall receive aid from this fund.

3d. No student shall receive more than fifty dollars in any one year, nor shall more than two hundred dollars in the aggregate be given to any one student.

4th. To entitle any student to aid from this fund he must have attended the Common school at least one year in the aggregate before he was fifteen years of age, and must have attended the University at least one term, or, if he has not attended the Common school as aforesaid, he must have attended the University at least one year.

5th. The President or acting President of the University, together with two of the Professors that the President may designate, shall constitute a committee to distribute the aid to the students under the provisions of this bequest, provided, that if the President cannot himself act he may designate a Professor to act for him, and provided also, that if there be a Professor in the Scandinavian Languages at the University, the President shall appoint him as one of the members of such committee, and two members of the committee shall constitute a quorum. . . .

6th. When the committee aforesaid have decided what students shall receive aid and the amount to be given to each, they shall record their decision in a book kept for that purpose, and upon the certificate of the President to the Treasurer, the student shall receive the amount allotted to him. The book thus kept may at any time be inspected by any member of the Faculty of the University, or by any member of the Board of Regents, or officer of the Board, but by no one else, without the consent of the committee, there being as I think no advantage in making public the fact that a student receives aid from the fund. It is my wish that applicants for aid be examined in a quiet and private way, unless the committee deem that there is some good reason for doing otherwise. The committee are authorized and directed to reject any and all applications for aid from students who they believe would not be materially benefitted thereby.

7th. If the income from this fund or any part thereof is not expended in any one year under the provisions herein, it may be expended the next succeeding year, but if it remain unexpended more than two years, such unexpended portion shall be added to the principal and be in like manner invested and treated.

8th. No distinction as to sex shall be made by the committee in giving aid, though the pronoun *he* has been used herein when applied to a student.

9th. If the Board of Regents of the University shall refuse or neglect to invest the money herein given, I reserve the right during my life time to give directions for its investment, or if I neglect to give such directions, and after my death, the President and Treasurer of the University and Secretary of the Board of Regents are authorized and requested to provide for the investment, but the Treasurer of the University shall under all circumstances be the custodian and Treasurer of the fund and shall hold all securities for it.

10th. In the event of my death before the money herein given is paid over as herein provided, I hereby direct my heirs, executors and administrators to pay the money herein bequeathed, in the manner herein named.

John A. Johnson

NOTE: From *Annual Report of the Board of Regents of the University of Wisconsin for the Fiscal Year Ending September 30, 1876*, 25-27.

I. PROPOSALS FOR A PROFESSORSHIP IN SCANDINAVIAN LANGUAGES AT UNIVERSITY OF WISCONSIN

Friends of education among the Scandinavian population of the Northwest have called a convention at this place [*Madison*] for the 4th of March next to consider what can be done to awaken a more general interest among countrymen in the cause of popular education and more particularly to consider the propriety and practicality of having Scandinavian languages taught in some of our colleges and high schools. The University of Wisconsin might not be disinclined to make Scandinavian languages a branch study placing them on equality with the German if a suitable person could be found. Such a one must have literary attainments and moral integrity but must also have the general confidence of the Scandinavians as well as the respect of his co-laborers in the University. Mr. Anderson of Albion Academy received an appointment to the University as a tutor about a year ago but didn't accept. He is now at Albion Academy. I am to be in the convention and would like to know your views in order to present them to the convention. I refer you to S. D. Hastings, C. L. Williams, A. J. Craig, Mr. Van Slyke or Governor Fairchild for reference in regard to me.

NOTE: Excerpt from a letter, John A. Johnson to President P. A. Chadbourne, February 20, 1869, in the Johnson Papers.

J. TABLE 1: MANUFACTURE OF AGRICULTURAL IMPLEMENTS, 1883, FULLER AND JOHNSON MANUFACTURING COMPANY

Implements	*Number Manufactured*
Stubble Plows (steel)	3,213
Breaking Plows (all kinds)	978
Stubble Plows (chilled)	312
Sulky Cultivators	1,540
Three-Shovel Cultivators	1,702
Five-Tooth Cultivators	1,530
Double-Shovel Cultivators (W.B.)	384
Double-Shovel Cultivators (L.B.)	480
Harrows	551
Sulky Rakes	1,416
Tobacco Hoes	300
Corn Cutters	5,045
Cane Mills	44
Mowers	200

NOTE: "Statement of Business for year ending Dec., 1883, Fuller and Johnson Manufacturing Company," in Division of Archives and Manuscripts, State Historical Society of Wisconsin, Madison.

K. TABLE 2: WHOLESALE PRICES OF IMPLEMENTS, 1883, FULLER AND JOHNSON MANUFACTURING COMPANY

Stubble Plows (chilled steel)	$ 7.20
Twelve-inch Bonanza Breaker Plows	15.90

Brush and Grub Breaker Plows	20.00
Casaday Sulky Plows	40.44
Harrows (all sizes)	8.92
Sulky Cultivators	22.50
Walking Cultivators	17.50
Sulky Rakes	20.75
Mowers	52.00

NOTE: "Statement of Business for year ending Dec., 1883, Fuller and Johnson Manufacturing Company," in Division of Archives and Manuscripts, State Historical Society of Wisconsin, Madison.

L. TABLE 3: REPORTED SALES OF FULLER AND JOHNSON SALESMEN IN THE FIELD AND COMMISSIONS PAID, 1888

	Sales	*Commission*
O. H. Swerig	$ 2,764.25	$ 900.00
C. S. Jackson	31,712.69	8,519.00
A. R. Chase	3,145.80	
J. H. Sigafoos	14,521.89	3,421.25
H. N. Timms	21,602.76	3,872.00
C. M. Closson	8,237.09	2,580.00
A. J. Coulee	9,472.63	2,375.00
C. F. Swain	1,593.96	268.75
L. D. Benner	5,515.80	65.00
E. M. McVicker	13,409.77	2,945.00
J. C. Thompson	5,528.43	

NOTE: "Statement of Business for year ending September 1, 1888, Fuller and Johnson Manufacturing Company," in Division of Archives and Manuscripts, State Historical Society of Wisconsin, Madison.

M. TABLE 4: STATEMENT OF CONDITION OF FULLER AND JOHNSON MANUFACTURING COMPANY, 1895

Resources

Notes Receivable	$ 288,952.97
Accounts Receivable	246,325.93
Cash	4,362.75

Real Estate	124,717.40
Tools & Machinery	87,214.94
Small Tools	6,025.67
Water & Steam Pipe	5,534.35
Office Furniture	1,499.66
Models	562.50
Patents	18,660.87
Patterns & Dies	20,392.18
Law Books	401.60
Insurance	1,173.66
Inventory	285,688.45
	$1,091,512.93

Liabilities

Capital Stock	$ 500,000.00
Surplus	252,650.88
Sinking Fund	5,204.13
Notes Payable	34,852.79
Accounts Payable	138,726.93
F. & J. Mfg. Co. Bonds	128,000.00
Interest Due on Bonds	5,226.67
Undivided Profits	3,523.23
Net Gain, year ending Aug. 31, 1895	23,328.30
	$1,091,512.93

NOTE: "Statement of the Condition of the Fuller and Johnson Manufacturing Company for year ending Aug. 31, 1895," in "Record of the Secretary," as reported to stockholders, January 19, 1896. See the Johnson Papers.

N. PROPOSAL BY PRESIDENT THAT FULLER AND JOHNSON MANUFACTURING COMPANY ISSUE $200,000 IN BONDS

Whereas I desire that the said Company issue its bonds in the sum of two hundred thousand dollars to be secured by a trust deed of all its property, and whereas the said Company will be unable to pay all the floating indebtedness with the proceeds of said bonds, including mine, now, therefore, I propose to this Company that the indebtedness held by me against said Company at this date, being the sum of seventy thousand dollars, shall be and remain a junior loan to each and every bond when issued, and the payment of said indebtedness and interest thereon shall be extended to such time when all said bonds shall have been freely paid with interest according to their tenor, provided, however, that in case this Company accepts this proposition, no dividend shall be declared or paid upon its capital stock during the existence of the bonded indebtedness without my consent, and I hereby agree to join in, and become a party to, the trust deed to be given to secure the said bonds in accordance with the proposition.

John A. Johnson

NOTE: "Record of the Secretary," as reported to stockholders, January 19, 1891. See the Johnson Papers.

O. OPENING REMARKS OF PRESIDENT JOHN A. JOHNSON, ASSOCIATION OF AGRICULTURAL IMPLEMENT MANUFACTURERS, DETROIT, OCTOBER 5, 1897

Sunbeams are forcing their path through the rifts in the industrial sky that has so long been lowering and gloomy. We dare not hope that the future shall be sunshine only. The effects of the disastrous storm have not yet disappeared. The fearful blasts are abating but the waves are not yet stilled, and they will roll on for some time to come. The wrecks are about us in ruined fortunes, in quiet wheels, in silent shops, in idle labor. But there is perceptible improvement. As man's own unreason and folly only brought on the storm, so may we hope that returning sense and knowledge acquired through stern adversity will, in the not distant future, assert their sway. But how deplorable that this land above all other lands showered with blessings by a bountiful Providence should ever have to pass through such trials. We always have more than abundance of all that makes life attractive. Whoever heard of famine under the American flag? Crop failures, such as to cause a want or even curtailment in the necessities of life, are absolutely unknown. Nature has provided us with resources that have no limit, that are infinitely more than ample to give employment to every willing hand at remuneration more than sufficient to satisfy reasonable demands.

The association is to be congratulated upon meeting under more auspicious conditions for its members as well as for those who depend upon its great industries. The manufacturers of agricultural implements and vehicles have had to bear their full share of the burdens and calamities of this industrial depression.

It is, however, much more agreeable to forecast a more hopeful future than to grieve over a disastrous past. This association can surely do much to accelerate the advent of prosperity that is now upon our threshold. Not only should we carefully consider what immediately concerns us; not only do we come in close contact with the greatest producing interest in our country, the agricultural, but we have very close relations with every other leading interest, and especially with the iron industry that is so intimately connected with the agricultural. Agriculture depends upon iron not only for implements and tools but in, if possible, a still greater degree for means of transportation. So closely are these branches of industry related that they are inter-dependent. When one suffers they all suffer. And when foundation industries prosper they all prosper. Whatever we may be able to accomplish to promote the interests of the tiller of the soil will also measurably promote our own.

NOTE: *Farm Implement News,* October 7, 1897. A copy of the address is in the Johnson Papers.

P. TABLE 5: BALANCE STATEMENT OF FULLER AND JOHNSON MANUFACTURING COMPANY, 1901

Resources	
Notes Receivable	$ 270,822.78
Accounts Receivable	503,154.63
Cash on Hand	7,903.18
Real Estate	145,999.22
Tools, Machinery and Shop Equipment	151,099.33
Office Equipment	4,384.72
Patents	19,516.23
Unearned Insurance	3,711.46
Manufactured Goods and Materials	550,004.61
	$1,656,596.16
Liabilities	
Capital Stock	$ 500,000.00
Surplus	405,981.50
Bonds	250,000.00
Notes Payable	254,708.83
Accounts Payable	155,826.51
Gains for Ten Months	90,079.32
	$1,656,596.16

NOTE: "Record of the Secretary" for the fiscal year ending June 30, 1901.

Q. EXCERPT FROM A STATEMENT BY THE GISHOLT MACHINE COMPANY

The demand for our turret lathes is constantly and rapidly increasing. Manufacturers are learning that much of their work, such as friction clutches, couplings for shaftings, Corliss engine bonnets, cone pulleys, etc. can be done on turret lathes for a fraction of what it costs in the usual way. The same is true of bar work.

On our machines bicycle wheel hubs are made from the end of the bar at almost nominal cost. We also make long pieces from the bar as we have a gripper that supports the out end.

We build machines of all sizes, from the small screw machine to those having a 4½″ hole through the spindle swinging 34″ and weighing about 14,000 pounds.

We are also building gap turret lathes swinging up to 50″. For bar work we have an automatic chuck and automatic wire feed that practically eliminates the time of feeding the bar.

We are now making the machines in large quantities, so as to reduce the cost to a minimum, jigs and templates being used, and all like pieces are absolutely interchangeable.

Our standard tool grinders are now made in lots of fifty, which, better than anything else, shows what the demand is for them.

NOTE: *American Machinist,* January 5, 1893.

R. TABLE 6: BALANCE STATEMENT OF GISHOLT MACHINE COMPANY, JANUARY 1, 1901

Assets	
Accounts Receivable	$ 61,954.85
Cash on Hand	2,830.83
Real Estate	27,600.00
Buildings	85,196.00
Power, Heating and Lighting Plant	33,327.00
Stationary Machinery	76,939.78
Small Tools and Shop Supplies	45,730.67
Office Furniture	1,717.00
Patents, Patterns and Drawings	25,400.00
Materials, manufactured and partly manufactured stock	83,817.25
	$444,513.38
Liabilities	
Capital Stock	$300,000.00
Notes Payable	40,133.00
Accounts Payable	20,198.42
Unpaid Dividends	9,000.00
Surplus	75,181.96
	$444,513.38

NOTE: From records of Gisholt Machine Company. Copies of the balance statement are in the Johnson Papers.

S. JOHN A. JOHNSON'S VIEW OF ANGLO-RUSSIAN RIVALRY AT TIME OF BOER WAR

But for England, Russia would long since have had a firm foothold on the Mediterranean and the Persian Gulf, in India and in China, and would have absorbed Norway and Sweden and thus had a firm footing on the Atlantic, and would then have been absolute . . . dictator of the world. And with such a despot at the head, where would human liberty be? Russia now has 130 million people. Had her ambition been gratified she would have had two or three times that number directly and many more indirectly. Her population is densely ignorant. Under present restrictions in order to increase her power she finds it to her interest to in some measure promote education. But she permits this to be done only under government supervision and leadership. Private enterprise in Russia seems to sleep the sleep that knows no awakening. Everything must come through the government or not at all.

NOTE: From an undated, unpublished typescript probably written early in 1901. A copy is in the Johnson Papers.

T. PETITION OF JOHN A. JOHNSON TO CONGRESS TO ABOLISH IMPORT DUTIES ON FARM MACHINERY

February 2, 1888

To the honorable, the Senate and the House of Representatives of the United States in Congress assembled:

The undersigned would respectfully petition your honorable body to abolish all import duties on agricultural machines, hay and grain harvesting machinery, threshing machines, straw cutting machines, feed grinding mills, farm vehicles, including farm wagons, that may be imported to the United States from countries that admit like machines manufactured in the United States free of duty.

Your petitioner would represent that he is a manufacturer of agricultural machinery at the City of Madison, Wisconsin, that he believes all import duties on all such articles of manufacture are superfluous and useless; that they can only harm the producer, and are of no value to anyone.

Your petitioner would further represent that the law imposing such duties works harm to the manufacturer of the goods named in this; that there are citizens who continually represent that the import duties on the goods named compel the agriculturist to pay much higher prices for them than he would if no duties were imposed, which allegations, while incorrect and untrue, nevertheless cause ill feeling on the part of the agriculturists toward the manufacturers of such implements, which ill feeling may be wholly avoided by abolishing the import duties on them.

Your petitioner would further represent that he believes that American workingmen should be protected against foreign cheap labor by suitable import duties, but that the manufacture of agricultural implements is in such advanced state, and that our implements are so superior to those of foreign manufacture, that none will be imported if the duties on them be wholly discontinued.

Trusting that Congress will take early action on this petition, your petitioner will ever remain

Your obedient servant
J. A. Johnson
President of Fuller & Johnson
Manufacturing Company
Madison, Wisconsin

NOTE: From *Congressional Record*, February 3, 1888.

Index